RURAL NON-FARM GROWTH
SIGN OF FARM SUCCESS OR FAILURE?

RURAL NON-FARM GROWTH

SIGN OF FARM SUCCESS OR FAILURE?

Dr. M. PRASADA RAO
Associate Professor
Department of Economics
Andhra University
Visakhapatnam-3, A.P. India
&
Honorary Director
A.P. Study Circle
Visakhapatnam-3

SERIALS PUBLICATIONS
NEW DELHI (INDIA)

First Published-2006

ISBN : 81-8387-009-0

Published by

SERIALS PUBLICATIONS
4830/24, Prahlad Street, Ansari Road
Darya Ganj, New Delhi-110002 (India)
Phone : 23245225
Fax : 91-11-23272135
E-mail: serials@satyar. net.in

This Book is Dedicated
to My Parents
Late Sri. M.Y. Ratnam and
Late Smt. M.N. Ratnam

CONTENTS

FOREWORD

This book is a pioneering effort to grapple with a key issue in development and poverty reduction, and its central results are of great importance.

The issue is as follows. Typically, in India and elsewhere in the developing world, from a quarter to half of rural incomes depend on 'rural non-farm income'–as opposed to farming, farm labour, remittances and transfers. Does this also work dynamically? In other words, under what conditions– and at what stage in the development process-are rural growth and poverty reduction critically dependent on what happens in the rural non-farm sector?.

One way to address this question is to ask why the rural non-farm sector looms larger in income and employment– overall, and for the poor - in some rural areas than in others. In India, two main explanations have been advanced. 'Distress diversification' implies that non-farm activity looms larger when, and where, people are forced into it because farming does badly. 'Rural growth linkages' imply that non-farm activity expands in response to prior agricultural success, and the supply and demand that it creates.

Much research has addressed these issues by research at the macro level, or by comparisons across countries or Indian states. At the other extreme, there are excellent highly localised studies, such as [Hazell and Ramasamy 1991]. This book reviews such research, but takes a new tack, concentrating on similarities and differences among areas and households in one Indian state, Andhra Pradesh. This permits a more discriminating approach to the issue of whether non-farm salience signals a dynamic response to farm success, or a survival strategy/in face of farm failure. It turns out to be crucial to distinguish different *types* of rural non-farm production and employment (RNFE) when investigating the relationships between non-farm production and trends in agricultural productivity growth and in farm employment.

The study shows that over-simplified generalisations about the roles played by RNFE can obscure a very important distinction. Traditional RNFE tends to act as a fall-back source of income for those who can find no other; hence it looms large for households, and places, where agriculture is doing relatively badly. More modern types of RNFE tend to develop under a range of conditions including, as this study shows, the presence of a dynamic agricultural sector. This distinction has important implications for the setting of policy priorities in different rural regions. We hope that Prasada Rao Mecharla and others will take forward the line of enquiry developed in this study, both by exploring the nature of RNFE, and of the farm-nonfarm linkages which influence it, in other parts of India and beyond, and by giving further attention to the policy implications which flow from the varied nature of rural non-farm employment.

We warmly congratulate Prasada Rao Mecharla on completing this important work, especially in view of the difficult personal circumstances, which included a long separation from his family. That it was completed says much for his determination and for his commitment to the study of India's development problems and opportunities.

Dr. Diana Hunt
School of African & Asian Studies
University of Sussex
Falmer, Brighton, BN 19 QN
U.K

Prof. Michael Lipton
Poverty Research Unit
School of African & Asian Studies
University of Sussex
Falmer, Brighton, BN 1 9 QNU.K

ACKNOWLEDGEMENTS

This thesis was supervised by the late Dr. Pramit K. Chaudhuri, and, in alphabetical order, by Dr. Diana Hunt and Professor Michael Lipton. I would like to express my gratitude for their patience, and generosity in advising me at every stage of this thesis. I am immensely indebted to them and words fail me to pay my deep debt of gratitude for their guidance at every stage of my work. They have been a constant source of inspiration and encouragement to me. They gave me very elaborate, systematic and useful comments on each chapter. Their broad outlook and experience made me work hard. Their encouragement and guidance will be invaluable for the rest of my career. Many other people have also assisted me in this endeavour. I would also like to place on record the help and encouragement I received from my colleagues in the School of Economics at Andhra University, India.

I am grateful to Professor Hans W. Singer, Professor G. Parthasarathy, Professor R. Radha Krishna, Professor G.K. Chadha, Professor M. Jagadeswara Rao, Professor B. Bhaskara Rao, M. Velia, A. de Haan, U. N. Moorthy, N. McCulloch, J. Litchfield, A. Lowden and T. Fisher, R. Goodrich for reading various chapters and offering their valuable suggestions at every stage of this work. I particularly thank them for sparing their precious time.

I would also like to thank the following individuals who have all contributed in one way or another to my completion of this D.Phil. Without them I would not have been able to have completed it. They are (in no particular order): Professor K. Venkateswarlu, Professor K. Sree Ram Murthy, Professor K. Siva Prasad, Professor K.C. Reddy, C. Samba Murthy,

R. Sudarsana Rao, M. Bhavani Sankar, Professor R. M. Mohan Rao, Professor C. Ratnam, Professor Ch. A. Krishna Rao, Professor Rani Gopal, Professor G. Ramachandrudu, Professor Krishna Murthy, Professor P. V. Sharma, Professor V. Gandhi Babu, Professor K. Ravi Babu, Professor S.K.V. Suryanarayana Raju, Professor Frank Ellis, Martin Greeley, Sumit Roy, M. Gopinath Reddy, Shaik Gallab, S. Sudhakar Reddy, Professor Ralf Grillo, Professor Biplab Dasgupta, Professor K. S. Chalam, Professor Chandu Subba Rao, Jim Fairburn, Julian Saurin, Surjit Singh, Sunil Ray, Ratna Reddy, Julia Tingle, Rachael Straub, Clare Rogers, Kiran K. Pandya, P. K. Mishra, Sanjoy K Nayak, Andy Newell, Mike Barrow, Barry Reilly, Tony Binns, V. Damodaran, M. Unnithan, Hilary Cook, K. C. Suri, C. Omergie, Peda Raju. Sarogini, Chinni Krishna, Ramanayya, Yedukondalu, Ramesh, Ramakrishna, Jayshree, Mohammad Razzaque, Grant Coleby, John Lewis, Imran Matin, Zahir Ahmad, Marie-Jo Cartijo, Henry Neale, Ravini, Dr. Tara Kumari, Dr T. Koteswara Rao, Dr V. Sheshagiri Rao, Ashwani, Mark Lacy and Lucy Ford, Satya Prasad, Raja, G. Ramesh, Tirumala Kumar, Eric Nyanjom.

I express my gratitude to David Hadrill & Christine Gent and their daughter, Mia Hadrill, for their invaluable affection, for providing me three years accommodation and kindness. Their constant vigilance has been crucial for my completion of this work.

I express my gratitude to Saurabh Sinha, Arti, and their daughter, Richa for providing me with a couple of months accommodation and their support. Annie, Jeff and their daughter, Tasmin for their friendship and support.

My sincere thanks are also due to Elizabeth Davis, Jason Bailey and other staff members of the computer centre, for their help in running the computer programmes. I thank the Poverty Research Unit at Sussex for providing me with work space.

My greatest debt is to the hundreds of the people of the two villages in AP who were generous in their affection and who talked to me without fear about their circumstances.

I am thankful to the Northern Dairies Educational Trust, Christian Overseas students fund,_Hammond Trust British

Council, and The Humanitarian Trust for providing me some financial help. The prompt help extended by the staff of the IDS library, University of Sussex library, Andhra University Library, and CESS library needs special appreciation.

I would like to place on record my gratitude to my mother, for her encouragement, throughout my academic career. I also thank V. R. Krishna Rao, Mohan Rao, Naga Rani, Leelavathi, Uma, Vijay, Vasu, Nandu, Narayana Rao for their moral support.

I will be failing in my duty if I do not place on record the co-operation I received from Chandrakala, Jayant and Prasant, my wife and sons. I extent my heartfelt thanks to them for their enthusiastic co-operation and support extended to me during my research work.

A special mention should also go to my trusty bicycle, which put in many miles transporting me to and from my house to the university!

I dedicate the thesis to the memory of my father and mother. Although they are no more, they are a constant inspiration to me and left behind imprints of sacrifice, dedication, hard work and honesty.

A large number of people have, in many ways, provided a great help to me while doing this thesis. I was born and brought up in Telaprolu village in Krishna District of Andhra Pradesh (AP). I was actively involved in student movements throughout my student career and worked as a Student Union President in Andhra University. I had an opportunity to study the socio-economic conditions of my surroundings in Visakhapatnam and in my native place in AP. The problem of chronic unemployment and under employment in rural areas interested me greatly. The possible solution to the problem was to develop rural non-farm activities. I desired to do research on the present state of rural non-farm activities in AP.

I was fortunate to be selected for a Commonwealth Academic Staff award for pursuing my D.Phil. in the U.K. This gave me an opportunity to study the state of rural non-farm activities in AP. I am grateful to the Association of Commonwealth Universities Commission for awarding me the Scholarship at the University of Sussex, England, and also to the Andhra University, Department of Economics, Visakhapatnam for granting me the necessary leave to complete my studies.

I participated in seminars/workshops on unemployment and rural non-farm employment during the period of my research in India and abroad. Professor G. Parthasarathy presided over a seminar at Andhra University from which many useful suggestions arose. At the annual Conference of the Development Studies Association held in Lancaster, England in 1994, a paper of mine based on the primary data of my research thesis was accepted and it was appreciated by the audience. In particular, the comments I received from Professor Malcolm Harper were extremely helpful.

I have the good fortune of meeting at an IDS seminar Peter Hazell, an expert in the field of rural development, and had an enlightening discussion with him on the subject.

After presenting a paper at Dublin University, Eire in 1995 I subsequently received suggestions from Barbara Harriss of Oxford University which were very useful.

This thesis seeks to test 'distress diversification' against 'growth linkages' to explain the propensity of rural people to be involved in the RNFS. This is done through (a) district level and (b) household level regressions of RNFE total shares and growth, and by sub-sectors in AP. Two different villages of the region, Veeravalli and Anandapuram, are chosen to represent the rural AP. The changing levels and nature of development are encapsulated by two purposively designed development situations. Situation 1 represents the backwardness of the village, Situation two has a highly developed agriculture sector and the incidence of non-farm expansions is high in both the cases. This study has been done through an extensive field survey in AP, spread over two villages and 819 households. I combined macro, micro level and some case studies to get a complete picture of the situation in A.P. I hope my sincere efforts would add, although in a very small proportion, to the already existing knowledge on the subject. Any error of analysis or interpretation within this D.Phil thesis remains entirely my responsibility.

LIST OF ABBREVIATIONS

ADD	:	Agricultural Distress Diversification
AERC	:	Agro-Economic Research Centre
AF	:	Agriculture First
AGE^2	:	Household Head Age Squared
AGL	:	Agricultural Growth Linkages
AGSPRs	:	Age/Gender-Specific Workforce Participation Rates
AISO	:	Area Irrigated More Than Once
AP	:	Andhra Pradesh
ARTEP	:	Asian Regional Team for Employment Promotion
ASLH	:	Average size of Land Possessed per Household
BC	:	Backward Caste
BLs	:	Backward Linkages
CD1	:	Dummy Variable for Scheduled Caste Household
CD2	:	Dummy Variable for Scheduled Tribes Household
CDAS	:	Current Daily Activity Status
CESS	:	Centre for Economic and Social Studies
CLs	:	Consumption Linkages
CV	:	Coefficient of Variation
CWAS	:	Current Weekly Activity Status
DRDA	:	District Rural Development Agency
EDUINT	:	Interactive Term between Levels of Education and Village Dummy
EPW	:	Economic and Political Weekly
FAO	:	Food and Agricultural Organisation
FC	:	Forward Caste
FLs	:	Forward Linkages
GCA	:	Gross Cropped Area

GDP : Gross Domestic Product
GIA : Gross Irrigated Area
GOI : Government of India
GR : Growth Rate
HH : Household
HHH : Household Head
HHI : Household Industry
H_o : The Null Hypothesis
HYV : High Yielding Variety
IAY : Indira Awaas Yojana (Indira Gandhi's housing scheme for the poor)
IDS : Institute of Development Studies
ILO : International Labour Organisation
IRDP : Integrated Rural Development Programme
ITI : Industrial Training Institute
JB : Jarque-Bera
JRY : Jawahar Rozgar Yojana (employment scheme)
K : Number of parameters used in c_K^2
Kg : Kilogram
Km : Kilometre
Km2 : Square Kilometre
LFPR : Labour Force Participation Rate
L^R : Log-Likelihood Ratio
MAMINT2 : Interactive term between March-May season and village dummy
NA : Not Available
NFE : Non-farm Employment
NFM : Non-farm Migrant
NFP : Non-farm Proper
NFS : Non-farm Sector
NIA : Net Irrigated Area
NSA : Net Sown Area
NSC : Non-subsistence Crops
NSS : National Sample Survey
NSSO : National Sample Survey Organisation
ODD : Overall Distress Diversification
ODL : Overall Development Linkage

OLS	:	Ordinary Least Squares
P (r)	:	Probability of Events r
p	:	Probability
PAAV	:	Per Acre average Value of Farm Output
PDUR	:	Person Day Unemployment rates
PWD	:	Public Works Department
RGL	:	Rural Growth Linkages
RMP	:	Registered Medical Practitioner
RMW	:	Rural Main Worker
RNFE	:	Rural Non-Farm Employment
RNFS	:	Rural Non-Farm Sector
Rs.	:	Indian Rupees
SC/ST	:	Scheduled Caste and Scheduled Tribe
SD	:	Standard Deviation
SE	:	Standard Error (of a regression)
SGDP	:	Sectoral Gross Domestic Product
SSC	:	Secondary School Certificate (new regulations)
SSLC	:	Secondary School Leaving Certificate (old regulations)
TRYSEM	:	Training of Rural Youth for Self Employment
u	:	Disturbance term with the classical properties
UPAS	:	Usual Principal Activity Status
UPSS	:	Usual Principal Subsidiary Status
χ_K^2	:	Chi- Squared

GLOSSARY FOR SELECTED NAMES AND TERMS IN THE THESIS

acre	: 2.45 acres = 1 hectare
adda leaves	: used for making plates for meals
anganwadi	: kindergarten helper
anicut	: irrigation barrage
ayacut	: command area of an irrigated system which provides the water from a deep reservoir
bajra	: chickpea
brahmin	: ceremonial caste, highest in the ritual order of the Hindu society
coir	: coconut fibre
crore	: ten million
gantilu	: a coarse cereal eaten as a staple food in the uplands
godown	: similar to a warehouse
golla	: shepherd community
gur	: sweetener derived from sugarcane juice
harijans	: the traditionally untouchable low castes
harijanwada	: a settlement of harijans at the end of village
jajmani	: a system of patron-client relationship in Indian traditional village social system defining civil liberties, rights and duties of different caste groups.
jowar	: a coarse cereal
kalasi	: porter
kamma	: a landowner business caste
kapu	: the leading caste
khadi	: hand-woven cloth made of hand-spun yarn

kharif (sarwa)	:	the first paddy autumn crop which is grown during June to September in the delta
kirana	:	store selling provisions (dry goods)
kutch	:	mud path
lakh	:	one hundred thousand
madiga/mala	:	traditionally an untouchable caste
mandals	:	revenue-cum development units
marvadies	:	a traditional and highly successful trading community from Marwadi region of Rajasthan
mutta maistry	:	foreman
paleru	:	permanent servant for farm as well as home
panchayat	:	the form of local elected council (self-government) at the village level.
panshop	:	a shop selling soft drinks, sweets and cigarettes
parishads	:	district peoples' council
purohit	:	person who conducts rituals of Hindu religion
rabi (dalwa)	:	the second paddy winter crop which is grown during November to March
shamiyana	:	a thick cloth for tents for functions
shandys	:	periodic village markets
tapi worker	:	mason
toddy	:	a drink made from the sap of the palmayra tree
tonne	:	metric ton
vaisya	:	traditional grocer trader in villages
zamindari	:	huge land owner who collected land revenue from the farmers until 1960s. There system exists a hierarchy of intermediaries between the state and the cultivators.

1
INTRODUCTION

1.1 Overview

Poverty eradication is a top priority for Andhra Pradesh (AP)[1], as stated in Andhra Pradesh: Vision 2020 by the Government of AP (1999). However, poverty, unemployment and underemploy-ment are often observed together where agriculture is unable to generate adequate employment opportunities for the rural population. Here the rural non-farm sector (RNFS) can play a very important role in the generation of employment and poverty reduction. This thesis examines the nature of rural non-farm employment (RNFE) in AP using secondary (district level) and primary (household level) data in two villages.

Without access to productive employment for the increasing labour force, it is not possible to increase either output or the purchasing power of the rural poor. A permanent solution to the problem of rural unemployment can be found only within the framework of rapid, employment-oriented economic growth [Planning Commission, India (1981:100)]. Yet AP presents some special features, which are a challenge to the prospects of such growth, based on RNFE.

- AP, unlike all-India, has a rising percentage of agricultural labourers in the rural workforce (Appendix Table 1.1).
- AP has India's highest and rising workforce participation rates, especially for females and children. This is partly due

to the age-structure, and partly to age/gender-specific workforce participation rates (AGSPRs) (Appendix Tables 1.2, 1.3 and 1.4).

- AP's high and rising age/gender-specific, and overall, workforce participation rates coexist with AP's smaller, and slower growing, share of RNFS in the rural workforce (Appendix Tables 1.5, 1.6 part 1 and part 2).
- These rates are linked to AP's unemployment rate which is higher and rising faster, than elsewhere in India (Appendix Table 1.7, 1.8 and 1.9).

In a recent study, by Fisher, Mahajan and Singha (1997), the authors note the following:

> The non-farm sector in Andhra Pradesh provides 17.1 per cent of employment compared to the national average of 17.7 per cent (1991), and has been growing relatively more slowly since 1981 (at 2.2per cent a year compared to 2.8per cent nationally). Within the agricultural sector there are disturbing employment trends: the proportion of cultivators has declined significantly while that of agricultural labourers has increased sharply. The latter now (in 1991) make up almost half of the rural labour force. (p. 249).

Previous studies on RNFE have examined the significance of agricultural development and other determinants for the growth of RNFE. Most studies have been based on secondary data and macro-level aggregates, although some have considered primary data at village and household level. There is a need for studies on RNFE at district level with disaggregated data and at household level to capture the influence of inter-district and inter-household differences on the composition and determinants of RNFE. The present study focuses on such data: secondary level at district level, primary at household level for two villages and case studies.

AP recorded a marginal positive growth rate in RNFE between 1981-91 (see Appendix Table 1.5 and 1.6 part 1 and part 2). During the corresponding period India recorded a small positive increase of 0.4per cent. In 1981 the RNFE of AP was 1per cent higher than the national average. By 1991 AP recorded a slightly higher share of RNFE at 16.8per cent compared to 17.1per cent in 1981. However AP's figures are nowhere near those of Kerala which recorded a share of 41.85 per cent in 1981 and 43.94 per cent in 1991. However, in some states the share of RNFE is much lower than that of AP, for instance Bihar recorded a share of 12.6per cent in 1981 and 11.7per cent in 1991. A few key points thus emerge:

- AP is very like all-India in RNFE share - some states have more, some less.
- But AP's share is falling while that of India is growing.
- Together with AP's high unemployment, rising agricultural labour share, and internal rural variations, the above suggests that AP is a good state to study what leads to rises or falls, high and low levels of RNFE share.

In AP the agricultural sector is dominant, and labour in this sector has grown enormously. Demographic pressures on agricultural land have increased and rural urban disparities have risen. Furthermore the incidence of poverty (in absolute numbers as a per cent of the population), though declining, remains quite high.

The percentage output share of the agricultural sector has declined in AP (at 1970-71 constant prices) from 64 per cent (1955-56) to 62 per cent(1960-61), to 57 per cent (1970-71) (Census of India, as cited in V11 plan Vol.1, AP).

The share of agricultural and allied sectors in State Net Domestic Product of AP at constant 1980-81 prices stood at 45.6 per cent in 1980-81 and subsequently declined to 39.8 per cent in 1990-91.[2] A distinctive feature of AP's agricultural economy is that its labour productivity remained stagnant between 1970-71 and 1986-87. The per worker income, at 1980-81 prices, in the agricultural sector was estimated to be Rs. 2,156 in the triennia ending 1971-72, and Rs. 2,088 in the triennia ending 1986-87. The corresponding estimates of per male worker income are Rs.3,265 and Rs.3,346 respectively. Labour productivity in the non-farm sector improved by 40 per cent. The per-worker income, at 1980-81 prices in the non-farm sector, increased from Rs. 4,899 in the triennium ending 1971-

72 to Rs. 6,886, in the triennium ending 1986-87. Therefore, higher labour productivity comes from non-farm activity in AP, but most extra employment comes from farming. But one can then conclude either that it's necessary to (a) get more workers into non-farm (rural or urban!) employment or (b) get farm labour productivity up.

In India, labour absorption in agriculture and in the urban-industrial sectors has not been fast enough to absorb the growing labour force. Unemployment has persisted and in some cases increased in both rural and urban areas. Surplus labour due to excess population growth is a major portion of this surplus. Though agriculture continues to be the largest employer, in the light of its declining employment elasticity any future rise in employment may have to be looked at beyond the agricultural, which is rural non-farm sector. Stagnant agricultural labour productivity, yet rising agricultural employment, in AP seem to imply high (though not necessarily rising) employment elasticities in agriculture in AP. To sum up :

- The share of the primary sector of agriculture in output fell for more than its share in employment in AP. This was also true in the rural sector alone i.e. RNFE growth was not employment generating; non-farm share growth was only urban so RNFE share stagnated.
- All these trends point to the need for new patterns of development which will lead to diversification and the absorption of more labour in non-farm employment within the rural sector.

1.2 The Importance of RNFE in AP

The growth of employment or output shares in the RNFS appears to be positively associated with absolute growth rates in rural districts of AP. In other words, the faster the growth of the share in employment of the RNFS among AP Districts, the faster the growth of total employment (see regression results 3.4.3 and 3.4.4). Mellor (1976), Hazell and Haggblade (1992)

Map 1.1 : Map of India and the Location of Andhra Pradesh

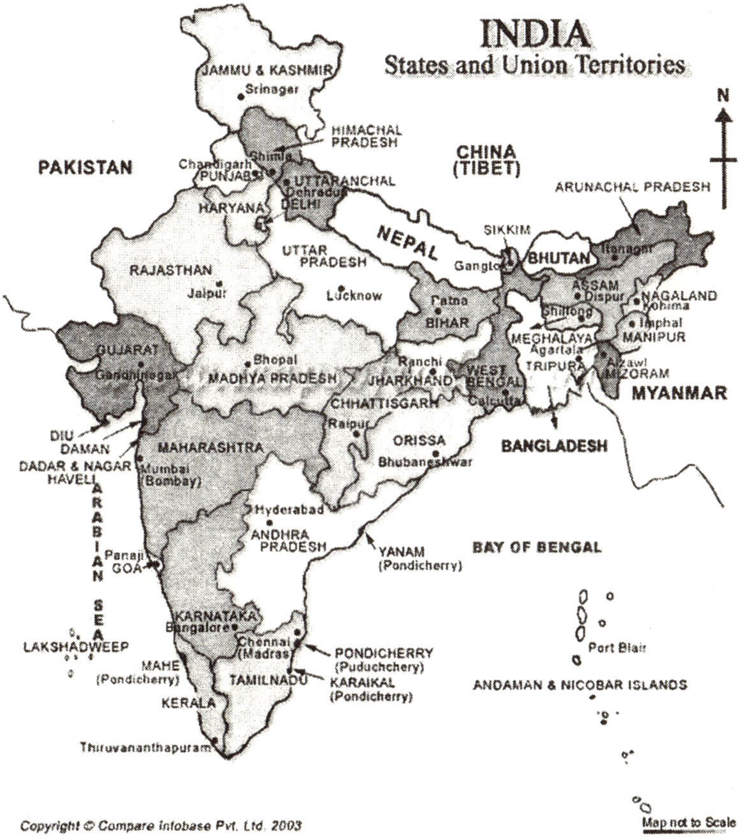

claim that RNFS growth happened where agricultural growth precedes.

One reason why RNFS is considered important is to counter the undersirable consequences of rapid urban population growth. Rural non-farm activity can successfully reduce large scale rural urban migration. This has many social benefits such as lower levels of congestion, and less pressure on infrastructure which had caused social and economic problems.

However, the expansion of the RNFE share can result from two different processes (see Figure 1.1), from (i) distress-diversification, as pressure on land cuts farm income and output per head, and forces people out of agriculture; or from (ii) linkage-diversification, as higher agricultural income and output (e.g. from technological improvement induced by pressure on land) induces more RNFE activity via 'growth linkages' from agriculture.

When agriculture grows slowly or shrinks relative to workforce growth, distress-diversification_into unproductive or low paid RNFS may take place. This occurs when labour is not fully absorbed in the farm sector and the RNFS acts as a sponge for excess labour.

Alternatively, rapid agricultural growth may induce growth in the RNFS through linkage diversification in 4 main ways. These are (a) backward production linkages, (b) forward production linkages, (c) consumption links and (d) farm accumulation, leading to the generation of a surplus which may be invested in the RNFS. Backward linkages are related to agricultural use of locally produced tools, equipment etc. Agricultural growth may lead to increased demand for the supply of produced goods and services (e.g. maintenance and repair of farm machinery). Forward production linkages occur from farming to the RNFS and entail activities such as agricultural processing and post-harvest activities. Farm growth raises the income of the rural community which can increase consumer demand for local non-farm consumer goods and services. Finally agricultural growth may generate surplus for investment in both farm and non-farm production.

Figure 1.1. What Evidence would Support 'Distress Diversification' or 'Growth Linkages'?

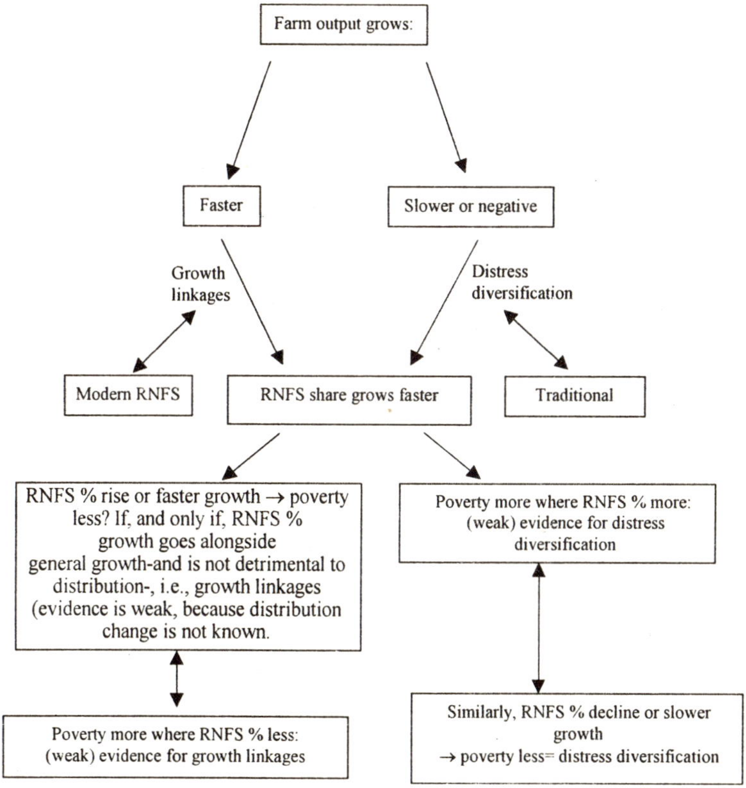

The argument of this thesis is that, if distress diversification is dominant, a rapid rise in the RNFS share of workers normally focused on 'traditional' occupations, such as household crafts (e.g. basket making, carpentry, blacksmith, handlooms, pottery, petty trade, toddy tapping, cotton carders, milk vending, butchers, barbers, cobblers) goes with slow agricultural and total growth. If linkage diversification dominates, a rapid rise in the RNFS share normally focuses on 'modern' occupations (e.g. transport, retail, construction, services) and goes with fast agricultural and total growth.

The main point we claim is that distress diversification out of unsuccessful agriculture lead to traditional RNFS. Growth linkages from successful agriculture leads to modern RNFS.

1.3 Sectoral Distribution of Workers in Rural AP

The labour market in AP has the highest proportion of agricultural labour households in all India (Appendix Table 1.1). Among such households, casual labour[3] (see Appendix Table 1.10.) forms the majority and its share of the agricultural labour force has been growing over the period. In Appendix Table 1.1 two important things are identified.

- The trends in AP relative to India are falling RNFE share; rising agricultural labour/cultivators ratio that stretch back to 1961, not just during the 1981-91 period.
- Even all-India has stagnant or slightly falling RNFS share. This is a peculiar feature given rural growth. This observation was also true between 1961-81 period.

AP has the highest AGSPRs in the country (Appendix Table 1.3). For example, the UPAS and UPSS rate (for definitions see Appendix Table 1.12) in the 15-59 years age group was 92.3 per cent among rural males in AP (1987-88) compared to an all-India 88.7 per cent. The corresponding rates for females were 72 per cent and 52 per cent. Male workforce participation rates are higher than the females, and rates are highest in the age group 15-59. AP would appear like everywhere else in these respects. High AGSPRs would mean low unemployment if people participate because there is a good chance of finding work. It can be shown that the AGSPRs are lower where unemployment is lower (Appendix Tables 1.3 and 1.7).

The gender composition of the work force changed slowly at the national level, but fast in the rural areas of AP (Appendix Table 1.3). The increase in the female percentage of labour force has also been faster in rural AP than in rural all-India. Because female participation rose faster than for males, there is a bigger gap between women in AP and all-India than for men.

Slow RNFE growth and low RNFE shares in AP is the core issue of this thesis, in part because they contribute to a key problem for AP that AGSPRs and unemployment rates[4] (UPSS)[5] are higher in AP than in India as a whole.

AP has the highest percentage of rural workers (defined as workers/population)[6] for total, males and females when compared with all-India according to the National Sample Survey (NSS) Daily Status, Weekly Status, and Usual Status.(See Appendix Table 1.4 for definitions of these concepts and Appendix 1.12 for the figures).

Possible reasons for the high participation rates in AP are first, it appears that the share of the population of working age in AP is growing faster than in other states.

Growth rates of rural working age population (15 years and above) in AP and India 1961-71 and 1971-81 are presented in Appendix Table 1.11. Census data for 1991 on working age population is not readily available and only 1971-81 Census data results are presented.

Between 1961 and 1971 growth rates of rural population in the age group of 15 and above was lower in AP than for all-India, for both men and women. However over the 1971-81 period the situation had reversed both for male and female workers which had higher growth rates in AP than in India. However, the caveat applies that the figures are average figures and do not allow clearly for the identification of a clear time trend.

The total population has grown by 2.2 per cent per year between 1981 and 1991. Over this period, the number of employed people (main workers) has also grown but by over 2.3 per cent per year (Final Population Census AP 1991: 23). Thus, the proportion of rural main workers in the total rural population of AP has increased by an annual 0.12 per cent.

By 1991 :

- India's rural crude participation rate for males in 1991 is 52.43 per cent.
- AP's rural crude participation rates for males in 1991 is 58.01 per cent.

- AP exceeds all-India by 5.58 per cent and AP has the highest crude participation rate for males in India, AP's high participation rates relative to all India may be explained by past demographic trends and AP's current demographic structure, in particular.
- AP has a higher share of people aged 15-59, and
- AP has higher age/gender-specific workforce participation rates.

1.4 Objectives of the Study

This thesis seeks to test 'distress diversification' against 'growth linkages' to explain the propensity of rural people to be involved in the RNFS. This is done through (a) district level and (b) household level regressions of RNFE total shares and growth, and by sub-sectors in AP.

The large differences in percentages of RNFE in AP and all-India provide the basis for investigating employment potentialities in non-farm activities. The main purpose of the thesis is to account for different levels and trends in the composition of RNFE in AP, and in the shares and growth of RNFE in Visakhapatnam and Krishna districts and in Veeravalli and Anandapuram villages during 1981-91, and to identify some of the factors that influence RNFE. The research examine and explain emerging patterns of employment in RNFE. Factors will also be identified which contribute to labour absorption in the non-farm sector at district and household levels. The thesis also identifies the determinants of inter-household differences in participation in RNFE for two villages of AP, and accounts for differences in the probability that a household has a member who has his or her primary occupation in the RNFS.

1.5 Questions Addressed by the Thesis

The central question of my research is whether, and how, the RNFS can contribute to the achievement of 'low levels of involuntary unemployment and/or higher workforce participation rates' in rural AP and to more equitable economic growth.

The research will attempt two things in distinct chapters. First, Chapter 3 identifies variables that account for inter-district variation in 1981 and 1991, in the level and growth of RNFE share. Second I identify (slightly different) variables to account for inter-household variation, in 1994-95 field survey, in the probability that a household contributes a worker to RNFE in Chapter 4.

As a consequence, it is proposed that the following hypotheses will be tested:

This thesis seeks to test 'distress diversification' against 'growth linkages' as explanations of employment viz., of the propensity of rural people to be involved in the RNFS. The strict agricultural growth linkages (AGL) is that higher (or a faster growing) agricultural income/output/employment tends to cause more (or faster-growing) nearby rural non-farm share. The agricultural distress diversification hypothesis (ADD) is that lower (or slower-growing) agricultural production (or 'performance' in agriculture) causes higher (or faster growing) RNFE shares. The research will also test a wider 'development linkage/diversification hypothesis'. This overall development linkage hypothesis (ODL) is that higher (or faster growing) development indicators such as literacy, bank branches and urbanisation tend to cause more (or faster growing) nearby RNFE. The converse overall distress diversification hypothesis (ODD) is that lower (or slower-growing) development indicators cause higher (or faster-growing) RNFE shares.

A central hypothesis that will be tested in Chapter 3 and Chapter 4 is that different factors determine 'traditional' and 'modern' RNFE shares in total employment. A high traditional rural non-farm share is likely to be associated with a low number of years of education of workers in a household, lower castes, and agricultural indicators suggesting distress diversification. A high modern rural non-farm share is likely to be associated with a higher number of years of education of workers, upper castes and agricultural indicators suggesting rural growth linkages from agriculture.

This thesis is intended to contribute to resolving the conflicting explanations of RNFE growth: is it due to 'distress-diversification' into non-farm activities, or to rural growth linkages? We argue that when rural labour is not fully absorbed in the farm sector, the traditional non-farm sector acts as a sponge for overload labour spillover into unproductive and low paid (compared with the prevailing wage rates/below subsistence relative to the farm wage) non-farm activities.

However the modern RNFS has strong backward and forward production growth linkages and consumption linkages with the farm sector.[7] The performance of the agricultural sector favourably influences modern non-farm employment and income.

The thesis also hypothesises that certain traditional industries, such as handloom weaving, cobbling, traditional gunny-bag making, basket-making, pottery, and toddy-tapping lose out to modern industries in the process of development. This loss results in a change in the occupational pattern of employment.

It appears logical to study the employment problem nature at the micro-level in a predominantly agricultural region, to get a clear picture of the level of the non-farm activities that prevail. There have been few micro level empirical analyses of these activities.

1.6 The Methodology and the Sample Areas

1.6.1 The Area of Study

The research proposes to study RNFE at household level in order to get a clear idea of the state and characteristics of RNFE in AP. In addition to the reasons given earlier and apart from the familiarity of the researcher with this region (whose districts are listed on Map 2, page 25), AP seems well suited for the present study for two reasons.

First, AP has three distinct regions in terms of modes of production, Coastal Andhra, Rayalaseema and Telengana. Whilst the coastal districts (except the tribal areas) are well-endowed, Rayalaseem is ecologically denuded and in the rain-shadow region. There has been no technological breakthrough in regard to agricultural growth in the semi-arid region and rain-fed districts are characterised by low land productivity. Telangana is considered socially under-developed. As for the cropping patterns, drought prone districts are characterised by low yield crops which give low returns. Moreover these districts have mixed cropping and rotations are more prominent so that their cropping patterns are more complex than those of the non-drought prone districts. The agricultural economy of the well-endowed region is dominated by paddy cultivation.

Second, there are marked regional variations in the non-farm sector. Commercialisation of the farm sector has especially developed in the Coastal Andhra region, compared to the Rayalaseema and Telangana regions.

1.6.2 Key Definitions

(a) Definition of RNFE

For rural non-farm employment we use the definition given by the 1991 Census, which is workers who have been "engaged in some economic activity only those who work over 183 days in a year, mainly in RNFE during the year preceding enumeration and who are neither cultivators or agricultural labourers but are 'other workers' (non-farm workers)".

The Census of India categorises all rural workers into nine 'industrial' categories. For our study we define as 'farm workers' as any engaged mainly only for 183 days in a year in categories I to III. (I) being cultivators, (II) agricultural labourers and (III) is agricultural allied activities i.e. livestock rearing, forestry, fishing, plantations, orchards and allied activities. Non-farming activities consist of: (IV) mining and quarrying; (V) manufacturing, processing, servicing, and repairs; (Va) in household (HH) industry; (Vb) in other than household industry; (VI) construction; (VII) trade and commerce; (VIII) transport, storage and communications and (IX) other services.

For our study, we shall define a RNF worker as: 'engaged in non-farm activities', any worker within a household who has, as a primary occupation one or several of the activities covered by the Census of India 1991 (occupational categories 1V-1X workers). In other words, all those who work in a primary occupation in any field of economic activity, other than cultivation or agricultural labour who, in turn, are deemed as 'non-farm workers'.

Principal occupations were determined on the basis of the time spent by the HH. Respondents (who were mainly the head of the HH but occasionally were all of the inhabitants within the HH) were asked to rank their occupation as being primary on the basis of what they spent the majority of the year employed as. So, a household may have several secondary occupations, but only one primary one. The occupation which was undertaken by working members of the HH most often and which required at least 183 or more days employment per person in a year (Census of India, 1991) was treated as primary and counted as a non-farm worker.

(b) Concept of rural areas :

The Census definition of a rural areas used here, requires: a population below 5,000; a population density of less than 400 persons per square kilometre; less than 75 per cent of the male working population engaged in non-agricultural pursuits.

1.6.3. Data Base and Sampling Procedure

The study uses district level and household data so as to estimate trends and determinants of RNFE by major industry groups and at household level.

(a) Secondary data sources:

Census data is used for estimating trends in aggregate and sub-sector RNFE at the state and district levels (Map 2).The data refers to main workers only, i.e. those who had worked for the major part of the year (183 days) or more. Marginal workers are those who had worked for less than six months (183 days) in the year (Census 1991:5).

The most important secondary data sources are the Census of AP published by the Census of India (1991), Series-2, Paper-1 of 1991 'Supplement Final Population Tables, AP', Census of India (1981) Series-2 AP part 11-A 'General Population Tables'. In addition information from Census of India (1961, and 1971) and from censuses carried out in 1961, 1971, 1981 and 1991 was used. National Sample Survey data available is from NSS for October 1972-September 1973, for July 1977-June 1978, for January-December 1983 and for July 1987-June 1988. Data for human labour is from, 'Cost of Cultivation of Principal Crops in India', Directorate of Economics and Statistics (1991), Department of Agriculture and Co-operation, Ministry of Agriculture, published in New Delhi.

Other data sources are from the Directorate of Economics and Statistics, Government of AP, Hyderabad, from the Centre for Economic and Social Studies (CESS) and from village studies from AERC (Agro-Economic Research Centre), Waltair, Hand Books of Statistics, Chief Planning Officer, Visakhapatnam and Krishna districts.

There are limitations with the data from Census and National Sample Survey Organisation (NSSO) that had to be relied upon. Census data is preferred to NSS data. Available secondary NSS data has limitations. In NSSO Rounds on unemployment, data is not presented in a uniform manner over the rounds, making comparisons over time difficult. NSS data for the district level is not available. The NSS data (presented at the national, state and regional) level is aggregated, limiting the use of such data. Disaggregated estimates will give a better insight into the problem. Data on RNFE is scant. Secondary data limitations have been experienced throughout the study.

Earlier studies of non-farm employment were mostly based on secondary data and to some extent primary data. The present study is different from the earlier ones in two respects. First, in its use of primary data and second, in that it analysed the existing situation at the micro level through an examination of case studies.

Map 1.2 : The districts of Andhra Pradesh.

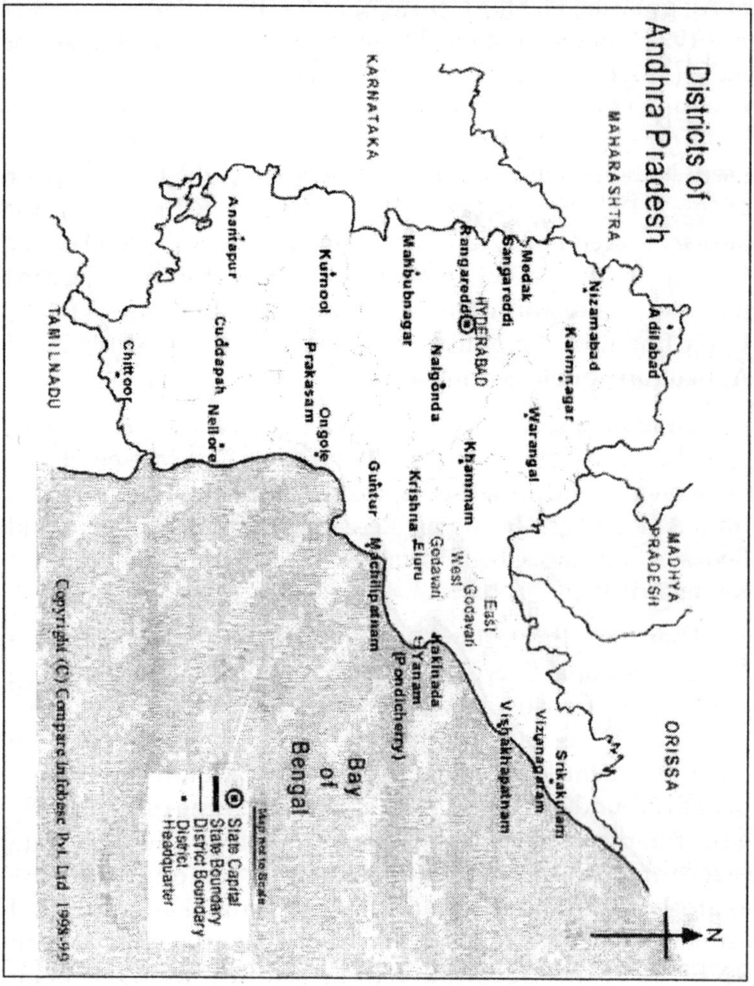

Note : The *Coastal Andhra* region is composed of the districts of Srikakulam, Vizianagaram, Visakhapatnam, East Godavari, West Godavari, Krishna, Guntur, Prakasam, and Nellore. The *Rayalaseema* region is composed of the districts of Kurnool, Anantapur, Cuddapah, and Chittoor. The *Telangana* region is formed of the remaining districts Ranga Reddy, Hyderabad, Nizamabad, Medak, Mahabubnagar, Nalgonda, Warangal, Khammam, Karimnagar, and Adilabad.

(b) Household level data

The household level data set covers two villages, one each (selected on the basis of the value of agricultural production per acre cultivated) in a high and a low-productivity district, that is respectively Visakhapatnam and Krishna.[8] Visakhapatnam is one of the agriculturally least developed of all coastal districts in AP and is in North coastal AP. Krishna is in central coastal AP and has better irrigation facilities, transport and communications, and educational institutions compared with Visakhapatnam. Krishna district is endowed with a rich variety of soils; rice is the main food crop. The delta area in the Krishna district occupies an important place in agriculture.

1.7 The Structure of the Thesis

The thesis consists of six chapters. This introductory chapter has outlined the problem, various concepts and empirical aspects of employment/unemployment categories in farm and non-farm sectors in rural areas of AP. It also presented the importance of RNFE, the structural distribution of rural workers, age/gender-specific participation rates in rural AP, and unemployment in AP. It then briefly introduced the objectives, the hypothesis, data base and methodology of the study.

Chapter 2 provides a survey of the literature dealing with RNFE, mostly for India and other South-Asian countries. It deals with the theoretical approach of the research and addresses the issues through a review of the results of theoretical and empirical research regarding non-farm employment. It mainly reviews the links between agricultural development and output and employment growth in the RNFE and also reviews the non-agricultural factors which influence RNFE.

Chapters 3 and 4 constitute the empirical core of the thesis. Chapter 3 describes, in total and by gender, district-wise trends in the share, patterns of change and growth of RNFE in AP between 1981+ and 1991.The model which will be used to explain RNFE is specified and the variables used in the subsequent empirical analysis are identified. The final sections of the Chapter identify the main determinants of aggregate RNFE and its major industry groups at district level through OLS and log linear estimates, and also uses the results to explore and analyse the hypotheses of distress-diversification vs. growth linkages. Questions relating to the role and performance of farm and non-farm activities in terms of employment in the light of the literature review in Chapter 2 are then raised.

Chapter 4 is divided into 2 parts. Part 1 provides, both at the district and village level (data from Mandal Revenue Offices; District Collector Offices; and the Directorate of Economics and Statistics, Government of AP), a general description of socio-economic characteristics of the two districts (Section 4.1) and villages (Section 4.2) under special study. Demographic characteristics, occupational structure, land-utilisation, cropping-pattern, irrigation sources, and land holding patterns are discussed. These profiles provide the background to understanding the role of rural non-farm activities in the area under study.

Chapter 4 part 2 seeks to identify differences, among households in the two villages, that account for differences in the probability that a household has a member who both (1) works for at least 183 days a year, and (2) has his or her main occupation (by time) in the RNFS. Next, we look for differences in the probability that a household has such a member in (a) modern, (b) traditional RNFE separately. The possible determinants of probability of a household having a main worker in RNFE are analysed through LOGIT models for the two villages.

Chapter 5 deals with special features of certain non-farm activities based on selected individual households (case-studies of RNFE) from two villages, Veeravalli and Anandapuram. The chapter also presents some of the problems of RNFE in the selected villages, elucidating specific issues and using some of the findings to discuss some policy implications.

Finally, Chapter 6 provides a short summary of main findings of the study and discusses the policy implications of the findings.

NOTES

1. A map of India with the location of Andhra Pradesh is presented on page 5. India is divided into 28 States. AP is a large Southern State with 66.5 million population (Census 1991). It is the fourth State in terms of area (276,254 sq. kms) and of population. The native language are Telugu and Urdu. AP has 23 districts. It is an agriculturally important state. In casual labour households it is the second in 17 major states in India (the first being Tamil Nadu). It is a state with fast urbanisation and industrialisation.
2. Statistical Abstract of Andhra Pradesh (1992:207).
3. 'Casual-wage labour' persons casually engaged in other's farm or non-farm enterprises (both household and non-household) and for wages, according to the terms of the daily or periodic work contract, are treated as casual wage labour.
4. 'Work participation rate' refers to the proportion of total workers in the population expressed as a percentage and not to the proportion of labour force or the economically active population which is conventionally used.
5. As defined by Usual Principal Activity Status (UPAS), by Usual Principal Subsidiary Status (UPSS) (main and marginal workers) all respondents are counted as either 'main workers' or 'marginal workers'. The UPAS of a respondent was defined as 'working' or 'employed' if, and only if, that respondent worked for 183 days or more in any gainful work activities (coded 11 to 51) during the 365 days preceding the day of the survey. These respondents are termed main workers.

   Usual Principal Subsidiary Status: the UPSS of a respondent was defined as 'marginal worker' if, and only if, that respondent worked in some gainful activity more or less regularly (but for less than 183 days), even if it was intermittent in nature. Only main workers can have UPAS, and only marginal workers can have UPSS.

   According to the usual status classification these two groups, viz. those workers with the UPAS status and those with UPSS status together constituted all workers.
6. The Census and NSS classify people as rural only when they live in locations with a population of less than 5000 [Census of India Series-2 AP (1991:6)]. The primary objective of the NSSO quinquennial surveys is to measure the extent of 'employment' and 'unemployment' in quantitative terms. This is disaggregated

by different population characteristics, such as age, sex, education for different geographical regions. To meet this objective, the surveys attempt to classify the population aged 5 years and above into different activity categories. The entire NSS survey of one year was divided into four sub-round periods of three months duration coinciding approximately with the four climatic seasons. Sub-round 1: July 87-September 87, Sub-round 2: October 87-December 87, Sub-round 3: January 88 - March 88, Sub-round 4: April 88 - June 88.

7. Mellor (1986) and Hazell (1988) suggest on the basis of empirical evidence that the strongest linkages originate from smaller farms (5-10 acres).

8. A study by the Agro-Economic Research Centre, Visakhapatnam (1974), selected indicators of resource base and of infrastructure so as to estimate input use and productivity for all the districts in AP. The districts were ranked and classified into high and low productivity districts on the basis of the value of agricultural production per acre cultivated. Of the two districts, Krishna emerged as an agriculturally developed and Visakhapatnam as agriculturally less developed district. The profile of these districts and of the villages Anandapuram and Veeravalli were selected so as to assess the differences in the pattern of non-farm employment at two development 'scales'.

   On the basis of levels of output and growth patterns (variation in the growth of output is analysed by the method of decomposition of output) the districts of Krishna, Guntur, East Godavari and West Godavari are identified as developed while Srikakulam, Vizianagaram and Visakhapatnam districts were identified as backward in terms of growth in agriculture. On the basis of a composite index, all Districts in AP were grouped according to their level of socio-economic development. Visakhapatnam is identified as one of the backward districts in AP.

2

RURAL NON-FARM EMPLOYMENT IN INDIA: A REVIEW OF THE EVIDENCE

INTRODUCTION

This chapter presents a survey of the literature on rural non-farm production and employment concentrating mainly on Indian and other south-Asian countries, but also including examples from Africa. The chapter is divided into three main sections and covers three sets of influences on the RNFS: 2.1 agricultural growth linkages to RNFE share and growth 2.2 general growth and development linkages to RNFE shares and growth 2.3 other possible causes in RNFE share and growth i.e. the distress diversification and finally 2.4 presents the key findings from the literature review.

2.1. Agricultural Growth Linkages to RNFE Shares and Growth

This section discusses the evidence on how RNFE is affected by agriculture-related factors such as the 'agriculture first' strategy, agricultural commercialisation, land holding size, and RNFE and irrigation. Is RNFS agriculture-linked?

In this section, 2.1.1 provides a description of the rural growth linkages (RGL) model, 2.1.2 the results of efforts to substantiate the RGL models, 2.1.3 counter-arguments regarding doubtful aspects of the method for substantiating the RGL hypothesis, 2.1.4 the distinction between sector-level diversification and household livelihood strategies, 2.1.5 trends in agricultural employment in A.P., 2.1.6 'Agriculture first' strategy for RNFE, 2.1.7 agricultural development and commercialisation and RNFE, 2.1.8 irrigation and RNFE and 2.1.9 farm-size structure and the quantitative significance of non-farm activities and employment.

2.1.1 A description of the rural growth linkages (RGL) Model

The rural non-farm sector was neglected by economists who were mainly working in the two sector growth models (Lewis, 1972; Ranis-Fei, 1961). In the two sector model it is assumed that employment in the modern industrial sector will expand and absorb the supply of labour from agriculture. This assumption has proved to be unrealistic. Lewis and Ranis-Fei both refer to two sectors as agriculture and non-agriculture, irrespective of whether these are rural or urban. However, the logic of their approach does not exclude the RNFS. Indeed, where (as in China, Taiwan and Korea) much early industrial growth was in the RNFS.

An explicit effort to incorporate RNFS into a growth paradigm was Mellor's (1976) topic of discussion of agricultural growth linkages (AGL): forward and backward and consumption linkages from agriculture to the non-farm sector. Forward linkages include those to processors and distributors in the non-farm sector (such as processing, transport and marketing of agricultural activities). Such linkages are frequently quite strong and the strength of such forward linkages depends crucially on the choice and location of the processing technology involved. The backward production linkages from agriculture to RNFE (rural input suppliers) are also crucial to agricultural performance and there may also be backward linkages to those who supply and maintain produced goods. Finally, consumer demand linkages are generated as a result of increasing farm incomes. Consumption linkages from agricultural income to non-farm sector are normally defined as one type of forward linkages. Push and pull factors are both important in influencing the level and growth of the RNFS. In some rural areas non-farm activities may be increasing because of agricultural growth and in some other areas, the workforce might have been pushed out of the farm sector because of lack of farm growth. The AGL model emphasises the pull factors.

Mellor, (1976 p.177) argued that:

> 'A rural-led strategy of development is likely to produce high average rates of return to investment in agriculture; rapid growth of small-scale rural industry receiving direct capital from cultivators; price relationships for industrial consumer goods which facilitate high profits and reinvestment; and an income base in agriculture sufficient to support taxes to self-finance much of the infrastructure requirements. The resulting substantial net outflow of resources from agriculture will spur growth in other sectors of the economy even while agriculture itself is expanding rapidly and profitably'.

Mellor also argued that increases in farm income stimulate demand for consumer goods and services. Agriculture must be given a leading role for a better employment-oriented strategy for economic growth. The larger agricultural production on medium and large farms increases cash incomes to these farmers. The bigger cash incomes provide a demand for increased non-agricultural production and a resultant rise in employment. The expanded employment of the lower-income classes that spend the bulk of increased income on food provides the demand for additional food production.

The focus is on increased employment through growth linkages and greater participation of the poor in economic growth rather than on the redistribution of existing output. Mellor focused on the concept of growth linkages. While the production linkages from economically backward agriculture may be low, technological innovation and intensification will enhance these linkages and rising agricultural incomes provide the impetus for consumption linkages. A non-farm employment oriented growth strategy requires emphasising agricultural development. Mellor's central argument is that RNFS growth is increasingly becoming vital because agriculture is income-inelastic in demand (which means a given proportionate change in income will not be matched by proportionate change in demand for agricultural products).

Following on from Mellor's work, Hazell & Haggblade (1991) developed a model designed to estimate the strength of farm and non-farm linkages, based on the hypothesis that the performance of the RNFS is linked to agricultural performance. A substantial share of RNFS involves agro-processing and consumer goods production through forward linkages, and repair and supply of farm inputs through backward linkages. Dominant sectors like trade and services provide largely for rural consumer demand. The growth of RNFE is driven primarily by agricultural growth, while infrastructure also showed a positive impact on RNFE.

Mellor also emphasised that non-farm linkages generated by bio-technical change on small and medium farms can accentuate both overall agricultural growth and its poverty-reducing effect. Besides stimulating national economic growth, the production and consumption linkages affect poverty and spatial growth patterns, particularly when the agricultural growth is concentrated on small and medium-size farms (Johnston and Kilby, 1975; Mellor, 1976; Mellor and Johnston, 1984) (this is due to the nature of the producer and consumer goods demanded by lower income farmers). The kinds of non-farm goods and services demanded by small and medium-size farms are often those produced by small, labour-intensive enterprises, whose growth can contribute to increased employment and income-earning opportunities for the poor (Hazell & Haggblade, 1991). Because much of the resulting growth in non-farm activity occurs in rural areas and small towns, it can help to contain rural to urban migration.

(Hazell & Hojjati 1995 p.1) argued that:

> "The rural non-farm economy is also intimately linked to agriculture. For example, a substantial share of rural manufacturing involves agro-processing and the production, repair and supply of farm inputs. Moreover, the dominant sectors in the RNFE consist of trade and services establishments that cater largely to rural consumer demand. The prospects for growth in

the RNFE will, therefore, hinge on future agricultural performance".

However, Unni (1991 p.30) argued that

> "A high incidence of poverty in a region could also result in distress diversification into non-agricultural activity. Households in the more impoverished regions, where agricultural development has not taken place, perhaps depend on some form of non-agricultural activity for their livelihood".

since such poverty is likely to be associated with weak agricultural performance, we also argue that the agricultural distress diversification (ADD) i.e., lower (or slower-growing) agricultural production or 'performance', on cause higher RNFE shares. A central task of this thesis is to assess which types of RNFE are associated with ADD and which types with growth linkages.

2.1.2 *The Results of efforts to Substantiate the Rural Growth Linkages Model*

Bell, Hazell and Slade (1982) used an input - output model derived from a social accounting matrix for the Muda region in order to measure the direct and indirect effects of the project. They estimated that every $1 of value added in agriculture generated directly from the project stimulated an additional 83 cents in the region's non-farm economy. Of these downstream effects, 40 per cent was due to production linkages (backward and forward), and 60 per cent to consumption linkages. Hazell and Roell (1983) claimed that larger farmers exhibit relatively strong demand for regional non-tradable commodities, and that their consumption behaviour is therefore a key source of growth in the regional economy. The example of North Arcot district of Tamil Nadu in India, also shows there are multiplier effects from agriculture (Hazell and Ramasamy, 1991). Haggblade *et al* (1989) estimated that African regional growth multipliers are approximately 60 per cent below those in Asia; a $1 increase in agriculture income in Africa produces only 50 cents of additional rural non-farm income, compared with more than 80 cents in Asia. The reasons they give for lower production and consumption linkages in Africa compared to Asia include ecology, low population densities, lower levels of commercialisation and urban-biased policies which constrain non-farm supply response.

'Empirical studies revealed the strength of farm non-farm growth linkages in Asia. Increases in agricultural output stimulate secondary rounds of growth in RNFE income that are 50-80 per cent larger than the initial increases in agricultural income (e.g. Bell, Hazell Slade, 1982; Hazell and Ramasamy, 1991; Hazell and Haggblade, 1991; and Rangarajan, 1982). Employment multipliers are also substantial, with evidence from the Philippines (Gibb, 1974) and India (Krishna, 1976; Mellor and Mudahar,1974) placing agriculture-to-non-farm employment elasticities between 1.0 and 1.3'.

Studies carried out in Sierra Leone, Nigeria, Malaysia and Bangladesh revealed a strong positive relationship between changes in rural household income and changes in the demand for rural small scale enterprise goods and services (Deb & Houssain, 1984; Hazell & Roell, 1983; King & Byerlee, 1978). The expenditure elasticities for (small scale) rural non-farm activities are consistently high, ranging from 1.34 in Nigeria, to 1.40 in Sierra Leone and 2.05 in Malaysia. A one per cent increase in rural household income in Sierra Leone would lead to a 1.4 per cent increase in spending on rural small scale non-farm activities. Moreover, in Nigeria and Malaysia, the expenditure elasiticities for these activities are higher than those for comparable products purchased from enterprises outside the region.

A semi-input-output model was used by Haggblade and Hazel, (1989) to estimate the multiplier effects of growth in agriculture on non-farm income. The agricultural income multiplier varies between 1.22 to 1.43. This means a Rs.1 increase in agricultural income due to technological change results in Rs. 0.22 to Rs. 0.43 additional income in the RNFS.

Time-series evidence comes from the moderately prosperous agricultural region of North Arcot. Using a simulation model for the region, Hazell and Ramasamy (1991) have estimated demand multipliers emanating from agricultural growth over the Seventies. They estimate that, as a result of production and consumption linkages, every Rs. 100 increase in agricultural income induced an additional Rs. 87 in income in other sectors of the rural economy. Production linkages accounted for about half the increase and consumption linkages the other half.

More generally, four things emerge from the literature. First, countries with more equal (smaller) farms tend to have larger RNFE shares. This is strongly visible for the more developed countries, such as the Republic of Korea, Japan and Taiwan (China), where the process of inter-sectoral labour transfer has been the most successful.

However, the presence or absence of measured local RNFE linkages depends heavily on whether rural towns, or places just across district borders, are included in RNFE income gains (a major criticism by B. Harriss, 1987).

In conclusion, these empirical studies indicate the importance of backward and forward linkages between farm and non-farm activities and point to the need for future research on the linkage question amongst several regions with different scales of development.

2.1.3 *Counter-Arguments Regarding Doubtful Aspects of the Method for Substantiating the RGL Hypothesis*

The purpose of this section is to examine whether there any evidence to suggest that regional growth linkage concepts misinterpret some of the key dynamics of rural industrialisation. In this regard the contributions made by Harriss (1987) and Hart (1998) are significant.

Harriss (1986, p.8) questioned whether consumption expenditure was a response to agricultural production or non-farm income and also argued that there were flows from agriculture to urban commercial centres. She found that:

> "Despite negative evidence of linkages from the newer industrial estates and despite the relative neglect of agro-industry in the

district's credit plans, it appears that North Arcot's "backward industrialisation" is strongly and directly linked to agricultural production, less strongly to consumption".

The main criticism about the growth linkages approach questions not only the quantitative importance of financial flows comprising consumption linkages but also the local location, small size and high labour intensity of units providing these goods and services. She noticed that much rural industry is not geared in terms of its product mix to local consumption, rather it is geared to local and non-local production.

In North Arcot, Harriss argues that RNFS production linkages were missed by Harriss and Ramasamy because they were considered out-of-district by being just over the border (in small rural towns).

Harriss (1993) concludes that the growth of the non-farm economy is also determined by the growth of the non-local home and national markets and increasing regional integration. Meanwhile, the interaction between large farms, banks and finances is increasing. There is also a flow of agricultural surplus to the urban commercial industrial economy.

Harriss (1987, p.276) examined the methodologies, assumptions and data base for the quantification of the local and non-local regional multiplier effects from agricultural development. The direction of causation in the pioneering growth linkages model exercises has been from agriculture to the rest of the economy, rather than the reverse, or allowing for full feedbacks (Rangarajan, 1982; Ahammed and Herdt, 1984).

Harriss (1987, p.276) asserted that "Controversial issues are (a) whether all these downstream effects or growth linkages of agriculture are stronger or weaker than those of industry; (b) whether consumption linkages are stronger or weaker than non-local linkages; (c) whether local linkages are stronger or weaker than non-local linkages; (d) whether local linkages are better than non-local linkages and thus whether state governments should implement policies with public investment in agriculture; (e) whether the generation of initial extra income for large farmers leads to more or less, and to better or worse, linkages than the generation of similar extra income for small farmers; and (f) whether the extra impact from these linkages leads to extra output, extra imports or higher prices (Johnston and Kilby, 1975; Mellor, 1976; 1983)". Further, Harriss raised the issue of the social accounting matrix which concerns the absence of sensitivity analyses and of discussions of measurement errors. In the case of commercial rice milling, which is the most important forward linkage, the values of paddy inputs and outputs have been scaled from surveys made in other years and provinces. Other inputs and components of value added were obtained from one or two rice mills in the region (Bell, Hazell and Slade, 1982; p. 297). These components have elsewhere been subject to great variation according to technology and capacity utilisation (Timmer, 1974; Harriss, 1979).

Hart (1998 p. 28, 31) also presents the criticism related to the assumptions underlying some of the growth linkage studies and the subsequent interpretation of results. She argues that:

> "diversification of local rural economies does not emerge automatically from agricultural growth and market expansion. Rather, intersectoral and spatial linkages depend crucially on the social logic of investment - that is, who gets the surplus and what they do with it - as well as on wider configurations of political economic forces".

She raised the question of:

> "whether agricultural growth can play a progressive role without prior redistribution along the lines of a Taiwanese-style land reform; particularly if larger farmers have preferential access to yield-increasing technology, consumption linkages can easily turn into import leakages if incremental income from agricultural growth is spent on luxury imports rather than labour-intensive, domestically produced goods and services".

She also argued that "in the Muda region of Malaysia, the growth of smallholder agriculture did not lead automatically to sustained diversification. In Taiwan, regional diversification cannot be attributed simply to agricultural growth. In Taiwan, and more recently in Malaysia, rising costs in urban areas have been a primary force propelling rural industrialisation. Yet the particular institutional forms and distributional outcomes are dramatically different. Ironically, the closest approximation to the outcome envisaged by the neoliberal regional growth linkage model is to be found in semi-socialist China. In certain parts of China, resources have indeed been retained within local circuits in ways that have dynamized some rural regions and sharply reduced poverty. Rural industrialisation in China since the 1980s is partly the product of a remarkable set of institutional innovations that combine collective ownership with market discipline".

One of the controversial aspects of the quantitative regional growth linkage models has been the estimates of consumption linkages. In particular, the contention that larger farmers display more multiplicative consumption patterns because they spend a higher proportion of incremental income on regional non-tradables (Haggblade *et al.*, 1989; Hazell and Roell, 1983). Accordingly, they should be the main targets of productivity increasing agricultural projects. This argument, which has been applied both to Asian and to African cases, flies in the face of the widely-held view that an agrarian structure dominated by egalitarian peasant agriculture (such as that in Taiwan) is most conducive to high levels of demand for labour-intensive, locally-produced goods (Ranis and Stewart, 1987, 1993).

Bhalla (1993) reports a decline in employment elasticities of agricultural output. However, this decline was accompanied by a rise in real wages which could partly be explained by a rise in demand for labour in non-farm activities (construction and services) (Bhalla, 1991; Hanumantha Rao, 1998).

The evidence available from the Census of India and NSS indicates that non-farm activities are an important component of primary and secondary employment in the rural areas of India (Census 1991). Non-farm activities in rural areas are defined by the Census as residual categories (i.e., all activities outside agriculture). Whilst some of these non-farm activities are linked directly or indirectly to agriculture, others are distinct, ranging from wage employment in industry or construction to self-employment in home-based handicrafts, trading and other services.

There is a growing recognition that non-agricultural activities in rural areas play a crucial role in providing simple consumer goods and services to the rural households. And also a big per cent of income and employment (Reardon 1998). The local provision of goods and services provides a humble but critical income to landless labour. Yet in developing countries the rural economy has until recently been viewed as an agricultural economy where in addition to crop production, fishing and forestry, a number of rural households may engage in a relatively limited amount of agro-processing, transporting and marketing of agricultural produce. The benefits are concentrated among the large farmers.

As Fisher *et al.* (1997: 25-6) stated:

> 'Comparisons across states, with their widely differing proportions of RNFS workers in the rural labour force, suggest that education, infrastructure and higher agricultural incomes all contribute towards the growth of rural non-farm employment........education is an important preparation for entry into the RNFS, and assists the mobility of workers within the sector. Better infrastructure promotes RNFS employment, for example by making transport of raw materials and products easier, or by providing electricity to RNFS units. Moreover, rural towns are often the focus of the growing RNFS, as units can enjoy better access to markets, services and infrastructure. Agricultural development provides more produce for processing and trading in the rural non-farm sector, and leads to greater demand for inputs and services supplied by the RNFS. By raising farm incomes, agricultural development also increases demand on the par of rural households for RNFS products. Finally, changes in the labour market in either sector influence the supply and demand for labour in the other'.

Likewise, the fact is that RNFE growth can result from a number of other stimuli than farm-based expenditures.

There is strong evidence to suggest that regional growth linkage concepts misinterpret some of the key dynamics of rural industrialisation. Taiwanese rural industrialisation was not simply a localised process operating directly via production linkages and demand for regional non-tradables, but was shaped in important ways by broader industrial dynamics. In addition, the specific forms of intersectoral and spatial linkages have been forged through institutional dynamics at different societal levels-in particular, the character of the coalition in control of the state and its relations with the peasantry, and the exercise of power through gender and kinship relations.

Conclusion: A high proportion of spending committed to goods and services which are locally produced, is equivalent to a high degree of labour intensity and therefore makes a 'good' impact upon poverty. However, the above review of literature questions the regional growth linkage argument that there is some best possible degree of agrarian inequality that will maximise consumption linkages, thereby generating non-farm expansion within the rural regions. Farm - non farm linkages do not emerge automatically from market expansion. Rather, they are shaped by the social relations of production, and forged through the exercise of power in many institutional arenas.

2.1.4 *The Distinction between Sector-level Diversification and Household Livelihood Strategies*

What has been reviewed in preceding sections has detailed only linkages between two sectors. Household-level analysis can help to enhance understanding of why individuals enter different types of non-farm production. Household-level studies point out that there are other factors, which may help explain total RNFE share and/or subsectors RNFE shares, not directly associated with either RGL or agricultural distress diversification such as household size, age, caste related to household livelihood strategies.

Reardon *et al.* (2000) argue that diversification of assets, activities and incomes is important to African rural households. They report that non-farm income constitutes on average about 45 per cent of rural incomes, and that push and pull factors drive diversification. The authors addressed some of the problems related to definitions and concepts, data collection, and the measurement of the nature and extent of diversification.

The livelihood is a term used frequently in recent diversification research, and while its meaning differs somewhat between studies, it generally applies to household and community behaviour, with respect to holdings and use of assets and the productive activities to which the assets are applied. The link between livelihoods and incomes needs to be made by valuing the output of livelihood activities at market and/or virtual prices. Also reviews the evidence on whether the poor are more reliant on RNFS income than the non-poor, or less reliant. There are quite region-specific conclusions and certainly there is no general trend for the poor to be more reliant on RNFS.

Nonetheless the rural non-farm economy is extremely important for the very poor section living in rural areas. The landless and the very small land holding sections of the rural population obtain more than 1/3 of their income from non-farm activities. These manufacturing and services activities use simple technology and very little investment e.g. making pots, gathering fuel, making food, weaving, domestic services and unskilled non-farm wage labour. On the other hand, for the better-off, non-farm production can include transport, commerce and certain manufacturing activities using high levels of investment such as metal works and milling.

Rural households in Africa base their economic welfare on a range of production activities: in self-employment and wage employment, producing for subsistence and the market, both within and outside agriculture (Diana Hunt, 1991, pp. 49-50). Further the author explored the theme for a new research and extension paradigm for complex, diverse and risk-prone (CDR) agriculture, exploring in particular detail its methodological implications. This is the need, particularly in CDR agriculture, for an intellectual framework that can facilitate analysis and interpretation of, and hence appropriate technological research planning and evaluation for small-scale multi-enterprise production units which are far from purely agricultural. Indeed, in sub-Saharan Africa farm household members are typically part-time farmers, and are simultaneously engaged in a variety of non-farm productive activities both for their own consumption and for the market. Yet the analytical frameworks that have been developed to explore the performance of these units reflect, on the production side, a strong bias towards the agricultural branches of household productive activity. They can be adapted to give equal weight to non-farm branches of production for rural development in terms of employment and income generation.

In many developing countries in Asia, there are 'severe limitations on the capacity of the agricultural sectors to absorb the existing supply of rural labour and to satisfy even minimum subsistence requirements of a large proportion of the rural population' (Shand, 1983: p.1). Rapid rural population growth has greatly increased the number of people that need to be absorbed into productive employment. Given agriculture's limited capacity to absorb labour, rural non-farm activity assumes increased importance as an alternative or supplementary source of rural employment and income.

There have been relatively few studies in which the household strategies towards RNFS are analysed. We shall try to provide empirical evidence which allows an insight into such household strategies.

2.1.5 Trends in Agricultural Employment in A.P.

Evidence from field studies on rice cultivation in AP suggests that over a period, employment per hectare of cropped area under HYV (high yielding varieties) has been falling. The hired labour days per hectare of irrigated paddy increased from 127 during 1957-60 to 161 for *kharif* and 198 for *rabi* in 1968-69, with the shift to HYV in the West Godavari district of AP initially. By the 1980s, there is a marked decline to almost pre-HYV level (Parthasarthy, 1987). This decline is associated with a rapid decline in bullock labour days per hectare of irrigated paddy, due to the replacement of bullock-labour by tractors in ploughing and transport (Mohan Rao, 1986: p.18). A similar picture is seen in the North Arcot district of Tamil Nadu (Chinnappa & Silva, 1980: p.210). The increase in the proportions of area under HYV since 1973-74 witnessed a continuous fall in the total labour use per hectare as seen from the data of Comprehensive Cost of Cultivation studies for West Godavari district. The index of labour use per hectare with 1973-74 as the base year showed a continuous fall and reached its lowest level of 72.13 hours by 1981-82. In terms of labour use per quintal of output, it was 79.20 hours in 1973-74 and only 49.50 hours in 1982-83. The decline reflects the increased mechanisation of agriculture, including in irrigation pumping and paddy threshing (Ramasamy *et al.*, 1986:p.9). However, the decline may also be in due to family labour inputs into HYV rising. If so, family labour is presumably moving away from non-paddy farming or RNFS, leaving landless or non-paddy families with better changes of work in those sectors. Appendix Table 2.1. and Figures 2.1., 2.2. and 2.3., which show the total rice area, production and yield. Total rice yield has been doing well between 1965-66 and 1992-93. Rice is the major staple food grain crop grown in AP. This crop is predominantly an irrigated crop and is grown in both seasons. Some times excessive rains and depression in Bay of Bengal in the month of September had caused considerable damage to the standing paddy crop.

Production and yield have generally increased, but with little changes in terms of the area under the crop. As yield per hectare increases demand for employment both in agriculture and in the RNFS is likely to increase.

Whilst fluctuation in production might occur, there has been no long run area decline although, some periods of decline can be identified for example; between 1983-84 and 1987-88 for both Kharif and rabi followed by sharp increase in 1988-89.

Area fluctuations were important for Kharif between 1968 and 1983 and became more cyclical from the mid 1970s (a 2 year cycle approximately). The fluctuations for Rabi are of a much lower magnitude but became more pronounced from the mid -1970s when a cycle of about 4 years appears. Given that rabi is produced between September and February and as the area under such rice is about 1/3 of that under kharif, it is possible that more seasonal RNFE may be generated (and sought) in that period. The caveat with such possibility is that the remaining 2/3 of the land might be devoted to other types of agricultural activities.

2.1.6 'Agriculture First' Strategy for Rural Non-Farm Employment

Mellor's proposed agriculture first (AF) strategy is expected to contribute to RNFE through a strategic shift in favour of agricultural development, based on small to medium sized farmers. This agriculture-biased pattern of development would create stronger mass demand linkages to RNFE. Following Mellor (1984), Hazell & Haggblade (1992) also argue that agriculture can influence non-farm activities through production, consumption and labour market linkages. 'Labour market linkages' can happen via FLs, BLs or CLs.(The Mellor, Hazell-Reardon claim is that labour's share of CLs in RNFS net income is higher than in FLs or BLs). The growth of production in agriculture leads to increasing demand for the supply of seeds, fertilisers, pesticides, sprays and repair services which are produced or supplied by non-farm activities. However, increases in agricultural production also give rise to increases of consumption of non-food items and thus non-farm activities become more relevant. In addition, growth in the agricultural sector may lead to an increase in farm wages to attract labour from non-farm activities and this in turn both leads to a tendency to increase mechanisation in farming and to pressures to raise labour productivity in the non-farm sector itself.

Agriculture output is controlled by the current state of technology, available land and climate. The improvement of agricultural technology will affect non-farm activities. On the other hand, development of non-farm activities such as transport, storage facilities, and intermediate goods demand can induce growth in agriculture. This indicates that developments in the farm and non-farm sector may influence each other. A major theme of the debate is: how does distribution of land (and farm income) affect linkages to (local) RNFE, especially to demand for RNFE labour? As shown by various research (e.g. Hazell & Roell, 1983; Mellor & Lele, 1973; Haggblade & Hazell, 1989), the multipliers are bigger for small to medium-sized farms than for very large farms or, they claim, than very small farms. Bell *et al* (1981) argued: the smaller and more equal the farm the more the local RNFE share and labour input. Mellor & Hazell and later Hazell & Ramasamy (1991) on

North.Arcot in Tamil Nadu said no, middle farmer households had more (CLs leads to local RNFE labour income) than small ones. A higher marginal budget share devoted to RNFS products.

The magnitude of the growth linkages can be increased through appropriate governmental policies and investments. Khandker (1997) has identified the importance of rural infrastructure (e.g., roads, electrification, banking services) in enhancing the size of the multipliers. Irrigated agriculture also has larger multipliers than rainfed agriculture. Therefore appropriate regional and farm targeting of agricultural technology and investments, supported by adequate investments in rural infrastructure, may significantly enhance the size of the indirect benefits emanating from agricultural growth (Hazell & Haggblade, 1991).

AF has also been proposed from the standpoint of generating higher levels of demand for modern urban industry. Adelman, (1984) on agriculture-development led industrialisation the min thrust is to support the development of small-medium farms (the small farm sector) in the first instance. In this case an AF version favouring the larger farmer could generally be expected to perform better. On the other hand, if AF was being construed as a better basis for generating that elusive trickle-down effect in favour of the rural poor, the class emphasis of AF might have to be different, with a special premium attached to linkages favouring the poorer sections of the rural economy.

However, even when non-farm linkages are substantially increased, the question may be raised about their sectoral destination: a distinction needs to be maintained between non-farm linkages which travel towards the modern industrial sector and the urban economy, and those which are captured and retained by the rural producers of goods and services.

Several studies have shown that technology-driven agricultural growth can contribute significantly to growth in national income (e.g. Adelman, 1984; Rangarajan, 1982; Cavallo and Mundlak, 1982; Byerlee, 1973). A large, if more contentious, body of literature discusses the poverty-reducing effect of technological change (e.g., Pinstrup-Andersen and Hazell, 1985; Lipton & Longhurst, 1989; Hazell & Ramasamy, 1991). Mellor (1976) emphasises the importance of divisible bio-technology as the basis for small to medium farm development and hence, for maximisation of farm non-farm demand linkages in rural regions. Technological change based on large-scale mechanisation does not provide the same linkage potential.

The experience of the Punjab is sometimes cited to illustrate the potential of spread to RNFS growth from an AF strategy based on medium size farm adoption of bio-technology. In Punjab fast growing agriculture made a far reaching impact on both farm and non-farm employment and income levels, besides strengthening agriculture industry relationships (Chadha, 1993: p.147). Through continuous expansions of irrigated cropped areas, rising levels of cropping intensity and the emergence of new labour intensive crop combinations on a large scale, on-farm employment has expanded impressively. With the expanding volume of agricultural produce, the many types of activities inside as well as outside the village have given rise to a high level of seasonal non-farm employment. Overall, income levels of all sections of the rural community have expanded gradually over time. Rising rural incomes have accelerated the demand for industrial output and employment, the benefits of which have occurred partially to the rural sector itself in terms of increased non-farm employment.

On the production side, the input structure has gradually changed with increased reliance on purchased inputs. This in turn has initiated the process of agro-industrialisation, with expansion in the numbers of small scale agro-industrial units and beneficial effects on off- farm incomes and employment. Further the availability of sizeable agricultural surpluses and the rising demand for processed food and non-food products have given a great fillip to the expansion of an agro-processing industry.

In brief, the Punjab development model shows that a fast-growing agriculture is capable of generating (1) high and rising levels of on-farm employment and income, (2) rising demands for purchased inputs to meet the requirements of technological changes, and for non-farm consumption goods arising out of higher income levels and structural changes in rural consumption patterns. It has also induced (3) new and expanding avenues of non-farm employment and income, especially for the weaker sections of the rural society, (4) a considerable industrial growth heavily biased towards agro-industrialisation which, by its very nature, is widely dispersed and strengths the rural-urban economic relationships (Papola, 1987).

2.1.7 Agricultural Development and Commercialisation and RNFE

It has been shown that both agricultural development in general and agricultural commercialisation are expected to encourage rural industrial activity. Generally, two variables can be used to capture levels of agricultural development: (a) the agricultural productivity per unit of land; and (b) the value of agricultural output per capita of agricultural population. *Prima facie* (b) is likely to be a better index of rural prosperity than (a) However, the available literature suggests that (a) is a better predictor of RNFE share (b) shows a significant positive relationship with the share of rural non-farm workers only at the state level-Vaidyanathan (1986)-and not at the NSS regional -Dev (1990); Unni (1991)-and district levels-Singh (1989); Jayraj (1989). In contrast, (a) shows a more significant positive association at all these 3 levels. The lack of correspondence between the two indices (output per capita and per unit of land) is mainly due to the fact that more fertile regions are also densely populated. Migration into more agriculturally productive areas (the 'suction process') may neutralise the per capita productivity advantages of these areas.

The RNFS is mainly influenced by two sets of factors broadly described as growth induced and distress induced. Kuznets (1966) observed that in most cases of successful sustained economic growth, the share of agriculture in both the labour force and the gross domestic product declined over time. On the supply side, when agricultural labour productivity improved, so did the overall economy. Kuznets and Lewis are about rising non-farm share. They say nothing about whether it is rural or urban. Similarly on the demand side, given a low income elasticity of food (Engel's law), any rise in income leads to a higher demand for non-farm output relative to food. (But this effect is much weaker for the very poor, who have a higher propensity to use income to raise diet quality and quantity-especially if the incomes is earned by extra physical effort needing more calories. (i.e. middle-income rural groups might do more, out of extra income, to promote RNFS than the poorest would do). This is the growth induced rise in the RNFS. Bhalla (1990) argued that the structural changes in output were not matched by similar changes in the employment of the workforce. The agricultural sector was unable to absorb the labour force causing rural unemployment and poverty. The RNFS is therefore seen as a labour absorbing counterpart via growth linkages of agriculture. These agricultural linkages are argued by the Mellor school to be the most useful to RNFS growth, while forward agricultural growth linkages mainly increase employment in processing industries (i.e. non-rural, capital heavy, and low-employment).

The separate issues are does agriculture, or RNFS, or urban non-farm sector, grow fastest when income per person (and hence demand) grow? where are employment effects highest, and where is extra employment most affordable (i.e. low capital cost per job)?

Kuznets' viewpoint is that in a growing economy the process of growth is accompanied by agricultural transformation leads to a rise in productivity leading to a surplus of labour. The next stage of development lies namely with the secondary and tertiary sectors. It is the service sector that absorbs more of these revealed inputs as the primary and secondary sector's demand for services increases. This directly leads to an expanding non-farm sector mainly propelled by growth and prosperity in the economy.

The degree of commercialisation of the rural economy would seem to be a major factor affecting the scale, and location of and technology used in rural non-farm activity. Traditionally, village communities were relatively self-sufficient and had an internal division of labour, based in India largely on caste and regulated by the *jajmani* system. Trade and transport activity was limited, and most of the transport was by bullock carts or on animals. The level of development of the transport network, as well as the size and density of village settlements, would seem to be relevant in determining the location, organisation and hence labour intensity of non-farm activities.

Empirical studies of farm and non-farm linkages have shown that the degree of commercialisation of agriculture influences the shares and growth of RNFE. Most studies (e.g., Basant and Parthasarathy, 1991; Murty and Durga, 1992) use the percentage of area under non-food crops as an index of commercialisation. The extent of commercialisation of agriculture helps to determine the extent of trading and transport activities in the rural areas. The larger the per capita output and the proportion of output which is sold outside the region the larger will be the volume of trade and trade-related activity. A high degree of commercialisation in production also often implies a greater degree of dependence on market purchases for intermediate and final goods, which adds to the volume of commercial and transport activity.

For these authors, growth of agricultural output and the degree of commercialisation of the rural area are the important factors in the rural economy which affect the growth of non-farm activities. Growth of agricultural output requires purchased inputs such as fertiliser, pesticides and efficient marketing. Delivering of purchased inputs at the farm gate, as well as marketing the increased output, requires the expansion of trading activities which result in the growth of rural non-farm activities.

Agricultural development and commercialisation are together expected to encourage rural non-farm activity by: supplying more raw materials; creating greater demand for inputs and allied services; raising demand for consumer goods and; generating surplus for investment. The variable used to capture levels of agricultural development is the value of agricultural output per agricultural worker.

Sankaranarayan (1980) argued that it is the degree of commercialisation of agriculture that determines the level of non-farm activity in rural areas. He suggests that the degree of commercialisation can be captured with two indices: exports from agriculture to the non-farm sector (FLs) and imports into agriculture from the non-farm sector (BLs). The percentage of area under non-food crops to total cropped area was used to measure the extent of exports from agriculture. This is a partial index since it does not capture the share of food crops that is marketed. The percentage of cash purchases of non-food goods to total consumer expenditure (both food and non-food) in rural areas was used to measure the imports into agriculture. Sankaranarayan found that both indices were highly positively correlated with the percentage of rural non-agricultural workers. An important dimension of commercialisation which was not incorporated in his study was the effect of differences in the spread of modern agricultural techniques which are intensive in the use of manufactured inputs (Vaidyanathan, 1986).

As noted above, most studies use the percentage of area under non-food crops as an index of commercialisation. However, this index is not found to be associated with the share of rural non-farm workers to any significant extent (e.g. Sankaranarayanan, 1980; Unni, 1991; Jayaraj, 1989; Shukla and Shukla, 1989). It can be argued that the area under non-food crops does not adequately capture commercialisation which encompasses all markets; a significant proportion of output of food grains is also marketed in many regions.

Between agricultural development and the growth of non-farm employment the linkages are dynamic. The RNFS is likely to grow in regions which have experienced high growth in agricultural production with a relatively stable trend over a period of time (Raj, 1976). However, the increases in RNFE are not always validated by empirical data. Improvements in physical infrastructure and urbanisation exert considerable influence on this relationship. Despite or because of agricultural growth, local non-farm activities may not expand due to the availability of agricultural work and/or the competition from goods (and even services) supplied from urban areas. Some of these issues are discussed below.

2.1.8 Irrigation and RNFE

Irrigation is considered to be an important factor which leads to an increase in the labour requirement in the non-farm sector. Irrigation needs more labour for the operation itself and indirectly it increases labour use through the use of other complementary inputs like fertilisers. The increase in irrigation leads to production in agriculture and increases demand for the supply of seeds, fertilisers, pesticides, and sprays and repair services which are produced or supplied by non-farm activities but not the local RNFS. Increases in agricultural production give rise to increases of consumption of non food items and thus non-farm activities become more relevant.

Kumar's village level study relating to Matar Taluk in Gujarat State during the period 1965-82, was an attempt to examine the relationship between the extent of irrigation and the level of non-farm employment across the sample of 28 villages using Census data of 1961-81. The cross section analysis does not suggest any meaningful relationship for any of the census years. The simple correlation coefficients were all negative though not statistically significant. Thus BL Kumar concludes his analysis does not suggest any relation between irrigation and RNFS.

Dhawan (1993) studied the relationship between yield impact of irrigation, and the impact on cropping pattern stabilisation in terms of crop yield, total crop output and farm income. The author suggests that there is a positive yield impact of irrigation similarly, the cropping pattern would become more market oriented with increased irrigation because the additional output due to irrigation cannot be fully absorbed in self consumption. Although market orientation of output may increase, the cropping pattern in favour of non-food crops may not occur. Dhawan specifically states that irrigation will not encourage the production of non-farm employment at the expense of food grains. According to Dhawan, irrigation has an influence on the stability of agricultural output, and states that one may conclude that irrigation is impact on output stability in the farm sector.

Sarden (1983) also studied non-farm employment in relation to irrigation development for the Philippines. His observation is that growth of agricultural production and income stimulate growth of non-farm employment. His studies of change in two communities find that the agriculturally prosperous regions use medium technology which is labour displacing. However, these workers are absorbed in non-farm employment. He also finds that when the demand for non-farm employment increases, the overall wage rate is pushed up. Further when non-farm employment is generated, income inequality in the agricultural sector is reduced because the poor who were mainly landless rural labourers, find employment in the non-farm sector, while small and marginal farmers have another source of income.

Jagadeswara Rao (1990) argued on the pattern of employment by noting that: In most of the tanks/ponds, own farm employment is the major source of employment. Employment in other farms is not more than 1/3 of the total. Non-farm employment is higher only in some tanks. He finds that the proportion of non-farm employment in total employment is higher in the largest farm size group (2.5 hectares and above).

2.1.9 Farm-size Structure and the Quantitative Significance of Non-Farm Activities and Employment

The quantitative significance of rural non-farm workers can be assessed by considering these relative to: (a) all rural workers; and, (b) all (rural and urban) non-farm workers. The present study is confined to all rural workers only[1].

Rural non-farm employment (RNFE) accounts, on average, for 10-20 per cent of all full-time employment in rural Sub-Saharan Africa, and 25-30 per cent of rural income (Hazell and Haggblade, 1993).

Liedholm & Kilby (1985) indicated that this is because a larger per cent of these workers are in agriculture and a low percentage of total rural labour force are in non-farm activities (14 per cent and 18 per cent respectively), whilst countries like Iran, particularly in rural areas, and Taiwan have a high percentage in non-farm activities (33 per cent and 49 per cent respectively).

India stands somewhere in between, with regional variations. The Census of India and NSS (National Sample Survey) reveals that the RNFS provides an important source of primary and secondary employment in the rural areas of India.

In Japan it appears that off-farm employment provides returns, per unit of labour time, which are not very different from farming.

Second, the cross-country evidence provided by Oshima (1985) shows that, for average farm families, the ratio of non-agricultural income to agricultural income is positively related to the level of income, and as such rises over time for countries and periods where income levels have been rising.

Third, time series data for Japan and Taiwan (China) also reveal that there is a steady increase of the percentage of farm households for whom on-farm income is less than off-farm income (Ho, 1985).

Fourth, for the Republic of Korea, the only country for which data is available, the inverse relationship in terms of income is far more pronounced when transfer incomes (constituting mostly inter-sectoral remittances) are excluded, which implies that remittances and dividend incomes are very much more unequally distributed over farm sizes than are other non-farm incomes (Ho, 1985: Table 2). The implication appears to be that the smaller the farm, the higher the proportion of transfers in total household income - even more so than is the proportionate role of other RNFS income. It is strange to call this "more unequally distributed".

In South Asian cases with lower levels of development, industrialisation and per capita incomes, the incidence of all wage-labour income, while forming the largest single component, is still very much lower than in the East Asian countries. The suggestion is that with development, the share of self-employment and sideline business incomes (assumed to be based mainly on self-employment) decline in favour of the category of pure wage-labour income.

Several recent studies (e.g. Fisher, 1997; FAO, 1998; Reardon *et al.*, 2000) have revealed that non-farm employment and income are quantitatively important. It has been estimated that RNFE accounts for one-third of rural employment in India by NSS and Census data.

2.2 Generalised Growth and Development Linkages to RNFE Shares and Growth

We discuss in this section factors such as infrastructure and rural-urban linkages, low agricultural development, poverty and distress diversification into RNFE. As well as the residual sector hypothesis, urbanisation and RNFE, farm seasonality and RNFE, levels of schooling, adoption of technology and gender composition of RNFS, which contribute to the growth of the RNFE.

The view point of McGee (1971) is distinct from that of Kuznets. The author considers the agricultural transformation and surplus of agricultural labour as a distress situation. The surplus of labour in the agricultural sector is not matched by any increase in the labour absorption capacity of the industrial sector. The surplus labour therefore has no other option but to enter into the low productivity service sector, which McGee calls 'the bloated service sector'. Such an expansion of the non-farm sector-if rural-is distress diversification into RNFS. The two viewpoints, i.e. Kuznet's growth-induced and McGee's distress induced nature of development, are clearly totally opposite explanations of the process of expansion of RNFS. Except that neither Kuznet not Mellor specifies whether non-farm growth is rural or urban.

The farm sector's demand for non-farm products consists of inputs for agriculture and animal husbandry, manufactured goods for final consumption and/or capital formation and services of various kinds including trading, transport and other consumers and producers services. Traditional agriculture uses mostly locally produced inputs, a large part of them being derived from agriculture and animal husbandry. The few non-farm inputs, such as making and repair of implements, are also produced by local artisans in India (usually under the *jajmani* system)[2]. With use of modern farm technology (fertilisers, pesticides, and mechanical equipment like pumps and tractors), dependence on non-local inputs increases greatly. Most modern inputs, except perhaps machine repair services, are produced by industries located outside and far away from the village where they are used. Consequently, the growth of traditional or modern agricultural production does not lead to a proportionate increase in the demand for locally-made inputs. The final demand for manufacture and services in a given rural area is, in part, a function of the level of prosperity of its population, of whom agriculturists constitute the most important segment.

The rural demand for personal and community services which are mostly locally produced in a given area again seems likely to be a function of the general prosperity of the rural population in that area. (Demand for such services - at least, those like education, transport, trade and construction, which normally are not traditional *jajmani* services - is indeed highly income-elastic. But we would expect the per cent of demand going to local providers normally to fall as local incomes rise). However, there are certain categories of community services (public administration, education and modern health services), whose level and location may be determined exogenously, for example by state policy. These have expanded very rapidly in the last three decades and there is some evidence that rural employment under this category has become quite sizeable in recent years. The level of state expenditure in rural areas obviously has secondary effects on the demand for the products of RNFS, and hence non-farm employment. The logic is that (1) demand for local RNFS grows with local rural prosperity, based in put on farm income. (2) but need it be local (3) state service provision is not necessarily local.

The level of farm incomes in a region will have a direct impact on non-farm activity in rural areas through an increased demand for diversified non-farm goods. However, a high level of farm incomes may inhibit the supply of labour from certain sections of the population, particularly among females for non-farm activities. This is possible since, with an increase in household income levels, female workers tend to withdraw form the workforce and engage in work within the household (Dasgupta, 1977). Thus, one can hypothesise a positive relation between the level of rural incomes and percentage (in total male workers) of male or overall non-farm employment, and a possible negative relation with the percentage (in total female workers) of female non-farm workers.

Our purpose is to examine the share and growth of RNFS in a specific context i.e. for AP between 1981-91. We need to bring together these two opposite hypotheses-growth linkages, and distress diversification - into a single framework.

Jayaraj (1989) separated several factors that have a bearing on the extent of RNFE into two broad internal and external factors. The internal factors are (1) the level and growth of agricultural output, (2) the distribution of agricultural income, (3) the degree of commercialisation of agriculture, (4) the amount of land availability in relation to the size of rural population, and lastly (5) the extent of irrigation. These are internal to the rural segment of the economy. As for the external factors they are external to the rural hinterland. Of these factors, growth of agricultural output and greater degree of commercialisation are also called growth induced factors, while low land man ratio and poor irrigation facilities are grouped as distress factors. Jayaraj's empirical findings are degree of urbanisation, size and nature of towns, level of income of male cultivators, level of literacy of rural males, pressure on land and proximity have significant positive impact on the level of non-farm employment of males across villages. Variables included to capture the impact of degree of commercialisation of agriculture have turned out to be insignificant. Furthermore, the results points to a non-linear relationship.

2.2.1 *Infrastructure and Rural-Urban Linkages*

Urbanisation and development of rural infrastructure are often complementary processes and occur simultaneously. They influence the growth of RNFE in many ways.

(1) Over time, several rural localities are classified as towns, while a few former towns may get declassified. The boundaries of cities can also expand to encompass surrounding 'rural areas'. Such increases in urban locations or towns are likely to lead to an apparent decline in the magnitude of rural non-farm activities. (2) Urbanisation and the associated improvements in infrastructure may render some rural non-farm activities non-viable through the competition of more attractive or less expensive substitutes. Agglomeration economies in urban areas contribute to this process. (3) Conversely urbanisation and the growth of infrastructure can encourage non-farm activities, both in the secondary and tertiary sectors in neighbouring rural areas to satisfy non-local demands. In fact, the relative shares of rural manufacturing employment in the districts of AP State are positively related to the relative shares of the districts in urban manufacturing. That is, districts having a high share in rural manufacturing employment in the State also have a high share in urban manufacturing, and *vice-versa*. (4) Better, and relatively inexpensive, transport facilities make it possible for many members of rural households to commute to non-farm occupations in neighbouring urban centres (Basant and Joshi, 1989).

Most studies (e.g. Unni, 1991) find a significant positive relationship between the rate of urbanisation and the proportion of non-farm workers in the rural areas at the cross-sectional level. The net impact of the processes associated with urbanisation is positive.

The impact of urbanisation can be mixed up with the impact of large villages in a region. Large villages can perform some of the functions which towns, especially smaller towns, usually perform. A variety of non-farm activities dependent on market size could become viable in large villages. Implicitly, the share of non-farm employment in these large villages is not high enough to warrant their reclassification as towns but nevertheless the share is higher than in other (smaller) villages. Besides, more densely populated regions usually have a higher proportion of large villages and are therefore indicative of higher population pressure on land. Thus, regions with a higher proportion of population residing in large villages may also have a high share of non-farm workers. Therefore, it will be useful to analyse the impact of large villages with our data.

Chadha (1993) reviews the process of rural industrialisation in post-reform China in deriving valuable conclusions relevant to India. The study identifies various determinants of non-farm growth, including the linkages between agricultural development and the non-farm sector which is mutual, development of suitable transport and communication systems, availability of electricity and the degree of education standards of both men and women in rural areas. A good transport system with flourishing transport activity is one of the indicators of the economic prosperity of the area. The study recommends rapid electrification.

The author points out that the infrastructure can encourage non-farm activities in rural areas. Under infrastructure support, four variables were formulated as: (1) electricity consumption in rural areas (million Kwh per head of rural population), (2) road development (paved road length per 1000 sq km. of areas); (3) improved road development (top and secondary grade paved road length per 1000 sq km of areas) and; (4) road-use intensity (number of private vehicles per 1000 sq km of area). In some sense the last variable reflects the degree of economic prosperity of local areas.

Binswanger and Khandker's (1995) main point is that, in India, the presence of a branch bank did little for agriculture but led to a lot of extra RNFS output and include that the impact of credit on expansion of agricultural output was modest but it induced demand for fertiliser, tractors and pump sets while reducing the requirement of labour. So the backward linkages are not as expected. We also test the hypothesis (of villages with bank branches leads to more RNFE) with the secondary data at district level. We are also defining the banking system as part of rural infrastructure.

The market for products of rural non-farm activity is in many cases clearly confined to the local villages. This is particularly true of trade, transport and services, but it is not always or necessarily so. Several products of rural industry (earthenware, leather footwear, processed farm produce like sugar and textiles) are sold in neighbouring urban markets and sometimes over a much wider area.

The level of RNFE (relative to the rural labour force) depends on the level of rural demand (relative to population) for various non-farm goods and services produced locally; the level of extra-local demand, from urban areas in the vicinity as well as from other regions, for rural products and services and location, scale and technology of activities catering to these demands. (i.e. the extent to which it is attractive to suppliers to locate these activities rurally and/or near consumers).

2.2.2 *Low Agricultural Development and Poverty and Distress Diversification into RNFE*

Parthasarthy *et al.* (1998) identify four factors that cause the shift of labour force from agriculture to RNFS in the contest of growth dynamic.

"A consistently high rate of overall agriculture growth; technology which facilitates high employment for a given output; a broad-based agriculture growth generating demand for non-agricultural goods; infrastructure development which facilitates location of non-agricultural industries. In the absence of these conditions, the observed rise in non-agricultural employment tends to be distress-induced (e.g. Vaidyanathan, 1986; Unni, 1991; Eapen, 1995; Saith, 1991; Chandrasekahar, 1993; Bhalla, 1993a, 1993b)".

Vaidyanathan (1986) wrote:

> "in India that non-farm activity acts as a residual sector so that rural workers, who are not absorbed fully in agriculture, spill over into non-farm activities, which act as a sponge for excess labour.

> This hypothesis is supported by a strong positive association between the NSS person-day unemployment rates (PDUR) and the percentage of rural non-farm agricultural workers. An excess labour situation should lead to a fall in the non-farm wage relative to the agricultural wage'. The growth of non-agricultural activities in the rural areas can be termed 'distress-diversification' into unproductive or low paid non-farm jobs. This occurs when labour is not fully absorbed in the agricultural sector and the non-farm sector acts as a sponge for the excess labour".

Bhalla (1992) elaborates this by identifying two kinds of distress diversification: Where workers have no main occupation but only work in household supplementary activities and where people are engaged in agriculture as main occupations but also engaged in secondary activities. In both cases there is distress diversification into non-farm activities, even though the wage rates are likely to be lower than the subsistence wage rates.

The excess labour situation in a region, leading to the growth of residual non-farm activities, was sought to be captured by the NSS person-day unemployment rate (Vaidyanathan, 1986). While the residual sector hypothesis appears promising, it needs to be emphasised that the NSS unemployment rate really captures only open and visible unemployment (Parthasarathy, 1979). Such reported unemployment is likely to be higher in regions where agricultural development is higher, as the expectation of obtaining employment is greater here than in an agriculturally undeveloped regions. Such reported unemployment is also expected to be higher among wage-dependent households or casual labourers (Sundarum and Tendulkar, 1988; Visaria, 1981) as opposed to self-employed households and self-employed persons. This is because it is easier for casual workers to perceive and report their unemployment. As Unni (1990: p. 11) put it:

> "in these regions, with high percentage of landless labour households and high incidence of poverty, the growth of the non-farm sector would depend upon whether there is a demand for such goods and services. If these regions are also highly impoverished then lack of demand may inhibit rather than facilitate non-farm employment".

We shall test whether poverty leads to high RNFE as suggested here.

This hypothesis views non-farm as a residual sector; rural workers who are not absorbed fully in agriculture overspill into non-farm activities, distress diversification. The RNFS acts as a sponge for the excess labour. A strong positive association between unemployment rates and the percentage of rural non-farm workers across the states has been taken as a validation of this hypothesis (Vaidyanathan, 1986; Mahendra Dev, 1990). Thus, the rate of unemployment, which is the reflection of poor labour absorptive capacity of agriculture, is another determinant for the extent to which people resort to non-farm employment. The rate of unemployment itself can be caused by unequal land distribution and associated farm mechanisation and/or population pressure on land.

Apart from problems of interpretation, data on unemployment rates is not available at the district and mandal level. Consequently, it is difficult to test this hypothesis at the district/mandal level.

The residual sector hypothesis becomes particularly relevant because at the all India level and for AP, most extra RNFE during 1961-91 is among casual non-farm workers. Also, participation in non-farm work varies inversely with size of land-holding possessed by households (Basant & Kumar, 1989; 1990). Thus, *ceteris paribus*, if distress-induced diversification is the dominant process contributing to the growth of rural non-farm employment, its share is likely to be high in those regions where the proportion of landless and land-poor casual labour households is high.

The second interesting feature which emerges is that much of the employment in non-farm activities is wage-employment. However, the "casualisation" of non-farm workers or higher participation of landless households in non-farm activities may not necessarily reflect a distress phenomenon if they are engaged in economically viable activities. As such, the residual sector hypothesis is difficult to test with cross sectional data for regions. This is so because only ex-post phenomena are observed, after all the adjustments have taken place. The validation of the distress diversification hypothesis may require detailed household level data. Different processes may be at work in different regions, (or with the same region for different types of households), and a general hypothesis may not be adequate to explain the regional variations in the share of non-farm employment.

Growing population pressure, the inability of rainfed agriculture to absorb surplus labour, and general economic development have brought about occupational diversification of a significant order in a semi-arid village like Mahudi. Broadly, two types of non-farm activities have emerged in the process. The first one is non-farm proper (NFP) and largely results from pull factors. The second one consists of non-farm migration (NFM) and largely results from push or distress factors. Both activities have now come to play a very significant role in the Mahudi village economy, touching about 90 per cent of households and 48 per cent of the labour force. Given the reality of rapidly growing population, inability of NFP activities to expand faster, and the inability of any intervention to bring about any drastic occupational changes, the NFM activity is therefore likely to remain one of the major sources of employment and livelihood in the near future in Mahudi as well as in all other neighbouring areas (Shylendra and Thomas, 1995).

Discussion in the literature regarding the association between poverty and RNFS is both interesting and troublesome. Researchers have argued for both positive and negative relations. Vaidyanathan (1986) suggests a positive relationship between poverty and RNFS. However, in a later study (1995) he changes his opinion because the increase in wage rates of agricultural compared to non-farm labour wage was quite high, ruling out distress conditions. Unni (1991) states that the relationship between poverty and RNFS is generally expected to be negative. The poor person can be easily absorbed only in agriculture even when there are distress conditions.

Fisher (1997: 3), however, points out,

> "The rural non-farm sector can also contribute to poverty reduction. Non-farm employment is particularly important to small and marginal farmers, as well as to the landless, who cannot derive sufficient income from the agricultural sector. In a recent World Bank study comparing the reduction of rural poverty across 15 of the most important states in India between 1957 and 1991, Datt and Ravallion (1996) show that the quantitative impact on rural poverty of above-trend growth in non-farm output is large".

A complication in interpreting regressions of poverty on RNFS and RNFE shares is that rural anti-poverty policies may deliberately emphasise RNFS/RNFE rather than agriculture (e.g. Integrated rural development programme, (IRDP) and Jawahar Rozgar Yojana (JRY employment scheme).

The nature of the relationship between the poverty ratio and RNFE is well expressed by Murty and Durga (1992).

> "As regards the poverty ratio, one may say that *a priori* its coefficient cannot have a positive influence on employment in HHI. As poverty ratio increases, the effective demand for rural manufactures may fall and therefore the extent of RNFE may decline. The fall in the demand for rural manufactures is unlikely to be as much as to lead to their disappearance from the consumption basket of the poor. However, one would expect that the desire of the poor to procure rural manufactures gets transformed into demand only for some inferior goods of local origin generally produced in the HHI sector. So the HHI shares in total RNFE are likely to increase as the ratio of people in poverty increases. A positive sign is therefore expected for the poverty coefficient".

We argue that poverty in a district or in a household is associated with distress diversification into traditional non-farm activities, whereas successful agriculture both reduces poverty and induces diversification into modern non-farm activities.

The Residual Sector Hypothesis

There are thus two arguments regarding the development of non-farm employment. One is based on agricultural development impacts, and the other on distress diversification.

In distress-diversification theory, there is an inverse relationship between agricultural development and non-farm employment. Development theory postulates a positive relationship between agricultural development and non-farm employment.

Figure 2.1. represents both these views. The line MM indicates a positive relationship between agricultural development and non-farm employment (development theory). As agricultural development increases, non-farm employment increases. The line NN indicates that non-farm employment decrease as agriculture develops (distress theory).

Figure 2.1: Possible Relation between RNFS Employment (per cent of rural total) and Agricultural Development, 1

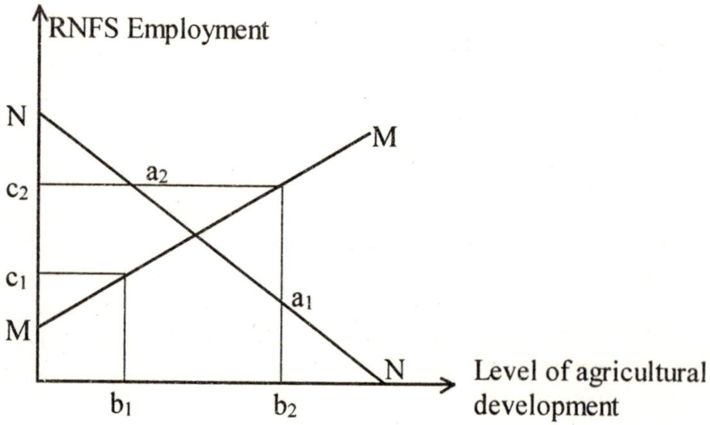

Figure 2.2. illustrates a third possibility: that the rural share of non-farm employment decreases when agriculture develops up to a certain level, and that, as agricultural development increases beyond that level, RNFS employment begins to increase. At a level to the left of a1, where there is an increase in agricultural development, non-farm employment decreases. After that level, as agricultural development increases, non-farm employment will also increase. The curve LL indicates this relationship.

The positive relationship between non-farm employment and agricultural development is not automatic. Regional agricultural development can reach a level where it can boost non-farm employment. However, a positive upward trend in non-farm employment also depends on other factors like demography, literacy, and infrastructure, in addition to agricultural development.

Figure 2.2: Possible Relation between RNFS Employment and Agricultural Development, 2

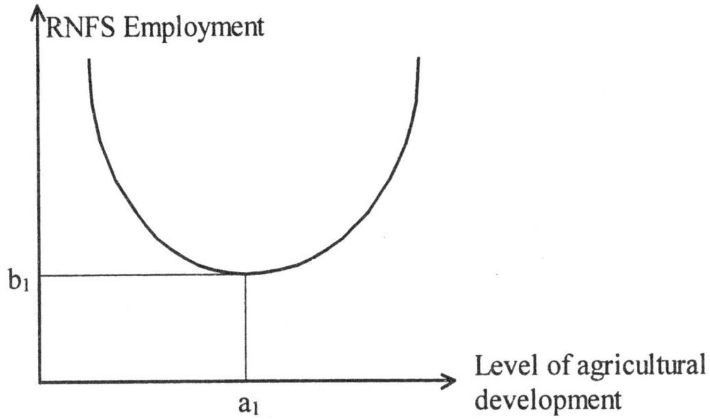

Figure 2.3. represents a general relationship between non-farm employment and agricultural development. Figure 2.4 indicates that farm size is negatively associated with RNFE at the household level. Haggblade and Hazell (1987) and Ho (1994) also suggest such a strong inverse relationship. However, as the economy develops, farm households have become increasingly involved in non-farm activities.

Figure 2.4. illustrates that there is an inverse relationship between RNFS employment and farm size. This is supported by the evidence given in Appendix Table 3.3 which shows that, with an increase in farm size from 0.01 to 8.00 hectares, the proportion of non-farm among farm households themselves in employment decreased from 33.3 per cent to 8.9 per cent. These figures refer to mean share of labour time per household allocated to non-farm employment.

Figure 2.3: Possible Relation between RNFS Employment and Agricultural Development, 3

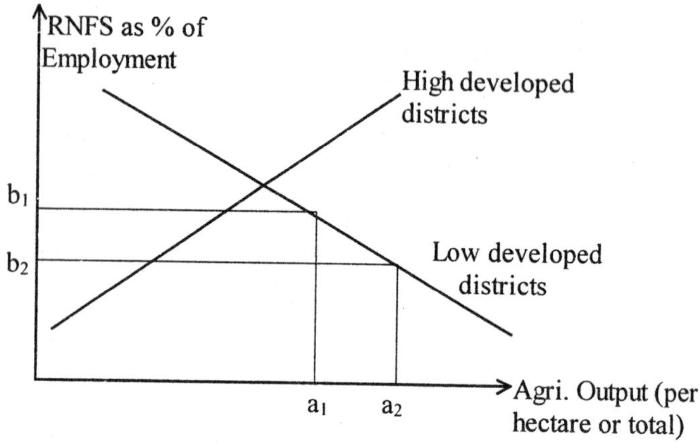

Figure 2.4:Possible Relation between RNFS Employment and Agricultural Development, 4

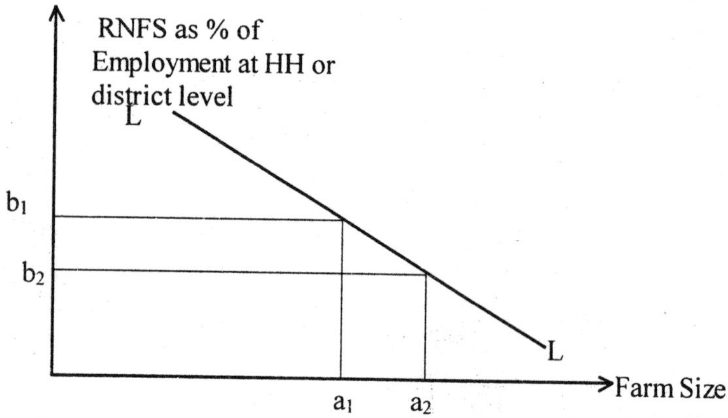

RNFS and RNFE cover many different things and, in particular, a modern or dynamic subsector that one would expect to be highly income-elastic in demand when agricultural income grows (construction, trade, transport, health/education services) and a traditional/static sector that one would expect to result in a negative, or at least below, the elasticity of demand to rising real agricultural income.

2.2.3 Urbanisation and RNFE

Urbanisation is one of the factors which influence the RNFS. Several studies e.g. Sharma and Saxena (1984) provided the empirical evidence by estimating the census of India data at the state level.

Unni (1990: 9) argues that:

> "the proximity to or existence of, a large urban population in the region may also facilitate the growth of non-farm employment in rural areas. This can affect the rural labour markets in two ways. The rural areas may cater to the demand for non-agricultural products or services in the nearby urban areas, or some of the residents of the rural areas may engage in non-farm occupations in the nearby urban areas and commute to their place of work regularly. Urbanisation can also be viewed as a proxy for availability of infrastructure facilities. While cropping pattern captures one facet of agriculture led growth, urbanisation is a force outside agriculture which may lead to the growth of non-farm activities in rural areas. To capture the impact of urbanisation percentage of urban population to total population in a region" was used.

Some studies (e.g. Unni, 1991) find a significant positive relationship between the rate of urbanisation and the share of RNFE (at the cross-sectional level). Parthasarathy (1998) discards the growth variable and experiments with urbanisation, while Murty and Durga (1992) try to explain why this variable is negatively related to the RNFS, both theoretically and empirically. Their argument is based on categorising the output of non-farm employment into local and non-local and suggests that the local variety of RNFS output is inferior. This view is difficult to accept because there is no clear-cut empirical basis to show a decline in consumption of traditional RNFS output as incomes increase. Jayaraj (1989) also concludes that of the external factors (outside of the rural areas) urbanisation is a dominant factor. Urbanisation has both push and pull effects. The pull effect arises from a growing urban manufacture and service sector leading to high demand for rural semiskilled and unskilled labour. Another way in which urbanisation has an impact on the RNFS is through increased demand for raw materials and simple manufactured consumer goods produced in rural areas. Rural areas very near to urban and semi urban areas are affected by this process. The nature of the urban centre (i.e., size and functional characteristics) determine the importance of this factor.

The above discussion broadly identifies the factors determining the share and growth of RNFS at the theoretical level. Appropriate measurable proxies need to be selected for which data is available and which are close to the theoretical factors and use them in our econometric exercise. The present study also considered urbanisation as an important factor in determining the non-farm employment.

But a thriving nearby town induces non-farm people to go there to work, cutting RNFE/S share. One would again expect opposite effects for traditional and modern RNFS/E. This hypothesis was tested with district level data in Chapter 3.

2.2.4 Farm Seasonality and Non-Farm Employment

Seasonality may be a constraint on both farm and non-farm activity. In general the RNFS is labour intensive, so labour moves between the agricultural peak season and the non-farm sector in a seasonally contercyclical manner.

There is some evidence that this happens (Hazell and Hojjati, 1995, p.7)

> "The average farm household in the valley earns 75 per cent of its total agricultural wage earnings between November and April, but earns nearly two-thirds of its non-agricultural wage earnings and non-farm business earnings between May and October. But this countercyclical pattern is less evident in the plateau where all three sources of income are about equally spread between the agricultural and non-agricultural seasons".

Basant and Kumar (1990: p.12) observed that

> 'employment in agriculture and non-agriculture move counter-cyclically i.e. during slack periods in the agricultural cycles a section of rural workers seek employment in non-agricultural sector. Further, as compared to self-employed and regular workers,

a large proportion of casual workers change their sector (agriculture/non-agriculture) of employment over sub-rounds'.

There is, however, no conclusive evidence on this issue and there are likely to be significant regional variations. Although non-farm activities provide a considerable amount of part-time employment to rural population, data on the pattern of labour utilisation among different types of non-farm activities for rural households is scarce. Part-time and periodic non-farm work is frequently not captured because of its seasonal nature. The World Bank (1978: 22) also cites data to suggest that agricultural and non-farm employment vary counter-cyclically and that the seasonal fluctuations in non-farm employment remain significant even in irrigated areas.

2.2.5 Levels of Schooling

Literacy plays a crucial role in the development process to generate employment. Levels of literacy can be expected to positively associate with modern RNFE and negatively associate with traditional RNFE. The present study tests this hypothesis with the district and household level data.

Chadha (1993) argues that levels of education can also play a significant role in raising the capability of entrepreneurs to see local opportunities, to promote workers' skills, and to forge better rural-urban or agriculture non-agriculture linkages. Under education and skill formation, the following variables were used through official data: (1) educational status of general rural public (percentage of literate persons, aged 12 years and more); (2) educational status of female rural population (percentage of literate females, aged 12 years and more) and; (3) higher educational rating (percentage of workers with junior middle and higher education).Chadha does find positive links of education to overall RNFS/E, but no support for the modern RNFS/E growth in Punjab.

Education not only improves an individual's qualifications for non-agricultural jobs, but also increases his ability to allocate his work time efficiently among income-producing activities (Huffman, 1980). The importance of education in determining rural involvement in non-farm activities in less developed countries is high. However, since in the early stages of development many rural non-farm activities require only unskilled labour, education probably only becomes important once 'high quality' and urban-type employment opportunities are available. Thus, education is probably more important in economies that have experienced some years of development than in those that are still in the early stages of growth. In developing countries, the younger generation is usually significantly better educated than the older generation. Thus, the effect of education on the participation rate in non-farm activities among the rural young is probably also more significant (Castillo *et al.*, 1983).

The present study recognised that the levels of schooling is an important factor which facilitates the younger generation to take up non-farm employment. Generally the impact of literacy on RNFS is expected to be positive (Chadha, 1991). However, non-farm activity is of two types (i.e. traditional and modern). In the case of traditional non-farm activity, literacy may not be a deciding factor while in modern RNFS it is essential. The disaggregated data results have to be examined to verify the hypothesis that modern sector non-farm employment may have a positive relationship. Seven different major categories have been considered in addition to the aggregate picture.

2.2.6 Adoption of Technology

For any given level of demand, the level of employment in the RNFS will vary depending on the technology used. The number of persons employed to process a given volume of, say, paddy will be much smaller with modern rice mills than with traditional hand pounding. Whether the non-farm activity is specialised or whether it is an adjunct to agriculture may also influence the magnitude of employment.

Stewart (1977, p. 234) examined the choice of technique in maize grinding on the basis of a survey conducted in 1969 in Kenya. She argues that

> 'The evidence from the survey shows that the most investment-intensive technique, the roller mill requires nearly 200 times as

much as investment per worker as the most labour-intensive method, the hand mill; over ten times as much as the water mill; and nearly 5 times as much as the local hammer mill, if we assume equal capacity utilisation for each technique'.

Further she shows that small scale investment opportunities may, to some extent, generate their own savings which has a bearing on the production and consumption linkage effect on RNFE.

Ellis (1988) argues that the induced innovation theory of technological change distinguishes two broad paths of technological development in agriculture. These correspond respectively to labour-saving and land-augmenting technical change and have implications for RNFE.

> 'In the labour abundant, land scarce, economy farmers seek innovations to raise the productivity of land. This induces a search for yield-increasing technologies by both private and public agencies.' (Ellis, 1988: p. 218).

For Bangladesh, Greeley (1987) notes that technological changes entail the substitution of traditional threshing methods in the farm-level post-harvest system.

> 'The rural growth linkages (the multiplier effects) of new agricultural technology are an important aspect of technology assessment... In the case of pedal threshers in Bangladesh the important content in manufacturing is low by Bangladesh standards and the backward linkages from local manufacture are therefore of potential importance.' (Greeley, 1987: p.196).

The above suggests that agricultural growth linkages are important for the growth of RNFE. The nature of non-farm activities is often described using 3 characteristics which are its location, the scale of production and the degree of capital intensity i.e. technology. The last two aspects are closely linked to one another. One factor which influences these characteristics is the commercialisation of agriculture which gives a boost to the scale of operations in RNFS. This in turn has impacts on labour costs, on industrial production units and so also on the type of technology used and the scale of RNFS employment.

Many studies (e.g. Adelman, 1984; Rangarajan, 1982) have shown that agricultural growth, especially "technology-driven agricultural growth", can contribute much to growth via its impact on other sectors (as well as directly). The strong linkages generated by technical change in agriculture towards the non-farm sector can lead to growth and poverty reduction, as growth in agriculture leads to more demand for input supply from the non-farm sector. It also provides inputs into transport, processing and marketing. These are the backward and forward production linkages respectively.

Farm income growth also leads to higher demand for consumer goods and services. This argument is developed by Johnston and Kilby (1975), Mellor (1976) and Mellor and Johnston (1984), who emphasised the potential for poverty reduction when agriculture growth is mainly among small and medium size farms: the type of non-farm goods and services demanded by small and medium farms are produced by small labour intensive non-farm units. Therefore, growth of incomes of small and medium size farms increases the demand for such labour intensive activities and therefore increases the employment as well as opportunities for earning more incomes by the poor. Hazell and Haggblade (1991) consider these as "indirect or down-stream, benefits of agricultural growth". Such indirect benefits are extremely important. Another beneficial effect is that rural urban migration is also reduced.

"Why do non-farm activities vary over time and across regions?". This question is raised and answered by Hazell and Haggblade (1991). "The resource endowments, location, ethnicity, historical happenstance and government policy all play a role. Yet agriculture, because of its size must be added to the list of key suspects". Three different routes link agriculture and non-farm activities: production, consumption and labour market links.

The labour market linkages have been studied by researchers such as Hossain (1988) and Ahmad and Hossain (1990). Labour market linkages can happen via FLs, BLs or CLs. Growth in agriculture leads to increased agricultural wages and consequently a rise in huge -earners' demand for non-farm production, so the composition of non-farm activities changes. Both labour intensive activities and low productive activities are reduced, while investment-intensive skill-intensive activities with high returns increase. A structural transformation of the rural non-farm sector is brought about by increasing agricultural products and incomes.

The labour market links between agricultural and rural non-farm activity seem consistently robust in the cross-section studies. All data have confirmed the positive relationship between earnings in agriculture and earnings in rural non-farm activity (Popola, 1985; Chadha, 1986; Radhakrishna *et al.*, 1988).

The above discussion brings out the importance of development in agriculture as a determinant of RNFE. If agriculture is prosperous, the RNFS can also be dynamic. Generally rural development such as agricultural infrastructure, like irrigation, power, roads, education, research and extra farm activity will lead to RNFE. Agriculture will grow and along with it the non-farm sector, usually the infrastructure will support both agriculture and non-farm activity. The evidence for the impact of technology on agricultural growth linkages between farm and non-farm can be seen with the case study analysis in Chapter 5.

2.2.7 *The Gender Composition of RNFE*

The literature on RNFE in India does not provide much evidence regarding gender effects. However, in the Indian context, two distinct features are observed at the village level.

Basant and Kumar (1990) argued that women's non-farm work being under-counted and classed as a secondary occupations may result in the under-estimation of the size of the RNFE. As these occupations are omitted from the Censuses and labour force surveys, the magnitude of the RNFE will be under-estimated. It is also true many women family farm workers are left out of labour force estimates, so the farm share of labour force could also be underestimated.

Basant and Kumar (1989) explored the nature of RNFE in India and some of its characteristics, using data collected from NSS Census of India and other social surveys. The authors dealt with the scope of rural non-farm activities and their importance in rural areas and the nature of employment. The study reveals that there has been a general growth of employment in the RNFS, which it is more pronounced for men than women.

2.3 Other Possible Causes in RNFE Share and Growth i.e. the Distress Diversification

Other factors such as farm-size, caste status, migration which influence the RNFS are discussed in this section.

2.3.1 Land-holding Size and Household Engagement in RNFE

In this sub-section we consider the relationship between farm size and RNFE. Islam (1987) hypothesised that the household dependence on non-farm employment varies inversely with the size of the operational holding. Further he pointed out that this relationship appears to be fairly strong for villages in Bangladesh, India, and Pakistan (i.e. villages with smaller holdings positive, villages with higher RNFS share). Even for villages in Sri Lanka and Thailand where the relationship is not so strong, the extent of dependence on non-farm employment is much higher for the landless and land poor households than for those with largest-size holdings. An inverse relationship is to be expected because under a system of private ownership of land, access to land becomes a prime determinant of farm employment. However, landless labourers and land-poor farmers could still have access to farm employment through wage employment, which is influenced by the interaction of technology (small holdings leads to more demand for labour per hectare which in turn leads to more farm opportunities of work, even for the landless). The limited labour-absorptive capacity of the agricultural sector compels the excess labour to seek alternative sources of rural employment.

Ho (1985) asserts that a strong inverse relationship exists between farm size per household and non-farm activity at village level. as farm size declines, farm households become more involved in non-farm activities, in terms of both income earned from and employment time associated to, non-farm activities. A strong inverse relation is also observed between farm size and non-farm income (as well as gainful earnings from non-farm activities). As the economy develops, farm households in general become increasingly involved in non-farm activities.

However, it is also arguable that at district level average land-holding size may have a positive relationship with non-farm employment. Agricultural output (or) income creates greater demand for non-farm goods and services (but there is no reason why the same household should therefore produce these RNFS goods), as well as generating surplus of income for investment in the non-farm sector. The present study is also intended to test these 2 hypotheses with the district and household level data.

The two separate hypotheses are (1) given total land (of given quality) and total village population; equal (smallish) farms lead to a larger RNFE share than unequal (biggish) farms; (2) for a given land distribution (Gini), if everybody has more land then demand for local non-farm products and, hence, the RNFE share is more.

2.3.2 Migration into Villages and RNFE

Migration can also be an important factor in the rural labour market. Education by itself stimulates out-migration as it raises the level of aspirations and unsatisfied needs in the population of rural areas. An individual who has attained a high level of education in rural areas or smaller centres may have difficulty in finding a position corresponding to their level of skill and may thus be prone to migrate.

However, because industrial development requires unskilled manpower as well as educated and skilled persons, migration consists of both the educated and uneducated. If we compare seasonal migrants, we can observe that large numbers of them are illiterate when compared with other migrants. Low wage rates prevailing at the place of origin and lack of continuous work are some of the major reasons given for migration (Murty, 1990). It is hypothesised that out-migration will be greater than in-migration because of limited occupational opportunities in rural areas. Inward-migration will have a positive influence on RNFS.

2.3.3 Caste Status

There are several demographic and social factors which can influence the supply of labour to the non-farm sector, including family size, age composition and caste status. For example if there are more adult members in the family, it is expected that there will be a greater supply of labour in the household. This provides the households with greater opportunities to diversify income and sources.

Caste position is important for entry into new jobs. Groups which belong to lower castes in the society have only inferior positions of influence in the village power structure. The Scheduled castes (SCs), Scheduled tribes (STs) and even artisan castes belong to this category. In areas where marginal farmers and landless labours are drawn from these castes they are in a disadvantageous position in terms of employment opportunities.

Krishna and Sharma (1998) further pointed out that there are sub-groups among rural labourers who are "even more vulnerable", and list bonded labour as the most exploited group; women workers are paid lower wages than male workers, migrant workers are exploited by their employers. SC and ST workers, deprived of land ownership and educational opportunities, are restricted to forms of labour with low returns and very low social status.

Murty (1996 p. 854) writes:

> 'SCs are a disadvantaged group. They have relatively little access to education. The inhibitions of the people of this social class leave them docile and generally less enterprising. This group may not share in the benefits that follow from the spread of certain non-agricultural activities. It is therefore plausible that SCs are relatively few in rural non-agricultural activities. They are distanced from RNFE'

These studies have highlighted the role of caste as an important issue in the occupational pattern. This study also focuses on this issue in the primary data analysis of LOGIT models in Chapter 4.

2.4 The KEY points which Emerge from the Literature Review

Although many studies have been carried out in the past on various aspects of RNFS, this review of literature on RNFS reveals the relative absence of studies identifying the determinants of RNFE at the micro level. Most empirical research on RNFE in India is based on secondary data at all-India or state levels. There are few studies on the determinants of RNFE at the household level and studies on the composition of the RNFS are rare. It appears from the past literature that no attempt has been made so far to examine the determinants of RNFE in the agriculturally developed regions vis-à-vis agriculturally less developed regions and traditional RNFE vis-a-vis modern RNFE. However, household surveys cover a wide range of information which can provide a greater understanding of the magnitude as well as the structure of RNFS. This review points to the need for further data disaggregated at the district level and household level in order to find out causes of growth of RNFE. One of the main issues is whether or not non-farm activities are quantitatively and qualitatively important for rural development in developing countries. Evidence of several studies in the Indian context indicate that RNFE is important for the poor. This study aims to contribute to the micro-level analysis of RNFE.

It can be concluded from the literature that the processes which encourage or prevent employment diversification in the rural economy are complex and difficult to analyse. However, the available studies and evidence show that there are possible hypotheses which can be tested. These cover various correlates and potential determinants of non-farm employment (such as seasonality, gender bias, linkages, migration, social factors like caste, urbanisation, commercialisation, poverty and distress diversification). Thus, the preceding discussion helps to formulate working hypotheses which can be tested in the context of the AP economy[3]. In order to examine the relationship between the growth of agriculture and non-farm employment, the study tries to analyse the level, structure and functioning of the non-farm sector in situations characterised by varying levels of development and agriculture growth.

Given these broad features of the labour market and the rural economy it is possible to highlight two dimensions of the growth of non-farm activities in rural areas. The non-agricultural sector may develop in rural areas under certain facilitating processes. These processes may emanate from either agriculture or outside it. The agriculture led growth model suggests that a sustained rise in farm output and incomes can act as a prime mover in initiating the development of non-farm activities in the rural areas. Other processes (general growth and development linkages to RNFE shares and growth) such as urbanisation and development of infrastructure, which emanate outside agriculture, levels of schooling, farm seasonality, adoption of technology can also lead to the growth of non-agricultural activity within rural areas. Both processes lead to the shift of rural workers to productive jobs in the non-farm sector.

The RNFS is influenced by distress diversification as third cause. From the literature review the diversity of results obtained from growth linkages or overall growth linkages or distress diversification suggests that possible growth in some parts of RNFS may be driven by agriculture or generalised growth linkages, whilst in other parts of RNFS the drive comes from the opposite lack of growth in agriculture or overall growth.

NOTES

1. For alternative definitions see the Appendix to this Chapter.
2. A system of patron and client relationship in Indian villages has been termed jajmani in the North Indian context. This involves reciprocal arrangements between landlords and tenants.
3. Chapter One, which is an introductory chapter, already presented these. I stress here that the hypotheses have emerged from the survey of the literature.

3

DETERMINANTS OF INTER-DISTRICT VARIATIONS IN RURAL NON-FARM EMPLOYMENT

Introduction

This chapter seeks to identify the determinants of inter-district variations in the shares and growth of rural non-farm employment (RNFE)[1] in Andhra Pradesh (AP). The focus is on non-farm main workers i.e. workers who had worked for the major part of the year (183 days or more), and whose principal work was in RNFE.[2] We will consider the changes between 1981 and 1991 and seek to identify some of the factors associated, across districts and over time, with relatively larger RNFE in AP. A study of the determinants of non-farm employment can help to interpret the structure and functioning of the labour markets.[3] This chapter attempts to identify these determinants and examines their inter-relationship with the help of district-wise data in the AP context. From the point of view of employment policy it is important to analyse the reasons for the large variations in non-farm employment which are observed across districts.

We can identify broadly two categories of RNFE: traditional and modern. In rural communities traditional non-farm activities (such as blacksmithy, carpentry, pottery, weaving, laundry, toddy tapping, barbering, cobbling, cotton cording) continue even though today some are declining. These activities may be grouped under seven headings: crafts, processing of crops, non-factory textiles, traditional forms of transportation and trade/commerce, personal services, repair and construction in homes and fields. For classification of non-farm activities see Appendix Table 3.1. The second category consists of modern manufacturing and processing, including sugar and textile factories, oil and grain mills, small factories producing engineering goods, shoes, paper, furniture, soap, matches and small scale quarries. A newly emerging third category consists of rural white-collar workers: public services, health and extension services, credit and marketing agencies, and public works construction.

This thesis seeks to test 'distress diversification' against 'growth linkages' as explanations of employment viz., of the propensity of rural people to be involved in the RNFS. The strict agricultural growth linkages (AGL) is that higher (or a faster growing) agricultural income/output/employment tends to cause more (or faster-growing) nearby rural non-farm share. The agricultural distress diversification hypothesis (ADD) is that lower (or slower-growing) agricultural production (or 'performance' in agriculture) causes higher (or faster growing] RNFE shares. The research will also test a wider 'development linkage/diversification hypothesis'. This overall development linkage hypothesis (ODL) is that higher (or faster growing] development indicators such as literacy, bank branches, urbanisation, tend to cause more (or faster growing] nearby RNFE. The converse overall distress diversification hypothesis (ODD) is that lower (or slower-growing] development indicators cause higher (or faster-growing] RNFE share.

A central hypothesis tested in this chapter is that a high traditional RNFE share is associated with low literacy and distress diversification, while a high modern RNFE share is associated with high literacy and rural growth linkages from agriculture. This issue is explored using a cross-sectional study of industrial categories IV to IX for 22 rural districts of AP

(a) pooled 1981 and 1991 cross-section data regressions and (b) growth of shares between 1981 and 1991 data regressions.

For our study we define as a RNFE household any household with at least one member in a primary occupation in categories 1V-1X of workers in the 1991 Census.

Parthasarathy (1998), Murthy and Durga (1989) analysed aggregate RNFE employment data for some categories of RNFE. The focus of our analysis bears on the importance of non-farm relative to agricultural employment. We have used the percentage of RNFE to the total employment variable and we have experimented with other structural differences (such as gender) between 1981-91.

Also by contrast, we have analysed RNFE in a disaggregated manner using all IV to IX categories (divisions) of RNFE for 1981 and for 1991. We have studied 1991 Census data and pooled data from both the 1981 and 1991 Censuses.

Methodology: Estimations of the shares of RNFE - and of both modern and traditional sub-sectors in total employment (main workers) and its determinants-were made for total workers (males and females) to explain district-level RNFE shares. For 1981 and 1991, regressions were run separately and pooled. Similar regressions were carried out with average annual growth rates over the decade used as the dependent and explanatory variabels for all the categories. Thus, we aim to explain (1) the level of RNFE across districts and (2) the growth of RNFE share between 1981-91. The econometric model used is the linear multiple regression (OLS) for growth rates between 1981 and 1991. A log linear model is used for pooled data 1981 and 1991. This is based on some strong key assumptions. We have checked for the violation of these assumptions.

As a preliminary step, means and standard deviations were computed for all the variables. T-tests were used to compare the difference in the means between 1981 and 1991 for all categories of RNFE, as well as for some of the independent variables. The results are given in Tables 3.10. and 3.11.

We are aware of the problems in comparing proportions between the districts. For example, suppose district 1 has 80 per cent of adults in the workforce on an average day, of whom 98 per cent are successful in obtaining work (including self-employment) but only 20 per cent of these are in the RNFS. District 2 has only 50 per cent of adults in the workforce, and on an average day only 80 per cent obtain work, but 25 per cent of these are in the RNFS. It does not really make sense to compare RNFE 1 (which has over 15 per cent adults normally working) and RNFE 2 (10 per cent) unless we also look at absolute figures.

The rest of this chapter is divided into three sections. 3.1. describes inter-district variations in shares, structure (by gender, by industry), and trends between 1981 and 1991 for RNFE. Section 3.2. summarises the hypotheses on inter-district variations in the RNFE share, the variables used in the subsequent empirical analysis, their specifications and the expected relationships. The model which will be used to explain RNFE is specified. This section also includes a summary of the changes to the explanatory variables used in the model between 1981 and 1991. Section 3.3. presents empirical results and relates to these the alternative hypotheses (distress diversification and growth linkages). The chapter concludes with a brief summary of findings.

3.1 Trends in the Composition and Shares of Rural Non-farm employment in AP Districts - A Comparison Between 1981 and 1991:

Why do districts *vary* in RNFS characteristics and growth? In order to provide some insight into this question, we first consider rural AP as a whole, and then the differences between districts.

Rural employment data is considered in this section. The data presented relates to the degree of labour absorption in the RNFS which is measured as the ratio of main workers in the RNFS to main workers in the rural areas. This is computed using Census data, as NSS data is lacking district-wise information.

Only about 18 per cent of total main workers are generally involved with non-farm activities. There are moreover few differences between the share of those involved with the non-farm sector in India and those involved with this sector in AP. Total main workers in the RNFS reached 23 million in 1991. At that time the RNFS share was 17.1 per cent and slightly higher than the 16.8 per cent calculated for 1981 (Table 3.1). There were 3.9 million workers in the RNFS, 75 per cent were males, compared to 76.3 per cent in 1981. Among all main workers, 61.4 per cent were males compared to 65.4 per cent in 1981. The female employment share in the labour force is higher in the farm sector than in the non-farm sector. Whilst changes occurred with the increasing rate of female labour, the RNFS still appears male-dominated. 39 per cent of all total main workers were females and 25 per cent of those involved with the RNFS were females.

In terms of the composition of RNFE for 1991, other services accounted for the highest share followed by trade, HHI and non-HHI. Rising trends could be seen in all sub sectors except for HHI for totals for males but not for females. The analysis of RNFE when deconstructed at the sub-sector level shows that the share of the construction sector is particularly low in total, for both males as well as females.

From Table 3.1., one can see that the proportion of males involved with the RNFS has slightly increased. The reverse holds for females. Comparisons of growth rates of the workforce by industry groups show that the total agricultural workforce in AP grew at around 2 per cent per annum while the rate of growth for non-farm employment was around 2.2 per cent per annum. For farming, the growth rate of females (3.2 per cent) was higher than that of males (1.2 per cent). In the non-farm sector an opposite trend can be marginally noted. The highest (per annum) rural employment growth-rate (between 1981 and 1991) was among agricultural labourers (3.3 per cent). The growth rate of cultivators was the lowest (0.6 per cent). All the sectors apart from agriculture and household manufacturing showed positive growth. Employment in the agricultural allied category declined.

The data shows that agriculture is the predominant activity in rural AP and that there appears to be a modest structural shift away from agriculture and allied categories to the RNFS. The significant growth of agricultural labourers is also a pointer to agricultural distress in the State.

Table 3.1 indicates that between 1981-1991 in AP there was an increase in mining and quarrying (category IV). This could be due to the liberalisation policies applied to cement production and the removal of subsidies to the granite industry. Storage and warehousing also increased from 1981 to 1991. This could be due to the increase in public construction of *godowns* for food grains and essential commodities in all marketing centres, and the encouragement by the authorities to private entrepreneurs to construct warehouses. The number of persons employed in the electricity, gas and water sectors decreased over the 10 year period. This could be due to the change in the billing system by the Electricity Department: the introduction of the slab system led to a considerable decrease in the number of bill collectors. Another reason for this decrease could lie with the introduction of machines in power projects.

Turning to employment trends by gender, the proportion of rural male main workers in agriculture declined. For females there was a marginal increase in the share. Regarding males in the RNFS, there is a continuous increase in mining and quarrying, manufacturing, trade and services, construction and transport. The largest increase for males is in transport, followed by services, trade and construction. For females it is to be seen in manufacturing, transport and services. A striking feature of this table is that overall female employment outgrew that of male employment. This feature was relatively pronounced in most RNFE sectors; indeed in 'allied' and household industry, female employment rose and male employment fell.

From the above discussion it would seem that the level and growth between 1981 and 1991 of rural employment in AP varies across different categories. The differences between males and females also requires explanation. Quantitative assessment of the possible influence and significance, of different factors that have shaped the 1991 scene can be provided by using an appropriate econometric model. At this stage, the overall conclusion regarding the employment changes

Table 3.1 : Growth Rate of Rural Employment in AP (1981 and 1991 Census Data):

Category	*Rural (1981)*	*Rural (1991) Rate*	*% Annual Growth Males*	*Rural (1981) Males*	*Rural (1991) Rate*	*% Annual Growth Females*	*Rural (1981) Females*	*Rural (1991) Rate*	*%Annual Growth*
I to IX Total Main Workers	18832869 (100.0)	23026505 (100.0)	2.0	12326971 (100.0)	14145823 (100.0)	1.4	6505898 (100.0)	8880682 (100.0)	3.2
Agriculture									
(I) Cultivators	7229577 (38.4)	7703384 (33.5)	0.6	5556880 (45.1)	5528638 (39.1)	-0.05	1672697 (25.7)	2174746 (24.5)	2.6
(II) Agri-labourers	7912322 (42.0)	10940275 (47.5)	3.3	3877712 (31.5)	5280400 (37.3)	3.1	4034610 (62.0)	5659875 (63.73)	3.4
(III) Agrl. Allied	515588 (2.7)	435471 (1.9)	-1.7	468345 (3.8)	376359 (2.66)	-2.2	47243 (0.7)	59112 (0.7)	2.3
(I to III) Total Farm workers	15657487 (83.1)	19079130 (82.9)	2.0	9902937 (80.4)	11185397 (79.1)	1.2	5754550 (88.4)	7893733 (88.9)	3.2
Rural Non-farm									
(IV) Mining	55028 (0.3)	153253 (0.7)	10.8	43904 (0.4)	119162 (0.8)	10.5	11125 (0.2)	34091 (0.4)	11.8
(Va) Household Mfg.	845866 (4.5)	742685 (3.2)	-1.3	556885 (4.5)	395536 (2.8)	-3.4	288981 (4.4)	347149 (3.9)	1.9

Contd...

Table 3.1 : (Contd....)

Category	*Rural (1981)*	*Rural (1991) Rate*	*% Annual Growth Males*	*Rural (1981) Males*	*Rural (1991) Rate*	*% Annual Growth Females*	*Rural (1981) Females*	*Rural (1991) Rate*	*%Annual Growth*
(Vb) Non-Household	526637	690240	2.7	421560	538409	2.5	105077	151831	3.7
Mfg	(2.8)	(3.0)		(3.4)	(3.8)		(1.6)	(1.7)	
(IV) Construction	155805	178854	1.4	136650	158331	1.5	19155	20523	0.7
	(0.8)	(0.8)		(1.1)	(1.1)		(0.3)	(0.2)	
(VII) Trade	589284	765788	2.7	472822	620850	2.8	116462	144938	2.2
	(3.1)	(3.3)		(3.8)	(4.4)		(1.8)	(1.6)	
(VIII) Transport	167276	236079	3.5	164870	232460	3.5	2406	3619	4.2
	(0.9)	(1.0)		(1.3)	(1.6)		(0.04)	(0.04)	
(IX) Other Services	835483	1180476	3.5	627344	895678	3.6	208139	284798	3.2
	(4.4)	(5.1)		(5.1)	(6.3)		(3.2)	(3.2)	
(IV to IX) Total RNFS	3175379	3947375	2.2	2424035	2960426	2.0	798588	986945	2.1
workers	(16.8)	(17.1)		(19.6)	(20.8)		(11.6)	(11.1)	

Notes : RMW: Rural Main Workers; Brackets indicate the percentage share of total main workers.

Sources : Census of India 1981, series-1 India, General Economic Tables, (Tables B.1 to B.5) pp. 242-245.
Census of India 1991, Andhra Pradesh, Population Totals, Series-2.

in rural AP is that the share of non-farm employment increased very marginally and less than all-India, both for the total and for males. This was mainly due to the increase in the tertiary sector (trade, transport, and construction). The share of non-farm employment for females has marginally declined due to the decline in household industry.

The industrial distribution of the workforce for males for the state as a whole shows that services was the major sector in terms of its share for total and for males in RNFS. For females, household industry had the highest share in RNFS.

RNFE shares and growth by district are shown in Tables 3.2, 3.3 and 3.4. Activities absorb varying proportions of workers across districts, and the annual change in the proportions involved in each sector points to a diversification of the rural economy during the decade. The expansion of sub-sectors of activities has resulted in wider opportunities in RNFE for both males and females. Yet, some districts seems to have performed better than others. In terms of growth rates, 12 of the 22 districts displayed increases for total as well as for males RNFE share.

In the analysis of rural employment for total (males and females combined) at the sectoral level, one can observe important changes in the growth rates between 1981 and 1991 for AP and India. Perhaps most striking is the difference for HH industry. The proportion of those employed in this sector has grown by 8.74 per cent per year in AP compared to 0.44 per cent for India. Other sectors which have absorbed employment more rapidly in AP than in India are agricultural labour (roughly twice the rate of India) and by decreasing order mining and quarrying and transport. The other sectors have grown either more slowly in AP than in India or declined more rapidly. Services and in particular trade (both are tertiary activities) have grown more slowly. The proportion involved in construction has declined over the period in AP whilst it has increased in India (-0.62 per cent compared to 0.19 per cent). In terms of decline, the proportion involved with agricultural allied activities has declined relatively substantially (a 3.65 per cent annual fall in AP compared to a 1.88 per cent fall for India).

Table 3.2 : District-wise Total Share and Growth Rates in Rural Employment (Farm and Non-farm) Activities (1981 and 91).

		Cultivators		*Agrl. Labour*		*Agrl. Allied Activities*		*HH Industry*		*Non-HH Industry*		*Mining & Quarrying*		*Construction*		*Trade*		*Transport*		*Services*	
District	*Growth of MW*	*% 91*	*GR*	*% 91*	*GR*	*% 91*	*GR*	*% 91*	*GR*	*% 91*	*GR*	*% 91*	*GR*	*% 91*	*GR*	*% 91*	*GR*	*% 91*	*GR*	*% 91*	*GR*
Srikakulam	1.69	35.19	-0.59	43.59	3.79	4.24	3.06	3.65	-1.04	1.50	-1.44	0.24	25.81	0.43	1.15	4.18	2.28	0.89	4.17	6.09	4.39
Vizianagar	1.96	42.74	0.71	37.08	3.14	2.25	2.04	3.39	0.52	2.39	-1.06	0.30	6.55	0.52	4.66	4.29	3.39	1.05	4.82	6.00	6.04
Visakhapt	1.72	50.15	1.33	30.79	3.60	2.30	-1.13	3.13	-0.62	1.94	-3.88	0.45	8.12	0.70	-1.78	3.61	0.78	1.40	-1.51	5.53	3.35
EastGoda	1.52	17.81	-2.04	59.23	3.30	2.34	-4.54	3.30	-1.72	2.85	-1.05	0.13	15.48	0.49	0.30	5.05	1.39	1.26	1.54	7.54	5.29
WestGoda	2.11	17.30	-1.51	61.38	3.15	1.87	0.90	2.08	-2.15	3.20	1.86	0.20	27.39	0.52	1.61	4.58	4.31	1.44	4.34	7.42	4.73
Krishna	2.11	20.49	-0.34	61.05	3.25	2.20	1.37	2.04	-1.75	2.98	2.41	0.38	27.84	0.66	-0.07	3.65	3.12	1.74	2.26	4.81	1.49
Guntur	2.18	25.01	0.02	59.08	3.46	1.50	0.49	0.92	-7.37	2.67	-0.26	0.59	12.29	0.75	3.89	3.49	3.66	1.20	4.39	4.79	3.13
Prakasam	2.01	29.23	0.40	54.57	3.59	2.26	0.33	1.56	-5.95	2.26	-0.47	0.30	9.73	0.94	0.33	2.98	1.40	0.91	1.33	4.98	3.18
Nellore	1.51	25.01	-0.73	54.62	2.55	3.24	1.51	2.47	-3.13	2.14	1.77	0.43	5.26	1.15	1.96	3.71	5.40	1.26	3.45	5.96	3.13
Chittor	1.75	43.16	0.49	38.86	2.84	2.20	1.75	2.26	-1.41	2.54	0.74	0.47	23.68	0.75	0.59	3.34	4.64	1.21	5.92	5.21	4.96
Cuddapah	1.03	35.24	0.53	46.30	1.78	1.88	0.26	2.67	-4.22	2.12	-1.64	0.59	0.08	0.96	-0.23	3.22	1.86	1.14	3.22	5.89	2.67
Anantapur	2.16	41.61	1.12	43.34	3.12	1.83	-0.36	2.19	-0.89	1.88	2.76	0.17	8.10	0.95	6.91	2.68	2.58	0.71	4.49	4.64	4.98
Kurnool	2.27	29.30	1.74	56.03	2.83	0.86	-1.38	1.65	-2.47	1.47	-1.24	2.01	5.99	0.73	2.97	2.61	1.02	0.73	2.29	4.60	2.93
Mahabub	2.68	41.80	1.41	43.59	4.66	1.86	-1.75	1.77	-6.47	3.00	7.76	0.34	13.71	0.81	4.98	2.68	2.44	0.72	5.78	3.44	2.90
RangaRed	1.38	38.32	1.07	40.52	3.23	2.43	-3.83	1.29	-10.83	4.45	1.13	1.68	19.19	1.28	-0.16	3.80	0.59	1.44	1.79	4.79	-0.85
Medak	2.53	43.41	1.41	38.82	4.10	1.42	-4.27	2.85	-3.13	5.08	8.67	0.54	43.53	0.60	4.04	2.76	3.26	0.66	3.73	3.88	2.62
Nizamaba	1.88	37.96	0.50	34.09	3.05	1.42	-3.30	13.39	3.32	3.82	1.05	0.21	12.50	0.74	2.22	3.22	2.53	0.66	4.90	4.49	4.19
Adilabad	1.87	39.17	1.16	39.14	1.77	1.20	-3.73	5.11	1.76	3.70	5.24	3.42	8.63	0.55	2.48	2.43	2.91	0.53	5.79	4.74	4.59

Contd...

Table 3.2 : (Contd...)

District	Growth of MW	*Cultivators* % 91	*Cultivators* GR	*Agrl. Labour* % 91	*Agrl. Labour* GR	*Agrl. Allied Activities* % 91	*Agrl. Allied Activities* GR	*HH Industry* % 91	*HH Industry* GR	*Non-HH Industry* % 91	*Non-HH Industry* GR	*Mining & Quarrying* % 91	*Mining & Quarrying* GR	*Construction* % 91	*Construction* GR	*Trade* % 91	*Trade* GR	*Transport* % 91	*Transport* GR	*Services* % 91	*Services* GR
Karimnaga	2.13	35.06	1.35	39.73	2.62	1.38	-6.96	7.05	0.32	6.30	9.90	1.22	9.19	0.87	-0.82	2.46	2.82	0.67	6.52	5.26	3.19
Warangal	2.52	36.55	1.60	46.83	4.05	1.03	-8.86	3.07	-3.32	3.63	8.42	0.46	33.51	0.87	2.16	2.28	1.91	0.81	2.53	4.47	2.55
Khammam	2.47	30.85	0.82	53.56	3.94	1.26	-2.35	1.87	-2.65	2.28	3.23	1.61	11.03	0.73	-5.73	2.67	3.06	1.83	4.99	4.34	2.32
Nalgonda	2.46	34.45	0.84	45.27	3.88	1.29	-7.29	5.49	1.71	3.50	7.28	0.33	46.96	1.24	2.93	3.34	3.39	1.20	9.33	3.88	3.10
AP	0.32	33.45	-1.37	47.51	1.24	1.89	-3.65	3.22	-3.27	3.00	0.69	0.67	3.61	0.78	-0.62	3.33	0.62	1.02	1.37	5.13	1.48
India	0.30	48.15	-0.56	32.17	0.67	1.96	-1.88	0.47	0.44	2.20	-3.28	3.60	0.49	1.04	0.19	3.26	1.57	1.23	1.12	5.92	2.27

	MW Growth	*Cultivators* % 91	*Cultivators* GR	*Agrl. Labour* % 91	*Agrl. Labour* GR	*Agrl.Allied Activity* % 91	*Agrl.Allied Activity* GR	*HH Industry* % 91	*HH Industry* GR	*Other than HH Industry* % 91	*Other than HH Industry* GR	*Mining* 91	*Mining* GR	*Construction* % 91	*Construction* GR	*Trade* % 91	*Trade* GR	*Transport* % 91	*Transport* GR	*Services* % 91	*Services* GR
Mean	2.00	34.08	0.51	46.70	3.26	1.92	-1.73	3.32	-2.34	3.03	2.33	0.73	17.03	0.78	1.56	3.32	2.67	1.02	3.91	5.13	3.40
SD	0.42	8.84	1.01	9.25	0.71	0.77	3.28	2.68	3.25	1.18	3.92	0.80	12.56	0.23	2.67	0.75	1.24	0.33	2.24	1.04	1.48
CV	0.21	0.26	1.97	0.20	0.22	0.40	-1.90	0.81	-1.39	0.39	1.69	1.10	0.74	0.30	1.71	0.22	0.47	0.32	0.57	0.20	0.43

Notes : MW = Main workers men+women. %: Percentage of all Rural main workers in 1991. GR: Average Annual Percentage Growth Rates of the proportion between 1981 and 1991.

CV: Coefficient of Variation (= Standard Deviation/Mean); SD = standard deviation.

Sources : Census of India (1991) Series -1, final population total paper2 of 1992 p.155. Census of India 1991 India Series-1, Provisional Population Totals: Workers and their Distribution, Paper-3 of 1991 pp. 443-448.

The shift away from cultivators has been more pronounced in AP. For non-HH industry the decrease occurred in AP and India by an almost similar magnitude. One can thus say that relatively, the involvement with the tertiary sector is different in AP than when compared with India. Moreover in terms of shares, one can say that cultivators and agricultural allied activities have experienced relatively more important declines in AP, compared to India, within these categories. Another sector whose performance would have been outstanding and distinct is the HHI.

The district-wise share and growth rates of rural employment (farm and non-farm) between 1981 and 1991 are also presented in the following tables. The difference in shares of males only among the districts grew between 1981and 1991. The biggest group of workers in 1991 was agricultural labourers but the sector which expanded most was mining and quarrying. As we have already seen, most sectors have expanded in AP during the decade with the exception of agricultural and allied activities and the HH industry. The districts in which agricultural and allied activities have declined the most are Warangal, Nalgonda, Karimnagar and East Godavari. These districts have not faced a decline of similar magnitude in HH industry. The biggest decline in this sector, albeit from a small base, was in Ranga Reddy.

For total, the largest variation in share across districts is for HH industry (CV = 0.81) in 1991. Differences across districts can also be observed in growth rates for the agricultural and allied sector (a difference of 11 per cent points change between Warangal and Srikakulam). The most pronounced uniformity (i.e. lowest subsector CV among districts) in terms of growth rate between 1981-91 is for agricultural labour. The proportion of workers involved as agricultural labourers has increased by a similar proportion across the districts. Besides the district-wise increase of the numbers of workers as agricultural labourers and in mining and quarrying, trade has grown throughout AP, with the exception of Visakhapatnam for transport and Ranga Reddy for the service sector.

District wise *male* share and growth rates in rural employment (farm and non-farm) activities between 1981 and 1991, presented in Table 3.3, show that mining and quarrying has most widely differing figures for both shares across districts in 1991 (CV = 1.29).

For males rural (farm and non-farm) breakdown, some changes are worth noting. The proportion of males involved with the HH industry has in fact declined for AP and India, although more for AP (-4.68 per cent per year compared to -3.74 per cent for India). On the other hand a shift might have occurred towards the non-HH industry sector where the signs are the opposite of those of the HHI (non-HHI for males increased by 1.09 per cent for AP and 0.54 per cent for India). Another sector which has expanded towards male employment between 1981 and 1991 has been mining and quarrying. The proportion of the shift in AP has been very pronounced for males compared to India (9.15 per cent compared to 0.79 per cent). On the other hand, the performance of agricultural allied activities for males is similar to that observed for totals, suggesting that what has happened to this sector has had relatively little effect for females (in fact confirmed by looking at Table 3.4). For the tertiary sector, the proportion of males has increased in AP but by less than India, with the exception of transport which has absorbed males increasing more rapidly in AP than in India. There thus appears to be some relatively important sectoral gender differences over the period which are specific to AP for HH industry (a female sector) and transport and mining and quarrying (a male sector).

Unlike for males, female main workers have grown between 1981-91 for both AP and India, although by slightly less in AP. Similarly to males, the share of female cultivators and in agricultural allied activities has resulted in a decrease in AP. Also similarly to males, the growth rate in agricultural labour is positive for females in AP. Yet the extent of all of these changes is much less pronounced for females than for males. This is contrasted with the pattern of positive growth in India for females for cultivators and agricultural allied activities. Contrasts with that is of the males in India, where it has been

Table 3.3: District-wise Male Share and Growth Rates in Rural Employment (Farm and Non-farm) Activities Between 1981 and 1991.

District	Growth of MW	Cultivators		Agrl. Labour		Agrl. Allied Activities		HH Industry		Non-HH Industry		Mining & Quarrying		Construction		Trade		Transport		Services	
		% 91	GR	% 91	GR	% 91	GR	% 91	GR	% 91	GR	% 91	GR	% 91	GR	% 91	GR	% 91	GR	% 91	GR
Srikakulam	1.18	38.14	-1.00	35.26	3.61	5.84	2.19	3.56	-2.24	2.06	-0.91	0.27	21.95	0.66	1.15	5.05	2.19	1.42	4.25	7.74	4.40
Vzianagaram	1.33	44.78	0.00	29.18	2.64	3.25	1.81	3.77	-0.76	3.50	-1.01	0.34	7.07	0.78	5.03	5.23	3.64	1.66	4.69	7.50	5.67
Visakhapatn	0.95	50.62	0.19	25.79	3.83	3.23	-1.11	3.20	-1.38	2.54	-4.19	0.52	7.92	0.95	-1.28	4.13	1.29	2.16	-1.48	6.87	3.31
EastGodavar	1.42	21.18	-2.15	53.27	3.92	3.00	-4.57	3.02	-2.79	3.41	-0.80	0.13	13.59	0.62	-0.07	5.83	1.31	1.66	1.57	7.89	5.59
WestGodav	1.82	23.50	-1.49	51.58	3.42	2.41	0.29	1.82	-4.02	4.06	1.88	0.21	22.79	0.74	1.45	5.66	3.99	2.10	4.26	7.92	4.80
Krishna	1.37	28.31	-0.83	48.26	2.77	3.03	1.06	2.12	-2.86	4.20	2.66	0.41	26.11	0.96	0.73	4.56	3.18	2.70	2.25	5.43	1.75
Guntur	1.42	32.15	-0.75	46.29	3.14	2.05	-0.39	0.98	-9.04	3.85	0.73	0.68	12.99	1.22	3.97	4.69	3.54	2.00	4.38	6.07	3.48
Prakasam	1.27	35.87	-0.37	41.91	3.32	3.23	0.04	1.77	-7.10	3.16	0.88	0.32	10.55	1.50	1.03	4.14	1.69	1.52	1.32	6.58	3.66
Nellore	1.02	31.93	-1.07	42.81	2.34	4.41	1.48	2.62	-4.14	2.86	1.90	0.40	4.14	1.73	2.65	4.26	5.38	1.94	3.39	7.04	3.19
Chittor	1.21	46.50	-0.23	31.29	2.70	2.27	0.55	2.50	-2.18	3.43	0.60	0.59	22.97	1.04	1.30	4.08	4.40	1.83	5.94	6.47	5.04
Cuddapah	0.78	42.49	0.18	35.07	1.79	2.21	-0.71	2.78	-4.31	2.82	-1.22	0.70	1.09	1.31	-0.69	4.03	2.45	1.68	3.25	6.91	2.99
Ananatapur	1.75	48.53	0.69	31.79	3.12	2.64	-0.21	2.55	-1.31	2.61	2.58	0.23	10.15	1.33	6.47	3.50	3.00	1.12	4.58	5.72	4.66
Kurnool	1.84	37.05	1.08	43.52	2.79	1.21	-2.10	1.80	-3.33	2.10	-0.85	2.30	6.59	1.14	2.66	3.70	1.38	1.24	2.27	5.93	2.97
Mahboobn	1.83	50.76	0.73	29.61	4.70	2.98	-2.04	1.79	-7.94	3.49	7.17	0.45	13.90	1.21	4.46	3.85	2.44	1.26	5.79	4.59	3.12
RangaRedd	0.75	42.98	0.64	28.28	3.31	3.43	-4.60	1.49	-11.44	6.33	1.50	1.87	20.03	1.84	-0.32	5.31	0.74	2.39	1.76	6.07	-1.33
Meddak	1.55	48.98	0.41	29.13	4.09	2.20	-4.95	2.26	-6.44	5.57	7.51	0.62	39.28	0.85	2.65	4.13	3.16	1.12	3.58	5.13	2.53
Nizamabad	1.25	44.42	0.01	30.20	3.51	2.55	-3.36	4.40	-0.67	3.99	0.44	0.24	11.14	1.11	1.32	5.55	2.65	1.23	4.95	6.31	3.64
Adilabad	1.22	45.34	0.55	29.98	1.25	1.90	-3.97	2.92	-1.89	2.86	1.02	5.58	8.52	0.76	1.67	3.60	3.01	0.88	5.79	6.18	4.71

Contd....

Table 3.3 (Contd....)

		Cultivators		*Agrl. Labour*		*Agrl. Allied Activities*		*HH Industry*		*Non-HH Industry*		*Mining & Quarrying*		*Construction*		*Trade*		*Transport*		*Services*	
District	*Growth of MW*	*% 91*	*GR*	*% 91*	*GR*	*% 91*	*GR*	*% 91*	*GR*	*% 91*	*GR*	*% 91*	*GR*	*% 91*	*GR*	*% 91*	*GR*	*% 91*	*GR*	*% 91*	*GR*
Karimnar	1.31	41.00	0.74	30.27	2.06	2.34	-7.07	4.49	-3.88	7.14	8.94	1.85	7.86	1.35	-0.44	3.75	3.37	1.20	6.50	6.60	3.12
Warrangal	1.33	44.15	0.50	33.09	3.10	1.60	-9.23	3.64	-4.37	5.42	9.34	0.61	33.19	1.28	2.52	3.20	2.09	1.36	2.47	5.64	2.58
Khamma	1.75	39.17	0.17	40.01	3.75	1.64	-3.45	2.31	-2.99	3.35	3.44	2.39	10.71	1.04	-4.67	3.47	2.89	1.31	5.02	5.31	2.65
Nalgonda	1.48	42.29	-0.01	31.17	2.91	1.77	-7.79	6.43	1.10	5.13	7.70	0.40	43.11	1.62	2.55	4.27	4.02	1.99	9.33	4.93	3.82
A.P	-0.35	39.08	-1.42	37.33	1.73	2.66	-3.50	2.80	-4.68	3.81	1.09	0.84	9.15	1.12	0.09	4.39	1.37	1.64	2.04	6.33	2.04
India	-0.14	51.40	-0.70	26.35	0.94	2.08	-1.94	1.96	-3.74	4.03	0.54	0.53	0.79	1.30	1.06	3.99	2.01	1.62	1.54	6.74	2.43
	MW	*Cultivators*		*Agrl. Labour*		*Agrl. Alled Activity*		*HH industry*		*Other than HH Industry*		*Mining*		*Construction*		*Trade*		*Transport*		*Services.*	
	Growth	*% 91*	*GR*	*% 91*	*GR*	*% 91*	*GR*	*% 91*	*GR*	*% 91*	*GR*	*% 91*	*GR*	*% 91*	*GR*	*% 91*	*GR*	*% 91*	*GR*	*% 91*	*GR*
Mean	1.36	40.01	-0.09	36.26	3.06	2.69	-2.19	2.83	-3.82	3.81	2.24	0.96	16.18	1.14	1.55	4.36	2.81	1.63	3.90	6.31	3.47
SD	0.32	8.32	0.82	8.23	0.82	1.02	3.22	1.22	2.99	1.35	3.68	1.24	11.29	0.34	2.38	0.77	1.14	0.47	2.24	0.95	1.49
CV	0.23	0.21	-9.00	0.23	0.27	0.38	-1.47	0.43	0.78	0.35	1.64	1.29	0.70	0.30	1.54	0.18	0.41	0.29	0.57	0.15	0.43

Notes and Sources : As previously.

Table 3.4 : District-wise Female Share and Growth Rates in Rural Employment (Farm and Non-farm) Activities Between 1981 and 91.

District	Growth of MW	Cultivators		Agrl. Labour		Agrl. Allied Activities		HH Industry		Non-HH Industry		Mining & Quarrying		Construction		Trade		Transport		Services	
		% 91	GR	% 91	GR	% 91	GR	% 91	GR	% 91	GR	% 91	GR	% 91	GR	% 91	GR	% 91	GR	% 91	GR
Srikakulam	2.57	30.44	0.31	57.02	3.96	1.65	10.52	3.79	1.14	0.60	-3.91	0.19	50.71	0.07	1.07	2.77	2.56	0.03	-0.81	3.43	4.34
Vzianagara	3.09	39.44	2.17	49.91	3.63	0.63	4.23	2.74	4.23	0.58	-1.45	0.23	5.40	0.11	1.18	2.75	2.65	0.05	15.64	3.56	7.46
Visakhapat	3.25	49.32	3.83	39.62	3.35	0.65	-1.30	3.01	1.01	0.88	-2.10	0.33	8.76	0.25	-4.48	2.71	-0.45	0.05	-3.37	3.19	3.52
EastGodav	1.82	7.90	-1.10	76.79	2.15	0.40	-3.88	4.12	1.14	1.20	-2.89	0.15	22.90	0.12	9.71	2.75	1.87	0.06	-0.88	6.51	4.31
WestGodav	2.72	4.36	-1.72	81.85	2.81	0.75	6.60	2.62	1.53	1.41	1.75	0.19	0.00	0.05	8.92	2.33	6.17	0.07	11.94	6.37	4.56
Krishna	3.56	6.80	4.29	83.44	3.76	0.74	4.05	1.90	0.96	0.85	0.54	0.33	32.87	0.14	-6.45	2.04	2.86	0.06	3.35	3.71	0.85
Guntur	3.40	14.61	3.02	77.67	3.73	0.69	3.72	0.84	-3.43	0.95	-4.57	0.46	19.16	0.07	2.18	1.74	4.15	0.04	5.56	2.93	2.13
Prakasam	3.19	19.74	2.78	72.66	3.81	0.87	2.04	1.26	-3.01	0.98	-4.93	0.28	8.53	0.14	-6.43	1.34	0.21	0.04	1.87	2.70	1.69
Nelllor	2.45	12.92	0.93	75.25	2.76	1.22	1.70	2.21	-0.57	0.89	1.04	0.48	7.20	0.14	-6.49	2.76	5.43	0.07	7.84	4.07	2.95
Chittor	2.86	36.89	2.45	53.10	3.00	2.06	4.87	1.81	0.93	0.87	1.87	0.23	22.96	0.19	-4.60	1.95	5.66	0.04	4.51	2.84	4.60
Cuddpah	1.56	20.42	2.14	69.25	1.78	1.21	5.15	2.43	-3.99	0.69	-4.54	0.37	-3.01	0.25	7.25	1.54	-0.75	0.05	1.28	3.80	1.57
Ananthapur	2.87	30.17	2.36	62.47	3.13	0.49	-1.57	1.58	0.33	0.68	4.01	0.08	2.09	0.32	10.55	1.33	0.98	0.03	-0.33	2.85	6.13
Kurnool	2.93	18.39	3.92	73.65	2.86	0.37	3.03	1.44	-0.73	0.59	-3.01	1.61	4.89	0.13	7.83	1.07	-0.55	0.02	3.38	2.73	2.81
Mahabubna	3.93	30.15	3.11	61.77	4.64	0.40	1.61	1.73	-3.99	2.35	9.01	0.19	13.15	0.29	8.49	1.16	2.44	0.03	5.32	1.94	2.25
Ranga Re	2.37	31.65	1.96	58.05	3.17	1.00	1.37	0.99	-9.35	1.75	-0.59	1.40	17.30	0.48	0.79	1.65	-0.05	0.09	3.35	2.95	0.72
Medak	4.08	35.76	3.67	52.13	4.10	0.34	6.46	3.65	1.21	4.40	11.08	0.42	62.67	0.25	16.35	0.86	3.91	0.03	17.19	2.16	2.91
Nizamabad	2.66	30.58	1.37	38.54	2.65	0.13	-1.84	23.68	4.45	3.62	1.88	0.18	15.09	0.31	7.13	0.56	1.27	0.01	0.77	2.40	6.09
Adilabad	2.93	29.99	2.73	52.75	2.24	0.16	2.10	8.36	4.43	4.97	11.40	0.22	14.38	0.24	7.46	0.69	2.17	0.02	6.29	2.61	4.18

Contd....

Table 3.4 : (Contd....)

		Cultivators		Agrl. Labour		Agrl. Allied Activities		HH Industry		Non-HH Industry		Mining & Quarrying		Construction		Trade		Transport		Services	
District	Growth of MW	% 91	GR	% 91	GR	% 91	GR	% 91	GR	% 91	GR	% 91	GR	% 91	GR	% 91	GR	% 91	GR	% 91	GR
Karimnar	3.26	27.76	2.56	51.37	3.05	0.19	-5.21	10.18	3.81	5.26	11.76	0.45	21.71	0.28	-2.77	0.86	0.33	0.03	7.18	3.62	3.36
Warngal	4.48	25.95	4.87	65.97	4.78	0.24	-4.40	2.27	-0.40	1.12	3.80	0.26	34.63	0.30	0.22	1.00	0.45	0.03	7.58	2.85	2.46
Khammam	3.79	17.33	3.73	75.59	4.12	0.64	4.69	1.16	-1.41	0.55	1.40	0.34	15.58	0.22	-11.13	1.35	3.80	0.04	3.54	2.77	1.37
Nalgonda	4.12	22.81	3.71	66.17	4.62	0.58	-4.58	4.09	3.29	1.09	4.78	0.23	71.49	0.69	4.36	1.97	1.61	0.04	9.04	2.33	1.15
AP	1.47	24.55	-0.46	63.23	0.19	0.67	-0.85	4.44	-1.26	1.71	0.54	0.38	8.38	0.23	-2.29	1.63	-0.93	0.04	0.00	3.21	0.03
INDIA	1.54	38.58	0.44	48.83	-0.31	2.14	1.47	2.90	-2.64	2.30	0.87	0.28	-0.69	0.27	-7.04	1.08	-0.27	0.08	-3.13	3.53	2.02
	MW	Cultivators		Agrl. Labour		Allied. Activities		HH Industry		Other than HH Industry		Mining		Construction		Trade		Transport		Services	
	Growth	% 91	GR	% 91	GR	% 91	GR	% 91	GR	% 91	GR	% 91	GR	% 91	GR	% 91	GR	% 91	GR	% 91	GR
Mean	3.09	24.70	2.41	63.41	3.55	0.70	1.79	3.90	-0.07	1.65	1.65	0.39	20.38	0.23	2.32	1.69	2.12	0.04	5.01	3.29	3.25
SD	0.73	11.35	1.65	13.06	0.83	0.49	4.15	4.97	3.34	1.49	5.28	0.38	19.58	0.15	7.07	0.74	2.07	0.02	5.19	1.16	1.82
CV	0.24	0.46	0.69	0.21	0.25	0.70	2.32	1.27	46.58	0.90	3.19	0.96	0.96	0.64	3.04	0.44	0.97	0.45	1.04	0.35	0.56

Notes and sources : As previously.

negative. The share of agricultural labour increased for males in India but decreased for females. The increase for males and females in the agricultural labour sector does not outweigh the decline in the other agricultural sectors. It is thus likely that employment has been found elsewhere.

Mining and quarrying is the sector with the highest growth for females in AP and in fact it is the only sector that would have absorbed females significantly. In AP, the tertiary sector such as trade, transport and services have declined or remain almost stagnant for females. The only noticeable sector of marginal experience has been non-HHI (which experienced 0.54 per cent annual income). Household industry, and construction have declined by over 1 per cent per year in AP. The observation for AP contrasts somewhat with the overall India pattern as mining and quarrying decline and services increase.

In terms of the sectors in decline for females, AP has performed better than India for HHI, construction and transport. In terms of the expanding sectors AP has done worse than India for non-HHI and services. Finally it remains that in 1991 there were relatively few differences in the share between AP and India for construction, trade, transport and services. For mining and quarrying AP had 1.35 times the proportion of India but for the non-HHI it had only 3/4 of the proportion that India had. The key sector for female employment would appear to have been HHI in which 4.44 per cent of females RNFE was concentrated. This was 1.5 times higher than in India in 1991. For the agricultural activities females are predominately engaged as agricultural labour (1.3 times India's proportions).

There is a positive growth rate for agricultural labour in all districts. The majority of districts experienced negative growth rates in agricultural and allied activities.

Table 3.5 presents some shares and growth rates of the traditional and modern RNFS. In relation to agriculture-related employment (cultivators, agricultural labour and agricultural allied activities), there are some differences across the districts and across gender. In total, Mahabubnagar has the largest

Table 3.5 : District-wise Shares and Growth Rates (GR) in Rural Employment (Farm and Non-farm Traditional and Modern) Activities (1981 and 91).

District	Cultivators +Agri. labour +Agri. Allied (total for 1991) %	1981 to 91 GR (%/y)	Tradition (total 91) (%)	1981 to 91 GR (%/y)	Modern 91 (total)	1981 to 91 GR (%/y)	Cultivator+ Agri. labour +Agri. Allied (males for 1991)%	1981 to 91 GR (%/y)	Traditional 91 (male)	1981 to 91 GR (%/y)	Modern 91 (male)	1981 to 91 GR (%/y)	c+Al+ Alli 91 (female)	1981 to 91 GR (%/y)	Traditional 91 (female)	1981 to 91 GR (%/y)	Modern 91 (female)	GR
Srikakula	83.02	-0.04	9.74	0.28	7.24	0.08	79.24	-0.15	11.74	0.95	9.46	0.67	89.11	0.05	7.22	-0.04	3.66	-1.03
Vizianagar	82.07	-0.20	9.39	1.69	8.55	0.25	77.21	-0.34	11.5	1.84	11.51	0.88	89.98	-0.12	6.3	2.74	3.72	-1.02
Visakhapt	83.24	0.30	8.66	-0.01	8.1	-2.59	79.64	0.20	10.87	1.37	10.3	-1.90	89.59	0.30	6.2	-0.99	4.22	-3.81
EastGoda	79.38	-0.02	10.84	1.01	9.78	-0.85	77.45	-0.02	11.89	1.86	11.65	-0.73	85.09	-0.07	10.63	1.109	4.28	-1.16
WestGoda	80.55	-0.22	9.5	0.61	9.94	1.35	77.49	-0.28	11.92	2.59	12.77	1.43	86.96	-0.17	8.99	0.83	4.05	2.13
Krishna	83.74	0.07	6.85	-1.67	9.41	0.70	79.6	-0.10	9.43	1.07	12.83	1.49	90.98	0.23	5.61	-2.57	3.42	-1.05
Guntur	85.59	0.08	5.71	-1.78	8.7	0.52	80.49	-0.12	10.07	2.48	12.44	1.59	92.97	0.21	3.77	-2.73	3.26	-1.93
Prakasam	86.06	0.27	6.54	-1.96	7.39	-1.14	81.01	0.10	10.58	1.18	10.64	0.20	93.27	0.37	3.96	-3.16	2.78	-4.91
Nellore	82.87	-0.12	8.43	-0.70	8.69	2.07	79.15	-0.25	11.04	0.87	11.19	2.53	89.39	0.004	6.28	-0.87	4.34	1.34
Chittor	84.22	-0.21	7.47	0.77	8.31	1.66	80.06	-0.37	10.47	2.75	10.97	2.10	92.05	-0.05	4.65	0.13	3.28	1.13
Cuddapah	83.42	0.17	8.56	-1.10	8.03	-0.44	79.77	0.05	10.91	0.65	10.54	0.15	90.88	0.33	6.23	-2.55	2.9	-3.14
Anantapur	86.78	-0.13	6.83	0.51	6.39	1.33	82.96	-0.23	9.72	2.26	8.79	1.89	93.13	-0.03	4.43	0.73	2.44	-0.24
Kurnool	86.19	0.12	6.25	-1.10	7.55	-0.40	81.78	0.05	9.93	1.76	10.48	0.15	92.41	0.14	4.17	-1.46	3.42	-1.58
Mahabub	87.25	0.12	5.21	-4.03	7.55	2.48	83.35	-0.002	8.59	-0.42	10.26	2.94	92.32	0.17	3.67	-4.95	4.02	2.63
RangaRed	81.27	0.48	6.08	-5.43	12.65	0.64	74.69	0.45	10.07	-2.45	17.74	1.21	90.7	0.33	3.94	-5.34	5.37	-0.13
Medak	83.65	-0.11	6.73	-2.72	9.64	3.49	80.31	-0.19	9.13	-0.70	12.29	3.89	88.23	-0.14	5.81	-2.19	5.96	6.22

Contd....

Table 3.5 : (Contd....)

District	*Cultivators +Agri. labour +Agri. Allied (total for 1991) %*	*1981 to 91 GR (%/y)*	*Tradition (total 91) (%)*	*1981 to 91 GR (%/y)*	*Modern 91 (total)*	*1981 to 91 GR (%/y)*	*Cultivator+ Agri. labour +Agri. Allied (males for 1991)%*	*1981 to 91 GR (%/y)*	*Traditional 91 (male)*	*1981 to 91 GR (%/y)*	*Modern 91 (male)*	*1981 to 91 GR (%/y)*	*c+Al+ Alli 91 (female)*	*1981 to 91 GR (%/y)*	*Traditional 91 (female)*	*1981 to 91 GR (%/y)*	*Modern 91 (female)*	*GR*
Nizamaba	73.47	-0.38	17.88	1.62	8.65	0.25	77.17	-0.17	10.31	-0.02	12.12	0.78	69.25	-0.60	26.08	1.88	4.68	-0.29
Adilabad	79.51	-0.50	9.85	1.11	10.63	3.48	77.22	-0.55	10.18	1.94	13.68	3.17	82.9	-0.51	10.97	1.41	6.14	6.57
Karimnaga	76.17	-0.40	12.31	-0.68	11.52	4.30	73.61	-0.45	10.6	-2.12	15.29	4.50	79.32	-0.40	13.8	0.42	6.88	5.16
Warangal	84.41	0.08	7.54	-2.76	8.05	2.61	78.84	-0.22	9.64	-1.74	11.87	4.16	92.16	0.27	5.12	-3.26	2.71	-1.56
Khammam	85.67	0.10	6.21	-1.91	9.12	1.73	80.82	-0.08	9.31	0.82	11.56	1.54	93.56	0.24	3.93	-3.20	2.5	-2.56
Nalgonda	81.01	-0.28	9.37	-0.19	9.61	3.09	75.23	-0.71	8.93	-1.70	13.41	4.57	89.56	0.15	6.42	-1.61	4.02	-0.53
AP	82.85	-0.04	8.35	-0.66	8.8	-1.32	79.07	-0.16	9.13	-0.03	11.80	1.62	88.89	0.05	7.12	-0.70	3.99	0.25
India	82.28	-0.14	9.6	2.10	8.12	1.03	79.83	-0.23	8.70	0.63	11.47	1.24	89.55	0.05	6.43	-0.38	4.02	-0.41

Notes and sources : As previously.

portion of workers involved in agriculture whilst Karimnagar has the lowest. For males also, these two extreme districts represents the same highest and lowest figures. For females, Karimnagar is again low whilst Khammam has the highest share of female workers in agriculture. Karimnagar thus has the highest proportion of workers for both sexes involved with non-farm activities. This district is also of high agricultural and infrastructural development and is part of a newly irrigated district.

In relation to changes in the proportion of main workers involved with the agricultural sector, a decline has occurred in more than half of the districts (in 12 for total, in 17 for males) with the exception of females. The average annual declines, where they have happened are, however, relatively small (0.5 per cent in Karimnagar for totals, 0.55 per cent for males and females in Adilabad). Again, Adilabad is the district which has witnessed the fastest increase in RNFE for both sexes.

Turning to the traditional and modern breakdown of district non-farm employment, recalling here that we have taken a somewhat arbitrary decision in the separation of the 2 sectors, males dominate both sectors. We have equated predominantly traditional RNFE with HHI and other services and predominantly modern RNFE with mining and quarrying, non-HHI, construction, trade and transport. AP out performs India for share of total labour force in modern RNFE. The same pattern occurs for males. In contrast, in AP a smaller share of total workers is involved with traditional non-farm activities than in all-India, but the pattern is reversed for males, (9.1 per cent in AP compared to 8.7 per cent for India). For totals, Nizamabad has the greatest proportion of non-farm workers involved with the traditional sector, while Ranga Reddy has the highest proportion of non-farm workers in the modern sector. The fact that 26.08 per cent of females are involved in Nizamabad in the traditional sector helps to explain the high total share of traditional overall in that district. The district with the greatest share of female workers in the modern sector is Karimnagar, although the 6.9 per cent figure is far behind that of males (15.3 per cent).

The average annual changes in modern sector RNFE have been important for both males and females (4.5 per cent and 5.2 per cent respectively per year over the decade). AP is the state where the rate of total modern RNFE growth has been highest. The most pronounced increase in the modern sector for females has been Medak (almost twice the increase of males). Acute declines have occurred for females in the modern sector in Visakhapatnam and for males in Ranga Reddy. There are important differences between males and females in their employment in the modern sector. As many as 15 districts have witnessed a decline in the number of females involved in the modern sector and in 11 districts there have been declines in both the modern and traditional sectors simultaneously. We see later that the female RNFE is linked to an increase in female agricultural employment. The pattern is more consistent in the traditional sector where the decline in RNFE has been important for males, females and total.

Table 3.6. separates the districts into 2 categories; those that have experienced an increase in the RNFS from those that have experienced a decrease. We are looking for some characteristics that can be easily identified to account for the RNFS performance. Neither the affluence nor the poverty of a district appears to be associated at the bivariate level with the share of non-farm employment within rural areas (through an examination of scatter plots and correlation matrices which is not reported in the thesis). As a first step towards multivariate analysis we plotted the RNFE share against irrigation as a proxy for agricultural development and poverty as well as urbanisation.

The highest percentage decline in RNFE is seen in those districts in which urban population has grown very fast, namely Visakhapatnam and Ranga Reddy. This may be due to the fact that there has been rural migration to urban areas as a result of a decline in traditional industries, or maybe it is a means of accessing urban employment. It was observed in the scatter plot of RNFE and growth of urbanisation that the slackening of the rate of growth of non-farm is mainly due to the slackening of urbanisation. The coefficient of variation of female RNFE across districts increased considerably between 1981-1991. Certain transformations have taken place in districts that seem to have facilitated the establishment of agro-based industries which were labour and female-intensive (for example cashew kernel processing, tobacco processing, and fruit juice manufacturing industries). However these were mostly confined to districts already leading in RNFS share.

There has been relatively little change between 1981 and 1991 in the agricultural sector in AP and India. The share for males has declined and has been little compensated by the small increase for females, generally the total annual decline is in the order of 0.04 per cent for AP and 0.14 per cent for India. However, a point worth noting is that the average annual decline for males for AP is about a third of that observed for India.

Table 3.6. shows that, in terms of the 1991 proportions involved, there is again little difference between AP and India; the proportion of males in rural farm employment and that of females is a little bit lower in AP compared to India (79.07 per cent) compared to 79.83 per cent and 88.89 per cent and 89.55 per cent respectively.

For total, the ratio for 1991 is reversed but again is small (82.85 per cent in AP compared to 82.28 per cent in India) differences are more pronounced in relation to the performance of the predominantly traditional and modern sectors. The biggest change happened for the modern sector where the increase has been in excess of 1 per cent per year over the period; AP has done better than India for males (1.62 per cent compared to 1.24 per cent). In contrast, the situation for females in the modern sector remained stable and even declined in India. The modern sector accounted for about 11.5 per cent for males compared to about 4 per cent for females. The performance in the traditional sector has not been very good for either males or females in AP. Both witnessed declines although the extent of the change has been more pronounced for females. The traditional sector accounted for 9 per cent of employment for males and about 7 per cent for females in AP standing slightly above the India average, which is in fact caused by a very pronounced dispersion for females.

Table 3.6 : Changes in RNFS Employment, in Urban Growth, in Poverty and Per capita Value of Agricultural Output Across as Districts Between 1981 and 1991:

Districts	% RNFE 1981	% RNFE 1991	Pattern of Change (percentage points)	% of urban Population 1981	% of urban Population 1991	Difference of urban Population (percentage points)	Decadal Growth rate of urban Population	% of Persons below Poverty line 1977-78	% of Persons below Poverty line 1987-88	Difference (percentage Points)	Per capita value of Agril. Output 1981	Per capita value of Agril. output 1991 (1981 Constant prices)	Difference Rupees
RNFS Decrease													
Ranga Reddy	22.51	18.95	-3.56	24.29	47.12	22.83	209.19	74.03	32.25	41.78	614.81	817.24	202.43
Visakhapatnam	19.21	16.72	-2.49	31.28	39.76	8.48	61.70	70.28	35.32	34.96	742.14	828.95	86.81
Prakasam	16.25	14.09	-2.16	14.99	16.45	1.46	29.66	58.56	44.14	14.42	1168.71	1238.95	70.24
Cuddapah	17.96	16.52	-1.44	19.40	24.00	4.6	45.11	54.21	24.20	30.01	697.40	1108.92	411.52
Kurnool	14.83	14.06	-0.77	24.49	25.85	1.36	30.12	74.42	38.74	35.68	1026.45	1350.15	323.7
Warangal	16.25	15.69	-0.56	17.24	19.40	2.16	37.66	76.12	56.57	19.55	661.15	888.01	226.86
Khammam	15.22	14.68	-0.54	16.98	20.19	3.21	50.44	42.12	34.97	7.15	739.37	1133.53	394.16
Guntur	15.09	14.63	-0.46	27.53	28.93	1.4	25.51	45.72	37.73	7.99	1398.75	1891.83	493.08
Krishna	16.88	16.46	-0.42	32.54	35.83	3.29	33.45	46.95	27.68	19.27	1412.12	1483.26	71.14
Mahabubnagar	13.76	13.38	-0.38	10.93	11.11	0.18	27.79	73.14	80.08	-6.94	708.52	825.82	117.3
Average	16.80	15.52	-1.28	21.97	26.86	4.83	55.06	66.56	41.17	20.39	916.94	1156.67	239.72
RNFS Increase													
Adilabad	16.35	20.5	4.15	19.32	23.14	3.82	51.80	82.15	49.14	33.01	586.41	605.30	18.89
Karimnagar	20.73	24.04	3.31	15.79	20.59	4.8	62.19	82.55	59.43	23.12	739.37	1133.53	394.16

Contd....

Table 3.6 : (Contdd....)

Districts	*% RNFE 1981*	*% RNFE 1991*	*Pattern of Change (percentage points)*	*% of urban Population 1981*	*% of urban Population 1991*	*Difference of urban Population (percentage points)*	*Decadal Growth rate of urban Population*	*% of Persons below Poverty line 1977-78*	*% of Persons below Poverty line 1987-88*	*Difference (percentage Points)*	*Per capita value of Agril. Output 1981*	*Per capita value of Agril. output 1991 (1981 Constant prices)*	*Difference Rupees*
Nizamabad	23.68	26.79	3.11	19.21	20.27	1.06	27.93	51.89	38.75	13.14	1040.88	1012.45	-28.43
Nalgonda	16.65	19.11	2.46	11.38	11.87	0.49	30.26	39.29	9.34	30.05	600.44	1733.49	1133.05
West Godavari	17.64	19.5	1.86	20.77	20.83	0.04	22.78	54.35	11.29	43.06	1701.61	1321.35	-380.26
Vizianagaram	16.3	18.11	1.81	15.94	17.20	1.26	25.90	-	51.52	-	742.14	828.95	86.81
Chittor	13.97	15.65	1.68	16.88	19.82	2.94	39.62	63.59	51.14	12.45	802.17	1103.44	301.27
Medak	15.4	16.76	1.36	11.97	14.50	2.33	51.49	77.54	41.39	36.15	658.92	726.26	67.34
Anantapur	12.1	13.28	1.18	20.81	23.51	2.7	40.81	77.84	74.51	3.33	866.76	1126.58	259.82
Nellore	16.12	17.32	1.20	20.76	23.81	6.05	35.95	60.66	60.05	0.61	873.66	1201.77	328.11
East Godavari	20.43	20.67	0.24	22.21	23.85	1.64	31.77	56.75	16.50	40.25	1114.09	1014.38	-99.71
Srikakulam	16.66	16.84	0.18	10.89	12.51	1.62	35.70	77.33	59.36	17.97	646.48	712.96	66.48
Average	17.17	19.05	1.88	17.16	19.33	2.17	38.02	66.81	43.54	21.10	864.41	1043.32	178.91
AP	16.8	17.1	0.3	23.32	26.84	3.52	42.69	63.54	40.78	22.76	N/A	N/A	N/A

Notes : % RNFS means Percentage of main workers in rural non-farm sector to total main workers in rural areas.
'Pattern of change' means percentage change in RNFS between 1981-1991.

Sources : Census of India 1991, Andhra Pradesh, Population Totals, Series-2, pp. 10, 66-73.
Sudhakar Reddy (1991) 'Poverty and Agricultural growth in Rural Andhra Pradesh Inter District Analysis', CESS, Hyderabad

Table 3.6 enables a rough separation of characteristics specific to the two groups of AP districts regarding their RNFS performance. Focussing on those districts where RNFS has reversed one sees that there are clear trends on average by higher urban population over the decade and by very fast growth in the urban population between 1981 and 1991. Whereas the two groups of districts started in 1977-78 with a similar percentage of people below the poverty line, the districts in which the RNFS has decreased has performed better in reducing its poverty. Some districts have had an excellent performance (such as Ranga Reddy and Kurnool) nevertheless the districts that belong to the 'RNFS increase' group have also done very well so that the pattern is not systematic. As for per capita value of agricultural output, the figure has increased in real terms for both groups, but it has increased by much more for the 'RNFS decrease group'. In particular no district in this group has experienced a decline (compared with 3 districts in the other group).

Finally as expected those districts where the RNFS has declined we have seen the proportions of those involved in RNFE fall by 1.28 percentage points over the 1981-91. The caveat existing with the data presented in the table which prevents one from drawing clear inferences is that fluctuations might have occurred during the decades considered.

In total the modern and traditional sectors had similar shares in AP (between 8 and 9 per cent in 1991), a breakdown hardly distinct from that of India (9.6 per cent and 8.12 per cent for modern and traditional) nevertheless there seems to be greater dispersion across districts for the traditional sector when compared to the modern sector.

Census of India 1991 Andhra Pradesh Series-2, Paper-1 of 1991 Supplement Provisional Population Totals.

It can be seen from the Table 3.7 there is an increasing disparity across the AP districts in 1981 compared to 1991 (CV has increase from 0.17 to 0.19). When we look at the pattern for males there is more uniformity in the recent period in terms of the proportion in RNFE. This time the change is quite

Table 3.7: Proportion of Rural Non- farm Employment to Total Workers Per District in Andhra Pradesh, 1981-1991

District	*% RNFE 1981 total (1)*	*% RNFE 1991 total (2)*	*Pattern of Change in percentage points Total* (3) = (2) - (1)	*% RNFE 1981 Males (4)*	*% RNFE 1991 Males (5)*	*Pattern of Change in percentage points Males* (6) = (5) - (4)	*% RNFE 1981 Females (7)*	*% RNFE 1991 Females (8)*	*Pattern of Change in percentage pointsfemales* (9) = (8) - (7)
Nizamabad	23.66	26.53 [1]	2.87	21.54	22.43 [8]	0.89	26.47	30.76 [1]	4.29
Karimnagar	20.74	23.83 [2]	3.09	22.98	25.89 [2]	2.91	17.4	20.68 [2]	3.28
EastGodavari	20.45	20.62 [3]	0.17	22.42	23.54 [5]	1.12	14.33	14.91 [4]	0.58
Adilabad	16.37	20.48 [4]	4.11	18.41	23.86 [4]	5.45	12.79	17.11 [3]	4.32
WestGodavari	17.63	19.44 [5]	1.81	20.31	24.69 [3]	4.38	11.56	13.04 [5]	1.48
Nalgonda	16.64	18.98 [6]	2.34	19.18	22.34 [9]	3.16	11.79	10.44 [9]	-1.35
Ranga Reddy	22.5	18.73 [7]	-3.77	28.63	27.81 [1]	-0.82	12.26	9.31 [12]	-2.95
Vizanagarm	16.28	17.94 [8]	1.66	20.12	23.01 [6]	2.89	8.93	10.02 [11]	1.09
Nellore	16.12	17.12 [9]	1	18.84	22.23 [11]	3.39	10.65	10.62 [8]	-0.03
Srikakulam	16.65	16.98 [10]	0.33	19.53	21.2 [17]	1.67	11.31	10.88 [7]	-0.43
Visakhaptnam	19.2	16.76 [11]	-2.44	21.97	21.17 [18]	-0.8	13.07	10.42 [10]	-2.65
Cuddapah	17.95	16.59 [12]	-1.36	20.61	21.45 [13]	0.84	12.06	9.13 [13]	-2.93
Medak	15.71	16.37 [13]	0.66	18.18	21.42 [15]	3.24	10.51	11.77 [6]	1.26
Krishna	16.89	16.26 [14]	-0.63	19.55	22.26 [10]	2.71	11.08	9.03 [14]	-2.05
Chittor	13.97	15.78 [15]	1.81	16.89	21.44 p14]	4.55	7.52	7.93 [15]	0.41
Warangal	16.2	15.59 [16]	-0.61	19.39	21.51 [12]	2.12	10.3	7.83 [16]	-2.47

Contd....

Table 3.7 : (Contd....)

District	*% RNFE 1981 total (1)*	*% RNFE 1991 total (2)*	*Pattern of Change in percentage points Total* (3) = (2) - (1)	*% RNFE 1981 Males (4)*	*% RNFE 1991 Males (5)*	*Pattern of Change in percentage points Males* (6) = (5) - (4)	*% RNFE 1981 Females (7)*	*% RNFE 1991 Females (8)*	*Pattern of Change in percentage pointsfemales* (9) = (8) - (7)
Khammam	15.21	15.33 [17]	0.12	18.5	20.87 [19]	2.37	8.68	6.43 [22]	-2.25
Guntur	15.09	14.41 [18]	-0.68	18.5	22.51 [7]	4.01	8.93	7.03 [19]	-1.9
Prakasam	16.26	13.93 [19]	-2.33	19.84	21.22 [16]	1.38	10.06	6.74 [21]	-3.32
Kurnool	14.84	13.8 [20]	-1.04	18.66	20.41 [20]	1.75	8.84	7.59 [18]	-1.25
Ananthapur	12.09	13.22 [21]	1.13	15.06	18.51 [22]	3.45	6.62	6.87 [20]	0.25
Mahhabubnag	13.77	12.76 [22]	-1.01	16.64	18.85 [21]	2.21	9.2	7.69 [17]	-1.51
Mean (AP)	17.0	17.3	0.3	19.8	22.2	1.2	11.6	11.2	-0.4
SD	2.8	3.4		2.7	2.1		4.1	5.6	
CV	0.17	0.19		0.14	0.09		0.35	0.5	

Notes : Figures in [ ] indicates the ranks. CV: Coefficient of Variation is (SD/Mean) and SD = standard deviation.

% RNFE Percentage of main workers in RNFS to total main workers in rural areas. % change in RNFS between 1981-91.

Sources : Census of India 1991 India Series-1, Provisional Population Totals: Workers and Their Distribution Paper-3 of 1991, pp. 443-448.

pronounced. The CV for males has gone down from 0.14 to 0.09 and for females has increased from 0.35 to 0.5. The pattern of RNFE is much more diverse across the AP districts than for males. It appears that there seems more spread in RNFE for females. The gender dimension of RNFE has become more pronounced during the decade which the data considered.

Differences between the districts which can be further seen show that there has been substantial variation across districts in the shares of non-farm employment in total employment. Differences in the proportionate changes on RNFE shares are summarised in Table 3.8.

For rural AP as a whole there is a small increase in the share in RNFS between 1981 and 1991 (Table 3.7). Even for males. there is a rise of just 0.18 percentage points. Thus there are some trends of variations in rural de-industrialisation.

The central point is that during the period 1980-81 to 1990-91 in the districts where the RNFS decreased, the per capita value of agricultural output is high compared with districts in which the RNFS has increased which suggests distress diversification overall. One possible inference is that in the districts where RNFS decreased, agriculture was booming and has successfully attracted workers out of the RNFS. This made them shift and become less poor, which could be encouraging.

Table 3.7 separates the AP districts according to the extent of the changes between 1981 and 1991 in the proportion of RNFE to total workers. These changes are also summarised for all workers (male plus female). Whilst there is a broad similarity in the changes in RNFS proportions for the total as well as males and females, there are some exceptions for female and male workers. 12 districts show positive growth in the share of RNFS in total workers ranging from a minimum of 0.18 per cent to 4.15 per cent. Similarly there were 10 districts showing declines ranging from 0.38 per cent to 3.56 per cent. The largest falls for the total occurred in the districts of Ranga Reddy and of Visakhapatnam. Adilabad in contrast experienced a big rise. The majority of the districts have experienced small changes (rise or decline); a smaller number of districts exhibited a

Table 3.8 : District Breakdown by Changes in the Proportion of RNFE to Total Workers, AP, 1981-1991.

Big falls in RNFS	*Big rise in RNFS*	*Medium fall in RNFS*	*Medium rise in RNFS*	*Small changes*
(> 2.44 percentage points)	(> 2.44 percentage points)	(1 to 2.44 percentage points)		(↑↓ < 1 percentage points)
		For total RNFS workers		
Ranga Reddy Visakhapatnam	Adilabad Nizamabad Karimnagar	Prakasam Cudapah Mahbubnagar Anantapur Kurnool	Chittor West-Godavari Viziana-garam Nalgonda	Srikakulam Nellore Krishna Medak Warangal East-Godavari Guntur Khammam
		For male workers		
	Adilabad Medak Krishna Karimnagar Guntur Nalgonda Vizianagaram Nellore Anantapur Chittor West-Godavari		Prakasam Srikakulam Warangal Khammam Kurnool Mahbubnagar East-Godavari	Ranga Reddy Cudapah Nizambad Visakhapatnam
		For female workers		
Prakasam Warangal Ranga Reddy Cudapah Visakhapatnam	Adilabad Karimnagar Nizamabad	Khammam Mahbubnagar Krishna Kurnool Nalgonda Guntur	Vizianagaram Medak West-Godavari	Anantapur Chittor Nellore Srikakulam East-Godavari

Source : Based on Table 3.7.

medium rise or fall: Ranga Reddy, Visakhapatnam and Adilabad districts for total and for females, although when females are considered, the district of Nizamabad needs to be added.

The grouping shows a heavy decline for the two districts of Ranga Reddy and of Visakhapatnam. A location effect, namely nearness to an urban industrial growth centre, might have caused this. On the other hand, Adilabad has distinct agro-climatic endowments. The district also has a large forest area (over 7 lakh hectares forming 43.6 per cent of the total geographical area) which is an important source of income to the state. The forest also provides building materials for some industries and is a major supplier of firewood. The bamboo forests are located in industrial complexes in Sirpur, Kagaj Nagar and provide employment to the household industry outside the farm sector. The Sirpur paper mills, the silk factories, the Bellampally chemical and fertiliser factory and the cement factory in Mamcherial, are important large scale industries in the state. The district is rich in resources (particularly forests and minerals) as well as possessing a vast potential for agriculture along with the potential for the development of related industries. All these conditions worked favourably towards the growth of the RNFS in the rural Adilabad district. The pattern of change in the other two groups, medium and small is very complex and can be analysed better through econometric methods such as the regression models exposed in this chapter.[4]

For total RNFE the CV suggests that there are increasing disparities across the state, whereas for males the CV shows that disparities are being reduced and a more uniform/ homogeneous pattern is appearing. On the other hand for females there is a marked increase in dispersion.

3.2 Factors Determining RNFE and Variables Used in the Regressions

This and the next section describe the determinants of a district's RNFE, viz., the ratio of RNFS main workers (those who have worked more than six months (183 days] in the year) to total rural main workers (throughout the chapter, 'workforce' refers to rural main workers). The hypothesised determinants are represented by variables listed in this section, and analysed by multiple regression. Section 3.3 provides further information on, and an evaluation of, the factors that are expected to determine the growth of RNFE share at the district level in AP. These factors can be grouped into two categories: agriculture related variables (1) commercialisation (2) irrigation (3) land holding size, and non-farm related variables: (4) urbanisation (5) incidence of poverty (6) village size (7) levels of literacy (8) infrastructure (9) per cent of bank branches in rural areas.

These independent variables are explained below.

Agriculture Related Variables

Commercialisation (X_1)**:** This is measured in districts where non-food commercial crops predominate, employment opportunities in non-farm activities like processing, grading, and marketing, may be more widespread. The hypothesis is that, since commercial crops are mostly market-oriented, a large area under commercial crops implies more opportunities for non-farm employment.

It may be observed that rice is often a commercial crop and that it involves a high proportion of RNFE activities. Greeley (1987) reports that about 25 per cent of the net value added that was embodied in rice at retail, in the Bangladesh villages in Chandina and Comilla that he surveyed, came from post-harvest local RNFS activity. Where one draws the line here is arbitrary: winnowing, threshing, drying, husking and milling are all essential to turn the farm product into a consumable, and are thus inherently agriculture-linked. However, the strength of local linkages depends on which commercial crops. Jute would generate more RNFE than rubber, processed usually far away for most added value. The main non-food commercial crops in AP are oil seed, groundnut and castor (occupying the first or second place in the country), sesamum, sunflower, chillies, sugarcane, mesta, cotton, and tobacco. These crops involve a lot of local processing employment for oil seeds, cotton and tobacco more than for rice. The importance of commercialisation can also be noted for those rural households whose income is in excess of Rs. 30.000. They derived 40.5 per cent of their income from farming and another 38.8 per cent from business (see Appendix Table 3.2.). Thus, this study expects a positive relation between non-farm employment and the proportion of area under commercial crops to total cropped area.

Irrigation (X_2): An increase in the irrigation ratio (percentage of gross irrigated area to gross cropped area) leads to changes in cropping patterns from less to more remunerative crops and to improvements in factor productivity. The net effect is increased value added, which, eventually increases incomes in the agricultural sector. The hypothesis is that irrigation increased incomes in agriculture and that this will lead to an increase in the demand for non-farm activities through production and consumption linkages, thereby increasing RNFE. A.S Sirohi pointed out that an increase in the irrigated area will increase the real per capita income of all classes. Over the period between 1956-57 to 1991-92 the percentage of irrigated area has been increased see Appendix Table 3.4.

A village level study of Matar Taluk in the State of Gujarat conducted by Kumar (1984) during the period 1965-82, attempted to examine the relationship between the extent of irrigation and the level of non-farm employment. A sample of 28 villages obtained from Census data of 1961-81 was used. The cross section analysis does not suggest any meaningful relationship for any of the census years. Simple correlation coefficients were all negative though not statistically significant. Thus Kumar concludes that his analysis does not suggest any relation between irrigation and RNFS. As will be seen this result is different from the one we obtained whilst studying inter-district analysis.

Irrigation always raises farm labour (whether by intensifying double crop which allows more fertility leading to higher investment or by extensifying more land). Very strong local linkages are needed, if irrigation is to raise non-farm labour even more than farm labour (Hazell, P. and C. Ramasamy (1992)].

The hypothesised impact of irrigation is *via* its impact on output factor productivity and agricultural income. On the other hand it is also possible that in highly irrigated areas seasonal variation in the demand for farm labour is greatly reduced. This reduces the need for looking for alternative RNFE. The net impact of irrigation on RNFE is therefore difficult to specify a *priori*. A positive relation is hypothesised based on the presumption that the linkage effects will dominate. (This also implies that as total demand for labour farm and non-farm rises there will be a tendency to introduce labour-saving innovations in both sectors).

I argue that irrigation works as separate effect only if, given agriculture output per person, and given yield, irrigation increases linkages to local RNFS. But irrigation also reduces seasonality of agricultural labour, cutting the need to seek RNFS work.

Land Holding Size (X_3)**:** The share of RNFE is hypothesised to vary inversely with the average size of the operational holding per person. The limited absorptive capacity of their operational holdings compels the poor, landless labourers and land poor farmers to go for RNFS. On the other hand the agricultural output or income creates greater demand for RNFS and generates surplus for investment in the RNFS. A substantial improvement will be to count irrigated land or the crop twice. Therefore it is argued that farm size may have positive or negative relationships with RNFE. Average farm size is estimated in hectares. (Appendix Table 3.3. provides some evidence for the fact that as land cultivated class (i.e. 4.01+ Hectares) by the household increases, their participation in RNFE decreases when compared to cultivated class which has fewer hectares, in particular poorer HHs with less land.

Non-farm Related Variables

Levels of Literacy (X_4) **:** Generally the impact of literacy on RNFS is expected to be positive (Chadha (1991)], but there is little evidence. However, non-farm activities are of two types, traditional and modern. In the case of traditional non-farm activities, literacy may be a deterring factor to participation or employment. In contrast it might have a favourable impact in the modern RNFS.

One would expect the level of education of a district to have a negative impact on labour supply. As the level of education increases, worker preferences for manual work changes. The level of education changes the workers attitude towards work. Disaggregated data results have to be examined to verify the hypothesis that modern sector non-farm employment may have a positive relationship with literacy.

We need to study the impact of literacy on RNFE separately for different categories, because some of them may require literate and skilled labour while others may require only unskilled labour. The sign may thus be positive for modern RNFE and negative for traditional RNFE. We have considered 7 different major categories of activities in addition to the aggregate picture. The level of literacy is estimated by calculating the proportion of literate population to total population.

Urbanisation (X_5) is the percentage of urban population to total population (see Table 3.9 for definition). There are two avenues through which urbanisation influences the rural share of workers in non-farm employment. On the supply side urban workplaces provide employment opportunities. Workers may actually reside in rural areas but physically move between these two segments. If rural-residing NFS workers commute to town, the RNFS proportion of rural activity and employment goes down but the proportion of rural residents engaged in non-farm production rises. Meanwhile, urban markets provide market opportunities for the products produced in the RNFS.

Urbanisation and infrastructure development are often complementary and occur simultaneously. Both can encourage non-farm activities in both the secondary and tertiary sectors and in neighbouring rural areas to satisfy non-local demands. Better and relatively inexpensive transport facilities enable members of rural households to commute to non-farm occupations in neighbouring urban centres (Basant and Joshi (1989)].

Urbanisation requires the services of rural artisans, semi skilled and illiterate casual labour to work in fast growing urban manufacturing and services; it creates demand for manufactured consumer goods and semi-finished raw materials of rural based.

There are two important ways in which urbanisation and RNFS are positively related. For the supply side urbanisation promotes the RNFS by providing production support as well as location advantage. Meanwhile demand for rural non-farm products originates in the urban area. Both, small towns and large cities generally provide good markets for rural non-farm products. Vibhooti Shukla's empirical study (1991) provides the necessary support: the share of small towns in district urban population acts favourably upon the magnitude and share of rural RNFE.

Urbanisation is per cent of urban population (in a district) over 5000 persons. If RNFS establishments create much work and output in such places, then supply and demand for labour in the rural hinterland is reduced. Thus, the hypothesis is that the level of urbanisation will have a positive impact on RNFE.

Incidence of Poverty (X_6): The incidence of poverty in a district is measured by the percentage of population below the poverty line.[5] The relationship between poverty and RNFE may be positive or negative. A high level of poverty may result in high level of RNFS due to 'distress diversification'. When agricultural development is not adequate, dependence on non-farm activity is likely to be relatively high, for survival. However, if these districts are extremely poor, effective demand may be so low that it prevents the development of RNFS rather than encouraging it. This may result in a non-linear relationship between incidence of poverty and the level of RNFE. In regions with a high incidence of poverty there will be a relative lack of demand for rural non-farm products, compared with regions of similar average consumption but less poverty i.e. the rich have higher savings/income ratio which inhibits the growth of non-farm opportunities while the poor have little effective demand. The initial hypothesis is that there will be an inverse relationship between the incidence of poverty and non-farm employment.

Villages Size (X_7) : The proxy variable used for measuring the agglomeration size is the percentage of villages with more than 1000 people in a district. This variable mainly operates on the production side, specifically in manufacturing activities. It is supposed that regional industrial agglomeration/clusters provide extra benefits for RNFE, possibly due to transfers of technology, the availability of special inputs and a better or more organised business atmosphere. For the above reasons, RNF labour is more productive. This creates a greater demand for labour in the RNFS, and perhaps a higher RNFS share at the district level. The coefficient of this variable may also be interpreted to reflect scope for scale economies or diseconomies in production as well as in distribution. The expected sign is positive.

If growth linkages matter more than distress diversification, then the help given to agriculture by good infrastructure in a district raises RNFS too.

Per cent of Bank Branches in Villages and Road Length in a Rural District (X_8 and $X_{9)}$: As proxy variables for the infrastructure we have used road length per 100 square kilometres and rural banks per 100,000 people. Rural infrastructure also influences the supply costs (farm and non-farm). It also affects the articulation of supply and demand via cheap transport and information. But again this might work both ways, allowing urban, for instance, to destroy rural competitions by cheaply entering at (low) marginal cost. In the case of Maharastra a negative relation was observed (Shukla, 1991). The author's explanation is interesting. He notes that investment in infrastructure in rural areas enhances the position of agriculture, at the cost of RNFE, through this is not counterproductive to RNFE. However, on balance we expect a positive sign for the coefficient.

Infrastructure is required for non-farm activities to develop. The availability of infrastructure facilities, such as roads, and banks will be high in areas which are developed. Rural infrastructure is hypothesised to have an influence upon the magnitude of NFE through the production or product supply side. I hypothesise that infrastructure help the growth of RNFS; therefore there is a positive relationship between ' per cent of villages with rural bank branches' and road length in square kilometres. The percentage of villages with rural bank branches was shown by Binswanger and Khandker (1995) to be a powerful explanatory of RNFS share and growth across districts in all-India (though not an explanation of agriculture variance).

Many studies (Hazell and Haggblade (1991); Shukla (1991 and 1992); H.P. Binswanger (1993) and G. Gangadhar (1996)] on RNFS emphasise the role of infrastructural facilities in promoting RNFS. One reason for such a positive relationship to exist is that infrastructure increases the responsiveness of non-farm economic activity to increased demand, derived from both agricultural and nearby urban growth centres. We have considered the two variables, road length and banking facilities to represent the available infrastructural facilities in a district. Transport and communications are vital links to the external world and the banking institution, which is a source of institutional credit, also facilitates RNFS. The earlier studies, especially Haggblade (1995), Shukla (1991) and Gangadhar (1996) all find a positive sign in their empirical exercise. We also expect a positive sign. In the study by Murthy and Durga (1992) agricultural development, infrastructural development and overall development are all expected *a priori* to have a negative relationship with RNFE, while a positive sign is expected for the poverty coefficient. Definitions are given in Table 3.9

3.3 Values and Key Characteristics of the Dependent and Explanatory Variables

A summary of the 1981 level, 1991 level, and pooled (1981-1991) values for all the dependent and independent variables are provided in Tables 3.10 and 3.11 respectively. Table 3.10 reports the results of tests for differences in means of the dependent variables among the 22 districts of AP between 1981 and 1991. The importance of these tests is to highlight which variables differed between 1981 and 1991.

Table 3.9: Description of the variables used in the regression analysis

	Variables	*Definitions*	*Sources*
X_1	% Commercial crops to total cropped area Commercialisation = % "non-food" crops / total crop.	Measures Commercialisation. % of area under commercial crops to GCA. The area under commercial crops in each district of AP for 1981-91 refers to crops which are used for Total condiments and spices (arecanuts, turmeric, ginger, garlic, coriander, tamarind); Total oilseeds Groundnut, sesamum, coconut, rape and mustard, sunflower, Total edible oil seeds (linseed, castor, niger seeds); Total drugs and Narcotics (coffee, Indian hemp, betel leaves, tobacco).	Season and crop reports 1980-81 and 1990-91, Directorate of Economics and Statistics, Govt. Of AP.
X_2	Irrigation ratio = % irrigated area / total cropped area	Measures the potential irrigation (takes into account existing or planned irrigation command areas. An irrigation command area is an area which receives or which is expected to receive water from an irrigation system).	Directorate of Economics and Statistics, Govt. Of AP 1981 and 1991.
X_3	Average Farm Size in Hectares (operated).	% gross areas irrigated to gross sown area (in '000 Hectares). Total operated land in a district/number of holdings in a district.	Statistical Abstracts of AP (1981 and 1991), Directorate of Economics & Statistics, Govt. of AP, pp.114-116.
	Non-farm Variables		
X_4	Literacy rate	% literate to total population (males, females, total).	Census series-2, AP Primary census abstract part II B.
X_5	Level of Urbanisation	Urban population as percentage of total population. Urban areas are defined to have the following characteristics: a minimum population of 5,000, a minimum population density	Census of India 1991, series-2 AP, paper-1 of 1991 final population

Contd....

Table 3.9 : (Contd...)

	Variables	*Definitions*	*Sources*
		of 400 persons per square kilometer, and at least 75 per cent of the male working population engaged in non-farm pursuits.	totals
X_6	% Rural Population below the Poverty line (CESS)	The poverty norm has been developed by Centre for Economic and Social Change (CESS) S. Sudhakar Reddy computed the head count measure which we have adopted. We have used the poverty line is Rs. 53.63 (per person) in the year 1980-81 and Rs. 107 in 1990-91. .	Center for Economic and Social Change, Hyderabad, poverty Project Monograph No.1, p. 60
X_7	% of Villages with population of 1,000 and above	% of villages with population 1000 and above in a district to total no. of inhabited villages.	Statistical Abstracts of AP (1981 and 1991) pp. 18-19.
X_8	Infrastructure / Banks % of Banks that are rural in total number of banks in a district.	Percentage of villages with bank branches per 100,000 population. Measures the district-wise spread of commercial bank offices in AP in 1981 and in 1991.	Statistical Abstracts of AP (1981 and 1991).
X_9	Road length. Total length of roads / 100 km^2 Geographical area	Road length per 100 square kilometres. (Roads maintained by the P.W.D (R&B), National Highways district-wise, 1990-91 (in Kms) and roads maintained by *zilla praja parishads* and by *Mandal praja parishads*).	Statistical Abstracts of AP (1981 and 1991), pp.189-190, 233-234.
Y_1	Rural Workers in non-farm Activities as a % of total workers	Non-farm employment is measured by primary occupational status. Individuals are asked whether they worked in agricultural or non-agricultural activities for at least 183 days during the previous year. It is defined as (the ratio of non-farm workers divided by total rural main workers) * 100. Rural non-farm workers are defined as rural main workers.[6]	Census of India 1991, series-2 Andhra Pradesh, Part II-B (I), Primary census Abstract general pp.110-129,
X_{10}	Dummy Variable	= 0 if t =1981 and = 1 if t =1991.	

Table 3.10 : Descriptive Statistics of the Dependent Variables (Cross District Averages of Rural Main Workers whose Primary Occupation is in the Sector) for 1981, 1991 and Pooled.

	Dependent Variable	*Mean for pooled sample 1981+91 (standard deviation) [C.V.]*	*Mean for 1981 (standard deviation) [C.V.]*	*Mean for 1991 (standard deviation) [C.V.]*	*t-value*
$Y1_{ilt}$	Mining and Quarrying	0.53 (0.68) [128.30]	0.33 (0.47) [142.42]	0.73 (0.80)	3.89***
$Y2_{ilt}$	Male Mining	0.69 (1.02) [147.83]	0.41 (0.66)[]	0.96 (1.24) [129.17]	0.47
$Y3_{ilt}$	Construction	0.82 (0.29) [35.37]	0.85 (0.34) [44.71]	0.78 (0.23) [29.11]	0.05
$Y4_{ilt}$	Male Construction	1.14 (0.38) [33.33]	1.14 (0.42) []	1.14 (0.34)[29.82]	0.00
$Y5_{ilt}$	Transport	0.95 (0.37) [1.37]	0.88 (0.40) [45.45]	1.02 (0.33)[32.35]	0.10
$Y6_{ilt}$	Male Transport	1.47 (0.53)[36.06]	1.32 (0.56) [	1.63 (0.47) [28.83]	0.18
$Y7_{ilt}$	Other than Household Industry	2.92 (0.98)[33.56]	2.81 (0.75) [26.69]	3.03 (1.18) [38.94]	0.09
$Y8_{ilt}$	Male Non-HHI	3.62 (1.15)[31.77]	3.43 (0.81) [	3.81 (1.35)[35.43]	0.14
$Y9_{ilt}$	Trade	3.22 (0.73) [22.67]	3.11 (0.72) [23.15]	3.32 (0.75) [22.59]	0.08
$Y10_{ilt}$	Male Trade	4.09 (0.83)[20.29]	3.81 (0.82) [	4.36 (0.77)[17.66]	0.19
$Y11_{ilt}$	Household Industry	3.94 (2.44) [61.93]	4.56 (2.06) [45.18]	3.32 (2.68)[80.72]	0.44
$Y12_{ilt}$	Male Household Industry	3.69 (1.49)[40.38]	4.56 (1.23) [	2.83 (1.22) [43.11]	0.64
$Y13_{ilt}$	Services	4.79 (0.95)[19.83]	4.45 (0.73) [16.40]	5.12 (1.04)[20.31]	0.22
$Y14_{ilt}$	Male Services	5.72 (1.04)[18.18]	5.13 (0.75) [	6.31 (0.95)[15.06]	0.35

Contd....

Table 3.10 : (Contd....)

	Dependent Variable	*Mean for pooled sample 1981+91 (standard deviation) [C.V.]*	*Mean for 1981 (standard deviation) [C.V.]*	*Mean for 1991 (standard deviation) [C.V.]*	*t-value*
$Y15_{ilt}$	% Female NFE to Total Main Workers	11.38 (4.87) [38.05]	11.56 (4.09) [32.38]	11.19 (5.63)[43.70]	0.002
$Y16_{ilt}$	% Rural non-farm Workers as a % of Total Main Workers	17.17 (3.08) [16.98]	16.8 (2.82) [16.57]	17.33 (3.38)[17.71]	0.07
$Y17_{il}$	%Male RNFE to Total Main Workers	21.00 (2.69)[13.31]	19.81 (2.72) [15.31]	22.21 (2.09)[11.39]	0.06
	Number of Observations	44	22	22	

Notes : CV: Coefficient of variation.

Differences between 1981 and 1991 means.

*** significant at 1 per cent, ** significant at 5 per cent * significant at 10 per cent.

First, we compare the means of dependent variables (at State level) between 1981 and 1991 to see if there are any statistically significant changes. t-values show that means for 1981 and 1991 for the dependent variables are not significantly different at 1 per cent except for mining and quarrying (see Table 3.10). Various types of non-farm employment, which are used in the OLS analysis as dependent variables, do not appear to have changed. There is also no significant difference between the 1981 and 1991 percentages of rural non-farm workers to either male or female workers.

Tables 3.11 reports the summary statistics for the independent variables. Descriptive statistics were computed and the mean difference was estimated by the t-ratio. Five independent variables are statistically significantly different at 1 per cent in 1981 and 1991: commercialisation, literacy, land holding size, percentage of population below the poverty line, and infrastructure (roads).

The reason why commercialisation is significantly higher in 1991, is that AP has emerged as one of the major rice surplus states and also as a major supplier of commercial crops such as tobacco, chillies, cotton, sugar-cane and groundnut. The area under sugar-cane has increased from 1.82 lakh hectares (1990-91) to 2.02 lakh hectares during 1991-92 (an increase of 11.0 per cent).[7] Groundnut, the most important oilseed crop in AP, accounts for a substantial portion of the total Indian area under such crop. In 1991-92 this crop formed 19 per cent of the total cropped area in AP. Groundnut is mostly rainfed during the kharif and irrigated in the rabi season. All four districts in the Rayalaseema region, and the Mahabubnagar and Warangal districts in the Telangana region, jointly together accounted for 77.6 per cent of the total area under groundnut in the State during 1991-92.[8]

3.4 Regression Analysis

The form of equation used for average annual growth rates between 1981 and 1991 and for shares for the 2 years combined (pooled) for total, males and females as well as for the sub-sectors is described below. The hypotheses mentioned in this

Table 3.11 : Descriptive Statistics of the Independent Variables for 1981, 1991 and Pooled.

	Independent Variables	*Mean for pooled sample 1981+91 (standard deviation) [C.V.]*	*Mean for 1981 (standard deviation) [C.V.]*	*Mean for 1991 (standard deviation) [C.V.]*	*t-value of the diff. between 1981-91*
X_1	% Commercial Crops to Total Cropped Area	25.06 (16.72) [66.72]	19.78 (11.21)[56.67]	30.35 (19.7)[64.91]	2.19***
X_{2it}	% Irrigation to Total Cropped Area	39.82 (19.52) [49.02]	36.80 (19.42)[52.77]	45.70 (19.58)[45.70]	1.03
X_{3it}	Average Farm Size (hectares)	1.77 (0.72) [40.68]	1.96 (0.82)[41.84]	1.58 (0.56)[35.44]	1.77**
X_{4it}	% Literacy to Total Population	28.68 (9.03) [31.49]	22.53 (6.08)[26.99]	34.93 (6.98)[90.98]	3.70***
X_{5it}	Urban Population as Percentage of Total Population	21.05 (7.69) [36.53]	19.35 (6.05)[31.27]	22.75 (8.85)[38.90]	1.49
X_{6it}	% Population below the Poverty Line	50.30 (19.00) [37.77]	58.14 (16.22)[27.90]	42.46 (18.63)[43.88]	2.98***
X_{7it}	Percentage of Villages >1000	57.87 (17.47) [30.19]	55.03 (17.61)[32.00]	60.71 (17.25)[28.41]	0.53
X_{8it}	Banks per 100000 Population	4.63 (1.21) [26.13]	3.82 (0.65)[17.02]	5.44 (1.10)[20.22]	0.53
X_{9it}	Infrastructure (total length roads) (kms)	0.60 (0.13) [21.67]	0.54 (0.13)[24.07]	0.67 (0.11)[16.42)	3.00***
X_{10it}	% Male Literacy to Total Population	39.11 (9.81) [25.08]	31.49 (5.91)[18.77]	46.73 (6.36)[13.61]	1.72
X_{11it}	% Female Literacy to Total Population	18.06 (8.86) [49.06]	13.29 (6.61)[49.74]	22.83 (8.33)[36.49]	1.59
	Number of Observations	44	22	22	

Notes : CV: Coefficient of variation.
Differences between 1981 and 1991 means.
*** significant at 1 per cent, ** significant at 5 per cent * significant at 10 per cent.

chapter were used to make inferences about the expected sign between the independent and dependent variables.

$$Y_{it} = a_o + b_1 X_{1it} + b_2 X_{2it} + b_3 X_{3it} + b_4 X_{4it} + b_5 X_{5it} \ldots\ldots b_9 X_{9it} + b_{10} X_{10it} + u_{it}$$

Where i denotes districts, and t the year of the observation (1981,1991) except for the growth equations.

Y_{it} = Rural workers in non-farm activities as a per cent of total workers

X_1 = Commercialisation defined as percentage of "non-food" crops / total crops

X_2 = Irrigation ratio defined as percentage of irrigated area / total cropped area

X_3 = Average land holding size in hectares

X_4 = Literacy rate (per cent)

X_5 = Urbanisation (per cent urban population)

X_6 = Percentage of persons below poverty line

X_7 = Per cent villages with 1000 population and above

X_8 = Banks per 100,000 (hundred thousand) population

X_9 = Total length of roads per 100 kilometres geographical area

X_{10} = Dummy variable = 0 if t =1981 and = 1 if t = 1991 - only applies to pooled data

u = Disturbance term with the classical properties.

The empirical results obtained from the regression analysis are discussed in this Section. A correlation matrix of all the variables discussed earlier was constructed and main findings are reported in Section 3.4.1. The small sample size of data for 1981 and 1991 led to pooling of the data and a time dummy variable (X_{10}) was used in the equation. The results of backward step-wise regressions are presented below.

First, the combined effect of the above variables on RNFE was estimated with the above equation. Given the analytical considerations discussed earlier, different combinations of independent variables were then introduced in the regression equations. For the combined analysis, district level data was used with 22 observations for 1981 and for 1991. One district (Hyderabad) was excluded from all the regressions since the entire district is urban.

3.4.1 The Determinants of Inter-District Variations in the Shares of RNFE (by totals and gender)

In order to understand the nature of the relationships between dependent and independent variables, a correlation matrix of all the variables was obtained (see Appendix 3.6). This exercise is helpful to check whether variables are "related" to each other, or move together. Typically a correlation coefficient r in excess of about 0.8 reflects a strong relation and indicates the risk of multicolinearity problems. RNFE in household industry, in the trade sector and in transport and services each exhibit some, albeit not too problematic a relation (r varies between 0.63 and 0.71) with the RNFE of other sectors (mining, non-HHI and construction) respectively. There is also some correlation for RNFE growth data between HHI and services (r = 0.64). With regard to the growth of HHI, some correlation appears with the growth of female literacy (r = 0.65). Moreover urban growth correlates negatively with the growth of RNFE in the services sector (r = 0.62).

The original data suggested a negative correlation between irrigation and farm size and between poverty and literacy (with r = 0.61). Whilst in log form the correlation coefficient between literacy and poverty increased (to r = 0.58) and between irrigation and farm it decreased (to r = 0.64). The correlation is not important but might affect some of the reduced model results. There are in fact no serious correlation problems.

Is the direction of causation to RNFE, from the "independent" variables listed in our equation. The RNFS in a district might, in turn, determine any one or more of the independent variables (for example poverty). Where appropriate we return to this issue in the discussion of the regression results.

In the model[9] there is a common intercept for all districts and for 1981 and 1991. The slope coefficients are also common for all districts and both years. This implies that disturbance terms are independently and identically distributed. The appropriate estimation method is OLS applied to panel data. Further assuming normality for the disturbance term, all the important statistical properties of the k-variable linear model are valid.[10]

Diagnostic tests were undertaken for all the regressions for normality of the disturbance term, heteroscedasticity and functional form. The heteroscedasticity test used was based on the regression of squared residuals on squared fitted values. It has a $\chi 2$ distribution with 1 degree of freedom. The computed values are presented in Table 3.12. The computed residuals are used to test for normality (based on the skewness and kurtosis of residuals). In a $\chi 2$ test with 2 degrees of freedom, the result possibly indicates a non-normal disturbance term. Similar results are observed for other categories of RNFE, as will be noted subsequently.

While estimating by OLS in most of the cases non-normality was encountered, implying that an inference cannot be made regarding the statistical significance of coefficients. To overcome this problem, **we** plotted the residuals and looked for outliers. Then dummy variables were introduced into the model for those outliers. For those results see Appendix Tables 3.7, 3.8, 3.9, 3.10, 3.10 Part 1 and 3.10 Part 2.

The next problem was heteroscedasticity, error of variance was not constant violating one of the central assumptions of classical linear regressions model. White's (1980) heteroscedasticity corrected variance-covariance matrix was used to find the appropriate standard errors and these were used to infer about the significance of the variables in the model.

As for functional form, although it can be detected, the solution is not straightforward. It was found that log linear specifications removed the problem except in one case (viz., mining and quarrying), where little more can be done.

The estimated coefficients of the log regression equations of the selected variables for pooled 1981 and 1991 data for total, males and females are presented in Table 3.12. The data were tested against different models (quadratic, semi-log and log functions). Log form results capture diminishing returns and are therefore preferred and presented.[11]

The right-hand side columns in the Table 3.12 give the most parsimonious model. This reports the results obtained from the stepwise procedure of SPSS where the variables are eliminated until the significance level of the remaining variables prevents further elimination.[12] The model passed all the diagnostic tests.

Total RNFE shares: The variables explain 52 per cent of the cross-district variation in total rural RNFE as a share of total employment. With the exception of the coefficients associated with commercial crops, literacy, big villages, and banks, all other coefficients have the expected signs. The irrigation ratio, significant at the 1 per cent level, is positively associated with non-farm employment. Urbanisation, road length and the year dummy are also positively associated with RNFE in AP although they are not significant. In the trimmed down version of the model, literacy rates become significant. For males it is significant in both versions. The negative sign for this variable might be related to literacy affecting the percentage of RNFE only once a certain level of development has been reached: traditional RNFE activities like toddy tapping, vegetable vending, canal labour and petty trade, require little education.

Farm size is significantly and as expected, negatively associated with RNFE.

The sign for commercialisation is the opposite of that predicted, but is not significant. This could imply that districts with rapid agricultural growth had better absorption of labour in the farm sector itself, and thus less spill-over effects into the RNFS. However the negative sign may be due to the fact that rural towns have not been included in the analysis. Hazell and Haggblade (1988) found a positive relationship between per capita value of agricultural output and non-farm employment, after including rural towns (see Appendix Table 3.5). Alternatively, the problem may be that rice is a strongly 'commercial crop' in some high RNFE districts, although in fact it is not here. The remaining variables (including road length, and people below poverty line), have the expected signs but are found be insignificant, even at the 10 per cent significance level.

The RNFE elasticity to literacy is -0.179. Such strong impact is unlikely to run causality from literacy to RNFE; a 1 per cent increase in the percent of literate population would decrease the percent of RNFE by 0.179 per cent. One possible explanation is that of the two types, modern and traditional RNFE, at the district level traditional RNFE outweighs the modern RNFE, where traditional RNFE require less education. The result for literacy support the wider/overall 'development linkage' (ODL) hypothesis that traditional RNFE share rises with lower levels of literacy.

Irrigation indicates overall economic growth and is expected to be positively related with the RNFS. In the case of totals, the regression coefficient for irrigation is 0.13, and is statistically significant at 1 per cent level in explaining district-level RNFE shares. This result for irrigation suggest that higher agricultural productivity (associated with irrigation) is linked to a high RNFE share. The analysis confirm the hypothesis that growth linkages from irrigated agriculture lead to modern RNFE.

When we look at male and female non-farm employment separately, the coefficient is significant at the 1 per cent level for males. This corroborates other research findings (e.g., Murty and Parthasarathy, 1998).

Average farm size elasticity of RNFE is -0.136. A 1 per cent increase in the average farm size would decrease the total share in RNFE by 0.136 per cent. This relationship is as expected and significant at the 5 per cent level. This implies support for the hypothesis (AGL) that the traditional RNFE share rises with distress diversification.

Further our results differ from those obtained by earlier researchers in the sense that they found no clear-cut significant relationship between poverty and RNFS.

When the percentage of males in RNFE is used as the dependent variable, the model explains 44 per cent of the variance. For males, our results show that irrigation, literacy, year dummy and district dummies for Ranga Reddy and Nizamabad are significant.

Irrigation is again positively associated with RNFE and now a 1 per cent increase in total irrigation would increase the RNFE by 0.13 per cent. Among male workers it is likely that increased agricultural development provided more avenues of RNFE compared to females. In contrast, however, there is again a negative association between literacy and the RNFE share. The results for males only support for the hypothesis (AGL) in the case of irrigation and ODL (overall development linkages) in the case of literacy.

When considering the share of *females* in non-farm employment, about 58 per cent of the variance was explained. In the reduced model, a negative relation between the percentage of people below the poverty line and percentage of RNFE was found (statistically significant at the 1 per cent level). Our model suggests that a 1 per cent decrease in female poverty will increase RNFE by 0.20 per cent. Poor women are less likely to be in the RNFS, but there is no such significant relationship for men (or for totals). A similar negative relation in the case of the percentage of villages was found, which is also statistically significant at the 1 per cent level. It implies that a 1 per cent increase of bigger villages will decrease RNFE by 0.21 per cent. It could be the case that (in rural villages) mobility among females is generally low and in small villages family norms are more likely to confine women to look after household activities.

For females three variables (per cent of banks, per cent of people below the poverty line and per cent of big villages) are significant at the 1 per cent level. The RNFE per cent of banks elasticity is -0.442. For females the coefficient associated with banks is negative and significant, an increase in banks would apparently decrease female RNFE. Similarly as female RNFE increases poverty decreases. The per cent of big villages shows a negative relationship with female RNFE. It is not likely to be a direct and negative causal relationship. The results for big villages and per cent of bank branches in the case of female labour (both for women only) oppose the hypothesised growth linkages (AGL) relationship. There is no apparent explanation for this result

We got a completely different set of significant explanatory variables for men and female RNFE shares and total, male year dummy and farm size.

From the results, it may be inferred that irrigation and poverty are important determinants of non-farm employment at the district (macro) level. However, the coefficients are not elastic and not consistent, depending on the variables considered. Meanwhile, the percentage of males in the RNFS is also significantly associated with agricultural development.

Initial results pointed out problems of normality with the residuals, which meant that valid inferences could not be made with the help of standard errors. In order to tackle this problem we identified the outliers in the initial model. Three districts, namely Ranga Reddy in 1981, Nizamabad in 1981 and Nizamabad in 1991 were outliers and as a result we included district dummy variables for them.

The estimates with the dummy variables resulted in normality of errors. The χ^2 (2) JB (Jarque-Bera) (1987) test for normality was computed at 1.86 against the critical value of 5.99 at the 5 per cent level. This made valid inferences possible (district dummies for the outliers were found to be highly significant at the conventional level, i.e. 5 per cent). One possible explanation for the 2 districts to be outliers is that they are very close to urban centres and are characterised by relatively important rural-urban migration. It might consequently, be possible that rural non-farm is being replaced by informal employment in the urban city centres. It is not captured by urbanisation variable for the pooled data but it captured with disaggregated data in Table 3.13.

A year dummy was included to see whether there was a significant change in RNFE between the 2 periods. For total and for female RNFE the year dummy was not significant, implying the absence of change. However, the dummy for males was significant at the 5 per cent level and the coefficient is positive indicating that male RNFE increased significantly between 1981 and 1991 reflecting some change. It means that the same explanatory variables led to more RNFE for men (but not for women or total) in 1991 than in 1981.

An interesting result for the pooled sample is that the variables which had a significant impact on male RNFS were different from those that mattered for female RNFS. It suggest that agricultural development as a proxy for irrigation may absorb more male labour in to the RNFS whereas distress conditions push females out of agriculture due to poverty.

Aspects affecting the male RNFE slope are as follows: irrigation is positively significant supporting growth linkages, literacy is negatively significant, 1991 year dummy is positively significant and the Ranga Reddy dummy for 1981 is negatively significant.

Areas affecting female RNFE are per cent of bank branches in villages, poverty, and big villages which are all negatively significant supporting distress diversification. For Nizamabad the district dummy for both years 1991 and 1981 negatively significant.

Areas affecting total RNFE are the following: irrigation is positively significant, literacy of males+females is negatively significant, farm size is negatively significant, and the district dummies for Ranga Reddy for 1981, and Nizamabad for 1991 are both negatively significant.

The district of Nizamabad is well endowed in the sense that the agricultural economy is dominated by paddy cultivation. Yet Nizamabad recorded high poverty levels by occupational classes in rural areas in 1977-78 and in 1987-88 (for agricultural labour, poverty levels were found to be above 55 per cent with a high incidence of poverty), (Sudhakar Reddy, 1991). This could explain the negative sign for 1991 for totals, and for both years' female figures.

The positive sign for Ranga Reddy for the year 1991 was probably caused by two reasons: (a) Self-employed in non-farm household occupational groups Ranga Reddy recorded with

Table 3.12 : Estimated Coefficients of Multiple Regression of the Logged Percentage of Non-farm to Total Employment in Rural areas and Selected Variables for 1981-91 (Pooled data):

Variables *lnY = %* RNFE	*Total* 1	*Male* 2	*Female* 3	*Total* 4	*Male* 5	*Female* 6
			Variables			
Constant	4.734	4.561	6.564	3.941	4.142	6.742
	(10.22)***	(10.36)***	(6.56)***	(14.06)***	(12.69)***	(10.39)***
ln Commercial Crops	-0.004	-0.008	-0.086			
	(-0.09)	(-0.20)	(-1.17)			
ln Farm Size	-0.069	-0.052	-0.036	-0.136		
	(-0.82)	(-0.73)	(-0.25)	(-2.19)**		
ln Irrigation	0.126	0.091	0.024	0.125	0.130	
	(2.14)**	(1.96)*	(0.21)	(2.63)***	(4.25)***	
ln Bank	-0.147	-0.090	-0.439			-0.442
	(-1.71)	(-1.32)	(-2.74)***			(-3.81)***
ln Poverty	-0.083	-0.058	-0.131			-0.199
	(-1.72)	(-1.44)	(-1.54)			(-2.87)***
ln Literacy	-0.274	-0.328	-0.030	-0.179	-0.277	
	(-1.85)	(-2.02)**	(-0.18)	(-2.88)***	(-2.84)***	
ln Urbanisation	0.058	0.069	-0.024			
	(0.88)	(1.26)	(-0.20)			
ln Road Length	0.083	0.007	0.138			
	(0.84)	(0.088)	(0.77)			

Contd...

Table 3.12 : (Contd....)

Variables *lnY = % RNFE*	*Total* 1	*Male* 2	*Female* 3	*Total* 4	*Male* 5	*Female* 6
ln Big Villages	-0.040	0.007	-0.174			-0.214
	(-0.53)	(0.10)	(-1.41)			(-2.60)***
Year dummy	0.071	0.142	0.086		0.133	
	(1.14)	(2.49)**	(0.83)		(2.79)***	
District Dummies						
Ranga Reddy 1981	-0.442	-0.494		-0.489	-0.523	
	(-3.48)***	(-4.62)***		(-3.98)***	(-5.21)***	
Nizamabad 1991	-0.312		-1.111	-0.294		-1.208
	(-2.37)***		(-4.54)***	(-2.44)**		(-5.80)***
Nizamabad 1981			-0.808			-0.849
			(-3.34)***			(-4.14)***
$\bar{R}^2$	0.52	0.44	0.56	0.49	0.44	0.58
F =	4.894***	4.049***	5.56***	9.364***	9.607***	12.63***
Heteroscedasticity $\chi^2(1)$	0.563	0.615	0.666	0.705	0.168	0.685
Normality χ^2 (2)	1.669	1.868	2.763	3.069	0.893	2.377
Functional Form χ^2 (1)	1.969	0.339	1.029	0.525	0.888E-3	0.394

Notes : The figures in brackets are t-values; - Number of observations: 44;
*** significant at 1 per cent; ** significant at 5 per cent; * significant at 10 per cent.

high poverty levels by occupational classes in rural areas in 1977-78 but not in 1987-88 (district with poverty levels above 55 per cent is the district with high incidence of poverty); (b) A change has taken place in the rank order of Ranga Reddy in poverty levels. Ranga Reddy improved its position following the percolation of industrial growth, and is moreover surrounded by the capital city Hyderabad.

3.4.2 The Determinants of Inter-District Variations in the Shares of RNFE (by industry (7 categories only)

The estimated coefficients of the multiple regression analysis of the district shares of RNFE (pooled) Log equation for seven distinct non-farm sectors are reported in Table 3.13. Four districts viz. Nizamabad, Ranga Reddy, Khammam and Kurnool were outliers and as a result we created four district dummy variables for them. These district dummies are significant at a conventional 5 per cent level.

A series of possible explanations for these to be outliers can be advanced. First, the dummy of Ranga Reddy is negatively significant. The district was adjacent to the 100 per cent urbanised state capital of Hyderabad. The rural people of Ranga Reddy district commuted in 1981 to take up the advantage of employment offered by the non-HHI and construction activities. Over the decade, development might have taken place in that district with the consequence that people shifted RNFE activities in that district. Another explanation for the dummy being significant in 1981 and not 1991 might lie with, progressive spillover effects induced by the Nagarjuna Sagar Project. Khammam is a newly irrigated district with increases in incomes which increases the demand for construction RNFE. For Nizamabad, a negative sign indicates that the possibility of involvement in RNFE HHI sector might be declining so that employment is available in the urban areas by commuting from the villages. Kurnool is in the Rayalaseema region. Tirupathi is a big Indian pilgrim centre. Activities in the pilgrim centre would give a boost to the non-HHI positively in the Kurnool rural district.

To explain the share of RNFE as well as the growth in the RNFS between 1981-91, **we** first used a multiple regression model and estimated coefficients using the standard OLS method. At this first stage some of the independent variables included in the regression equation were not significant. The number of independent variables was then reduced using step-wise backward regression as before.

In disaggregating total RNFS into seven categories we followed the categories specified in the 1981 and 1991 Census: mining, household industry (HHI), other than household industry (NON-HHI), construction, trade, transport and services. Of these, some are wholly or predominantly modern (i.e. non-HHI. trade, Transport and services) whilst others are wholly or predominantly traditional (i.e. HHI, construction) groups of activities. The present results have a higher adjusted $\bar{R}^2$ as well as a consistent pattern of signs and level of significance for many variables.

The variables eliminated in the backward stepwise regression procedure as not significant in influencing the dependent variable were urbanisation, road length and commercial crops. One reason for this may be that some of the included variables (e.g., irrigation, poverty and literacy) may have captured the influence of these factors. A second reason is that total non-farm employment may only capture the net impact of certain sectors. This aspect will be clarified in the disaggregated picture.

The estimated coefficients for logged (pooled) districts shares of RNFE in total employment are presented in Table 3.13. for seven sectors. The coefficients of irrigation at the 1 per cent level and urbanisation at the 5 per cent level are found significant in the RNFE mining sector. For this sector we found functional problems and heteroscedasticity problems. We tried to solve it by using different models such as semi-log, and quadratic functions and by identifying the outliers.

For the HHI sector, banks, irrigation, literacy, poverty and district dummy Nizamabad are significant. HHI is considered as mostly a traditional activity. As expected this variable is negative and significant at 5 per cent level. Literacy has a positive effect for the modern sectors such as those mostly covered: trade, transport and services. The hypothesis we considered was proved. Banks for HHI on the other hand show a negative relationship.

Urbanisation has a positive effect on mining, non-household industry and transport as expected. The outliers of district dummies Ranga Reddy, Khammam 21, and Nizamabad are significant. Ranga Reddy district is situated in a suburban area of 100 per cent urbanised district i.e. Hyderabad. This dummy for Ranga Reddy has a negative effect on RNFE. It is understandable that the rural people of Ranga Reddy district can very easily commute to the urbanised district of Hyderabad and take the available transport facilities, so the relationships are negatively affected. The four districts of Kurnool, Ananthapur, Chittor (Tirupathi) and Cuddapah are collectively known as Rayalaseema. In the case of Chittor (Tirupathi), as it is the biggest pilgrim centre in India, it contributes to a host of informal trades and commercial activities such as milk, flower, fruit and vegetable vending; transport; petty trade; pan shops; and hotels, which account for the highest concentration of non-farm activities in the rural Kurnool and urban Ananthapur.

In the district of Kurnool, self-employed categories in non-farm household occupations were experiencing high poverty levels across different occupational classes, especially within rural areas, in 1977-78. By 1987-88, poverty levels in this category declined. Also 'Other labour' and all occupational groups combined (self-employed in non-farm, agricultural labour, other labour, self-employed in agriculture, others, all occupational groups) recorded high poverty in 1977-78 but which was reduced by 1987-88. This could explain the positive sign in 1991 for non-HHI activities. In 1981, the Khammam district, the dummy variable was negatively significant but was not so in 1991. The reason could be Khammam is a newly irrigated district. More irrigation provides more incomes and thus leads to construction. Moreover Khammam district was recorded with high poverty levels (above 55 per cent) by occupation classes in rural areas in 1987-88 in the group of agricultural labour and other labour but not in 1977-78.

It can be concluded this subsection by looking at the significant variables which we have identified. We separate those variables depending on whether they support or oppose our central hypothesis which is 'distress diversification' to traditional RNFE, or growth linkages to modern RNFE. We also emphasised that it is not always possible to identify for each variable whether there will be support either for or against the hypothesis we tested. The per cent of bank branches, negatively significant for HHI was important for regression for regressions of RNFE logged (pooled) sub-sectors. Farm size was positively significant for construction (which supports the hypothesis) and negatively significant for trade and services (which also supports the hypothesis). Irrigation is negatively significant for mining and positively significant for HHI, non-HHI and construction. Literacy is negatively significant for HHI (supporting the hypothesis), non-HHI, and positively significant for the trade and transport sectors (which also supports the hypothesis). However, literacy is also positively significant for service sectors (which opposes the stated hypothesis). Poverty is negatively significant in affecting HHI, trade and transport RNFE. Urbanisation effects are positively significant for mining, non-HHI and transport sectors. The percentage of bigger villages is positively significant for non-HHI, and negatively significant for trade and transport sectors. The year dummy is positively significant for non-HHI and negatively significant for trade and transport sectors.

The conclusion is that irrigation is significant positively for HHI supporting the strict growth linkages hypothesis (AGL) to modern RNFE. The percentage of villages with banks is negatively significant for HHI which supports the wider development linkages (ODL) hypothesis. Farm size is positively significant for construction and may suggest that distress linkages decline as average farm size rises. it is negatively significant for other services sector against suggesting agricultural distress linkages to this traditional RNFE sub-sector. Poverty is negatively significant for trade and thus

Table 3.13 : Districts Shares of RNFE in total Employment : Estimated Coefficients Logged (Pooled) for Seven Sectors

ln (Y) (X)	*Mining*	*HHI*	*NON-HHI*	*const-ruction*	*Trade*	*Transport*	*Services*	*Mini*	*HHI*	*NON-HHI*	*Constrict*	*Trade*	*Trans-port*	*Services*
Constant	-2.113	8.261	1.839	-0.743	1.303	-2.056	0.989	-1.815	7.177	0.568	0.142	1.501	-1.517	1.121
	(-0.55)	(6.02)***	(1.62)	(-0.62)	(1.99)*	(-2.37)**	(2.02)**	(-1.11)	(6.51)***	(0.72)	(0.23)	(2.70)***	(-1.89)*	(4.85)***
ln banks	-0.567	-0.609	-0.232	0.128	0.097	0.202	-0.131		-0.529					
	(-0.79)	(-2.38)**	(-1.16)	(0.58)	(0.79)	(1.24)	(-1.43)		(-2.34)**					
ln comm. crops	-0.523	0.174	0.023	0.225	-0.004	0.087	-0.315							
	(-1.35)	(1.32)	(0.21)	(1.83)	(-0.06)	(0.99)	(-0.63)							
ln farm size	0.008	-0.144	-0.083	0.231	-0.103	-0.014	-0.104				0.424	-0.144		-0.241
	(0.01)	(-0.59)	(-0.41)	(1.02)	(-0.83)	(-0.09)	(-1.12)				(2.69)***	(-1.89)		(-4.77)***
ln Irrigation	-0.913	0.196	0.179	0.304	0.073	0.186	-0.010	-1.044	0.231	0.277	0.194			
	(-1.84)	(1.12)	(1.30)	(2.03)**	(0.86)	(1.66)	(-0.16)	(-3.60)***	(1.96)*	(2.87)***	(1.77)*			
ln literacy	0.282	-1.149	-0.876	-0.586	0.358	0.668	0.560		-1.100	-0.844		0.372	1.039	0.302
	(0.23)	(-2.61)**	(-2.63)***	(-1.60)	(1.74)	(2.45)**	(3.65)***		(-4.59)***	(-3.16)***		(2.62)***	(4.93)***	(5.30)***
ln poverty	0.471	-0.325	-0.148	-0.005	-0.128	-0.209	-0.035		-0.240			-0.143	-0.208	
	(1.11)	(-2.28)**	(-1.25)	(-0.04)	(-1.77)	(-2.19)**	(-0.65)		(-1.86)*			(-2.28)**	(-2.39)**	
ln road length	-1.435	0.193	0.134	-0.064	-0.097	0.036	-0.055							
	(-1.64)	(0.65)	(0.541)	(-0.24)	(-0.64)	(0.18)	(0-49)							
ln urbanisa-tion	1.208	-0.165	0.337	0.345	-0.048	0.293	0.012	1.167		0.336			0.213	
	(2.13)*	(-0.85)	(2.13)**	(2.00)*	(-0.50)	(2.29)**	(0.17)	(2.55)**		(2.31)**			(1.78)*	
ln villages	-0.436	-0.431	0.307	0.226	-0.256	-0.345	-0.204			0.284		-0.222	-0.425	
	(-0.69)	(-0.20)	(1.74)	(1.16)	(-2.35)**	(-2.40)**	(-2.51)**			(2.14)**		(-2.74)***	(-3.86)***	

Contd....

Table 3.13 : (Contd....)

ln (Y) *(X)*	*Mining*	*HHI*	*NON-HHI*	*const-ruction*	*Trade*	*Transport*	*Services*	*Mini*	*HHI*	*NON-HHI*	*Constrict*	*Trade*	*Trans-port*	*Services*
Year dumm	2.123	-0.045	0.354	0.101	-0.155	-0.351	-0.063	1.333		0.361		-0.163	-0.355	
	(3.98)***	(-0.24)	(2.34)**	(0.62)	(-1.69)	(-2.90)***	(-0.92)	(4.22)***		(2.76)***		(-2.26)**	(-3.44)***	
Nizamabad		-1.488							-1.463					
1991		(-3.80)***							(-4.04)***					
Ranga Reddy			-0.683	-0.715						-0.723	-0.587			-0.461
1981			(-2.21)**	(-2.12)**						(-2.51)**	(-1.89)*			(-3.78)***
Khammam				-0.977							-0.748			
1981				(-2.87)***							(2.47)**			
Kurnool 1991			0.668							0.660				
			(2.15)**							(2.28)**				
$\bar{R}^2$	0.45	0.60	0.25	0.24	0.38	0.66	0.54	0.44	0.62	0.29	0.27	0.43	0.65	0.62
F	4.51***	6.87***	2.20**	2.16**	3.63***	9.251***	6.134***	12.33***	14.750***	3.483***	4.926***	7.53***	17.22***	24.69***
Hete $\chi^2(1)$	0.976	0.710	0.033	1.262	1.742	0.563	0.010	2.432	1.655	0.148	0.087	0.607	0.249	3.066
Normality $\chi^2(2)$	0.211	1.948	0.116	0.818	0.672	0.759	1.76	0.209	1.402	0.749	1.622	2.167	0.228	1.008
Function. $\chi^2(1)$	2.576	0.008	1.924	1.474	1.398	0.351	2.448	1.718	0.985	1.822	1.067	1.993	0.148	1.710

supports the 'wider linkages hypothesis' (ODL). Literacy is positively significant for trade and transport sectors but negative for HHI supporting the 'wider overall distress diversification hypothesis. Literacy, positively significant for services, which lead to distress diversification (ODD).

Urbanisation is positively significant for mining, non-HHI and transport and this positive connection support the wider hypothesis (ODL), that development raises the modern RNFE share. The size of villages is positively significant for non-HHI, which supports only the wider hypothesis (ODL) not AGL. The results showed irrigation has a significant bearing on the composition of RNFE.

3.4.3 The Determinants of Inter-District Variations in the Growth (1981-91) of RNFE

Table 3.14 reports the estimates of the RNFE growth model. Three separate regressions were run: one each for total, males and females in RNFE. Columns 1, 2, and 3 give the estimates of the full model and columns 4, 5 and 6 report the results of our most parsimonious model. Looking at these columns only, it is found that for the whole sample (male+female) the growth of RNFE is significantly associated with commercial crops, literacy, road length and urbanisation. However, both the commercial crops and urbanisation variables bear unexpected signs. The results suggest that a 1 per cent increase of commercial crops in total crops decreases the growth of RNFE by 0.119 and that a 1 per cent increase of urban population in the total population decreases the growth of RNFE by 0.4 per cent. The literacy rate came out very strongly to influence the RNFE positively. A 1 per cent increase in literacy will apparently increase the growth of non-farm employment by 0.5 per cent.

The estimated model was significant and explained 47 per cent of the variation in the dependent variable. The diagnostics for the final results did not show any problem at the conventional level. The initial model specification proved to be problematic. In particular the test for normality failed, making it impossible to infer anything about the significance of the variables. However, this problem could be tracked down to one important outlier. When we added a dummy variable for this district, the problem was removed. As can be seen in Table 3.14, the district dummy Warangal is positively significant justifying the use of a dummy variable in the model. Warangal has a big railway junction which connects Hyderabad to Vijayawada and leads to the new Delhi route. The floating traffic creates more RNFE in small rural towns. With this reason Warangal shows a positive sign and relatively high RNFE growth.

Separate regressions for males and females were also estimated. For males the growth of RNFE is significantly influenced by road length and urbanisation (column 5). However, once again the urbanisation variable bears an unexpected sign. The result suggests that a 1 per cent increase in urbanisation decreases the growth of RNFE by 0.343 per cent. This implies that more RNFE is available in rural towns. Road length appears to influence RNFE positively as a 1 per cent increase in road length will increase the growth of RNFE by 0.21 per cent. The estimated model was relatively more significant than total explaining 55 per cent variation of the dependent variable. The district dummy was negatively significant. The reason is in Srikakulam (outlier) district may be that the predominance of *Khadi* (cloth manufacturing) and village industries, cashew industry and coconut fibre is available outside the villages.

A separate regression for females is also estimated. Column 6 shows that for females the growth of RNFE is influenced by growth of female literacy, growth of per cent of rural banks and growth of irrigation. The important point is that growth of irrigation bears an unexpected sign. The result suggests that a 1 per cent increase in the growth of irrigation decreases the growth of female RNFE by 0.3 per cent. On the other hand, a one percent increase in the growth of female literacy increases the growth of female RNFE by 0.3 per cent. 1 per cent increase in the proportion of commercial crops in total crops is associated with a decrease in the growth of female RNFE by 1 per cent. This is also possible because commercial centres are located near rural towns. Females might not be in a position to take the advantage of rural town employment. The results also suggest that 1 per cent increase in the growth of banks increases the growth of female growth of RNFE by 6 per cent. Location of banks will solve some of the financial constraints and induces the growth of female RNFE.

The district dummy Karimnagar is negatively significant. This could be due to the sharp contrast between the district's north-west zone (comprising mandals Jagtial, Vemulavada) and north-east zone (comprising mandals viz., Dharmpur Mahadevpur and Mahamamtram). The former zone has recently experienced agricultural transition. Its labour market is well developed; the daily wage rate is around Rs. 40 for males and Rs. 22 for females, which are both higher than their corresponding minimum wage rates fixed by the government. Underemployment is virtually absent and the bargaining strength of labour is strong. The labourers in JRY works are paid the ruling market wage rate rather than the recommended minimum wage rate. There is no visible poverty in the developed pocket and poverty alleviation programmes seem to be efficient. For instance, the living conditions of traditional communities such as 'golla' (shepherd community) and 'yerukala' (pig rearing community) improved due to both overall development of the region and the support given under IRDP. Incidentally, the absence of rural industrialisation in this developed zone is clearly visible. In contrast to the developed belt of Karimnagar, the economic activities in the tribal belt (Kharmapur, Mahadevpur, Mahamantram) are underdeveloped and are mostly subsistence oriented. A labourer gets employment for about four months during the busy season at a wage rate of Rs.15 for males and Rs. 10 for females. One can see survival mechanisms being adopted by the labourers in the offseason.

The incidence of poverty is the highest recorded for all classes in Srikakulam in coastal Andhra in 1978-88. This could be the reason for the negatively significant district dummy.

The conclusion is that for males, RNFE growth between 1981 and 1991 is adversely and significantly affected by urbanisation. This result opposes the narrow growth linkages (ADD) hypothesis whereas the fact that infrastructure (road

Table 3.14 : District Growth Rates of RNFE in Total Employment : Estimated Regression Coefficients for 1981-91 for Total, Males and Females

Y = % RNFE	*Total (col.1)*	*Males (col.2)*	*Females (col.3)*	*Total (col.4)*	*Males (col.5)*	*Females (col.6)*
Constant	-5.204	1.763	4.371	-4.118	3.003	4.282
	(-3.91)***	(1.48)	(1.84)**	(-3.39)***	(4.19)***	(2.26)**
Banks	0.088	0.078	0.621			0.561
	(1.32)	(1.25)	(3.88)***			(4.69)***
Commercial crops	-0.118	-0.052	-0.116	-0.119		-0.174
	(-1.63)	(-0.84)	(-1.03)	(-1.91)*		(-2.44)**
Farm size	0.002	-0.038	-0.150			
	(0.02)	(-0.52)	(-1.19)			
Irrigation	-0.048	-0.084	-0.358			-0.328
	(-0.49)	(-0.95)	(-2.43)**			(-3.04)***
Literacy	0.735	0.420	0.233	0.535		0.277
	(3.44)***	(2.06)**	(1.18)	(2.96)***		(1.75)*
Poverty	0.036	-0.015	0.039			
	(0.90)	(-0.46)	(-0.71)			
Road Length	0.159	0.218	-0.062	0.270	0.207	
	(1.22)	(1.86)	(-0.29)	(2.38)**	(2.36)**	
Urbanisation	-0.280	-0.222	0.038	-0.407	-0.343	
	(-1.71)	(-1.50)	(0.15)	(-3.37)***	(-3.12)***	

Contd....

Table 3.14 : (Contd....)

Y = % RNFE	*Total (col.1)*	*Males (col.2)*	*Females (col.3)*	*Total (col.4)*	*Males (col.5)*	*Females (col.6)*
Bigger Villages	-0.479 (-2.01)**	-0.357 (-1.54)	-0.070 (-0.21)			
District Dummies						
Warangal 20	2.634 (2.73)**			1.911 (2.42)**		
Srikakulam 1		-3.249 (-3.97)***			-2.906 (-4.11)***	
Karimnagar 19			-7.709 (-3.87)***			-7.232 (-4.49)***
$\bar{R}^2$	0.48	0.59	0.57	0.47	0.55	0.65
F =	2.963***	4.041***	3.743***	4.668***	9.469***	8.775***
Heteroscedasticity. $\chi^2(1)$	3.065	1.449	2.164	2.563	0.478	1.401
Normality $\chi^2(2)$	1.072	1.052	1.417	1.144	0.046	0.916
Functional Form $\chi^2(1)$	0.101	0.00753	1.807	0.221	3.855	2.616

Notes : The figures in brackets are t-values;
Number of observations: 44.
*** significant at 1 per cent ** significant at 5 per cent * significant at 10 per cent.

length), which is positively significant which, in turn, supports the wider (ODL) hypothesis. For females the percentage of bank branches and literacy are positively significant, which also supports the wider (ODL) hypothesis. However, commercialisation and irrigation is negatively significant which opposes the narrow growth linkages (AGL). For totals the commercial crops and urbanisation are negatively significant. This suggests distress diversification (ADD). Literacy and infrastructure (road length) are positively significant, which supports the ODL hypothesis. We emphasise that log pooled data and growth regression results differ in some of the signs of the independent variables. For instance, literacy is positively significant in growth models whilst negatively significant for log pooled data. Urbanisation is negatively significant for growth models but positively significant for log linear models. There are possible explanation for these different results. These models are different and use different degrees of freedom (smaller degrees of freedom for the growth models). Nevertheless, the differences in the sign for literacy can possibly be explained as follows: in log linear models certain non-farm occupations where traditional non-farm dominates may not require much education whereas in the growth process of growth (where growth linkages are strong) higher literacy levels might be required which induces modern non-farm employment. Another caveat of our analysis might lie with omitted variable(s) that could further explain some of the variation of the dependent variable.

3.4.4 The Determinants of Inter-District Variations in the Growth (1981-91) of RNFE (by industry 7 categories)

Table 3.15 presents the RNFE growth regressions by industry (7 categories). Here also the method used for explaining the growth of RNFE by categories between 1981-91 is the standard OLS method. In these models also we found the problems of normality of residuals and identified outliers in the initial models. We included district dummies for them. The estimates with the district dummies made valid inferences possible. However, there is a functional form problem for the mining equation. The crucial problem is that the statistical test can only identify problem but cannot suggest any solution to it. The alternative is to try different kinds of functional forms and to check whether the problem remains. In our case, we tried logarithmic and semi-logarithmic transformations of the model. Different kinds of quadratic forms were also estimated. In none of the attempts could the problem of the functional form be tackled. Thus although **we** acknowledge the problem, given the information at hand probably **we** can do very little about it. Diagnostics did not show any problems at the conventional level except for the mining sector, so **we** are cautious in interpreting this particular model.

The most striking result is that urbanisation was found to be robustly significant in all 7 sectors. In all the sectors it has an unexpected sign. A 1 per cent increase in per cent of urbanisation is associated with a decrease in the growth of RNFE by 4.7 per cent for mining, although in other sectors the relationship is less strong. Once again, this implies that urbanisation (whether or not it creates non-farm employment in rural towns only), tends to reduce the growth of its share in villages.

Irrigation is significantly positively associated with mining, non-household and transport sectors and with the service sector negatively. The growth of mining and quarrying is significant at the 1 per cent level influenced by commercial crops, irrigation and urbanisation. The coefficient for mining is very big. The district dummy Khammam is significant and positive at the 10 per cent level. Khammam district is newly irrigated one. The hypothesis is that the new irrigation provides extra income for rural people and that income enhances demand for construction. For the household industry model the growth of HHI is significantly influenced by urbanisation and literacy. The result suggests that a 1 per cent increase in urban population decreases the growth of HHI by 1.2 percent. Surprisingly, literacy growth came out very strongly to influence the HHI positively. A 1 per cent increase in literacy will increase the growth of HHI by 1.8 per cent. For the non-household industry only 3 variables irrigation, poverty and urbanisation influenced non-HHI. The surprising result is poverty, which is positively significant only in non-HHI model. This suggests that a 1 per cent increase in poverty increases the growth of non-HHI by 0.2 per cent. Though the coefficient is small, there is the possibility of absorbing casual labour in the non-HHI. For the construction model banks, road length, and urbanisation are significant. We can see a positive relationship between infrastructure and construction. Urbanisation may on the other hand negatively influence construction in rural areas. Trade, commercial crops, urbanisation, bigger villages, and the Nellore district dummy are negatively significant. Whereas road length and literacy are positively significant. This result suggests that literacy and infrastructure are essential for modern trade RNFE. For commercialisation, urbanisation and bigger villages the negative effect suggests that trade employment is urban based. For the transport sector, irrigation, road length and literacy, the positive effect suggests that linkages from agricultural development and infrastructure are significant.

The impact of commercialisation, urbanisation and bigger villages has a negatively significant effect on transport, the reason being that transport is urban based. The Warangal district dummy is positive because it has a big railway junction which might have caused the growth/expansion of rural transport. For services, which is also a modern sector, model literacy is positively encouraging. This result is as we expected. Urbanisation and irrigation are negatively associated with services. In this service sector irrigation generates more farm employment.

The conclusion for this sub section for the subsectors is that the per cent of bank branches is positively significantly for the growth of construction RNFE, this supports the wider (ODL) hypothesis to modern RNFE. Commercial crops is negatively significantly for mining, trade and transport sectors. Agricultural development (irrigation) is positively significant for mining, non-HHI transport supports growth linkages (AGL) and negatively significant for services (which supports our central hypothesis). Poverty is negatively significant for non-HHI growth. Urbanisation is negatively significant for all the sectors and bigger villages for trade and transport is also

Table 3.15 : Regression Results for Growth in the Share of Rural Non-farm Employment to Total Employment (1981-91):

(Y) (X)	*Mining*	*HHI*	*NON-HHI*	*const-ruction*	*Trade*	*Transport*	*Services*	*Mining*	*HHI*	*NON-HHI*	*Constrict*	*Trade*	*Trans-port*	*Services*
Constant	-22.663	-11.440	0.674	1.331	1.629	-6.075	0.261	-8.971	-9.320	2.206	0.133	4.378	-5.640	1.025
	(-1.17)	(-3.82)***	(0.21)	(0.47)	(0.80)	(-2.86)***	(0.28)	(-0.67)	(-3.96)***	(2.29)**	(0.06)	(3.35)***	(-2.29)**	(1.17)
Banks	1.274	0.004	-0.150	0.220	0.089	-0.063	0.040				0.285			
	(1.36)	(0.02)	(-0.60)	(1.54)	(1.05)	(-0.43)	(0.54)				(2.25)**			
Commercial	-2.255	-0.215	-0.356	-0.169	-0.191	-0.394	-0.030	-2.410				-0.207	-0.348	
crops	(-2.20)*	(-0.84)	(-1.31)	(-1.11)	(-2.10)**	(-2.52)**	(-0.36)	(-4.11)***				(-2.73)***	(-2.83)***	
Farm size	-0.730	0.027	0.154	0.004	-0.031	0.094	-0.120							
	(-0.66)	(0.10)	(0.50)	(0.02)	(-0.30)	(0.54)	(-1.32)							
Irrigation	4.270	-0.378	1.55	0.466	0.112	0.634	-0.460	4.769		1.537			0.582	-0.427
	(3.17)***	(-1.14)	(4.41)***	(2.11)*	(0.90)	(2.97)***	(-4.40)***	(4.37)***		(5.66)***			(3.11)***	(-4.32)***
Poverty	-0.359	-0.120	0.284	0.067	0.038	0.069	-0.028			0.212				
	(-0.74)	(-0.94)	(2.12)**	(0.88)	(0.74)	(0.81)	(-0.70)			(1.87)*				
Road length	-0.762	0.211	0.071	0.265	0.170	0.462	0.180				0.492	0.285	0.450	
	(-0.44)	(0.46)	(0.15)	(0.96)	(1.04)	(1.64)	(1.25)				(2.07)**	(2.05)*	(2.03)**	
Urban	-3.605	-0.821	-1.447	-1.097	-0.409	-1.061	-0.324	-4.694	-1.068	1.312	-0.547	-0.382	-0.926	-0.378
	(-1.60)	(-1.44)	(-2.39)**	(-3.24)***	(-1.99)	(-3.02)***	(-1.80)*	(-2.91)***	(-2.94)***	(-2.94)***	(-2.26)**	(-2.50)**	(-3.25)***	(-2.65)***
Villages	0.518	-0.003	-0.641	0.364	-0.716	-1.203	-0.229					-0.474	-1.149	
	(0.17)	(-0.003)	(-0.78)	(0.79)	(-2.37)**	(-2.34)**	(-0.93)					(-1.80)*	(-2.54)**	
Literacy	0.829	2.33	1.003	-0.303	0.511	1.436	0.840		1.820			0.419	1.283	0.791
	(0.30)	(3.25)***	(1.33)	(-0.72)	(1.90)	(3.13)***	(3.73)***		(3.77)***			(1.88)*	(3.29)***	(4.20)***

Contd....

Table 3.15 : (Contd....)

(Y) (X)	*Mining*	*HHI*	*NON-HHI*	*const-ruction*	*Trade*	*Transport*	*Services*	*Mining*	*HHI*	*NON-HHI*	*Constrict*	*Trade*	*Trans-port*	*Services*
District Dummies														
Nellore					-2.219 (-2.27)**							-2.575 (-2.79)***		
Nizamabad	20.689 (1.88)*							16.931 (1.79)*						
Warangal					2.172 (1.77)*	6.372 (3.07)***							5.663 (3.29)***	
Khammam	16.861 (1.57)			7.528 (4.52)***				18.180 (1.91)*			6.730 (4.21)***			
Ananthapur				-5.971 (-3.21)***							-5.433 (-3.41)***			
$\overline{R}^2$	0.40	0.39	0.53	0.69	0.47	0.52	0.71	0.51	0.48	0.60	0.67	0.49	0.60	0.70
F=	2.28**	2.48**	3.63***	5.189***	2.718**	3.303***	6.589***	5.447***	10.84***	11.302***	11.462***	4.370***	5.41***	17.26***
Heterosk.	0.018	0.362	1.149	0.534	0.016	1.609	0.241	3.060	0.216	0.301	1.901	0.071	2.814*	2.398
Normality	0.722	0.426	1.448	0.161	0.927	0.702	0.247	0.960	1.417	0.755	0.786	0.067	0.414	0.437
Functional	4.341**	0.033	0.495	1.033	0.819	0.310	1.449	3.915*	0.202	0.190	2.068	0.805	0.186	1.830

Notes : The figures in brackets are t-values; - Number of observations: 44;
*** significant at 1 per cent; ** significant at 5 per cent and * significant at 10 per cent.
For construction, corrected Normality Khammam 21 has coefficient. = 7.172 and t = (3.74)***.
For males White's Heteroscedasticity adjusted S.E's (not reported here) only changed the significance of the dummy variables.

negatively significant.Infrastructure development (road length) is positively significant for construction, trade and transport. supporting 'wider' overall development linkages for these modern sectors and the central hypothesis Literacy is positively significant for trade, and transport and services are negatively significant for HHI (which supports the wider (ODL) hypothesis).

3.3.5 Elasticities of RNFE for Total, Males, Females and for 7 Sectors

Table 3.16 part-2. To find out the size of the separated impact of each variable on the RNFS we have calculated partial elasticities of different significant explanatory variables with respect to the growth of RNFE for total, males and females and for 7 sectors. Elasticities have been calculated only for the significant variables up to the 10 per cent level. This has been done by comparing the mean scores obtained for each variable. They are at the point of means.

Irrigation is elastic for mining, non-HHI, transport and inelastic for females and services sectors.

A 1 per cent increase in irrigation increases the growth of RNFE by 0.51 per cent in trade, by 1.21 per cent in non-HHI, and by 0.27 per cent in transport. On the other hand, irrigation decreases the growth of RNFE by 3.05 per cent for females and by 0.23 per cent for other services. Women who are in a poor household are less likely to be in the RNFS. A 1 per cent increase in urbanisation will result in a decrease of the RNFE trade sector by 0.21 percent, in other words trade elasticities of RNFE is 0.21 (i.e. relatively inelastic). Table 3.16 Part I : presents estimated significant coefficients of multiple regression of the districts shares of RNFE is total employment logged data results for 1981-1991.

Summary and Conclusions

18 per cent of the rural labour force in AP in 1990-91 was engaged in RNFE as their prime occupation. As such, RNFE plays a crucial role in providing additional employment and in generating additional income to rural people, particularly

Table 3.16 Part 1 : Estimated Significant Coefficients of Multiple Regression of the Districts Shares of RNFE in Total Employment: Logged data Results for 1981-1991 (Pooled) Total, Male, Female and for Seven Sectors

Variables Y = % RNFS	*Pooled Total*	*Pooled Males*	*Pooled Females*	*Mining & Quarrying*	*HHI*	*NON - HHI*	*Constru- ction*	*trade*	*Trans- port*	*Services*
Constant	+(***)	+ (***)	+ (***)		+ (***)			+ (***)		+ (***)
comcrp										
villages			- (***)			+ (**)		- (***)	-(***)	
Irrigation	+ (***)	+ (***)		- (***)	+ (*)	+ (***)	+ (*)			
farm size	- (**)						+ (***)	- (***)	- (**)	- (***)
Poverty			- (***)		-(*)			- (**)	-(**)	
Literacy	- (***)	-(***)			- (***)	- (***)		+ (***)	+ (***)	+ (***)
Urbanisation				+ (**)		+ (**)			+ (*)	
Road length										
Bank			- (***)		-(**)					
Year dummy		+ (***)		+ (***)		+ (***)		- (**)	- (***)	
RangaR	- (***)	-(***)				- (**)	-(*)			- (***)
NIzamabad	- (**)		-(***)		-(***)					
Khammam							+(**)			
Kurnool						+ (**)				

Notes : The signs of the significant variables only are reported above.
*** Significant at 1 per cent; ** Significant at 5 per cent and * Significant at 10 per cent.

Table 3.16 Part 2: Regression Results for Growth in the Share of Non-farm Employment to Total Employment (1981-1991) [Elasticities Shown in Brackets)

Variables (1980-81) Growth rates)	*Total*	*Males*	*Females*	*Mining*	*HHI*	*NON - HHI*	*Construction*	*trade*	*Transport*	*Services*
Constant	- (***)	+ (***)	+ (**)	+ (***)	-(***)	+ (**)		+ (***)	- (**)	
Banks			+ (***)				+ (**)			
			[0.38]				[0.63]			
Commercial crops	- (*)		- (**)	- (***)				- (***)	- (***)	
			[3.35]	[0.54]				[3.88]	[0.34]	
Irrigation			- (***)	+ (***)		+ (***)			+ (***)	- (***)
			[3.05]	[0.51]		[1.21]			[0.27]	[0.23]
Literacy	+ (***)		+(*)		+ (***)			+(*)	+ (***)	+ (***)
	[12.71]				[3.65]				[1.54]	[1.09]
Poverty						+(*)				
Road length	+ (**)	+ (**)					+ (**)	+ (*)	+ (**)	
	[3.20]	[2.25]					[1.80	[1.78]	[0.27]	
Urbanisation	- (***)	-(***)		- (***)	- (***)	- (***)	- (**)	- (**)	- (***)	- (**)
	[3.00]	[2.32]		[0.40]	[0.66]	[0.82]	[0.51]	[0.21]	[0.34]	[0.16]
Size of Villages								-(*)	- (**)	
									[0.34]	

Contd....

Table 3.16 Part 2: (Contd....)

Variables (1980-81) Growth rates)	*Total*	*Males*	*Females*	*Mining*	*HHI*	*NON - HHI*	*Construction*	*trade*	*Transport*	*Services*
Srikakulam		- (***)								
Nizamabad				+(*)						
Warangal	+ (**)								+ (***)	
Khammam							+ (***)			
Ananthapur							- (***)			
Karimnagar			- (***)							
Nellore								- (***)		

Notes : Elasticities have been calculated from the regression coefficients: Elasticity = Mean value of the Variable / Mean RNFE multiplied by the regression coefficient of the variable. The signs of the significant variables only are reported above.

*** Significant at 1 per cent, ** -Significant at 5 per cent, * Significant at 10 per cent.

to the poor and to those with little land. RNFE encompasses a wide variety of activities, although services, trade and manufacturing predominate.

The main conclusions of this chapter is that the share of RNFE is lower in the 1980s in AP than in India. Moreover, the share of RNFE has grown more slowly in the 1980s in AP than elsewhere in India, despite slower improvement in output (and in labour absorption) in agriculture.

The analysis of the share of RNFE in total employment (farm + non-farm) reveals that the share of RNFE in AP increased marginally between 1981 and 1991. While employment in the manufacturing sector has increased sharply, employment in household industry witnessed a decline. However, considerable differences are seen across districts, both in RNFE structure and trend: 12 out of 22 districts experienced a decline in the shares of RNFE in total employment between the two periods. In the period and for these districts, the proportion of people below the poverty line has also decreased: the falling rural non-farm share may be due to the facts that (1) urbanisation has possibly absorbed some of those engaged in RNFS (more than in the other 10 districts) activities and (2) the per capita value of agricultural output and employment has also increased faster 1981-1991, the share of the RNFS in the total rural workforce has increased faster for male than for female employment. The analysis of the changes in RNFE omits possible effects of urban non-farm employment on the rural workforce.

The regression results reported in this chapter are summarised in Table 4.15 Part 1 & 2. Linkages between the RNFS and the levels and growth of agricultural productivity in the districts of AP are either weak, or else there are positive linkages in some districts but negative (distress) in others, so overall no strong link is found.

Conclusions for Log Total RNFE Shares, Males and Females

There are here a series of distinct issues. (1) The variables which explain inter-district differences in RNFE are not the same for males and females. (2) Females have a lower mean

RNFE share than men. One interesting result (for the pooled sample for 1980 and 1990) is that the variables significantly associated with male RNFE were different from those that were significant for female RNFE. The conclusion (for the log pooled sample for 1980-90) for totals (males+females) is that irrigation is positively significant, and farm size and literacy negatively significant, in explaining a district RNFE share. For males also irrigation is positively significant and literacy is negatively significant. However, for females only infrastructure (per cent of villages with bank branches), big villages and poverty are negatively significant. The results for irrigation suggest that higher agricultural productivity (related to irrigation) is linked to a high RNFE share growth for male workers. The analysis of determinants of RNFE confirm the hypothesis that growth linkages from irrigated agriculture lead to modern RNFE. The results for farm size support the hypothesis (AGL) that traditional RNFE share rises with distress diversification for those with little or no land.

Literacy supports the wider/overall 'development linkage' (ODL) hypothesis that traditional RNFE share rises with lower levels of literacy. The result, for males only, supports the AGL hypothesis in the case of irrigation and ODL in the case of literacy.

The results for big villages and per cent of bank branches in the case of female labour oppose the hypothesised growth linkages (AGL) relationship. There is no obvious explanation for this result. Some other variables which we could not consider might be of importance and, could explain further variations in the dependent variable.

It seems that females tend to be absorbed more in agricultural work whereas males tend to seek opportunities in RNFE perhaps because, in seeking the available limited opportunities in RNFS, males take advantage of their greater mobility. Also individual behaviour is affected by social norms and those norms differ between sexes. Ellis (1988:167) points out that the division of labour between women and men is socially, not biologically, determined, and that it is also susceptible to change. What we observe in AP today is the outcome of past and current social conventions which emphasise the productive role of women within the household and family unit (i.e. make them less mobile). I assume that mobility matters more in seeking work in RNFE than in agriculture. The reason is non-farm employment is limited.

Conclusions for Disaggregating Sub-sectors of RNFE

The conclusion for the log pooled sample for the share of the 7 sub-sectors is that irrigation is significant positively for HHI, supporting the strict growth linkages (AGL) hypothesis to modern RNFE.

Non-HHI and construction RNFE categories are significantly negative on mining. The mining link is strong can be explained by technical reasons. Mining requires lots of water, and much harder in very watery soils. Per cent of villages with banks is negatively significant for HHI, which supports the wider 'development' linkages (ODL) hypothesis. For traditional household industry the fact is that irrigation is significantly positive. This is surprising, but per cent of villages with banks is negatively significant for HHI and supports ODL. If HHI is 'modern' the reverse is true. Binswanger and Khandker (1995) find that the per cent of villages with banks at all India level highly positively significant for total RNFS per cent - credit may be a key constraint on modern and traditional RNFS alike (but not on agriculture as argued by Binswanger and Khandker), cutting across the "growth linkages versus distress diversification" debate. Farm size is positively significant for construction (and may suggest that distress linkages decline as average farm size rises) and negatively significant for other services, again suggesting agricultural distress linkages (ADL) to this traditional RNFE sub sector.

Poverty is negatively associated with per cent of employment in trade, which tends to rise as poverty falls; if trade is a 'modern' subsector of RNFE this supports the 'wider linkages hypothesis' (ODL). For such sectors so does the fact that RNFE literacy is positively significant for growth in such sectors as trade and transport. Conversely, it is negative for HHI, supporting the 'wider' ODD distress diversification hypothesis. The fact that the literacy is positively significant for services, however, opposes my hypothesis that rural services, which are predominantly tradition-oriented, are linked to distress diversification (ODD).

Urbanisation is positively significant for mining, non-HHI and transport; since for non-HHI urban options may pull away rural non-farm workers, this positive net link provides a specially strong indication in support of the wider hypothesis (ODL), that development raises the modern RNFE share. As urbanisation increases employment is generated for the remaining resident rural non-farm people; nearby villages take advantage of modern local-not just urban-employment opportunities.

The size of villages is positively significant for non-HHI, which supports only the wider hypothesis (ODL), not AGL. The argument is that demand for the products of RNFS is higher in larger villages. The real argument is that different bits of activities, in a big village, provide enough demand to 'take in each other's working' across sub-sectors of RNFE. This is plausible a sort of 'economies of scope' but has nothing obvious to do with strict 'growth linkages' from agriculture to RNFE.

However, village size is negatively significant for trade and transport shares in employment-so, if big villages are those with prosperous agricultural development, these sectors are mainly 'modern', not 'traditional'.

The strict agricultural growth-linkages (AGL) and ODL hypothesis is supported for total RNFE share and male RNFE but not for ADD. For females RNFE share opposes the AGL hypothesis and supports the ODD hypothesis.

Conclusion from the Growth of RNFE Shares Regressions

The results for the total labour force is that urbanisation and commercialisation are negatively significant. This implies that the districts with high growth of urban share, and of agricultural commercialisation, tend to show slower growth of total RNFE. This suggests that distress diversification (ADD) supports. Literacy and infrastructure, being positively significant, support the ODL hypothesis. For males, infrastructure is also positively significant, as are growth infrastructure (banks) and literacy for females, also supporting the wider (ODL) hypothesis, but commercialisation and irrigation are negatively associated which opposes the growth linkages hypothesis. It seems that as irrigation expands women wage workers find additional employment chiefly in farming itself.

The agricultural distress diversification (ADD) and overall growth linkages (ODL) hypotheses are supported for total RNFE growth. For males growth, the ODL hypothesis is supported but not the AGL hypothesis. For females, there is some support for the wider (ODL) hypothesis but not for the AGL hypothesis.

Conclusions for all the Seven Sub-sectors Growth Regression Results

Urbanisation is strongly negatively significant. In explaining district level RNFE shares of mining, non-HHI transport urbanisation is positive whereas for growth, the association with urbanisation is negative in all the sub-sectors. The negative growth relationship implies that NFE is mostly urban based. There is no obvious explanation for this negative relationship but lack of urbanisation may be linked, which implies that less non-farm employment opportunities for rural residents (because they can not commute to town centres) may be associated with greater distress diversification in rural RNFE. There is a positive link for levels but negative link for growth across districts.

The growth in per cent of villages with banks has a positive association with RNFE growth for construction only, supporting the wider (ODL) hypothesis to modern RNFE. Agricultural commercialisation growth is negatively significant for growth in mining, trade and transport. In the case of mining one would not expect a direct link to agriculture. The negative relationship suggests that mining employment has grown fastest in areas of low agricultural potential supporting ADD. The negative relationship between agricultural commercialisation and employment growth in trade and transport is very surprising. More agricultural surplus surely has to mean more trade and transport, not less. On the other hand agricultural development (irrigation growth) is positively significant for non-HHI and transport employment growth supporting growth linkages (AGL), but is negatively significant for services. This also supports our central hypothesis, that agricultural development leads to growth linkages in modern RNFE and distress diversification in traditional RNFE.

Poverty growth is positively significant for non-HHI growth. However, this pattern runs against the hypothesis stated. Infrastructure development (road length) is positively significant for construction, trade and transport supporting 'wider' ODL for these modern sectors and hence our central hypothesis. Growth of literacy is positively significant for HHI, which is surprising, and has no obvious explanation. For transport and services employment growth however, literacy is positively significant, supporting the wider (ODL) hypothesis for these modern sectors. However, districts with faster growing "village size" tend to have slower growing employment shares in trade and transport, opposing ODL and the central hypothesis.

From the RNFE growth we have obtained partial elasticities (the size of proportionate effects at the mean). From the results, it may be inferred that RNFE is a positive effect from relatively high levels of rural bank branches, from irrigation. From literacy and from infrastructure. Negative effects are obtained from commercialisation is wholly negatively signed. The percentage of big villages and poverty is negatively signed, literacy positively, infrastructure (roads) positively, whereas locations in areas with more urbanisation are negatively related to RNFE growth.

The elasticities indicate that growth in some of the RNFS variables does not have a strong effect on RNFE (totals and sub-sectors) growth. Perhaps in most cases the effects of the variables on employers' demand for RNFS labour, absolutely or relatively to farm labour, are of opposite sign to the effect on the employees' willingness to supply such labour, absolutely or as compared to farm work. However, literacy should raise both supply of and demand for, modern RNFE labour.

The overall results for total RNFE share support the hypothesis that there is a positive linkage effect from expanded irrigation (i.e. districts with 1 per cent more irrigation increase RNFE share by 0.13 per cent shaie at point of mean, or districts with (A) per cent faster growth in irrigation area secured (B) per cent faster growth in RNFE share or both to RNFE). This is especially true for male RNFE compared to females in both modern and traditional sectors. Similarly, poverty reduction has quite a high impact in promoting RNFE.

One of the other findings is that growth of literacy is positively associated with modern RNFE growth in districts, and negatively associated with traditional RNFE growth in districts. The problem, though, is that education affects both labour supply and labour demand in different stages of socio-economic and technological development. Making inferences about its effect and relation with development level can only be tentative; in other words, its influence needs to be considered cautiously. We expect education to raise modern RNFE share, lower traditional RNFE share, in early and late stages of development.

The district level data analysis in most respects supports the hypothesis that growth linkages (AGL) are the main explanation for high shares in, and the growth of, 'modern' RNFE, and distress diversification (ADD) for 'traditional' RNFE. Also in most respects this supports the wider hypothesis (ODL) that linkages are the main explanation for high shares in and growth of , modern RNFE, and overall distress diversification (ODD) for traditional RNFE.

NOTES

1. Rural areas are defined as rural in the decennial Census of India as meeting three criteria: that the population is below 5,000; that these areas have a population density of less than 400 persons

per square kilometer; and that less than 75 per cent of the male working population should be engaged in non-agricultural pursuits. The definition for rural non-farm employment in the 1991 Census is those workers who have been "engaged in some economic activity during the year preceding enumeration and who are neither cultivators or agricultural labourers but are 'other workers' (non-farm workers)".

2. Marginal workers: are those who had worked for less than six months (183 days) in the year (Census of India, 1991 p.5).

3. For instance Parthasarathy (1998), Vibhooti Shukla (1991), and Unni (1991) have identified and suggested certain factors associated with high RNFS, output and employment and have examined the inter-relationship using either state-wise or district-wise data.

4. Deccan Chronicle Survey on Wednesday 19th April 2000 revealed that the villages in Mahabubnagar districts employ youth who are migrating to urban areas for work. Drought relief is also provided by the AP state government. There is hardly any agricultural work going on the villages, except in a few pockets where groundnut is being harvested. Vast stretches of dried-up fields lie fallow everywhere. As a result of lack of adequate and continuous power supply whatever crop was required in certain areas is almost lost. The voltage is too low to draw water from deep borewells and cannot water the crop. It is difficult to strike water in the borewell even at 200 feet. Severe drought causes the younger people to move away from Mahabubnagar.

5. The poverty norm has worked at the Centre for Economic and Social Change (CESS) S. Sudhakar Reddy who has computed the head count measure which we have adopted. These are poverty ratios. Figures for 1980-81 and 1990-91 at district level used the available data. The alternative proxy for poverty in a district is the ratio of Scheduled caste and Scheduled Tribe population to total population. This variable is available for the year 1980-81 and 1990-91. However, the former is considered much better and is therefore used. The poverty line is Rs. 53.63 in the year 1980-81 and Rs. 107 in 1990-91.

6. An alternative definition of workers includes subsidiary workers along with main workers. Such a definition was used by C. Samba Murty and C. Durga, 1989. I have chosen to use main workers only excluding subsidiary workers which is also the definition used by H.P. Binswanger and Khendkar (1995).

7. This, coupled with an increase in yield rate of 7 per cent in 1991-92, resulted in an all-time record of 150.57 lakh tonnes of cane (from 126.68 lakh tonnes of cane in 1990-91, an increase of 18.9 per cent).
8. Over the years the area under oilseed cultivation (particularly groundnut), has expanded following a shift in the cropping pattern away from low-value food crops to cash crops. The area increased from 19.11 lakh hectares in 1987- 88 to 23.94 lakh hectares in 1990-91 and to 24.81 lakh hectares in 1991-92.
9. Our model corresponds to model (a) given in Table 10.1. of Johnston (1984 p. 797).
10. J. Johnston Econometric Methods 3rd edition, (1984)
11. All other results are with the author and can be shown upon request.
12. These results were also obtained from Microfit 4.0. F-statistics suggest the significance of the model.

4

THE DETERMINANTS OF RURAL NON-FARM EMPLOYMENT IN TWO VILLAGES

The preceding chapter examined the factors influencing RNFE at aggregate level (district) for AP. In this chapter an attempt is made to examine the determinants of RNFE at household level in two villages. Part 1 presents a profile of the study area. Part 2 examines the determinants of RNFE at the household level.

PART ONE

Introduction

This part provides an account of the general features of the districts of Krishna and Visakhapatnam[1] from which the two villages for study are chosen (Section 4.1), and of the selected villages (section 4.2). Demographic characteristics, occupational structure, land-utilisation, cropping-pattern, irrigation sources, and land holding patterns are discussed. These profiles provide the background to understanding the role of rural non-farm activities in the area under study.

4. 1 The Districts

4.1.1 Location

The district of Krishna is located on the east coast of AP (Map 4.1). There is an important railway junction at the city of

Vijayawada, which is a large commercial centre with many trading activities. It is also a principal trading centre for rice exports. Following recent re-organisation of administrative lines by the State Government, Krishna is divided into forty eight mandals.[2]

Agriculture (cultivators, agricultural labour and agricultural allied activities) is the most important occupation of the people of the district; being the main employment of 83.7 per cent of the rural workforce in 1991, and paddy is the main food and main crop produced. The delta area in Krishna occupies an important place in agriculture, as the Krishna delta system and the Nagarjunasagar Project are the main sources of irrigation. The river Krishna flows through the district, and a part of upland mandals as well as the delta mandals now use river water for irrigation. Muniyeru is the chief tributary of the river Krishna and is an additional irrigation source, and the Budameru, a hill stream which flows through several mandals. Average rainfall in the district is 1080mm, almost all from the south-west monsoon (June-September).

The district of Visakhapatnam is one of the north-eastern coastal districts of AP (Map 4.2), divided into forty three mandals. Agriculture (cultivators, agricultural labour and agricultural allied activities) is the main occupation for a large proportion of rural people in the district being the main employment of 83.2 per cent of the rural workforce in 1991. The government of AP (1993) states that 'though the city of Visakhapatnam is developing industrially, the rural areas are backward'.[3] The Agro Economic Research Centre (AERC) reports confirm this. Also there is considerable imbalance between rural and urban parts of the district in respect of economic and social development.

Rice is the main staple, both produced and consumed, and other important crops are *ragi, bajra, jowar,* sugar-cane, groundnut, sesame and chillies. Since there is no major irrigation system, only about 30 per cent of the cropped area is irrigated under the *ayacut*[4] of the medium irrigation system and minor irrigation tanks and the rest of the cultivated area is rain-fed. Next to draught animals, which are the main source of

Map 4.1 : Krishna District with Mandals

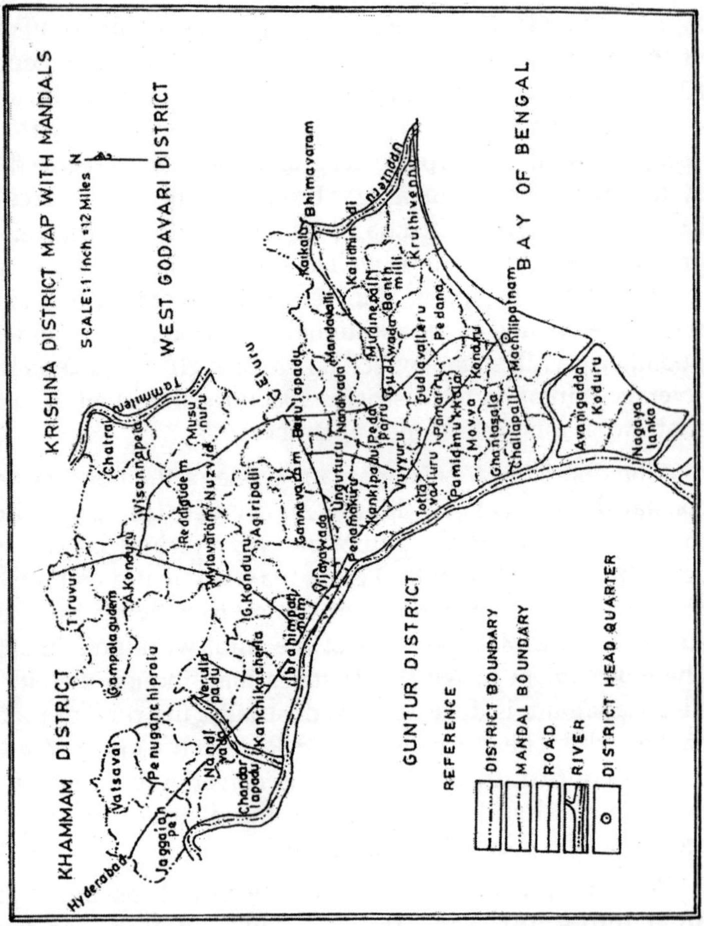

Map 4.2 : Visakhapatnam District with Mandals

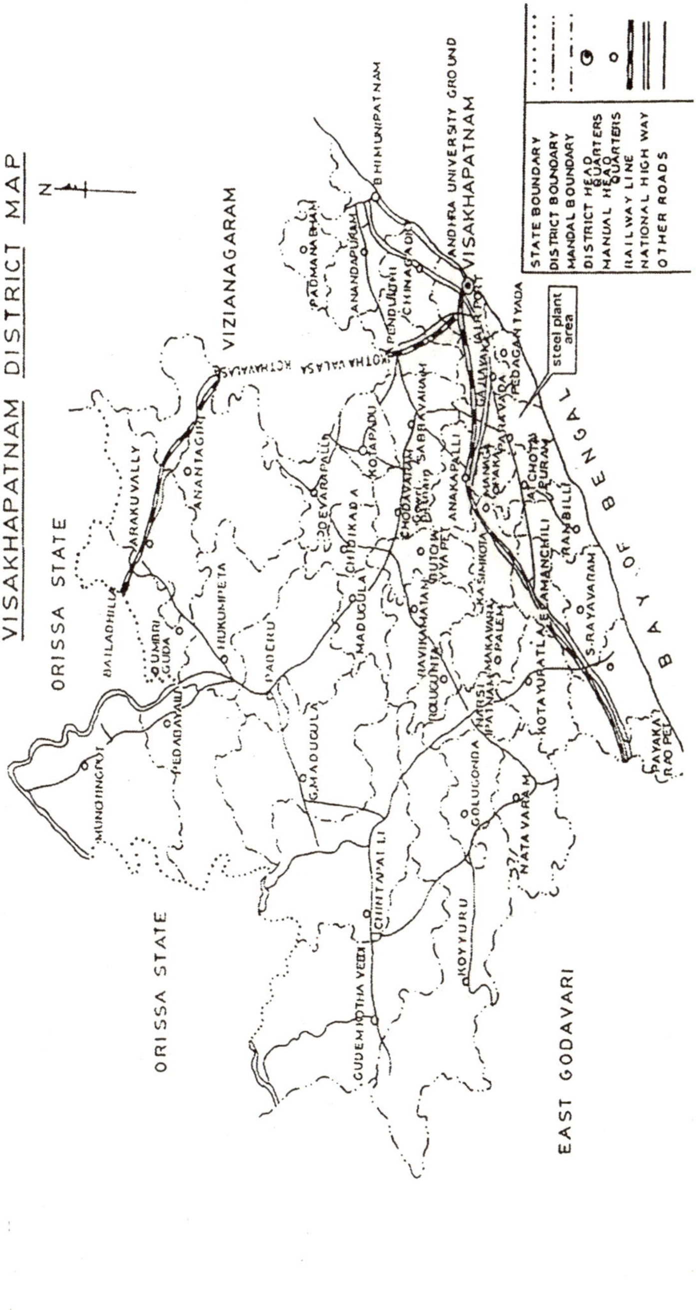

power for agriculture, milk animals, sheep and goats are important for income generation. Many rural households earn subsidiary income by selling milk to the Visakha-Dairy and in local markets. Fishing is another important economic activity.

4.1.2 Selected Socio-economic Characteristics of the two Districts

4.1.2.1 Demographic Features

Non-farm activities, as will be shown on page 5, are influenced by demographic characteristics such as population levels/numbers, gender composition, density of population, and literacy levels. Key figures for the districts are given in Table 4.1.

Aggregate growth rates between 1981and 1991 have been calculated and shown in Table 4.1. It is seen from the table that the population growth rate of Visakhapatnam is less than that of Krishna, AP, and India with respect to males, females and totals. This situation could be explained by the overall backwardness of the area which might be the cause of migration movements away from Visakhapatnam.

According to the 1991 Census, literacy in Visakhapatnam was slightly lower than that in Krishna for both genders because much of Visakhapatnam has a more 'tribal' population and inadequate transport and communication facilities. The villages in Visakhapatnam are smaller and located farther apart. There are fewer schools, often not easily reached on foot, and a large proportion of the people are uneducated. One would expect a smaller percentage of rural people to be in the modern non-farm sector. As for most of India, males are a dominant group in the total literate population in both these districts. A high level of literacy with good educational infrastructure in a district may also result in diversification into rural non-farm activities. Rural gender balance and literacy are relevant for non-farm employment.

In terms of per capita income and agricultural surplus Krishna is an advanced district in AP. This agricultural surplus has been used by the people to upgrade their occupational skills and knowledge. Education is important for the upward

Table 4.1 : Rural Demographic Characteristics 1991 Census[5]

	Krishna	Visakhapatnam	Andhra Pradesh	All-India
Total Rural Population	2373879	19,76,509	48,620,882	622,812,376
(TRP)	100%	100%	100%	100%
% Annual Growth Rate (1981-91) of TRP	**1.45**	**1.11**	**1.70**	**2.07**
Rural Males	1207092	9,91,687	24,591,875	321,279,405
% of Males in TRP	50.85	50.17	50.58	51.59
% Annual Growth rate (1981-91) of Males Rural Workers	**1.49**	**1.12**	**1.74**	**2.14**
Rural Females	1166787	9,84,822	24,029,007	301,532,971
% of females in tot rur. pop	49.15	49.83	49.42	48.41
% Annual Growth Rate (1981-91) of females rur. workers	**1.40**	**1.09**	**1.67**	**1.99**
Scheduled Tribes Population	70767	460882	3,880,254	62,751,026
% of ST in TRP.	2.98	23.32	7.98	10.08
Total No. of Households	558503	445975	10,326,962	111591326
Average HH size	4.25	4.43	4.71	5.58
Literate in TRP	890283	470583	14,438,253	226144087
% of literate in TRP	37.50	23.81	29.70	36.31
% of literate in TRP aged>10 in 1981	9.70	5.40	7.15	N/A

Contd....

Table 4.1 : (Contd....)

	Krishna	Visakhapatnam	Andhra Pradesh	All-India
% Annual Growth Rate (1981-91) of Total Literate	**2.45**	**5.00**	**4.23**	**4.15**
Literate males in TRP	531556	320844	9,663,607	151216579
Literate Male as % of TRP	44.04	32.35	39.30	47.07
% of males literate in tot. rural pop. aged > 10 in 1981	12.13	8.22	10.13	N/A
% Annual Growth rate (1981-91) of male literate	**2.32**	**4.15**	**3.77**	**3.61**
Literate females in TRP	358727	142539	4,774,646	74,927,508
Lit. fem. as % of TRP	15.11	14.47	19.87	24.85
% of female lit. in TRP aged > 10 in 1981	7.17	2.58	4.01	N/A
% Annual Growth Rate (1981-91) of female Literate	**2.66**	**6.60**	**5.23**	**5.36**
Population Density (per Km^2)	349	294	180	N/A

Notes : fem.: females - Data for literate as percentage of population aged above 10 are for 1981 only. Sources: - Census of India 1981 part1 XIII - A & B (1) volume 1 series 2 handbook Village & town districts, Visakhapatnam.. - Census of India 1981, series-1 India part II B(i), primary census abstract general population p. 31 and p.37. - Census of India 1981, Series-Andhra Pradesh, part - 1V -A Social and Cultural Tables pp.322-334.. - Census.

mobility of the civil society. The agricultural surplus and the surplus income available at the household level motivates families to send their children to school. There is also a demonstration effect in Krishna, in that many people of the district become non-resident Indians (doctors, engineers and scientists in USA and UK). This has provided an impetus to others to utilise the education facilities provided by the AP State. This has resulted in literacy levels in Krishna being the highest. (The percentage of literate persons in the total population aged above ten is highest in Krishna compared to Visakhapatnam and AP as whole).

From the middle of the 19th Century until 1960s Visakhapatnam was under the influence of feudal landlords (*Zamindaris*) who spent very little on the education of the people. The income level of the people in rural areas is low and there are few cases of upward mobility (income, occupation).

4.1.2.2 Occupational Distribution

The rural working population has been divided into ten categories according to the type of work. It is important, in a study of RNFE, to present a disaggregated picture of the labour force as there is a wide array of activities undertaken within the RNFS.

In order to identify the factors that influence RNFE the employment pattern of the agriculturally less developed district will be compared to that of Krishna which is agriculturally developed. In the 1991 Census, workers were broadly classified as cultivators, agricultural labourers and non-farm workers. 50.2 per cent of the workers in Visakhapatnam were cultivators compared to 20.5 percent in Krishna. Agricultural workers, (cultivators and agricultural labourers combined), formed the bulk of rural workforce. They constituted 80.9 and 81.5 percent respectively of the workers in the districts of Visakhapatnam and of Krishna.

In the case of Visakhapatnam, land distribution is comparatively equally distributed and most cultivators are marginal farmers. These are more likely to work their own land and do not hire such a large proportion of labour as do the

Table 4.2 : Occupation-wise Distribution of Rural Workers in the Districts Under Study

	Krishna			*Visakhapatnam*		
Occupation	*Total*	*Males*	*Females*	*Total*	*Males*	*Females*
Total	1125171 (100.00)	716110 (100.00)	409061 (100.00)	933805 (100.00)	596070 (100.00)	337735 (100.00)
Cultivators	230571 (20.49)	202757 (28.31)	27814 (6.80)	468293 (50.15)	301727 (50.62)	166566 (49.32)
Agricultural labourers	686909 (61.05)	345599 (48.26)	341310 (83.43)	287535 (30.79)	153725 (25.79)	133810 (39.62)
Livestock, Forestry, Fishing, Hunting and Plantation, Orchards & allied Activities	24724 (2.20)	21710 (3.03)	3014 (0.74)	21464 (2.30)	19262 (3.23)	2202 (0.65)
Total farm	83.74	79.6	90,97	83.24	79.64	89.59
Mining and Quarrying	4325 (0.38)	2970 (0.41)	1355 (0.33)	4212 (0.45)	3105 (0.52)	1107 (0.33)
Manufacturing Processing, Servicing (maintenance) and Repairs in Household Industry	22967 (2.04)	15196 (2.21)	7771 (1.90)	29238 (3.13)	19070 (3.20)	10168 (3.01)

Contd....

Table 4.2 : (Contd....)

Occupation	Krishna Total	Krishna Males	Krishna Females	Visakhapatnam Total	Visakhapatnam Males	Visakhapatnam Females
Manufacturing Processing, Servicing and Repairs in other than Household Industry	33575 (2.98)	30095 (4.20)	3480 (0.85)	18091 (1.94)	15125 (2.54)	2966 (0.88)
Construction	7420 (0.66)	6858 (0.96)	562 (0.14)	6518 (0.70)	5676 (0.95)	842 (0.25)
Trade and Commerce	41041 (3.65)	32679 (4.56)	8362 (2.04)	33741 (3.61)	24603 (4.13)	9138 (2.71
Transport, Storage, Communication	19564 (3.65)	19336 (2.70)	228 (0.06)	13028 (1.40)	12852 (2.16)	176 (0.05)
Other Services	54075 (1.74)	38910 (5.43)	15165 (3.71)	51685 (5.53)	40925 (6.87)	10760 (3.19)
Total non-farm	15.10	20.47	9.03	16.76	20.37	10.42

Source : Andhra Pradesh Final Population 1991, Office of the Director of Census Operations, Andhra Pradesh, Hyderabad.

bigger farmers in Krishna. Thus, the number of agricultural labourers in Visakhapatnam is found to be less than when compared to Krishna. The difference in the proportion of agricultural labourers to cultivators thus depends on the different distribution it uses land. With a higher proportion of agricultural labourers in Krishna, the amount of income derived from agriculture would be supplemented by non-farm activities. This would lead to a more pronounced diversification of the non-farm activities. It is also the case that agricultural income is available only during the cultivation period some of the year. In other months people obtain employment in the RNFS.

In Visakhapatnam the cultivator is attached to land which s/he owns. The cultivator does not frequently find the time to go out to work. In the less developed districts the social status and stigma (caste) attached to manual labour and non-farm work inhibits farmers from seeking work in the RNFS. In Visakhapatnam the cultivator therefore uses family labour on a small piece of marginal land.

The gender distribution amongst the agricultural labour force in general terms is similar in both districts. In Krishna, 50 per cent of the agricultural labour force is female and in Visakhapatnam it is 46 per cent. When it comes to cultivation, however, the figures indicate that males dominate. In Krishna only 12 per cent of cultivators are females and in Visakhapatnam 35 per cent.

Employment in agriculture is the major source of livelihood in both the agriculturally less developed and agriculturally more developed districts. It is assumed that in the agriculturally less developed area people who work on farms may not earn sufficient income. In Krishna the following activities seem to dominate: agricultural labourers, cultivators, services, trade and commerce, and other than household industries. The order is the same in Visakhapatnam, except that cultivators outnumber agricultural labourers. The potential for developing forest-based industries in the rural sector appears to be missing.

As mentioned earlier, Visakhapatnam was under the control of the *Zamindari* system (erstwhile *Zamindars*).[6] After the abolition of this system, the State introduced the notion of private property in the region and cultivators were granted ownership rights. This led to an even distribution of land; each land holding is no more than three acres in Visakhapatnam. In contrast, land in Krishna is concentrated in the hands of landlords and even after the implementation of the Land Ceiling Act and litigation initiated by landlords, little land was available for distribution. Availability of irrigation and of HYVs helped to provide employment opportunities to agricultural labourers in the Krishna. Therefore, the two districts are different in many respects.

4.1.2.3 *Land Utilisation*

Land utilisation particulars are given in Table 4.3. The area forested, barren and uncultivable land, land under miscellaneous use is less in the district of Krishna compared to that of Visakhapatnam. This resulted in more net sown area in Krishna than in Visakhapatnam.

Table 4.3 : Land-Utilisation Particulars of Study Districts (1991-92): Area in '000' Hectares.

Category	*Krishna*	*Visakhapatnam*
Total geographical area, of which:	880 (100)	1134 (100)
- Forest	66 (7.5)	478 (42.15)
- Barren and un-cultivable land	65 (7.37)	153 (13.49)
- Land put to non-farm uses[7]	120 (13.64)	86 (7,58)
- Cultivable waste	43 (4.89)	14 (1.23)
- Permanent pastures and grazing lands	18 (2.05)	4 (0.35)
- Land under miscellaneous tree crops and groves not included in the Net area sown	7 (0.8)	21 (1.85)
- Other fallow land	31 (3.52)	23 (2.03)
- Current fallow land	27 (3.07)	25 (2.2)
- Net area sown	503 (57.16.)	330 (29.1)

Source : "An Outline of Agricultural Situation in Andhra Pradesh 1993-94", Directorate of Economics and Statistics, Government of Andhra Pradesh, January 1993.

It could mean that better land in Krishna is used by more people and hence there are more inequalities in Krishna, so no greater widespread prosperity leads to fewer non-farm chances of work. In contrast, Visakhapatnam did not have better land and as more people depended on land and lesser inequalities are possible. Thereby greater widespread prosperity leads to higher non-farm opportunities.

Visakhapatnam has a relatively higher proportion of forest area. Forests provide a livelihood particularly to the poor tribal population. There is a lot of scope for forest resources in Visakhapatnam compared to Krishna. Land utilisation in the Krishna district is oriented towards agricultural development whereas in the Visakhapatnam district it is oriented towards forest products.

4.1.2.4 Irrigation

The sources of irrigation, and the area irrigated in 1993-94 under each source, are given in Table 4.4. The state of irrigation development in the districts under study can be understood by examining the gross irrigated area (GIA), the net irrigated area (NIA), and the area irrigated more than once in an year (AIMO).

The Krishna district has a good system of canal irrigation. There are no 'perennial' sources of irrigation like rivers in the Visakhapatnam district which results in the absence of any major irrigation system there. Visakhapatnam is completely dependent for medium and minor irrigation sources upon the rivers intermittent in the district Sarada, Varaha and Tandava.

A feature of irrigation is that the GIA, NIA and AIMO in Krishna are more than twice that of the Visakhapatnam district: people use land more intensively for irrigation in Krishna than in Visakhapatnam. The distribution of AIMO (irrigated area under canals) is very high in Krishna, where agriculture has a dependable source of irrigation. In Visakhapatnam AIMO is mostly dependent on unreliable sources of irrigation such as wells. This phenomenon can be explained as tanks and tube wells as sources of irrigation are indicators of the commercialisation of agriculture in the upland and agency areas (dry and forest) in the Visakhapatnam. This have been in improvements in the intensity of land use and the area irrigated more than once in a year.

Table 4.4: Area Irrigated by Different Sources in the Districts Under Study (area in '1000' hectares) (1993-1994):

Sources of Irrigation	*Krishna*			*Visakhapatnam*		
	GIA (1)	*NIA (2)*	*AIMO (3)*	*GIA (1)*	*NIA (2)*	*AIMO (3)*
Canal	338 (79.62)	272 (76.62)	66 (91.67)	49 (37.12)	48 (38.1)	1 (16.67)
Tanks	41 (9.60)	40 (11.27)	1 (1.39)	39 (29.55)	39 (30.95)	Nil
Tube wells	16 (3.75)	14 (3.94)	2 (2.78)	4 (3.03)	3 (2,38)	1 (16.67)
Other wells	19 (4.45)	16 (4.51)	3 (4.17)	20 (15.15)	18 (14.29)	2 (33.33)
Other sources	13 (3.04)	13 (3.66)	Nil	20 (15.15)	18 (14.29)	2 (33.33)
Total	427 (100.0)	355 (100.0)	72 (100.0)	132 (100.0)	126 (100.0)	6 (100.0)
Intensity of Irrigation (GIA/NIA*100)		120.28			104.76	
GIA/GCA		63 %			34 %	
NIA/NSA		71 %			38 %	

Note : The figures in brackets indicate percentages of the Gross area irrigated.

Source : Computed from data in Table 4.4 An Outline of Agricultural Situation in Andhra Pradesh 1993-94, Directorate of Economics and Statistics, Government of Andhra Pradesh Hyderabad.

Irrigation development can be understood by examining the ratios of Irrigation Indicators (1993-94) of GIA/GCA (gross cropped area) to NIA/NSA, where NSA is the Net Sown Area sown under crops and orchards, counting areas sown more than once.[8] These are estimated for both districts and reported in Table 4.5

4.1.2.5 Food and Non-Food Crops

The percentage of area under food and non-food crops in Krishna and Visakhapatnam is presented in Table 4.5. The trends in cropping pattern of food crops and non-food crops in the two districts are not similar. The area under non-food crops is larger in Visakhapatnam than in Krishna. It suggests that there is a tendency on the part of cultivators to take up the non-food crops in backward districts. Commercialisation is expected to encourage rural non-farm activities by supplying more raw materials, creating more demand for inputs and allied services, raising demand for consumption goods and generating surpluses for investment. The changes involved in agricultural development include the use of new bio-chemical inputs, irrigation, and mechanisation of various agricultural operations. Such changes are usually accompanied by increases in marketable surplus and the commercialisation of rural markets, particularly in the product market.

The predominance of non-subsistence crops in the cropping pattern (NSC/TC) has a direct positive impact on male employment in transport, storage and communications. This relationship supports the hypothesis of agriculture led growth of non-farm employment. Many studies such as that of Durga and Murthy (1992) use the percentage of area under non-food crops as an index of commercialisation. The food crops are predominantly grown in both regions. Cropping intensity in Krishna is higher than in the district of Visakhapatnam.

Table 4.5 : Area Under Food Crops and Non-food Crops in the Districts Under Study (1991-92). (Area in 1000 Hectares).

	Krishna	*Visakhapatnam*
Total area under food crops	662	336
(% of total food crops)	(88.27)	(79.43)
Total non-food crops	88	87
	(11.73)	(20.57)
Total cropped area	750	423
	(100)	(100)
Net area sown	503	330
Area sown more than once	247	93
Cropping intensity	149.11	128.18

Source : Directorate of Economics and Statistics, Government of Andhra Pradesh, Hyderabad.

4.1.3 Summary

The study of the two selected districts (Krishna and Visakhapatnam) presents a picture of contrasts. Demographic characteristics, according to the 1991 Census, show that the population of Visakhapatnam is less than that of Krishna. Literacy rates for both males and females is also lower, indicating the backwardness of rural Visakhapatnam.

The total geographical area of Visakhapatnam is greater than that of Krishna but the NSA is only 29.1 per cent compared to 57.1 per cent for Krishna.

The area irrigated by different sources (canals, tanks and wells of different types) is much higher for Krishna (427,000 hectares), compared to in Visakhapatnam (132,000 hectares). The cropping intensity of the Krishna district (partly because of the good irrigation system) is 149.1 per cent and 128.18 per cent for the Visakhapatnam district.

The area taken up by food crops is 88.3 percent of the total cropped area in Krishna and 79.4 per cent in Visakhapatnam, but the NSA, even per rural person or worker, is itself much higher in the Krishna district. The food crops in Krishna are a commercial link to greater land inequalities than in Visakhapatnam.

Considering the demographic characteristics, cropping patterns and the available irrigation facilities in the two districts, we find that the district of Krishna is relatively more developed compared with the district of Visakhapatnam. Similar differences are noted in the two villages (Veeravalli and Anandapuram respectively) that have been selected from the two districts which are discussed in section 4.2.

4. 2. Profile of The Villages

This section presents a profile of the two villages which covers demographic features, occupational distribution, land-utilisation, irrigation, land-holding, cropping pattern, and intensity of cropping and highlights the differences between the two villages.

4.2.1 *Anandapuram in the Visakhapatnam District*

The village (Map 1) is near the National Highway No. 5 that connects Madras and Calcutta. It is 22 Km away from Visakhapatnam (Map 4.3). A *kutch* (mud path) leads to the village. The nearest big railway station is in Visakhapatnam. Anandapuram is agriculturally little developed, with predominant wage employment in quarrying, and self employment in *shandy* business, *toddy* tapping, poultry, petty trade, vegetable vending and a variety of other non-farm activities.

The average annual rainfall in the village is 952 mm, about 60 per cent during the south-west monsoon, (June-September), and almost all the rest during the north-east monsoons (October-December). The main source of water for agriculture is the south-west monsoon. The main food crops grown are paddy, *bajra, ragi* (all grown mainly for subsistence), chillies, groundnut, mango, sesame, vegetables, banana, cashew and flowers.

Irrigation in the village is not sufficient to meet the agricultural requirements. Every farmer would like more, or more reliable, water control. The absence of rivers means that there is no perennial source of irrigation in the area. Irrigation mostly depends on surface water conserved in tanks, and on ground water from wells. There is a small reservoir (*gambhiram*) located in the *mandal* which irrigates about 495 hectares. Most of the tanks are themselves rainfed as is the major portion of land; both depend on erratic monsoon rainfall. Therefore, the cropping pattern in the village resembles that of a dry region and most of the farmers in the area are marginal farmers.

Shandys (periodic village markets) are the key exchange places for both goods and services. Groundnut and vegetables yield a marketable surplus and help to generate the farmers' cash income. Money gained from the sale of these crops is invested for further cropping.

The wage for agricultural labour is low and women are paid nearly half the men's wage. Due to low productivity in rainfed agriculture, a major part of the production is used for

Map 4.3 : Location map of Anandapuram in the Visakhapatnam District

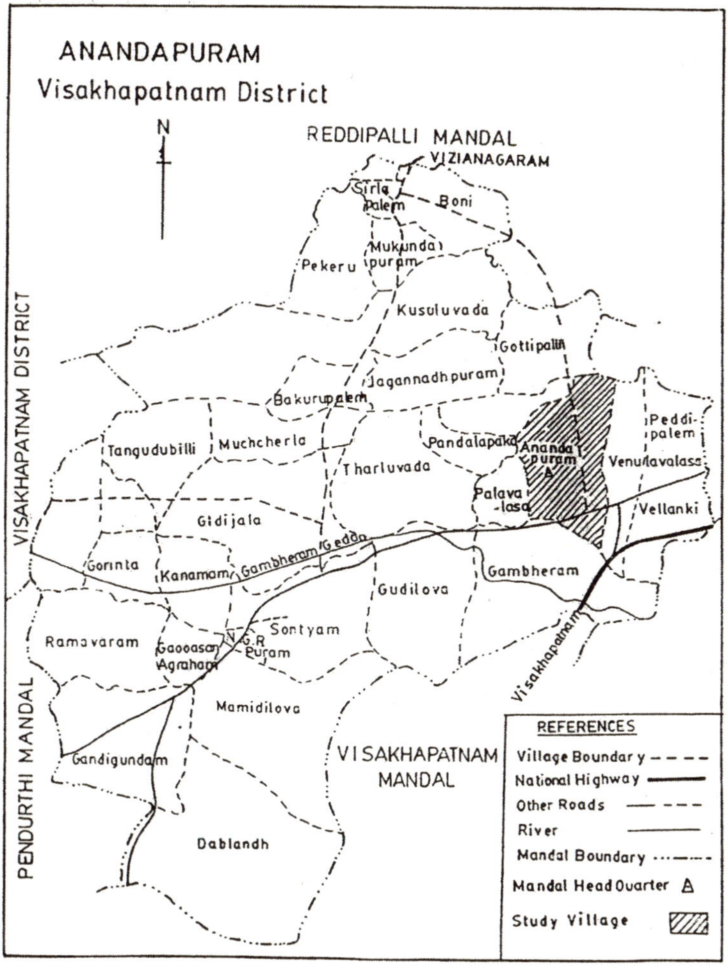

consumption. Food consumption habits have changed of late, and the people are consuming modern crop varieties.

There are a few small-scale industries: an oil mill, a rice mill, some factories and repair shops, Andhra Plywood Products, Visakha Electricals (diesel motors repairs), Coastal cartons (card board manufacturers), Aqua Marine Food Products, Gayatri Plastic Company, *coir* and jute, and a *gudaku*[9] factory. Traditional sources of employment like weaving, cobbling, carding cotton and other handicrafts are losing their importance. According to one cobbler, personal communication, (1994) in Anandapuram, many years ago there were 10 cobblers but now only he remains. People prefer to buy rubber-made foot wear from a factory rather than ones made by a cobbler. Weavers and cotton carders people have been replaced by factory made cloth.

4.2.2 The Profile of Veeravalli

The village of Veeravalli, in the Krishna district, is agriculturally developed. Veeravalli is adjacent to Hanuman Junction (rural town) which is a busy commercial centre. The land is fertile and yields are better when compared to those of other villages in the area. Veeravalli has commercial sugar cane plantations and a sugar factory. Veeravalli is an agriculturally rich area. The main commercial crop is sugar-cane. The establishment of sugar-cane processing factories in this area has provided further incentives to expand cane production. This village comes under Bapulapadu *Mandal* (see Map-4.4). The population density is 269 persons/Km^2. According to the meteorological centre (in Nuzvid) the average rainfall per year is 1007 mm. A major part of rainfall for this area is caused by the South-west monsoon.

Three types of soils are present viz., black cotton (which covers around 57 per cent of the village), sand-clay loams (22 per cent) and red loams (19 per cent). Irrigation in this village is facilitated through rivers, ponds, wells and tube wells. The canal is one of the main sources of water and it meets all the major irrigation demand of the area. Due to the perennial supply of water, multiple cropping has developed in various combinations.

Map 4.4 : Location map of Veeravalli in the Krishna District

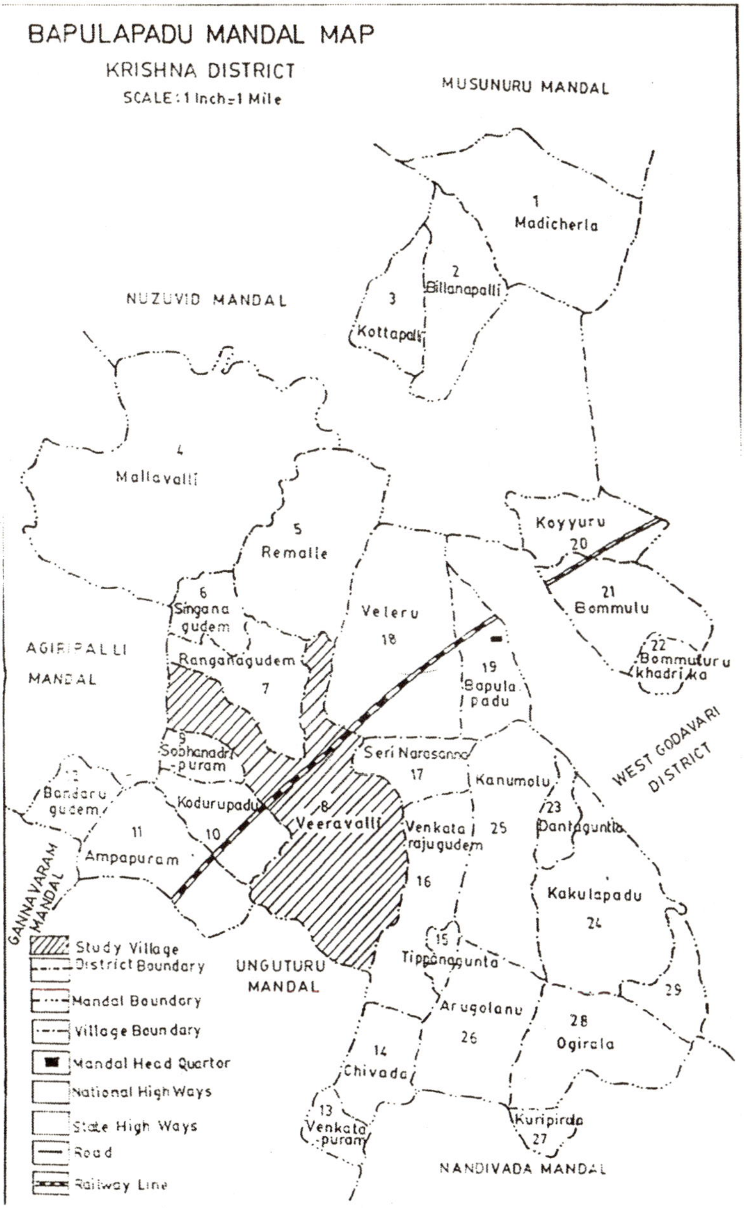

A good number of factories are located within a 5 km range including well developed traditional pot making units. Further, there are the Hanuman sugar industry, a cardboard paper mill, a milk cooler plant, the Rajasree paper mill, two rice mills, a jute factory, the Lifco Factory (which manufactures transport equipment for lorries), an acid and a spirit factory. Veeravalli has more industries than any other village of the *mandal*.

4.2.3 Socio-economic Indicators of the Surveyed Villages

This section provides the basic features such as demography and literacy that influence the socio-economic activities at village level in order to identify the factors for the development of RNFS.

4.2.3.1 Demographic Characteristics:

Table 4.6 gives the population structure by gender (including growth rates between 1981 and 1991), the average size of household, and literacy rate in the two villages.

Regarding the growth of population, what was observed at the district level is confirmed in the respective villages. The average household size is slightly (0.25 per cent) higher in Anandapuram. There is a difference in the levels of literacy between the two villages. Literacy levels in Veeravalli are higher than in Anandapuram. Male literacy in both villages is greater than female literacy. Increasing literacy may be helpful for the generation of skills which are essential for the development of modern RNFE; we explore this in the econometric analysis.

4.2.3.2 Occupational Structure

Table 4.7 shows that, between 1971 and in 1991, the proportion of main workers to the total population has also increased from 34 to 43 per cent, despite an actual decline in male workers. In the case of agricultural labourers a decline is noticed for both groups (males and females).

In Anandapuram the percentage of workers engaged in unskilled non-farm activities has increased over the reference period. There was a big shift (1971-91) of male workforce

Table 4.6: Demographic Characteristics for 1971, 1981, and 1991

	1971		*1981*		*1991*	
	Veeravalli	*Anandapuram*	*Veeravalli*	*Anandapuram*	*Veeravalli*	*Anandapuram*
Area of village in Hectares			2255.71	950.60	2255.71	950.60
Total Population	3395	5991	4278	4442	5440	5583
(in thousands)	(100.0)	(100.0)	(100.0)	(100.0)	(100.0) [2.43]	(100.0) [2.31]
Males	1707	3994	2185	2237	2735	2788
	(50.28)	(66.67)	(51.05)	(50.36)	(50.27) [2.27]	(49.79) [2.23]
Females	1688	1997	2093	2205	2705	2795
	(49.72)	(33.33)	(48.95)	(49.64)	(49.73) [2.60]	(50.20) [2.40]
Total No. of Households	N/A	N/A	949	860	1296	1060
Average size of HH	N/A	N/A	4.51	5.17	4.20	5.27
Total/Literacy	1218	669	1852	755	2467	1425
	(35.88)	(11.17)	(43.29)	(17.00)	(45.35)[2.91]	(25.52)[6.56]
Males	687	412	1072	567	1424	819
	(40.25)	(10.32)	(49.06)	(25.35)	(52.65)[2.88]	(29.38)[3.75]
Females	531	157	780	188	1030	501
	(31.46)	(7.86)	(37.27)	(4.23)	(38.08)[2.82]	(17.92)[10.30]

Notes : Literacy in percentages to the total population;
- The first figure is the absolute number for 1991;
- The second figure in bracket is a percentage of a total;
- The third figure here is the growth rate between 1981 and 1991;
- N/A: not available.

Source : Census of India (1991), Series -2, Andhra Pradesh, part XII - A&B, District Census Handbook, Visakhapatnam, Volume II, Analytical Note: Village and Town-wise, pp. 370-373.

percentages out of cultivation of farm labour towards animal husbandry, mining/quarrying, livestock, trade and commerce, transport and other services. One explanation could lie in the growth of Visakhapatnam, which is close to this village. This has led to an increasing demand for services and the increase in construction activities has led to increases in quarrying (a steel plant is located in Visakhapatnam city). The improvement of incomes in the village is likely to generate demand for additional items and further provide an incentive for people to take up petty trade and commerce.

There is no sharp difference in the occupation-wise distribution of workers in Veeravalli. The number of workers directly engaged in agriculture has not changed over the reference period. However, cultivators (as a percentage of total workers) have decreased in contrast to an increase in agricultural labourers. Non-farm activities record no change overall; among them the number of workers engaged in other-than household-industry activities has considerably increased, while there has been a parallel decrease in other services.

In order to analyse the occupational structure of the workers the working population of the study villages have been divided according to the types of work. Percentages are given in table 4.7, which reports the occupational pattern in the rural areas in 1971, 1981 and 1991.

The gender balance is an important aspect of the population structure. Table 4.7 points to relatively little change in the number of males and females in Veeravalli between the 1971 and 1991 Census. It is interesting to note, however, that the proportion of female workers has almost doubled from 16.94 per cent to 31.59 per cent.

In Anandapuram, the proportion of males exceeded that of females in 1971. But it has already been seen in Table 4.7. that there has been a tremendous change in the gender proportion of the population of Anandapuram, all in the 1980s. There is a change in both the gender composition of the population and of the workers during the reference period. There is an increase in the proportion of females.

Table 4.7 : Distribution of Workers in the Villages Under Study

	Veeravalli									*Anandapuram*								
	1971			*1981*			*1991*			*1971*			*1981*			*1991*		
	Males	*Females*	*Total*	*Males*	*Females*	*Total*	*Males*	*Females*	*Total*	*Males*	*Females*	*Total*	*Males*	*Females*	*Total*	*Males*	*Females*	*Total*
Total Pop.	1707	1688		2185	2093	4278	2735	2705		3994	1997		4442	2237	6679	2788	2795	
Total main workers	956	195	1151	1316	639	1955	1592	735	2327	1175	132	1307	1337	573	1910	1563	738	2301
	(100)	(100)	(100)	(100)	(100)	(100)	(100)	(100)	(100)	(100)	(100)	(100)	(100.0)	(100.0)	(100.)	(100)	(100)	(100)
			(33.90)*	(60.23)*	(30.5)*	(45.68)*			(42.78)*			(21.85)*	(30.1)	(25.61)*	(28.6)*			(41.21)*
1. Cultivator	311	0	311	336	1	337	263	26	289	584	40	626	673	211	884	586	281	867
	(32.53)	(-)	(27.02)	(25.53)	(0.16)	(17.24)	(16.52)	(3.54)	(12.42)	(49.70)	(30.3)	(47.74)	(50.34)	(36.82)	(46.28)	(37.49)	(38.08)	(37.68)
2. Agriculture labourers	364	164	528	549	572	1121	817	632	1449	310	75	385	128	226	354	255	294	549
	(38.08)	(84.1)	(45.87)	(41.72)	(89.51)	(57.34)	(51.32)	(85.99)	(62.27)	(26.38)	(56.82)	(29.46)	(9.57)	(39.44)	(18.53)	(16.31)	(39.84)	(23.86)
3. Livestock	17	0	17				24	0	24	1	Nil	1				67	12	79
	(1.78)	(-)	(1.48)				(1.51)	(-)	(1.03)	(0.09)		(0.07)				(4.29)	(1.63)	(3.43)
Total-farm	72.39	84.1	74.37	67.25	89.67	74.58	69.35	89.55	75.72	76.17	87.12	77.27	59.91	76.26	64.81	58.09	79.55	64.97
4. Mining	nil	0	0				0	0	0	1	nil	1				79	0	79
		(-)	(-)				(-)	(-)	(-)	(0.09)		(0.07)				(5.05)	(-)	(3.43)
(5 a) HH	86	6	92	41	27	68	62	22	84	63	nil	63	115	31	146	75	17	92
	(8.10)	(3.08)	(7.99)	(3.12)	(4.23)	(3.48)	(3.89)	(2.99)	(3.61)	(5.36)		(4.82)	(8.6)	(5.41)	(7.64)	(4.8)	(2.3)	(3.1)
(5 b) Other than HH	11	0	11	390	39	429	183	9	192	38	2	40	421	105	526	59	6	65
	(1.15)	(-)	(0.95)	(29.64)	(6.1)	(21.94)	(11.49)	(1.22)	(8.25)	(3.23)	(1.52)	(3.06)	(31.49)	(18.32)	(27.54)	(3.77)	(0.81)	(2.82)
6. Construc.	18	0	18				9	0	9	4	nil	4				14	1	15
	(1.88)	(-)	(1.56)				(0.57)	(-)	(0.39)	(0.34)		(0.31)				(0.9)	(0.14)	(0.65)
7. Trade and commerce	20	3	23				62	15	77	92	10	102				203	65	268
	(2.09)	(1.54)	(1.99)				(3.89)	(2.04)	(3.31)	(7.83)	(7.58)	(7.80)				(12.99)	(8.81)	(11.65)
8. Transport	20	nil	20				47	0	47	17	nil	17				84	3	87
	(2.09)		(1.74)				(2.95)	(-)	(2.02)	(1.45)		(1.30)				(5.37)	(0.41)	(3.78)

Contd....

Table 4.7 : (Contd....)

	Veeravalli									Anandapuram								
	1971			1981			1991			1971			1981			1991		
	Males	Females	Total	Males	Females	Total	Males	Females	Total	Males	Females	Total	Males	Females	Total	Males	Females	Total
9. Other Services	109 (11.4)	22 (11.28)	131 (11.38)				125 (7.85)	31 (4.22)	156 (6.70)	65 (5.53)	5 (3.79)	70 (5.36)				141 (9.02)	59 (7.99)	200 (8.69)
Total non-farm	27.61	15.9	25.61	32.76	10.33	25.42	30.64	10.47	24.28	23.83	12.89	22.72	40.09	23.73	35.18	41.9	20.46	34.12
Non-workers	751 (33.47)	1493 (66.53)	3395	868	1403		1135	1943	5440	822 (30.59)	1865 (6941)	5991	860 (38.12)	1396 (61.88)		255	1662	5583

Notes : Figures in the brackets indicate percentages with reference to total main workers.
- * Percentage to total population.

Sources : Census 1971, District census handbook Series 2, Andhra Pradesh Parts X- A &B, Visakhapatnam district.
- Census 1971 Series 2 Andhra Pradesh District Census handbook parts X A & B Village & Town Primary Census Abstract Krishna District.
- Census of India 1981, Series-2 Andhra Pradesh District Census handbook Parts X111- A & B (11) Visakhapatnam District, Volume 2.
- Census of India, 1981 Series-2, Andhra Pradesh, District Census handbook Parts *XIII* - A&B, Village & town Primary Census abstract, Krishna District.
- Data for 1991 Village/Town primary census abstract 1991 Krishna district, Visakhapatnam district.

The details of the gender breakdown of workers may show that the development process absorbs more male labour than female labour in the non-farm sector.

In Veeravalli only marginal changes in the case of males can be noted. In Anandapuram, there has been a sharp increase in the proportion of workers of both genders. The change in females is more than marginal.

Data from the 1981 Census does not provide a disaggregate picture of non-farm employment and there are problems of comparability with the Census of 1991. It was observed that according to the 1981 Census count, workers constituted 45.68 per cent of the total population in Veeravalli against 28.6 per cent for Anandapuram. Thus, there were wide variations in the proportion of the working population of the total population. There were wide variations in the proportion of male workers of the male population between the two villages as well.

The percentage of female workers in the female population in Veeravalli (30.5) was higher than in Anandapuram (25.61). 17.24 per cent of the workers in Veeravalli were cultivators against 46.28 per cent in Anandapuram. Agricultural labourers constituted 57.34 per cent in Veeravalli against 18.53 per cent in Anandapuram. Non-farm employment constitutes 25 per cent in Veeravalli and 36 per cent in Anandapuram indicating that non-farm opportunities are relatively higher in Anandapuram due to the proximity of this village to the urban area of the city of Visakhapatnam .

4.2.3.3 *Land Utilisation*

The utilisation of land (Table 4.8) influences the area under crops in the total area available and shows the development culture of a particular village.

Proportions have been used because of the difference in the total geographical area of the two villages. The pattern of land use in both villages signals some differences between the villages. Although for both villages forest area is nil, the area under non-agricultural use is lower in the village of Veeravalli, where arable land[10] is relatively higher. This indicates that more land could be put to agricultural use in Veeravalli. However, the extent to which arable land is used is marginally higher in Anandapuram as indicated by a higher NSA as a percentage of total geographical area in Veeravalli. This is mainly because of the early rainfall and its impact on the land utilisation pattern.

Table 4.8 : Land Utilisation, 1994 (in acres)

	Anandapuram	*Veeravalli*
Total geographical area	2347 (100.0)	5580 (100.0)
Forests	0	0
Barren & Uncultivable	43 (1.83%)	0
Land put to non-agricultural uses	519 (22.11%)	744 (13.33%)
Permanent pastures	8 (0.34%)	21 (0.38%)
Land under miscellaneous tree crops and groves not included in NSA	177 (7.54%)	15 (0.27%)
Cultivable waste	9 (0.38%)	0
Other fallow land	104 (4.43%)	265 (4.75%)
Current fallow land	15 (0.64%)	216 (3.87%)
Net sown area (NSA)	1472 (62.72%)	4319 (77.40%)

Source : *Mandal* Revenue Office.

4.2.3.4 *Irrigation*

The breakdown of irrigation sources is shown in table 4.9. Irrigation is crucial for the development of agriculture, which provides a livelihood for the majority of the people in the rural areas. Irrigation needs more labour for the operation itself and indirectly it increases labour use through other complementary inputs like fertilisers. With the availability of irrigation, more land can be cultivated extensively and also intensively. The increase in irrigation leads to increased production in agriculture and increases the demand for the supply of seeds, fertilisers, pesticides, sprays and repair services, which are produced or supplied by non-farm activities. This study shows that irrigation has a positive influence on non-farm employment.

Table 4.9 : Irrigated Area Under Different Sources 1993-94 (in acres)

	Canals	*Tanks*	*Tube wells (a)*	*Dug wells (b)*	*Total wells (a+b)*	*Others*	*Total*
Anandapuram	0	382 (77.8)	10	107	117 (23.83)	0	491 (100.0)
Veeravalli	3229 (66.59)	0	971	234	1205 (24.85)	415* (8.56)	4849 (100.0)

Notes : The figures in brackets indicate percentages of total irrigated area.
- *: Lift Irrigation.

Source : Mandal Revenue Offices, Anandapuram, Bapulapadu.

The total irrigated area in Veeravalli exceeds that of Anandapuram. In Veeravalli canals are the predominant source of irrigation, while in Anandapuram tanks are predominant. Wells are the next important source in both villages. On the whole, Veeravalli has a more dependable source of irrigation than Anandapuram as tanks, which mostly rainfed, are undependable.

4.2.3.5 Distribution of Land Holdings

The distribution of land holdings by size of 'standard' acres operated is shown in table 4.10. As the population increases, the average size of land holding decreases. Moreover, the distribution of cultivated land is uneven. It is difficult to earn adequate income from very small holdings and it is well known that labour use, often even hired labour use, per hectare is less on big farms than on small ones. Therefore, especially as the workforce grows, it is essential to supplement the incomes of the small marginal farmers, and agricultural labourers through non-farm activities. This study also considered farm size as one of the key factors in determining the rural non-farm activities.

Table 4.10 : Land Holding Pattern

	Veeravalli			Anandapuram		
Cultivator Households' Sub-groups	*No. of House-holds*	*Total Land of the Sub-Groups*	*Average*	*No. of House-holds*	*Total Land of the Sub-Groups*	*Average*
Landless HHs	84	-		273	-	
Marginal Farmers 0.5 to 2.46	530 (51.16)	677.57 (17.11)	1.26	551 (77.93)	868.36 (47.25)	1.58
Small Farmers 2.47 to 4.93	262 (25.29)	1061.49 (26.80)	4.05	90 (12.73)	353.41 (19.23)	3.93
Semi Medium 4.94 to 9.87	156 (15.06)	1007.07 (25.43)	6.46	46 (6.51)	349.3 (19.00)	7.59
Medium Farmers 9.88 tc 24.70	87 (8.40)	1213.38 (30.64)	13.95	20 (2.83)	266.91 (14.52)	13.35
Total	1036 (100)	3959.51 (100)	3.82	707 (100)	1837.98 (100)	2.60

Notes : Farm size was measured by the extent of total holding.
- Figures in brackets are percentages.
- In the two villages there are no large farmers (with a land holding in excess of 24.70 acres) over the period 193-94.
- Calculations of Gini-coefficients seem to suggest land is distributed more unequally for the marginal farmers group when compare that of other farmer's groups. The Gini for Veeravalli is 0.343, and for Anandapuram it is 0.336. Differences between the two villages are marginal once small to medium farmers are considered.

Source : *Mandal* Revenue Offices of respective villages.

The distribution of farms according to their total holdings is presented in Table 4.10. The average size of land possessed per household (ASLH) is 3.82 and 2.60 acres respectively for Veeravalli and Anandapuram. This suggests that, in terms of the smallness of their land holdings, the cultivator class is less disadvantaged than in Veeravalli. Another significant feature is that contrary to the general pattern, small, semi-medium and medium-farmers constitute the biggest group (in percentage) compared to large farmers in Anandapuram. It can be inferred that farmers in the developed village are better placed in terms of both their land holding sizes and land quality (better irrigation facilities). It can be observed from the table that the majority of the land holdings (51.16 per cent in Veeravalli and 77.93 per cent in Anandapuram) are concentrated in the lowest size groups viz., 0.5 to 2.46 acres. In the case of the largest holdings viz., 9.88 to 24.70 acres, they account for only 2.83 per cent in Anandapuram compared to 8.40 per cent of all holdings in Veeravalli. More than three quarters of farmers belong to the marginal and small farmers category in Veeravalli village while 90 per cent of the farmers in Anandapuram are small and marginal farmers. Thus, marginal farmers dominate the farm sector of Anandapuram and agriculture remains backward with predominance of family farms.

4.2.3.6 Cropping Pattern

The cropping pattern of the villages is influenced by the availability of irrigation. Details are shown in table 4.11. One of the important factors contributing to output is the land allocated to a particular crop.[1]Cropping pattern details are useful to assess agricultural development and commercialisation in the study villages.

Farmers allocate their land to different crops in accordance with local climate, soil, knowledge, and availability of other resources together with a number of additional considerations. The latter may include an attempt to increase the income, to minimise the risk of crop failures, or to maximise employment for themselves and their family members. Thus, the cropping pattern in any region is the outcome of trials and adjustments in respect of farm enterprises and practices. The same is true for the cropping pattern of the area under study. Table 4.11 shows the area statistics of crops for the two selected villages for one agricultural year (1993-94). Figures in brackets are the percentages of the total cropped area.

Veeravalli's cropping pattern is dominated by food and commercial crops. Among food crops, paddy accounts for 52.42 per cent of the gross cropped area, followed by black Gram

Table 4.11 Area Under Principal Crops - Season wise 1993-94 (Acres)

	Veeravalli			*Anandapuram*		
Crops	Kharif	Rabi	Total	Kharif	Rabi	Total
Rice	3565	270	3835	382	0	382
	(84.6)	(8.52)	(51.95)	(25.13)	(-)	(19.74)
Sugarcane	299	293	592	0	0	0
	(7.1)	(9.25)	(8.02)	(-)	(-)	(-)
Bajra	0	0	0	150	0	150
	(-)	(-)		(9.87)	(-)	(7.75)
Ragi	0	0	0	60	79	139
	(-)	(-)	(-)	(3.95)	(19.04)	(7.18)
Maize	15	0	15	0	0	0
	(0.36)	(-)	(0.2)	(-)	(-)	(-)
Chillies	31	105	136	15	45	60
	(0.74)	(3.22)	(1.84)	(0.99)	(10.84)	(3.1)
Groundnut	254	250	504	650	102	752
	(6.03)	(7.89)	(6.82)	(42.76)	(24.58)	(38.86)
Sesamum	0	0	0	48	20	68
	(-)	(-)	(-)	(3.16)	(4.82)	(3.51)
Mango	20	0	20	65	0	65
	(0.47)	(-)	(0.27)	(4.28)	(-)	(3.36)
Vegetables	0	17	17	40	96	136
	(-)	(0.54)	(0.23)	(2.63)	(23.13)	(7.03)
Banana	0	0	0	20	15	35
	(-)	(-)	(-)	(1.32)	(3.61)	(1.81)
Coconut	4	0	4	0	0	0
	(0.09)	(-)	(0.05)	(-)	(-)	(-)
Cashew	0	0	0	20	0	20
	(-)	(-)	(-)	(1.32)	(-)	(1.03)
Flowers	0	0	0	50	0	50
	(-)	(-)	(-)	(3.29)	(-)	(2.58)
Other Fodder	6	311	317	0	0	0
Crops	(0.14)	(9.82)	(4.29)	(-)	(-)	(-)
Pulses	20	1922	1942	20	58	78
	(0.47)	(60.67)	(26.31)	(1.32)	(13.98)	(4.03)
Total	4214	3168	7382	1520	415	1935
	(100.0)	(100.0)	(100.0)	(100.0)	(100.0)	(100.0)

Source : *Mandal* Revenue Offices.

(32.72 per cent). Sugar cane is another important commercial crop accounting for 5.68 per cent of the GCA and the area under sugarcane is increasing. Groundnut accounts for another 4.27 per cent. The cropping pattern of Anandapuram is dominated by food crop (paddy) with 30.84 per cent of the GCA. Bajra is the second most important crop among food grains. Since the village agriculture is mainly unreliably irrigated, these crops are typical. Groundnut is another important crop grown in the area and with 30.84 per cent (as a single crop) it accounts for GCA of the village. One can conclude by reporting that dry crops thus dominate the cropping pattern of Anandapuram whereas food crops and commercial crops dominate of Veeravalli.

4.2.3.7 *Intensity of Cropping and Irrigation*

Table 4.12 presents the intensity of cropping and irrigation (1993-94) for the villages under study.

Table 4.12 : Intensity of Cropping and Irrigation 1993-94 (in acres).

	Anandapuram	*Veeravalli*
Net sown area (NSA)	1472	4319
Area sown more than once	415	3063
Total cropped area	1887	7382
Intensity of cropping (= GCA/Net area operated (i.e. cropped during the year) *100)	128.19	170.92
Net Irrigated area	511	4019
Area Irrigated more than once	61	830
Total Irrigated Area	572	4849
Intensity of Irrigation (= GIA/NIA*100)	112.9	120.65
NIA/NSA*	34.71	93.05

Note : *Indicates the extent of NIA being irrigated.
Source : Mandal Revenue offices.

Irrigation in Anandapuram is mostly dependent on surface water conserved in tanks and groundwater. In terms of the intensity of cropping and total cropped area, Veeravalli shows a higher average than Anandapuram. Veeravalli has a location advantage being situated in an irrigation area. In Anandapuram dry crops (unirrigated) are predominant. Generally irrigated crops are grown in one season. Therefore the intensity of cropping is low. The NIA/NSA ratio is relatively high for Veeravalli village whilst for Anandapuram only one third of the NSA is irrigated. These differences can be attributed to the differences in the sources of irrigation and confirm the low level of agricultural development in the Anandapuram compared to Veeravalli. This has a direct impact on the cropping pattern and agricultural production of the village.

4.2.4 Summary

Rural Visakhapatnam is less developed than rural Krishna. This difference in development is also apparent in the two villages selected for our study. The literacy rate in Visakhapatnam is lower than that in Krishna. A larger proportion of workers are dependent on agriculture in the district of Visakhapatnam than in the district of Krishna. Visakhapatnam has also a vast area dedicated to forestry. On the other hand, the area sown is small. The soils of Visakhapatnam are mostly red-earth whereas large tracts of fertile alluviums are present in Krishna.

There is no perennial source of irrigation in Visakhapatnam where agriculture depends mostly on tanks (largely rain-fed) and wells. The Krishna district is dominated by paddy cultivation on irrigated land. In contrast, the agricultural economy of the Visakhapatnam district is dominated by dry-crops such as *bazra, ragi, jowar,* and groundnut, which are affected by the re-occurrence of droughts. The percentage of area irrigated to total cropped area differs widely between the two districts, since tanks in Anandapuram irrigate most of the area and since tank irrigation is only possible when rainfall is good. The type of irrigation influences the cropping pattern. The major crops grown in Anandapuram are paddy, millet, oil seeds, pulses and sugar cane. In view of these, it is possible to say that Visakhapatnam is relatively under-developed when compared to Krishna.

Similar features distinguish the two villages, Anandapuram and Veeravalli. Also, in Veeravalli, there was no change in 1971-

91 in the gender composition of population, while gender composition of workers indicate important changes in Anandapuram; the proportion of female workers to total female population has increased. In fact in Anandapuram, both population and the composition of workers have changed. There has been an increase in the proportion of workers to total workers. The number of workers engaged in non-farm activities has increased in occupations which are predominantly unskilled. In Veeravalli there is much change in the occupation-wise distribution of workers. The proximity of an urban area has important implications, by affecting the distribution of workers' wealth. Differences in irrigation sources and cropping patterns in the two villages conform to the differences that are observed at district-wide level for Krishna and Visakhapatnam.

PART TWO

Introduction

This part seeks to identify differences among households in two villages, that account for differences in the probability that a household has a member who both (1) works for at least 183 days a year, and (2) has his or her main occupation by time in the rural non-farm sector. Next, we look for determinants of differences in probability of a household have such a member in (a) modern, (b) traditional RNFE separately.

The second part of this chapter analyses the determinants of inter-household differences in RNFE for two villages of AP, and highlights households' basic characteristics. Two villages have been analysed in order to see whether there are differences between the villages in the factors influencing non-farm activities. Two broad groups of determinants of RNFE participation have been identified in the review of literature: growth linkages from development in agriculture, and distress diversification.

A central hypothesis that will be tested in this second part is that quite different factors determine 'traditional' and 'modern' RNFE shares in the total employment. A high traditional rural non-farm share is likely to be associated with low years of education of workers in a household, lower castes, and agricultural indicators suggesting distress diversification. A high modern rural non-farm share is likely to be associated with higher years of education of workers, upper castes and agricultural indicators suggesting rural growth linkages from agriculture.

We therefore hope to contribute to resolving the conflicting explanations of RNFE growth: is it due to 'distress-diversification' into non-farm activities, or to rural growth linkages as explanations of rural non-farm employment, or-more precisely-of the propensity of rural workforce participants in AP to be involved in the RNFS. The 'strict' growth linkages hypothesis is that of agricultural growth linkages (AGL): higher (or a faster growing] agricultural income/output/employment tends to cause more (or faster-growing) nearby rural non-farm share. Then on the agricultural distress diversification hypothesis (ADD) is the opposite hypothesis that lower (or slower growing) agricultural production (or 'performance' in agriculture) causes a higher (or faster-growing) RNFE share.

The research will also test a wider 'development linkage/ diversification hypothesis' is that of this overall development linkage hypothesis (ODL) is that higher (or faster-growing) development indicators such as literacy, bank branches, urbanisation, tend to cause more (or faster-growing) nearby RNFE. Then on the converse, overall distress diversification hypothesis (ODD) is that lower (or slower-growing) development indicators cause higher (or faster-growing) RNFE share.

Our results suggest that when rural labour is not fully absorbed in the farm sector, the traditional non-farm sector acts as a sponge for overload labour spillover into unproductive and low paid (lower than the prevailing wage rates/below subsistence relative to the farm wage) non-farm activities. But the modern RNFS has strong backward and forward production growth linkages and consumption linkages with the farm sector.[12]

The factors that influence RNFE at macro (district) and micro (household) levels may be broadly similar but some are particularly significant at the household level. District level studies, by using aggregate data, may miss some of the factors. We discuss the comparison of distinct and household determinants of RNFE shares at the end of this part of the chapter.

In order to analyse the socio-economic characteristics of sample households, we have used simple descriptive statistics: sample mean, coefficient of variations, and t-test of differences in means. To estimate the impact of various factors on non-farm employment at the household level, logit regression analysis for the entire sample of households as well as for sub-samples are used. Marginal effects and impact effects at the mean have been calculated with the help of regression coefficients.

Following some remarks about the HHs, village and district selection, this second part of Chapter Four is divided into three sections. Section 4.1 (Part 2) reviews the socio-economic characteristics of the sample households. Section 4.2 (Part 2) shows that some of these characteristics differ substantially between the two villages whilst others do not; separates HHs into self-employed and wage employed, involvement in modern and traditional RNF employment, and introduces the discussion of determinants of RNFE at the household level, describing the variables which are thought to matter and their expected link with RNFE. Section 4.3 (Part 2) presents the results of logit analyses of data gathered for the two villages and compares the household-level with the district-level determinants of RNFE and explains the differences obtained. Section 4.4 (Part 2) summarises the messages of chapter 4.

The Method of Data Collection

We define a household as 'engaged in non-farm activities' if any member has a primary (at least 183 days a year) occupation, one (a primary occupation always in just one) Census of India 1991 occupational categories 1V-1X.[13] For simplicity we shall refer to such households as 'non-farm households' even though they may also derive part of their income from farming. The probability that a household will fit this definition can then be determined by certain location/ village specific factors and household-specific variables. The logit model is used to estimate the probability, (conditional on the HH specific independent variables being at the mean) of a household in a village being engaged in rural non-farm activity. All beta elasticity, etc. estimates are at the point of means in any set of linear best fits either OLS-regression based or logit. Thus the combined effect of more than one variable on the conditional probability of a household being a non-farm household can be calculated. In addition, the marginal effect of a unit change in a single variable, holding all other variables constant (normally at their means) on the probability of a household being non-farm household can be computed.

In the villages surveyed, the household and not the individual was taken as the unit of enumeration and also in fact we had find out whether each working individual had a primary occupation in the RNFS. This was done because occupations such as cultivation, trade, household industry, services, arts and crafts (non-farm activities) are often carried out jointly within the household. Whilst such a view of the household is perhaps not accurate, it is difficult to calculate an individual's efforts in any activity on the basis of standard interviews. We do rely on each HH member's 'primary occupation' being RNFS. For further details see Appendix to Chapter 4 (a).

Principal occupations were determined on the basis of the time spent by the HH members. Respondents (who were mainly the HH head but occasionally all of the inhabitants within the HH) were asked to rank their occupation as being primary on the basis of what they spent the majority of the year employed as. So, a household may have several secondary occupations, but only one primary one. The occupation which was occupied by working members of the HH most often and which required at least 183 or more days employment per person in a year (Census of India, 1991) was treated as primary. If all members of the HHs were found to work less than 184 days each, then they were treated as being involved with a subsidiary occupation. The occupation which was selected was the one which the working HH member(s) spent most time employed in.

We seek to account for a household's involvement in the RNFS by reference to its demographic features (e.g. male/female and child/adult ratios, household size) and to other household specific characteristics (occupation, education level, poor non-poor, caste, seasonality, family size, land holding size).

District and Village Selection Criteria

Most data was not publicly available (e.g. household head age; level of schooling of the workers). Hence primary data was collected from July 1993 to January 1994. Data for 819 households was gathered from two villages (Anandapuram 354, Veeravalli 465), the former from a more agriculturally developed district (see part one of this chapter). Once a district had been selected, all the *Mandals* of the district were listed and one *Mandal* was randomly drawn. In selecting the village a similar procedure was adopted. The selection of the village was based on village characteristics.[14] In other words, we looked for villages near the district average for certain characteristics. Considerations of a logistics nature also mattered as we needed to be able to access the nearby villages.

Selection of Households

The households[15] were a random sample of 35 per cent taken from our list of all the HHs in the village, prepared with the help of the *gram panchayat* (village council) administrative officer.

The analysis is at an aggregated and disaggregated level. In order to capture the impact of RNFE share increase and decrease, entry and exit, it is necessary to separate them. Thus, we develop four models using a different set of variables.

The households were divided into those spending the longest proportion of working time (1) RNFE and farm employed, (2) modern or traditional RNFE.

4.1 The Salient Characteristics Of The Selected Households

4.1.1 Demographic Characteristics

Table 4.13 provides some basic statistics about the selected HHs in the 2 villages. A caveat here is that little can be inferred about the participation rates because we do not have information about the proportion of (1) persons who are of normal working age, or (2) persons in work (of whatever age) as proportion of the number of persons who are of normal working age. The determinants of (1) and (2) are different so that our comments here are limited. Percentages in the table below relate to proportions of total population (workers and non-workers, all age groups), therefore, not to proportions of persons of working age or of persons in work.

The average size of the household is significantly lower (at 1 per cent) in the developed village. The proportion of male workers in main occupation is higher (and conversely lower for females) although the total number of main workers in the developed village forms a smaller proportion of all workers than in the underdeveloped village.

Table: 4.13 : Primary Statistical Information of the Sample Households

	Veeravalli	*Anandapuram*
Total number of households surveyed (around 35% of households in each village)	465	354
Total population	1974	1713
Total number of main workers (least 183 days a year) in the sample	795	825
% of main workers in total population (Main workers/total)	40.27%	48.16%
Male main (least 183 days a year) workers % of total main workers	588 74.8%	556 67.5%
Female main (least 183 days a year) workers % of total main workers	207 25.2%	269 32.5%
Average size of sample households [no of households]	4.25 [465]	4.84 [354]

Note : Main workers are those that work 183 days in one or more occupations for males and females. Source: Field-work.

4.2.2 *Age- and Gender Distribution of Total Workers in Sample Households:*

The age- and gender- distribution of the sample households are given in Table 4.14. The table shows that there is a higher proportion of child workers (aged 5 to 15) in Anandapuram than in Veeravalli. In both villages, most workers are aged 16 to 45; the ratio of females to males is also highest in that age group. While approximately 83 per cent of female workers (in both villages) fall in the 16 to 45 years category, the corresponding percentage for male workers is 69 per cent to 73 per cent (depending on the village). Interestingly, a higher proportion of child workers (8.6 per cent) is found in Anandapuram than in the more-developed Veeravalli (3.1 per cent). This may also be directly linked to a higher incidence of poverty in Anandapuram. Lower levels of income in the less developed village might have forced parents to send their children to work.

Table 4.14 : Age Group and Gender Distribution of Household Total Workers:

	Age groups (In years)				
	5-15	*16-45*	*46-60*	*60 above*	*Total*
Veeravalli					
No. of Males (%)	8 (1.36)	408 (69.39)	139 (23.64)	33 (5.61)	588 (100)
No. of Females (%)	2 (0.97)	173 (83.57)	28 (13.53)	4 (1.93)	207 (100)
Total (%)	10 (1.26)	581 (73.08)	167 (21.00)	37 (4.65)	795 (100)
Anandapuram					
No. of Males (%)	23 (4.14)	405 (72.84)	102 (18.35)	26 (4.68)	556 (100)
No. of Females (%)	12 (4.46)	222 (82.53)	34 (12.64)	1 (0.37)	269 (100)
Total (%)	35 (4.24)	627 (76.00)	136 (16.48)	27 (3.27)	825 (100)

Note : The figures in brackets are the percentages of total sample population of the specified age plus gender.

Source : Field Survey.

4.1.3 *Literacy*

There are wide variations in educational attainment among the sampled workers in both villages. In Veeravalli, 55 per cent of the 795 sample workers are literate, as against only 31 per cent of the 825 workers in Anandapuram. The probability of being illiterate is two and half times greater for women workers when compared to men workers in the developed Veeravalli but only one and half times as high in the less-developed Anandapuram.

The Table 4.15 indicates those workers who have completed some years of schooling. Levels of schooling might affect the RNFS by increasing the length of time spent in education. More education might lead to longer duration of RNFS, or it might provide better RNFS opportunities in terms of quality and quantity (i.e., employees work more days and therefore obtain

Table 4.15 : Distribution of main Workers by Educational Attainment:

	Primary (1-5 yrs)	*Upper Primary (6-7 yrs)*	*High School (8-10 yrs)*	*Post Secondary (higher) 10+2+3+2 years*	*Literate total*	*Illiterate total*	*Total*
Veeravalli							
Males	113 (19.22)	60 (10.20)	137 (23.3)	82 (13.95)	392 (66.67)	196 (33.33)	588 (100)
Females	31 (14.98)	5 (2.42)	7 (3.38)	2 (0.97)	45 (21.74)	162 (78.26)	207 (100)
Total	144 (18.11)	65 (8.18)	144 (18.11)	84 (10.57)	437 (54.97)	358 (45.03)	795 (100)
Anandapuram							
Males	101 (18.17)	44 (7.91)	53 (9.53)	25 (4.5)	223 (40.11)	333 (59.89)	556 (100)
Females	18 (6.69)	1 (0.37)	12 (4.46)	3 (1.12)	34 (12.64)	235 (87.36)	269 (100)
Total	119 (14.42)	45 (5.45)	65 (7.88)	28 (3.39)	257 (31.15)	568 (68.85)	825 (100)

Note : Figures in brackets are percentages.
Source : Field-work

a higher income). A third possibility is that it is faster growth, which leads both to greater literacy and a diversification of employment into RNFS. Graph 4.1 indicates also that percentage of distribution of workers by education is higher in developed village compared to less developed village.

Those with post-secondary education form around 11 per cent of the workers in the developed village compared to around 3.5 per cent in the less developed village. Also, as noted in several studies, post-primary education (upper primary, high school and post-secondary) is an important contribution factor for productivity in agriculture. (Chalam (1986)) As can be seen from table 4.15 the less developed village has fewer members of workers with post-primary education compared to the developed village.

The educational background of workers in different occupations is given in Table 4.16. This table specifies the average number of years of schooling by occupation and economic status (poor/ non-poor).

The occupational background of the workers can be broadly divided into cultivators, agricultural labours and non-farm workers. Each group of workers is also categorised further into poor and non-poor, partly so as to examine to what extent educational background of workers is related to this distinction.[16] Non-poor workers have more years of schooling in all the categories of occupations. It is further observed that the average years of schooling is higher in the developed village.

4.1.4 Distribution of Sample Households-Worker By Caste Groups

Backward castes outnumber other caste groups in both Veeravalli and Anandapuram sample groups (Table 4.17). In the less developed village, backward castes are significantly more represented, and forward and scheduled castes[17] less, than in the developed village. However Anandapuram has 4.3 per cent of scheduled tribes compared to Veeravalli 1.5 per cent.

The Indian caste is rigid in its influence on occupational structure. A person born in a barber caste may become either a barber (traditional occupation) or if educated can get into a

Table 4.16: Occupation and Literacy (Males and Females) - below - and above the Poverty Line

	Anandapuram				*Veeravalli*			
	No of Males	*Average years of schooling*	*No of Females*	*Average years of schooling*	*No of Males*	*Average years of schooling*	*No of Females*	*Average years of schooling*
Cultivator								
Poor	13	0.29	5	2.0	5	1	0	0
Non-poor	98	2.39	35	0.42	150	5.45	16	2.88
Agricultural Labourers								
Poor	106	1.23	86	0.16	124	2.33	104	0.69
Non-poor	41	1.92	35	0	21	1.95	19	0.37
Non-farm activities								
Poor	85	1.65	29	0.37	42	4.05	5	1.4
Non poor	476	2.62	77	2.13	294	6.85	52	3.15

Source : Field-work.

Graph 4.1

Percentage Distribution of Workers by Education in Veeravali

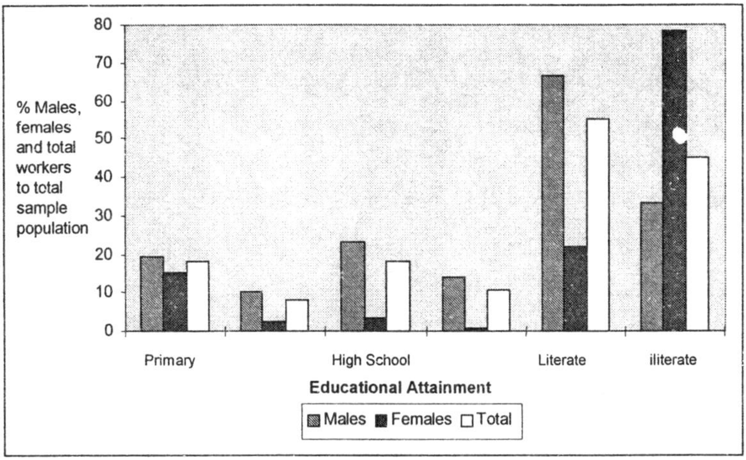

Graph 4.2

Percentage Distribution of Workers by Education in Anandapuram

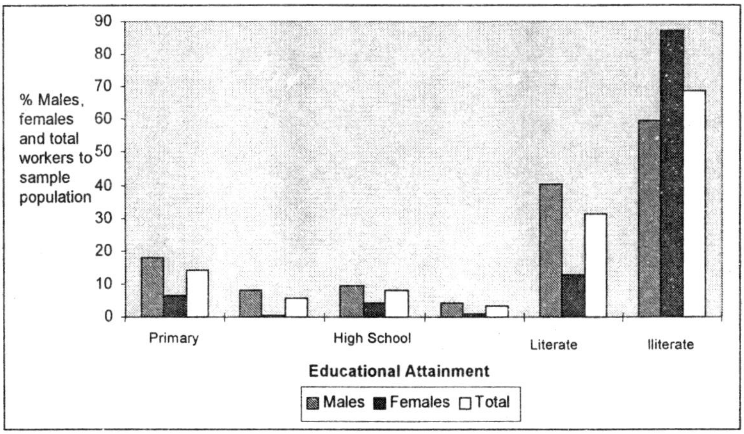

non-traditional occupation. However a person born in a caste other than that of barber will not become a barber. Here is a difference between the Indian caste structure and the Western occupational structure. The same is applicable to other caste-based occupations (e.g. potters, fishermen, carpenters, goldsmiths, basket makers, cotton carders, tinkering families, cobblers, washermen, toddy tapers, earth diggers (who level the fields during the harvest season), shepherds, piggery and butchers). Therefore the predominance of backward, SC and ST casts among the workers in a less developed village is again due to the caste related occupations.[18] But, in fact SCs are much less represented in Anandapuram. In general a less developed village is likely to retain a much larger per cent hanging on to traditional occupations (often with little work for low income).

Table 4.17: Caste-Wise Distribution of Sample Households

	FC	*BC*	*SC*	*ST*	*Total*
Veeravalli	155	236	67	7	465
(Total HHs)	(33.33)	(50.75)	(14.41)	(1.51)	(100.0)
Anandapuram	51	264	25	15	355
(Total HHs)	(14.37)	(74.37)	(7.040)	(4.26)	(100.0)

Notes : Figures in brackets indicate the percentage to total sample households.
FC: Forward caste, BC: Backward Caste, SC: Scheduled caste, ST: Scheduled Tribe.

Source : Field survey

4.1.5 Land Holding

The distribution of land holdings among the sample households are presented in Table 4.18. In Anandapuram as much as 86 per cent of households is concentrated in the lowest two land-holding size groups of 0 - 2.50 acres (marginal and small farmers). In Veeravalli 54 per cent of households are in these size groups.

In Veeravalli, of the total 742.65 acres of cultivated land, a meagre 40.5 acres belong to farmers in the size class of between 0 - 1.25 acres, with a per HH (average) holding of 0.71 acres. 225 acres of cultivable land belong to farmers in the size class of 10 and above acres, with a per household holding of 20.45 acres. In Anandapuram, of the total 135.60 acres of cultivable land, 37 per cent land belongs to farmers in the size class of 2.25 - 5 while 32.45 acres belong to farmers in the size class of 2.5 to 5 acres with a mean per HH holding size of 4.20 acres.

Table 4.18 : Operational distribution of Holding held by Farmers and Tenants (in acres):

	0 to <= 1.25		*> 1.25 to<= 2.5*		*> 2.5 to <= 5*		*>5 to <= 10*		*> 10*		*total*	
	V	*A*	*V*	*A*	*V*	*A*	*V*	*A*	*V*	*A*	*V*	*A*
No. of households in each land group (% of total)	57 (30.3)	52 (57.1)	44 (23.4)	26 (28.6)	47 (25.0)	12 (13.2)	29 (15.4)	1 (1.1)	11 (5.9)	nil	188 (100)	91 (100)
Total amount of land (acres) in each land group (% of total land in village)	40.45 (5.45)	32.1 (23.7)	86.9 (11.7)	47 (34.7)	172 (23.2)	50.5 (37.2)	218.3 (29.4)	6 (4.42)	225 (30.3)	nil	742.65 (100)	135.6 (100)
Average land size in acres	0.71	0.62	1.98	1.81	3.66	4.20	7.53	6	20.45	0	3.95	1.49

Notes : The term 'operational' has been used because tenants do not own the land Figures in brackets are percentages.
- V = Veeravalli, A = Anandapuram.

Source : Field survey

From the observations reported in the Table one can say that the distribution of land holdings is highly skewed with most of the cultivable land distributed among relatively wealthy farmers. Because of the relatively high proportion of small size land holdings, households in Anandapuram mainly operate subsistence farms. It can be seen from the data and from figure 4.2 that there are no large farmers in the less developed village, while there are some in the developed village (30 per cent of the land is operated by 11 households; 6 per cent of the sample). In the less developed village there is a slightly higher mean farm size in the 2.5 to 5 acre range; it should be noted though that these represent some of the wealthiest households in this village (with only 1 household operating more than 5 acres).

The Gini coefficients associated with operational distribution of the operational holding held by farmers have been calculated for the 2 villages. The figure obtained (a Gini coefficient of 40.6 per cent for Anandapuram and of 51 per cent for Veeravalli) point that the land holding is more unequal in Veeravalli than in Anandapuram. What one observes from the data is that a greater proportion of households holds smaller plot but that these plots account for a greater proportion of the total land available across all groups. Disparities are relatively acute in Veeravalli towards bigger holding from 5 acres onwards.

We expect land distribution to affect RNFS participation via operated land per household.

4.1.6 Occupational Pattern

The main point percentage of employed persons where main occupation (timewise) RNFE is more, for both male and female in Anandapuram than in Veeravalli.

Data relating to the farm and non-farm occupational distribution of the sample households are presented in Table 4.19. The Table shows that for males, there are more cultivators than agricultural labourers in Veeravalli, and *vice versa* in Anandapuram. Whilst there are more female agricultural labour than cultivators in both villages, the excess is much larger (proportionately) in Veeravalli than in Anandapuram.

Table 4.19: Occupational Distribution of the Total Sample Workers

	Number of employed persons					
Main occupation of households	*Veeravalli*		*Ananda-puram*		*Veera-valli*	*Ananda-puram*
FARM	*Males*	*Females*	*Males*	*Females*	*Total*	*Total*
Cultivators	145 (24.5%)	15 (7.4%)	90 (16.1%)	43 (16.1%)	160 (20.1%)	133 (16.1%)
Agricultural labourers[19]	105 (17.7%)	126 (62.4%)	97 (17.3%)	120 (44.9%)	231 (29.1%)	217 (26.3%)
Total	250 (42.2%)	141 (69.8%)	187 (33.4%)	163 (61.0%)	391 (49.2%)	350 (42.4%)
Non-farm	354 (58.6%)	61 (30.2%)	371 (66.5%)	104 (39.0%)	407 (51.0%)	475 (57.0%)
Total employed persons	604 (100%)	202 (100%)	558 (100%)	267 (100%)	798 (100%)	825 (100%)

Source : Field Survey

The farm labourer/cultivator ratio is greater for men in Anandapuram, less for women, and somewhat more for both together. In both villages, there is more RNFE than farm employment for males and females. Occupational distribution signals that there was a trend towards transformation of employment and much more diversification in Anandapuram than Veeravalli. The higher generation of male RNFE in Veeravalli is due to agro-processing industries like sugar, rice and jute factories which surrounded the village. The higher shares of RNFE females in Anandapuram compared to Veeravalli indicates diversification into petty trade and traditional non-farm occupations like toddy tapping, clothes washing, milk vending, tailoring. Usually these activities were undertaken by the poorer sections of the village.

4.1.7 Non-farm Occupations of Selected Households' Members in the two Villages

Tables 4.21 and 4.22 show that different kinds of traditional and modern non-farm activities are undertaken in the two villages. The type of activity people undertake in these villages also reveals that there are direct linkages between agriculture and non-farm activities.

The traditional non-farm employment in household enterprises are persons who operate their own non-farm enterprises, or are engaged independently in a profession or trade (on their own account or with one or a few partners).

For the purpose of these tables "traditional" is taken to mean pre-industrial. There is no specific time point at which "modern" starts as some industrial innovations were introduced prior to independence and others afterwards.

A close look at Table 4.20 parts 1 and 2 (traditional and modern non-farm occupations of members of selected households in Anandapuram) reveals that there are more workers in traditional non-farm occupations than in modern occupations. The majority of males and females are traditional such as milk vendors, washer women, *toddy* tapping, and *shandy* business which are all traditional occupations. A higher number of male workers are found in traditional occupations such as *shandy* business, *kirana*, rickshaw pulling, *toddy* tapping, and tailoring. But there is diversification in occupations, due to changing consumer demand for tailoring and *kirana* businesses.

Forty occupations are listed for modern non-farm employment. Of these, quarrying records the highest percentage of male and female workers. Other important occupations are doctor, teacher, and nurse for both males and females.

The total number of non-farm occupations (traditio-0nal+modern) observed in our sample study in Anandapuram is found to be 77 in total. The number of persons going in for these non-farm activities is still found to be higher among the traditional occupations based on caste such as *purohit* (a person who performs marriages) or astrologer. It appears that economic pressure in less developed villages is strengthening the traditional occupations rather than diversifying these occupations into modern occupations. At the same time non-farm occupations are expanding into both traditional and modern occupations providing scope for the breaking up of the structure of the rural society.

Table 4.20 Part 1 : Traditional Rural Non-farm Occupations of Selected Households' Members (in Anandapuram)

	Occupations	*Males*	*Females*	*Total*
1.	Tailoring	19	4	23
2.	Panshop, soft drinks (soda sales) Shop selling sweets, tobacco, cigarettes.	8	2	10
3.	Kirana (dry goods) store Selling provisions, soaps, detergents.	25	8	33
4.	Servant maiden household	1	2	3
5.	Shandy business	29	7	36
6.	Milk vendor	14	16	30
7.	Rickshaw puller	21	0	21
8.	Shepherding	11	2	13
9.	Vegetable vendor	4	1	5
10.	Poorohit (Person who conducts rituals of Hindu Religion).	4	0	4
11.	Tea Stall	10	5	15
12.	Porter (local names mutta worker Maistry)	4	0	4
13.	Fishing	3	1	4
14.	Fostering	1	0	1
15.	Fruit vending	3	1	4
16.	Mutton vending	8	0	8
17.	Barber	9	0	9
18.	Mediator (who buys and sells paddy, pulses) (not legal)	3	0	3
19.	Onion vending (exclusively)	3	0	3
20.	Carpenter (mill repair helper)	16	1	17
21.	Mango vending	1	0	1
22.	Washermen	7	10	17
23.	Butcher	1	0	1
24.	Toddy tapping	23	9	32
25.	Tapi worker (mason)	4	0	4
26.	Middle man (sale of commercial crops yield)	2	0	2
27.	Butter milk vending (exclusively)	0	2	2
28.	Astrologist	8	8	16
29.	Banana coconuts seller (exclusively)	0	2	2
30.	Kalasi (porter)	3	0	3
31.	Sweet vendor	1	0	1
32.	Petty Trade	3	1	4

Contd...

Table 4.20 Part 1 : (Contd....)

Occupations	Males	Females	Total
33. Cloth business	1	0	1
34. Cleaner	1	0	1
35. Harikatha (traditional profession entertaining people)	1	0	1
36. Tobacco business +Soda only	10	6	16
37. Hostel worker	1	0	1
Total	**263 (70.5)**	**88 (84.6)**	**351 (73.6)**

Source : Field Survey.

Table 4.20 Part 2: Modern Non-farm occupations[20] of Selected Households' Members (Anandapuram)

Occupations	Males	Females	Total
38. RTC (Road Transport Corporation) Driver and conductor	2	0	2
39. Quarrying	29	6	35
40. Convent Principal (teacher)	7	3	10
41. Gooddaku factory worker	2	0	2
42. Jute mill worker	4	0	4
43. Hotel worker	3	2	5
44. Factory employee	3	0	3
45. Plastic worker	1	1	2
46. Security	1	0	1
47 RMP Registered Medical Practitioner Doctor + veterinary	3	0	3
48. Govt. Hospital attender & Co-operative	2	0	2
49. Plywood factory worker	1	0.	1
50. Supervisors	1	0	1
51. Hospital Nurse	0	1	1
52. Co-operative	1	0	1
53. Post master	1	0	1
54. Rice mill worker	3	0	3
55. Lorry driver	1	0	1
56. Co-operative Society	1	0	1
57. Cycle repair	6	0	6
58. Cycle vendor	3	1	4
59. Medical shop (trade medicine)	2	1	3

Contd....

Table 4.20 Part 2: (Contd....)

	Occupations	*Males*	*Females*	*Total*
60.	Cycle parts vending	1	0	1
61.	Construction (building work for public)	1	0	1
62.	Lodge worker (freemasons)	3	0	3
63.	Lorry cleaner	2	0	2
64.	Ice selling on bicycle	3	0	3
65.	Electrician Mike (audio) set & lighting	2	0	2
66.	Mini contracts (low budget) in irrigation	1	0	1
67.	Auto driver	4	0	4
68.	Scooter Mechanic	1	0	1
69	Photography	1	0	1
70.	Worker in sea food company	1	0	1
71.	Bed making worker	1	0	1
72.	Painter	1	0	1
73.	Poultry keeping	3	1	4
74.	Timber Department (private)	1	0	1
75.	Oil business	1	0	1
76.	Radio repair	1	0	1
77	Ganuga Oil extraction from seasmum and ground nut	5	0	5
	Total	**110 (29.5)**	**16 (15.4)**	**126 (26.4)**
	Grand Total	**373 (100)**	**104 (100)**	**477 (100)**

Note : The figures in brackets are percentages.
Source : Field survey.

Table 4.21 parts land & (traditional and modern non-farm occupations of members of selected households in veeravali) shows the overall occupational structure in Veeravalli is more diversified than in Anandapuram, but less so for the traditional comprising 35 different occupations. Potters, carpenters, tea-stall owners, and barbers account for the highest percentage of male self-employment. For women pottery is the most important occupation. Fifty modern RNFE occupations were recorded in Veeravalli. Among males, employment in the local sugar factory accounts for the highest percentage. Other important modern non-farm occupations for men are lorry driver and cleaner, jute mill worker, other factory worker, electrician and teacher respectively. Among females, teachers constitute the highest percentage.

Table 4.21 Part 1 : Traditional Non-farm Occupations of Members of Selected Households in Veeravalli

	Occupations	*Males*	*Females*	*Total*
1.	Kirana (dry goods) store	7	1	8
2.	Cloth selling (mobile)	4	1	5
3.	Petty trade	1	0	1
4.	Carpenter	14	1	15
5.	Pottery	32	20	52
6.	Rickshaw pullers	9	0	9
7.	Tea stall	10	2	12
8.	Mastry	2	0	2
9.	Dairy milk	6	0	6
10.	Priest	2	0	2
11.	Pan business	9	5	14
12.	Tailor	7	4	11
13.	Fish vending/pisciculture/processing	1	1	2
14.	Poorohit	2	0	2
15.	Banana + fruit seller	6	1	7
16.	Cobbler	1	0	1
17.	Milk seller	5	5	10
18.	Washer man	4	3	7
19.	Adda Leaves selling for use of tiffin and meals plates made by Bauhinia vahlii or ternihalia catappa leaves.	1	4	5
20.	Toddy tapping	2	1	3
21.	Barbers	8	0	8
22.	Butcher	5	1	6
23.	Soda shop	4	0	4
24.	Vegetable vending	6	0	6
25.	Animal Husbandry	1	0	1
26.	Curtain Stitching	4	0	4
27.	Rice Business	1	0	1
28.	Basket making	1	1	2
29.	Ration shop	1	0	1
30.	Cook	3	0	3
31.	Anganwadi work (Kindergarten helper)	0	1	1

Contd....

Table 4.21 Part 1 : (Contd....)

	Occupations	*Males*	*Females*	*Total*
32.	Attender	6	0	6
33.	Village servant (Administrative)	2	0	2
34.	Sweeper	2	0	2
35.	Bill collector	1	0	1
	Total	**170** **(49.3)**	**53** **(85.5)**	**221** **(54.3)**

Source : Field survey

Table 4.21 Part 2: Modern Non-farm Occupations of Members of Selected HHs in Veeravalli

	Occupations	*Males*	*Females*	*Total*
36.	Worker tyre shop	1	0	1
37.	Lorry labour drivers & cleaners	18	1	19
38.	Paints Company	1	0	1
39.	Jute mill	16	0	16
40.	Tractor driver	4	0	4
41.	Rice mill	8	1	9
42.	Paper mill	2	0	2
43.	Teacher	10	4	14
44.	Railway worker	6	0	6
45.	Assistant Engineer	2	0	2
46.	Sugar factory	23	1	24
47.	Private job apprenticeship	1	0	1
48.	Health Inspector	2	0	2
49.	Clerks	5	0	5
50.	Factory employ	10	1	11
51.	Field supervisors	1	0	1
52.	Leafco (lorry equipment) factory	2	0	2
53.	Co-operative Bank + clerk	2	0	2
54.	Operator (machine)	2	0	2
55.	Village Administrative Officer	2	0	2
56.	Supervisors	1	0	1
57.	Bank supervisors	1	0	1
58.	Instructor in training institute	1	0	1
59.	Mechanic operator	2	0	2

Contd....

Table 4.21 Part 2 : (Contd....)

Occupations	Males	Females	Total
60. Post master	3	0	3
61. Telephone worker	1	0	1
62. RMP Doctor	1	0	1
63. Alcohol factory	3	0	3
64. Chemical factory	1	0	1
65. Bus driver (tourist)	1	0	1
66. Librarian	1	0	1
67. Security	1	0	1
68. Public works Department (PWD) employee	1	0	1
69. Operator in agro industry	1	0	1
70. Excise Constable	1	0	1
71. Electrician	10	0	10
72. Oil engine operator	2	0	2
73. Oil mill	2	0	2
74. Contract	2	0	2
75. Cycle shop	1	0	1
76. Grinding	0	1	1
77. Medical shop	1	0	1
78. Wine shop	1	0	1
79. Cycle shop	5	0	5
80. Welder	1	0	1
81. Construction	5	0	5
82. Technician	1	0	1
83. Motor Mechanic	2	0	2
84. Painting	1	0	1
85. Wood cutter	3	0	3
Sub-Total	**175** **(50.7)**	**9** **(14.5)**	**184** **(45.2)**
Total	**345** **(100)**	**62** **(100)**	**407** **(100)**

Note : The figures in brackets are percentages
Source : Field-survey.

In contrast to traditional RNFE, modern employment is more diversified in the developed village of Veeravalli, but female work participation is limited to the educational service sector, rice mill, sugar factory, and other factory employees only. This could reflect that families are financially sounder, because they obtain regular wage employment and there is less need for family income supplementation.

The number of occupations in the RNFS in a developed village suggests that it is possible to strengthen employment in such a village rather than in an under developed village. It may also be concluded that non-diversification of occupations in a traditional village reflects underdevelopment of the village and that non-diversification in RNFS could result in further underdevelopment.

4.2 Testing For Household Involvement In RNFE as a Main Occupation : Key Features of the Models

To analyse the determinants of involvement in RNFE as a main occupation among a sample of households and to attribute a weight to these determinants we have used a logit model, in view of the discontinuation, of the dependent variable - i.e. whether or not a household contained a main worker (≥ 183 days of work per year whose primary occupation was RNFE, or in some cases modern or traditional RNFE). In logit models, the dependent variable is a dummy (i.e. a dichotomous variable which takes a value of 0 and 1). Here, it takes the value 0 if the household has no main worker whose primary occupation was RNFE in the year 1993-94 prior to the survey, and 1 otherwise. If a HH has no main worker at all, they are excluded from all analysis because we are trying to discover determinants of RNFE among HHs with main worker (s), not determinants of having a main worker of all. Several cases are modelled; (i) whether the household is engaged in a non-farm activity; (ii) whether the HH is engaged in traditional or modern non-farm activities;

A list of explanatory variables used in the regression along with some descriptive notes are given in Table 4.22.

4.2.1 The explanatory Variables:

Three logit functions were found to generate the best fit and were used for the purpose of our analysis. The determinants of non-farm employment for both village, (Eq.1 and Eq.2), are

Table 4.22 Description of the Variables Used in the Logit Model

Variable	*Variables notation*	*Description*
X_1	Farm size **LAND**	Number of acres operated by the household.
X_2	Educational levels **EDUC**	Levels of educational attainment in terms of years of schooling. The potential figure is between 0 for (illiteracy) and 20 years of schooling (including University). Average years achieved by all the workers in the household.
X_3	Per acre value of agricultural output **AGR** etc	Market average value of agricultural products (paddy, pulses, cereals and vegetables) produced by the household (prices are supplied by the Food Corporation of India, Krishna District Office, Vijayawada, in Rupees per year).
$X_4 X_5$	Household head age AGE. Also used as squared, AGE^2	Household head age in years.
X_6	Family size of the household FAMILYS	Number of family members (including children) in the household.
X_7	Caste dummy 1 CD1	If the household is from a backward caste the dummy takes the value of 1, or 0 otherwise.
X_8	Caste dummy 2 CD2	If the household is from a Scheduled caste or from a Scheduled Tribe, the dummy takes the value 1, or 0 otherwise.
X_9	Migration into the village by the HH; MIGIN	Value 1 the household/ one or two members/ may be head of HH has migrated into the village at any point in time prior to the interview, or 0 if not.
$X_{10} X_{11} X_{12}$	Seasonality September-November, December-February, March-May Denoted SON, DJF, MAM.	The year is divided into four seasons. The response of the head of the HH was considered and dummies were attributed depending on the month during which the HH works the most days. I have used 3 dummy variables with June to August as the base case. Then a dummy is attributed to September to November, X_{10}, December to February X_{11}, March to May X_{12}.

Contd....

Table 4.22 (Contd....)

Variable	*Variables notation*	*Description*
X_{13}	Skilled/unskilled SK	If the household is skilled the dummy takes 1, or 0 if it is not skilled. The definition of skills will be given subsequently in the main text
X_{14}	Poor/non-poor POOR (see last row)	Based on the average per person household income per month compared to a poverty line. If the household is poor the dummy takes 1, 0 otherwise. (see p.)
X_{15}	Village dummy VD	If the household is in the developed village (Veeravalli) it takes 0 and 1 otherwise (Anandapuram).
X_{16} X_{17}	Interaction variable: X_2*X_{15} Interaction variable: X_{12}* X_{15}	This is a set of two interaction variables. Village dummy has been multiplied (interacted) with education, and the March-May season.
X_{18}	modern/traditional (see last row) MODERN	If the HH is most of the time involved in the modern RNFS (Census criteria of a minimum of 183 days in a year) then the dummy takes the value 1, or 0 if involved with the traditional RNFS
Y_i	Dependent variable Rural non-farm employment 0R - X_{14}	Poor/non-poor, 0R X_{18} modern/traditional 0R X_{19} Self-employed and wage-employed have been used A household engaged in non-farm activity, if any working member has, as a primary (183 days in year) occupation, one or several activities covered by the Census of India 1991 occupational categories IV-IX.

Note : u_i = Disturbance term with the classical properties where i denotes the household interviewed.

reported in Table 4.26 (p. 229 and sec. 4.3) Pooled village level data on all 819 households are considered in Eq.3 (Table 4.27, p. 233 and sec.4.3). Disaggregated RNFE determinants for Modern/Traditional RNFS Eq.4. The basis for pooling the data is given later on as the decision relied on results obtained from the regressions themselves.

The expected relationship between the dependent variable (denoted y) and the independent variables is

Y = f [Farm Size operated X_1 (-ve), Levels of schooling X_2 (+ve Modern RNFS, -ve traditional rnfs), Per acre value of agri-output (Rs) (AGR) X_3 (-ve), Household head age X_4 (-ve), Household head age^2 X_5 (+ve), Size of household X_6 (+ve), Caste dummy1 X_7 (-ve), Caste dummy2 X_8 (-ve), Migration-in X_9 (+ve), September-November X_{10} (-ve), December-February X_{11} (-ve), March-May X_{12} (-ve), Skilled/unskilled X_{13} (+ve), Poor/non-poor X_{14} (-ve for the Whole sample or +ve for traditional RNFS, -ve for modern RNFS), Village dummy X_{15} (-ve)). The variables listed above are for each of the logit regressions estimated. Before reporting the estimated the equations, the predicted nature of the relationship between the dependent and explanatory variables is discussed.

However, the relationship may differ between the aggregate tests for the entire sample of rural households and the disaggregated tests on subsets of households

The probability of being engaged in non-farm occupation is measured by the logarithm of the odds ratio for the household to be engaged in non-farm employment, and this is explained by a set of explanatory variables, whose definition and selection are given next.

Size of Land Holdings (X_1) : The size of agricultural land holding operated by the household measured in acres can tell us about the economic status of the household member. Land holding increases the involvement in the RNFS (for instance machinery, fertilisers, pesticides, repairs and services). We expect owned and operated holding to affect probability of HH involvement in RNFE in the same way. Land access per person of working age, not per HH, that affects (or is affected by) RNFE participation. If a HH's workers have lots of own/operate land each they are less likely to do RNFE. Direction of causation: strong RNFE activity cuts the incentive to rent in (and hence operate more) land. We expect the regression to provide information as to whether larger holdings tend to raise the propensity to work in supplying RNFS goods and services.

Level of Schooling (X_2) : Education is a potentially important determinant of RNFE. Education improves an individual's prospects for non-farm jobs as well as increases his or her ability to allocate time to work efficiently among income producing activities. However, in early development phases many rural non-farm activities require only low levels of schooling.

We expect a positive relationship between modern non-farm occupations (like mechanical repairs of tractors, services, modern textiles, jute, ply-wood factory) and level of education, but a negative relationship between level of education and traditional non-farm occupations (like *toddy* tapers, rickshaw pullers, basket makers, barbers, clothes washing, shepherds, tailors, quarry workers, potters, carpenters, goldsmiths, gunny bag makers).

Per Acre Average Value of Agricultural Output (X_3) : A household's per acre agricultural output may affect its members' decision to be engaged in non-farm activities. Per acre value of agricultural output is treated as a proxy for the accumulation of savings for investment in RNFS capital. A high value possibly means that the household has the resources necessary to train for RNFS activities. In addition to training, the money can be used to purchase the equipment necessary to be involved in the RNFS (for example, TV and radio repairs, scooter and moped repairs, welding, cycle shop, tractor repairs, purchase of a sewing machine, thrift organisation, or cultivation of prawns and pond fish). It can also generally induce a greater demand for education with long run spillovers.

Therefore, a positive relationship is expected between per acre value of agricultural output and RNFE. Per acre value of agricultural production is estimated as the gross value of agricultural output per acre value in rupees. On the other hand, HHs that fail in agriculture may also be pushed into RNFE due to distress diversification. The direction of the link is much clearer when RNFS HHs are separated. We hypothesise a positive link from agriculture output to modern RNFE and negative link to traditional RNFE.

Household Head Age (X_4) and **Household Head Age² (X_5)**: We expect that household head age is inversely related to non-farm employment. Here, household head age is treated as proxy of the working age in a HH. There are two reasons for this. First, a large proportion of HH heads comprise a large proportion of HH workers as a whole. It was observed during my fieldwork that for a large proportion of HH, the head of the HH is the only earning member. (2) Young household heads tend to have younger working members (spouse, working children).

It is expected that the head of HH age is positively related to modern non-farm employment, but negatively for traditional and total non-farm employment especially for self-employed. The positive relationship for modern RNFE is mainly attributed to the fact that non-farm work generally requires a certain amount of skill, mobility, and training. Moreover opportunities in the non-farm sector are more scarce than in the farm sector which requires information and greater efforts on the behalf of the HH to establish and confirm the opportunities.

The head of the HH might try and persuade the other members (e.g. their sons/daughters) of the HH that are of working age to act in a way (if not too risky) in which household income can be increased (the head behaves like a 'dictator'). In other words HH head wants other members to be part of RNFE, but not if their interest is against it. Nevertheless, although potential income is higher in the non-farm sector, older farm heads may not be themselves able to shift from farm to non-farm work. Therefore, we expect a negative relationship with total non-farm employment.

It is expected that the head of Age² negatively related to modern RNFE but positively for traditional RNFE.

Size of the Household (X_6) : The expected relationship between the household size and the probability of the household being engaged in RNFE is positive. This is the result of two factors. First, even if RNFE activities is randomly distributed across persons, there are more persons in larger households, so there is a relatively greater chance that at least one working member will be in non-farm employment. Secondly it was observed during field work that once a member of the HH is engaged in RNFS, other younger members tend to follow him/her. The parents in most HH also encourage their children to be educated and employed in better non-farm occupations. Since large family size has a genetic component it is likely to be 'interested' alongside access to modern RNFE.

1. If non-farm activity is random among persons, HHs with more persons have more likelihood of a member in RNFE.
2. If all HHs have the same land area, than in bigger HHs one (or two) working members can 'mind the farm' while other member(s) go to the RNFS.
3. If a large family size is in part 'genetic', RNFS large-family descendants will be more likely to go to the RNFS and to have large farms.
4. One-worker HHs cannot have 2 specialisations, are in age one within RNFS, 2 worker HH can, 3 worker HH, etc. Thus, economic factors as well as demographic factors go together with the RNFS.

Social status (X_7) and (X_8) : (Caste) In the Indian context, the majority of occupations are linked to caste. While upper castes predominate in certain activities such as priesthood, trade and education, other backward castes are engaged in agricultural and allied activities. Many are engaged in traditional RNFE (for example leather work, sweeping, butchering). As such, it will be of interest to know whether there is any impact of caste on employment in the RNFS. In this study, we have classified all the sample workers into three Caste Groups. Caste Group1 includes all the upper castes such as *Brahmin, Kshatriya, Vysyas, Kammas* and *Kapu Naidu* (*Telaga*). Caste Group2 contains all the backward castes such as *Kummari,*

Blacksmith, Gowda, Yadava, Koppulavelama, Turupukapu, Uppari, Rajaka, Jalari, Goldsmith, Settibalija, Mangali, Senapathi, Indian Muslims and other minorities. Caste Group3 includes the Scheduled Castes/Harijans (SCs live in a settlement of harijanwada at the end of villages even after 50 years of independence) and the Scheduled Tribes (STs) such as Madiga, Mala, Relli and Lambadi (nomadic tribe). Generally caste, occupation, and levels of schooling and income of a household determine the HH socio-economic status. Moreover most of the BCs can shift occupations if they are given the employment skills that are necessary. They do not want to go for lower occupations but for higher occupations and they lack resources (STs belong to the landless illiterate group in rural areas). It can be hypothesised that households that belong to BCs and SCs and STs will have the least chances to opt for modern, skilled non-farm employment.

Migration (X_9) : Migration into the villages does have an impact on RNFS. Agricultural poverty (of which lack of cash crops is often a sign) stimulates emigration; inadequate access to income-generating land in a village then encourages emigration. Complete households from poorer sections of the population will migrate. It is hypothesised that migration into the villages will lead to greater non-farm opportunities in rural areas. It was noticed during my field work that those migrants (in the sample) found seasonal employment in villages and also were mostly in the RNFS. It is expected that households which have migrated into the villages will be more likely to take up RNFS employment because of better chances of finding employment in this sector. We expect most to enter wage or self employment.

Seasonality (X_{10}), (X_{11}) and (X_{12}) : With the agricultural sector dominating the AP economy seasonality may affect RNFE. During the lean season (in terms of agricultural activities) there is a decline in work opportunities in the agricultural sector. Particularly women are withdrawn from the labour force. In rural areas farm-work is available at a peak in the July-September period, and at its lowest in April-June, the lean season. In order to study these fluctuations, the year is divided into 4 seasons. The *kharif* or monsoon season lasts from June to August (planting time), September to November (threshing time). The *rabi* or winter season starts in December and ends in February (harvesting time). The summer season is from March to May. The response of the head of the household has been used to classify household. It was asked of the head and other workers when they were working most. Three dummies were used, for season one (September to November), for season two (December to February) and for season 3 (March to May). The base is June to August.[21]

Since labourers find local farm employment largely at the beginning and at the end of the monsoon, unemployment in the rural areas is seasonal. In some traditional activities (for example *toddy* tapping, carpentry, pot making, *shandy* business (periodic markets), goldsmithy, basket making, construction activity), work is available for few months. People are unemployed during the rest of the year. In the present study, seasonal employment means that certain occupations, like agricultural employment are available only during June-August, and September to December. In the remaining six months people are unemployed in the farm sector and hence people are more likely go to the RNFS between January and June as this period is the main season for traditional occupations and petty trade.

Occupation (X_{13}): The sample households are divided into two pairs of categories: 'unskilled' and 'skilled',[22] modern and traditional. People who are trained for skilled occupations, will generally have better opportunities of employment and their productivity is said to be higher which in turn is reflected in their relatively higher earnings. It is expected that skilled household members will have a better chance of taking up non-farm employment, so that the expected relationship between skilled and RNFE is positive.

Poor and non-poor (X_{14}): The poverty line cut off point which differentiates the poor from the non-poor households is Rs.187.39 per person per month, which is the figure for 1993-94 rural per capita monthly expenditure used by the Directorate of Economics and Statistics, Government of AP, as its poverty line. Household income was determined by income derived from the occupation, eliciting information from the head of the household in the presence of neighbours, village elders that acted as a deterrent from providing misinformation. Each household's income was divided by the number of people in the household. This is a simple unweighted count. The dummy if the household is poor takes the value 1 or 0 if it is not poor.

We expect the sign with modern sector RNFE to be negative because modern sector activities require certain amount of skills, education and mobility. Poor people can not afford such investments. However, this effect might not apply or might be reversed, for traditional RNFS (thus we expect a positive sign).

Village Dummy (X_{15}) : If the household is in the developed village (Veeravalli) it takes 0 and 1 otherwise (Anandapuram). Since residence in the less developed village is expected to diverse the propensity of RNFE involvement, we expect the sign to be negative for both modern and traditional RNFE.

4.2.2 Basic Sample Characteristics

The results of tests for differences in means of variables between the two villages are presented in Tables 4.23 and 4.24. The purpose of these tests is to point out whether the villages differ in terms of some basic characteristics. This exercise is a useful complement to the logit analysis which we have used and whose results we will report in the following section. Unfortunately one limitation of the data is that we do not have comprehensive secondary data for other villages of AP, and thus we cannot decide whether the sample is representative of the broader context of AP.

First, we compare the whole sample i.e. pooled data between the two villages and then the two villages taken separately using all the variables we have used in the logit models. Second, we separated the sample between all farm and non-farm households (i.e. equal to main working time) and excluded all 274 farm households, thereby focusing on the characteristics of those HHs involved with the RNFS as primary time criteria. Third, we separated the whole sample between the 'self-employed' and wage-wage employed between the villages and compared them with all the variables we have used in the logit model. The idea was to see if there were any variations among the variables, which we used in the logit models.

Table 4.23 : Summary Statistics and Test of Differences in Means for Independent Variables between the Two Study Villages

Variable	*Mean for whole sample [N =.819]*	*Mean for Ananda-puram [N = 354]*	*Mean for Veeravalli [N = 465]*	*t-value Anada/ Veerva*
LAND HOLDING SIZE	1.07	0.38	1.60	5.96***
(in acres operated)	(8.70)	(0.89)	(14.02)	
C.V.	2.76	2.47	2.34	
EDUCATION				
[average (years of education)	3.81	2.29	4.97	9.14***
of the workers in sample)]	(19.02)	(11.98)	(21.30)	
C.V.	1.14	1.51	0.93	
PER ACRE AVERAGE VALUE	3192	2757	3524	0.57
[of agri- output (Rupees)]	(29573833)	(32447093)	(27196938)	
C.V.	1.70	2.07	1.48	
HH HEAD AGE	44.01	43.77	44.19	0.46
	(170.09)	(169.59)	(170.76)	
C.V.	0.30	0.30	0.30	
FAMILY SIZE	4.50	4.84	4.25	4.95***
	(2.94)	(3.23)	(2.59)	
	0.38	0.37	0.38	
CASTE DUMMY 1	0.61	0.75	0.51	7.22***
	(0.24)	(0.19)	(0.25)	
C.V.	0.80	0.57	0.98	
CASTE DUMMY 2	0.14	0.11	0.16	2.18**
	(1.16)	(0.10)	(0.14)	
C.V.	2.5	2.81	2.31	
MIGRATION IN	0.16	0.14	0.18	1.43
	(0.14)	(0.12)	(0.15)	
C.V.	2.31	2.5	2.11	
SEPTEMBER - NOVEMBER	0.25	0.29	0.22	2.10**
Season 1	(0.19)	(0.20)	(0.17)	
C.V.	1.72	1.55	1.91	
DECEMBER - FEBRUARY	0.28	0.27	0.29	0.72
Season 2	(0.20)	(0.20)	(0.21)	
C.V.	1.61	1.63	1.55	

Contd....

Table 4.23 : (Contd....)

Variable	*Mean for whole sample [N =.819]*	*Mean for Ananda-puram [N = 354]*	*Mean for Veeravalli [N = 465]*	*t-value Anada/ Veerva*
MARCH - MAY Season 3	0.39	0.34	0.43	2.70***
	(0.24)	(0.23)	(0.25)	
C.V.	1.26	1.38	1.16	
POOR (1 for poor HH)	0.38	0.47	0.31	4.80***
	(0.24)	(0.25)	(0.21)	
C.V.	1.29	1.06	1.48	
VILLAGE DUMMY	0.43	N/A	N/A	
(1 for Anandapuram)	(0.25)			
C.V.	1.16	N/A	N/A	
SKILLED (proportions of	.57	0.47	0.65	5.02***
main workers who are skilled)	(.25)	(0.25)	(0.23)	
(1 for skilled)				
C.V.	0.86	1.06	0.74	
MODER1 (1 for modern	0.25	0.15	0.32	5.48***
employment)	(0.19)	(0.13)	(0.22)	
C.V.	1.72	2.4	1.47	
NON-FARM	0.67	0.80	0.57	7.15***
	(0.22)	(0.16)	(0.25)	
C.V.	0.70	0.5	0.88	

Notes : The figures in brackets are the variance. The variance considered with the mean has been used to calculate the of each coefficient of variation (CV). The t-tests assume equal variance as were obtained from SPSS.
*** Significant at 1 per cent, ** significant at 5 per cent, * significant at 10 per cent.

Table 4.23 reports the means (some of the results are proportions), coefficients of variation (CVs) as well as the values of t-statistics for the selected variables for the villages under study, as well as for the pooled data set that are used in the logit models.

A cursory analysis shows that there are differences between the two villages that match the developed and less developed prediction pattern. Veeravalli is much wealthier than Anandapuram with regard to education, mean land holding size, and per acre average value of agricultural output. HHs

Table 4.24 : Summary Statistics and Test of Differences in Means for Households with a Main Worker Principally Engaged in Rural Non-farm Employment only

Variable	*Mean for whole sample [N = 545]*	*Mean for Ananda-puram [N = 282]*	*Mean for Veeravalli [N = 263]*	*t-value Ananda-puram Veeravali*
LAND HOLDING SIZE	0.38	0.25	0.52	2.91***
(in acres)	(1.18)	(0.61)	(1.76)	
C.V.	2.86	3.13	2.55	
EDUCATION (Average literacy	4.18	2.65	5.81	8.64***
of the workers in sample)	(20.64)	(13.80)	(22.88)	
C.V.	1.09	1.40	0.82	
PER ACRE VALUE	1931.44	1966.71	1893.62	0.19
[of agri- output (Rupees)]	(21103372)	(25366610)	(16608742)	
C.V.	2.38	2.56	2.15	
HH HEAD AGE	43.06	43.05	43.19	0.33
	(164.97)	(166.98)	(164.3)	
C.V.	0.30	0.30	0.30	
FAMILY SIZE	4.52	4.80	4.21	3.75***
	(3.24)	(3.40)	(2.89)	
C.V.	0.40	0.38	0.40	
CASTE DUMMY 1	0.64	0.73	0.54	4.81***
	(0.23)	(0.20)	(0.25)	
C.V.	0.76	0.61	0.93	
CASTE DUMMY 2	0.12	0.10	0.14	1.48
	(0.11)	(0.09)	(0.12)	
C.V.	2.72	3.02	2.48	
MIGRATION IN	0.20	0.16	0.24	2.13**
	(0.16)	(0.14)	(0.18)	
C.V.	2.01	2.27	1.80	
SEPTEMBER-NOVEMBER	0.15	0.20	0.10	3.18***
	(0.13)	(0.16)	(0.09)	
C.V.	2.40	2.04	3.02	
DECEMBER - FEBRUARY	0.23	0.26	0.21	1.17
	(0.18)	(0.44)	(0.17)	
C.V.	1.81	1.71	1.93	
MARCH -MAY	0.54	0.42	0.67	6.05***
	(0.25)	(0.24)	(0.22)	
C.V.	0.92	1.18	0.7	
POOR	0.38	0.45	0.30	3.83***
	(0.24)	(0.25)	(0.21)	
C.V.	1.28	1.10	1.54	

Contd....

Table 4.24 : (Contd....)

Variable	*Mean for whole sample [N = 545]*	*Mean for Ananda-puram [N = 282]*	*Mean for Veeravalli [N = 263]*	*t-value Ananda-puram Veeravali*
VILLAGE DUMMY	0.52	N/A	N/A	
(1 for Anandapuram)	(0.25)			
C.V.	0.97	N/A	N/A	
SK SKILLED/UNSKILLED	0.55	0.46	0.65	4.33***
(1 for skilled)	(0.25)	(0.25)	(0.23)	
C.V.	0.90	1.08	0.74	
MODER1 MODERN/	0.32	0.19	0.45	6.80***
TRADITIONAL	(0.22)	(0.16)	(0.25)	
(1 for modern)				
C.V.	1.47	2.06	1.10	

Note : As for Table 4.24.

from Veeravalli are somewhat better off than those in Anandapuram [although PAAV (per acre average value of farm output) is not significantly different from poverty incidence, at 31 per cent versus 47 per cent is significant (at the 1 per cent level). In Veeravalli the average household (the proportion of households with a main worker whose primary work is in the modern non-farm sector) is more than double that of Anandapuram; and Veeravalli has a significantly higher proportion of its main workers who are skilled, but a lower proportion self employed.

The significant differences between the villages are visible not only in terms of mean values but also within the CV. The distribution of 'years of education per worker' is much less spread in Veeravalli than in Anandapuram, as is that of PAAV and (to a lesser extent) landholding size. The differences between the villages set out in part one of this chapter reflect these results. There are both higher levels of small holdings and a larger area under small holdings in Anandapuram compared to Veeravalli. The type of crops in Veeravalli is also different giving a higher gross value of output/acre. We can see the links much more clearly. Lower PAAV in Veeravalli (i.e. less variability) in Veeravalli presumably reflects wider access to water control. All of these trends explain the differences between the two villages. Besides the economic variables, seasonality in agriculture is important in the villages. In particular the involvement of people in the RNFS in the March-May period is greater. It shows the non-farm signs of distress diversification in Anandapuram. RNFS has a greater proportion of HH in Anandapuram compared to Veeravalli because of distress diversification. Partly the farm sector is not prosperous which is responsible for this distress diversification. Basic sample characteristics for HHs engaged in the RNFS only are presented in table 4.24.

Table 4.24 reports the means, proportions and coefficients of variation (CVs) of the selected variables for the villages and pooled sample only for households with at least one member whose primary employment is in the RNFS. These households only were used in logit models in which the dependent variable was modern/traditional.

Households involved only with the RNFS appear (fróm comparing Tables 4.23 and 4.24) to be on average "worse off" in economic terms; the mean land holding, and per acre value of agricultural output are lower. Yet, the comparison would be misleading as a guide to per capita income in that such HHs could get their income from predominantly non-farm sources. Indeed, literacy which is somewhat higher for those involved in the RNFS.

The RNFS as a whole thus either requires or attracts on average slightly more educated HHs, but this too may be misleading, i.e. time of modern RNFS, but the reverse of the truth for traditional. Also, however, this sample contains a similar proportion of poor people to the entire sample, signalling that belonging to the RNFS does not necessarily improve poverty incidence.

Whilst social and demographic characteristics appear relatively similar (family size, caste dummies, skill), a greater proportion of households with RNFS main workers contain people that work in March-May (54 per cent, compared to 39 per cent for the entire sample).

Focusing next on Table 4.24, we find that the indicators of HHs engaged in the RNFS being worse off in terms of farm income than those that do not is more pronounced for Veeravalli than in Anandapuram. Thus, land size holding of those HHs in Veeravalli engaged in the RNFS whilst greater than that of those HHs in Anandapuram engaged in the RNFS is substantially smaller than the full sample averages. Also when comparing the per acre value of agricultural output of those HHs engaged in the RNFS in Veeravalli to that of the entire sample of per acre value.

RNFS HHs differ between the two villages in a number of characteristics. RNFS households in Veeravalli are significantly (at 1 per cent) more educated, have larger land holdings, are older, more skilled, are more involved in the modern sectors than in Anandapuram. RNFS HHs in Anandapuram are more likely than in Veeravalli to have a large family size, to be poor, to work as self employed and in December-February and are more likely to belong to backward castes. The proportion of those belonging to Scheduled castes and Tribes and working in the September-November season, however, do not differ significantly between the two villages.

In relation to the caste composition, 73 per cent of the HHs in the RNFS in Anandapuram belong to CD1 (backward caste HH takes the value of 1, and forward caste 0), 10 per cent belong to CD2 (scheduled caste and scheduled tribe caste HH takes the value of 1, and forward caste 0) and another 17 per cent to the base case which is the upper castes. In Veeravalli, the breakdown is of 54 per cent, 14 per cent and 32 per cent respectively. Thus the RNFS is the preserve of CD1 followed by the base. There is comparatively little involvement of those HHs which belong to CD2. As for the seasons, most of the RNFS HHs in Veeravalli work most in March-May (67 per cent) whilst in Anandapuram 42 per cent work most in March-May. Overall 32 per cent of those involved with the RNFS (only) work in the modern sector, an average between the figure of 45 per cent for Veeravalli and that of 19 per cent for Anandapuram.

HHs with main workers primarily committed to RNFS are 'more advanced' in Veeravalli than in Anandapuram (agriculturally, land size and productivity, and otherwise) reflecting their 'more advanced' village and suggesting agricultural growth linkages, not distress diversification, as the mainspring of RNFS involvement of a household. But these RNFS households are, on the whole behind the levels of their agricultural fellow-villages both in agriculture (land size and productivity) and otherwise - and this is more so in the 'advanced' Veeravalli than in Anandapuram village suggesting the opposite to the above. The apparent contradiction will be resolved in the logit analysis 4.3.

4. 3 The Logit Results

We have identified two distinct categories of non-farm employment: modern wage-employed and traditional wage-employed. Moreover data for farm households (households with no main worker principally in non-farm employment, i.e. 'pure' farm HHs) have been collected. It is useful to separate these categories in order to capture the dynamics of both growth linkages from agriculture and distress diversification whilst bearing in mind that multiple factors influence the labour market. The equation used is of the form[23] (Appendix Table 4.1 pooled data correlation matrix).

$$Y_i = a_o + b_1 X_{1i} + b_2 X_{2i} + b_3 X_{3i} + b_4 X_{4i} + b_5 X_{5i} \ldots\ldots b_{14} X_{14i} + b_{17} X_{17i} + u_i$$

Where i denotes households, and

Y_i = A HH is engaged in non-farm activity, if any working member has, as a primary occupation at least 183 days in a year (in one or several activities).

X_1 = Farm Size operated (number of acres operated by the HH)

X_2 = Levels of schooling (number of years of schooling)

X_3 = Per acre value of agri-output per year (in Indian Rs)

X_4 = Household head age in years

X_5 = Household head age^2 in years

X_6 = Size of household (Number of family members including children in the HH).

X_7 = Caste dummy 1 (if the HH is from a backward caste the dummy takes the value of 1, 0 otherwise)

X_8 = Caste dummy 2 (if the HH is from a scheduled caste or scheduled tribe the dummy takes the value of 1, 0 otherwise)

X_9 = Migration-in (if the HH has migrated - at any point in time prior to being interviewed into the village the dummy takes the value 1 or 0 otherwise).

X_{10} = September-November (Dummy takes value 1, if this is the period during which the HH works the most days)

X_{11} = December-February (as above)

X_{12} = March-May (as above)

X_{13} = Skilled/unskilled (if the household is skilled the dummy takes 1, 0 otherwise)

X_{14} = Poor/non-poor (if the HH is poor the dummy takes 1, 0 otherwise)

X_{15} = Village Dummy if the HH is in the developed Veeravalli it takes 0 and 1 otherwise

X_{16} = Interaction variable $X_2 \cdot X_{15}$

X_{17} = Interaction variable $X_{12} \cdot X_{15}$

u = Disturbance term with the classical properties.

In the logit regressions the log likelihood function is maximised using interactive techniques given in the programme LIMDEP. For the model specification details see [Appendix Table to chapter 4 (b)]. The interpretation of coefficients in the logit model is less straightforward than in OLS. Usually, a positive coefficient for an independent variable reveals that a high value of that variable will increase the probability of a household being upwardly mobile. The marginal effects of the regressors, X, on the probabilities are not equal to the coefficients. Instead, a further calculation is required to obtain the marginal effects (for continuous variables) or impact effects (for the dummy variables). We report the marginal effects by estimating them at the mean values of the explanatory variables and likewise for the impact effects.[24] The intercepts are not significant, which suggests that no important variable has been omitted from the model. The overall predictability of the model is given by the frequencies of the "predicted" outcomes[25] although a Mac Fadden R^2 has also been calculated.

Log-likelihood ratio tests were carried out to eliminate some of the variables of the model with pooled data (see Table 4.25).

4.3.1 General Results

Given these equations each of them will have to be estimated for two villages. But before estimating separately for each of the villages we can impose a restriction that the villages can be pooled together and thus that the data can be considered jointly. If these restrictions cannot be statistically rejected, the pooled model would then be the more efficient procedure. In order to test these restrictions we have carried the necessary statistical tests. The results are reported in Table 2.25. These statistics are derived from the standard log likelihood ratio test statistic. Our results suggest that in the case of 3 models the restrictions of pooled estimation cannot be rejected. We have therefore estimated these models with pooled data. For other models we need to estimate the models separately for each of the village.

4.3.1.1 Results for Anandapuram:

Logit regressions for which dependent variable have been estimated separately for Anandapuram and Veeravalli because the log likelihood ratio is higher than the critical value for NF1 model (see Table 4.25)-i.e. we accept NF2 where (see Table 4.26) the pooling hypothesis is rejected. We provide interpretations only where the variables are significant. We have not used any interaction dummies for these variables.[26]

The coefficient on the land holding is negative. This implies a negative correlation between the size of land operated and the probability of being involved with non-farm employment. This suggests that the growth (AGL) linkage impact on modern RNFE dominates the distress diversification (ADD) impact on traditional RNFE. This may be attributed to the predominance

Table 4.25 : Log-likelihood Ratios to Test the Relevance of Pooling Data

Models	*Pooled data Log-Likelihood* L^R	*Ananda-puram Log-Likelihood* L''_1	*Veeravalli Log-Likelihood* L''_2	*Log-Likelihood Ratio Formula* $-2[L^R_{-(}L''_{1+}L''_{2)}]$	*No. of Explanatory Variables for Pooled data [1]*	*No. Explanatory Variables for the Villages [2] Village1 + Village 2*	*K [3]*	χ_K^2 *at 5%*	*Reject Y/N 5%*
Non Farm 1	-308.31	-111.12	-184.79	24.8	16	15+15	14	23.68	yes
Non Farm 2	-301.77	-111.12	-184.79	11.72	18	15+15	12	21.03	no
Moder 1	-231.25	-105.28	-117.13	17.68	16	15+15	14	23.68	no
Moder 2	-228.24	-105.28	-117.13	11.66	18	15+15	12	21.03	no

Notes : Modern 2 and Non Farm 2 include interaction variables.

- K = number of parameters used in χ_K^2.
- Column [3]: column [2] - column [1] - the constant.
- H_o: *the null hypothesis* that the pooled villages data and the data of the separate villages are the same.
- The last column relates as to whether we can/cannot reject the null hypothesis. "NO" stands for rejection.
- Note that although L''_1 and L''_2 are the same for some of the columns, the difference lies in the pooled data model (L^R) which contains interaction variables.

Table 4.26: Logit Model of the Probability of a Household Engaged in Non-farm Employment in Sample Households in each Village, 1993-94, [the Dependent is Non-farm 1, all farm = 0].

Variables	*Result [Eq.1] Anandapuram*		*Eq. [2] Veeravalli*	
	Coefficients	*Marginal/ Impact Effects*	*Coefficients*	*Marginal/ Impact Effects*
Constant	3.45		1.04	
	(1.41)		(0.68)	
Land Holding	-0.642	-0.0391	-0.538	-0.131
Size	(-3.09)***	(-2.74)***	(-4.78)***	(-4.58)***
Education (years	0.428	0.0261	0.136	0.0332
of education)	(4.06)***	(3.75)***	(3.74)***	(3.76)***
AGR (per acre	-0.0000619	-0.00000377	-0.000114	-0.0000276
value of agri.output)	(-1.85)*	(-1.79)*	(-2.96)***	(-2.99)***
HH Head Age	0.0207	0.00126	-0.0924	-0.0225
	(0.24)	(0.24)	(-1.58)	(-1.58)
HH Head Age^2	-0.000241	-0.0000147	0.000890	0.000217
	(-0.27)	(-0.27)	(1.51)	(1.51)
Family Size	0.0623	0.00380	0.148	0.0360
	(0.54)	(0.54)	(1.58)	(1.58)
Caste Dummy 1	-0.0295	-0.0180	-0.653	-0.159
	(-0.34)	(-0.34)	(-1.88)*	(-1.88)*
Caste Dummy 2	-0.652	-0.0397	-0.755	-0.183
	(-0.68)	(-0.68)	(-1.73)*	(-1.73)*
Migration In	0.916	0.0558	0.867	0.211
	(1.39)	(1.38)	(2.31)**	(2.31)**
September -	-3.489	-0.213	0.226	0.0549
November	(-3.15)***	(-2.93)***	(0.37)	(0.37)
December -	-2.459	-0.150	0.759	0.184
February	(-2.19)**	(-2.20)**	(1.27)	(1.27)
March - May	0.0708	0.00431	2.71	0.659
	(0.06)	(0.06)	(4.48)***	(4.47)***
Skilled 1,	-0.0109	-0.000663	0.865	0.210
Unskilled 0	(-0.02)	(-0.02)	(2.41)**	(2.41)**
Poor 1, Non-	-0.537	-0.0327	-0.865	-0.210
Poor 0	(-1.31)	(-1.25)	(-2.56)***	(-2.55)***
Log - Likelihood	-111.12		- 184.79	
Chi - Squared (14)	135.35***		267.02***	
Number of Observations	354		465	
Mac Fadden R^2	0.38		0.42	
% Correct Prediction	86.16		84.52	

Notes : The t-ratios are in brackets.
- *** Significant at 1 per cent level; ** Significant at 5 per cent level, * Significant at 10 per cent level.

of small and marginal farmers in this village. As such the lower the farm size the higher the probability will be of it being engaged in non-farm employment.

The marginal effect of a unit increase in landholding on non-farm employment at the means[27] of all variables is -0.04. This implies that, at the means, if land holding increases by one unit (one acre in this exercise) the probability of non-farm employment decreases by 4 percentage points.

Similarly at the means of the data if education increases by 1 year the probability of RNFE increases by 2.6 percentage points. The coefficient has the expected relationship and is statistically significant at the 1 per cent level. Therefore, it can be said that the higher the years of schooling, the greater will be the likelihood of being engaged in the RNFS. Later on we shall argue that this is a net effect; the impact of schooling via higher 'modern' RNFE exceeds its impact via lower 'traditional' RNFE.

We found a negative link between land productivity (per-acre agricultural output produced by the households) and non-farm employment. However, the estimated coefficient is very small. However, even when agricultural output increases this creates a somewhat negative influence on non-farm employment.

We inserted three dummy variables to assess the seasonal impact of non-farm employment. September-November and December-February are the peak seasons when there are numerous agricultural activities to perform. As a result we would expect a negative sign on the coefficients of these two dummy variables. The results are similar to our expectations, since the coefficients on these dummies are negative as well as being significant. These results imply that a household with an average set of characteristics is 21.3 percentage points less likely to be involved in RNFE in the peak September to November period i.e. if HH works more days in September-November than in March-May or December-February; or 0 otherwise. On the other hand, the impact of December to February peak season reduces the possibility of RNFE of a typical household by 15 percentage points. The season March to May is considered to be a slack period in agricultural activities and, as a result, there is not enough scope for agricultural employment. So ideally the impact of this season on non-farm employment should be positive. In our case the coefficient of March to May is positive but fails to be significant.

Our analysis in the context of the relatively less developed village suggests that land holding size and agricultural output per acre have a negative effect on RNFE. This suggests that for RNFE as a whole growth linkages to the modern sector. On the other hand education has a positive impact. The link between education and RNFS is strong. This supports wider (ODL) hypothesis.

4.3.1.2 *Logit Analysis for Veeravalli*

It is observed from the estimates that the coefficient on the land holding for Veeravalli is also negative. The marginal effect obtained from (results [2] Table 4.26) is -0.13. This indicates that at the means of the data if the land holding increases by one acre the probability of non-farm employment decreases by 13 percentage points. The coefficient obtained implies that even in the relatively more developed village there is also a negative link between the size of land ownership and the probability of non-farm employment. We observed a similar relationship in the literature review. This suggests either that, the growth (AGL) linkage impact on modern RNFE dominates the distress diversification (ADD) impact on traditional RNFE.

On the other hand, the means of the data obtained show that with one extra year of schooling the probability of RNFE increases by 3.3 percentage points. For Anandapuram the increase was 2.6 percentage points. The difference between the two villages may have been due to (a) because there are differences between the means of the education obtained by villagers, increase in education in Anandapuram, for work in more RNFS, compared to Veeravalli. In Veeravalli the mean is higher and thereby induces less RNFE. This supports wider (ODL) hypothesis.

Per acre value of agricultural output the coefficients are significant at 10 per cent level for Anandapuram, so size can be usefully compared. All we can compared is that in Anandapuram there is no effect, but on Veeravalli a significant though small, effect. This suggests that for RNFE as a whole growth linkages (AGL) to the modern sector.

The migration-in dummy is found to be positively associated with RNFE as expected. A HH that has migrated into the village increases the probability of RNF by 21.1 percentage points. This is particularly true in the case of relatively more developed Veeravalli, this shows growth linkages (AGL) and expansion of RNFE which might in turn induce migration.

The season dummy March to May is found to be significant at the 1 per cent level and the coefficient has the expected positive sign. It may be inferred that the "doing most work in agricultural slack season March to May" has an "household that HH has a main worker principally engaged in non-farm employment. But the causality is the other way round. This supports the wider (ODL) hypothesis.

We included two dummies to consider the caste impact of caste on non-farm employment. Caste dummy two is found to be negatively associated with RNFS as expected but not significant.

The coefficient related to skill has as expected a positive sign and is significant at the 5 per cent level. The impact effect is 0.21. This implies that if the HH has acquired skills by way of training and education the probability of non-farm employment increases 21 percentage points. This variable is significant only in Veeravalli, not in Anandapuram perhaps because most RNFE is modern in Veeravalli but traditional in Anandapuram. The developed village supporting the growth linkages (AGL) hypothesis, into modern non-farm sector.

On the other hand the coefficient for the poor/non-poor dummy variable reveals a negative link between being poor and the probability of non-farm employment. This can be attributed to the RNFS requiring certain levels of skills as well

Table 4.27: Logit Analysis of the Probability of a Household Engaged in Non-farm Employment in pooled Sample Households in Each Village, 1993-94. [the Dependent is Non-farm is 1 and all farm = 0].

Variables	*Result [3] Coefficients*	*Marginal/ Impact effects*
Constant	1.388	
	(1.14)	
Land Holding Size	-0.555	-0.0898
	(-5.82)***	(-5.06)***
EDUCATION (Years of Education)	0.153	0.0247
	(4.33)***	(4.14)***
AGR (per acre value of agri. output)	-0.0000860	-0.0000139
	(-3.47)***	(-3.52)***
Household Head Age	-0.637E-01	-0.0103
	(-1.33)	(-1.33)
Household Head Age^2	0.630E-03	0.000102
	(1.29)	(1.29)
Family Size	0.111	0.179
	(1.54)	(1.54)
Caste Dummy 1	-0.643	-0.0104
	(-2.07)**	(-2.08)**
Caste Dummy 2	-0.873	-0.141
	(-2.31)**	(-2.30)**
Migration In	0.881	0.142
	(2.78)***	(2.76)***
September - November	-0.919	-0.148
	(-2.26)**	(-2.22)**
December - January	-0.113	-0.0183
	(-0.28)	(-0.28)
March-may	1.78	0.288
	(4.08)***	(4.05)***
SK	0.529	0.856
	(1.87)*	(1.86)*
Poor	-0.716	-0.116
	(-2.79)***	(-2.74)***
Village Dummy 2	1.56 (5.38)***	0.253 (4.89)***
Mamint2	1.570	
	(2.30)**	
Eduint	0.239	
	(2.41)**	
Log - Likelihood	-301.77	
Chi- Squared (13)	440.45***	
Number of Observations	819	
Mac Fadden R^2	0.42	
% Correct Prediction	85.10	

Notes : As before (for Table 4.26).

as a specific amount of education. Poor people do not obtain these skills and, as such, the probability of RNFS decreases by up to 21 percentage points for poor household. By implication this suggests that household development out of poverty is associated with increased RNFE prospects (ODL).

The coefficients associated with household head age, household head age^2 and family size have expected signs but are not significant, even at the 10 per cent significant level. This indicates a weak relationship with RNFE in this model. Seasonal dummies September to November and December to February also not significant and have unexpected positive signs. This may be because consumption linkages induce little scope for RNFS in those periods.

4.3.1.3 The aggregate (pooled) results:

The results of the aggregate exercises (for which data for Veeravalli and Anandapuram have been pooled) and the statistical significance of the variables are presented in Table 4.27. To identify the factors which are responsible for RNFE at the household level, one logit model is estimated. When interaction variables are included the log likelihood ratio is less than the critical value (NF2 see Table 4.25). Interaction variables were introduced to test changes of the relationship between (1) the village dummy and education and (2) the village dummy and March-May season variables. This is to observe whether the slope of the line is changing or not.

We shall now discuss these results in turn. The chi-squared test of the log likelihood values for this model is significant at the 1 per cent level. We observe that some variables (land holding size, education, per acre value of agricultural output, migration into the villages, season March-May, poor and village dummy) are significant at 1 per cent, and two variables (caste dummy one and two, season September-November, Mam interaction and education interaction) at the 5 per cent significance level.

The coefficients of land holding size, education, per acre value of agricultural output, caste dummy1, caste dummy2, migration in, September to November, March to May, Skill, poor, and village dummy have the expected signs and are significant.

In general we get the results which we expected for Veeravalli for the pooled data - but for Anandapuram alone the expected effects are obtained only for landholding size, years of education, and seasonality.

For the pooled sample, the land variable is found to be negatively associated with RNFE (as expected and statistically significant at the 1 per cent level). As land size increases the participation of the household in non-farm activities declines. To some extent this relationship may capture distress-diversification. Land concentration can lead to an overspill of surplus labour into unproductive non-farm jobs

The important result of this model from the RNFS point of view is found to be the coefficient for education. It may be noted that the coefficient is positive and significant at the 1 per cent level, indicating a rather strong relationship with RNFE. Its marginal effect is positive, suggesting that households with higher education are more likely to seek non-farm employment in rural villages. The marginal affect is 0.0247. One year of education increases the probability of non-farm employment by 2.47 percentage points. But this is more in Veeravalli and less in Anandapuram It is understandable that, where the education of household workers is higher, they are (a) reluctant to work in the farm sector as they have better prospects elsewhere (b) more attractive to RNFE employers. Education is robustly significant.

The coefficient for per acre value of agricultural output is significant at the 1 per cent significance level indicating a strong negative relationship with RNFE - but the effect is tiny

As expected the caste (social background) variables CD1 and CD2 (upper caste being the base) is found to be negatively associated with non-farm employment. If the worker belongs to a SC or a ST community - or even to a Backward caste - s/he has relatively less scope for non-farm employment compared to a worker from the upper castes. This may be due to low levels of literacy; skill, training and social structure among these caste groups are lacking. The present caste system would seem not to encourage the diversification of these caste groups into the RNFS.

The village dummy (Anandapuram = 1, Veeravalli = 0) is statistically significant. This shows there are significant differences between the two villages. The model of rural RNFE spelled out here is that households are more inclined to non-farm activities in Anandapuram, with the coefficient being positive. This is as expected, in the sense that in Anandapuram, which is agriculturally backward. "Agricultural backwardness" is already captured in "output per acre" (i.e. gross land productivity) in Table 4.31 and 'skills' and 'years of education' captured other 'backwardness' variables. Perhaps it is the nearness of Visakhapatnam which causes that people of given skills and literacy in Anandapuram to move to Visakhapatnam city. In Veeravalli they would stay in their work in the RNFS. People are more likely to move towards more types of RNFS - perhaps mainly traditional RNFS we explore this below.

Two interaction variables were used: education with village dummy (EDUINT), and the season March-May with village dummy (MAMINT2). They are significant at the 5 per cent level. If the households in less developed villages engage in non-farm employment during March-May, the household scores 1 on the interaction March-May * village dummy. This result indicate an increased probability of being employed within a non- farm in March-May in less developed Anandapuram. This shows that the seasonal effect varies across the villages. This result indicates an increased probability of employment in less developed village compared with those in more developed village. To summarise it may thus be inferred from the results, that per acre value of agricultural output (growth linkages between farm and non-farm), social background such as caste and seasonality are important factors of non-farm employment at the household level. It suggests that economic, environmental and social factors would matter for the RNFS.

Skilled variable significant at 5 per cent in Veeravalli, not significant in Anandapuram.

Table 4.28 : Logit Analysis of the Probability of a Household being Engaged in Modern RNFE only for Sample Households with a main Worker Principally Engaged in Non-farm Employment in Villages, 1993-94, pooled data: [the Dependent Variable is Modern RNFS = 1, Traditional RNFS = 0]

Variables	*Result. [4] Coefficients*	*Marginal/ Impact effects*	*Result [5] Coefficient*	*Marginal/ Impact effects*
Constant	-0.998		-1.261	
	(-0.74)		(-0.93)	
Land Holding Size	-0.222	-0.0417	-0.253	-0.0480
(In acres owned)	(-1.95)**	(-1.95)**	(-2.14)**	(-2.13)**
Education	0.28	0.0528	0.313	0.0592
(Years of education)	(8.56)***	(8.22)***	(7.41)***	(6.89)***
AGR (per acre value	0.0000491	0.00000921	0.0000463	0.00000876
of agri.output)	(1.75)*	(1.76)*	(1.63)	(1.64)
HH Head Age	-0.0963	-0.0181	-0.0917	-0.0174
	(-1.83)*	(-1.82)*	(-1.72)*	(-1.72)*
HH Head Age^2	0.00115	0.000215	0.00112	0.000212
	(2.08)**	(2.07)**	(2.01)**	(2.00)**
Family Size	0.0587	0.0110	0.0485	0.00919
	(0.80)	(0.81)	(0.66)	(0.66)
Caste Dummy 1	-0.0327	-0.00613	-0.0522	-0.00989
	(-0.11)	(-0.11)	(-0.18)	(-0.18)
Caste Dummy 2	0.500	0.0938	0.453	0.0859
	(1.19)	(1.19)	(1.06)	(1.06)
Migration in	0.590	0.111	0.630	0.119
	(1.98)**	(1.97)**	(2.08)**	(2.08)**
Skilled 1, Unskilled 0	0.764	0.143	0.889	0.168
	(2.84)***	(2.87)***	(3.18)***	(3.20)***
Poor 1, Non-Poor 0	-0.555	-0.104	-0.535	-0.101
	(-1.89)*	(-1.91)*	(-1.81)*	(-1.83)*
Village Dummy	-0.469	-0.0879	-0.547	-0.104
(Anandapurm1)	(-1.73)*	(-1.74)*	(-1.19)	(-1.20)
September-November	-0.505	-0.946	-0.332	-0.629
	(-0.90)	(-0.90)	(-0.58)	(-0.58)
December-February	0.478	0.0897	0.586	0.111
	(0.95)	(0.95)	(1.11)	(1.11)

Contd....

Table 4.28 : (Contd....)

Variables	*Result. [4] Coefficients*	*Marginal/ Impact effects*	*Result [5] Coefficient*	*Marginal/ Impact effects*
March-May	0.194 (0.39)	0.0930 (0.37)	0.0191 (0.04)	0.00362 (0.04)
Eduinter 2			-0.0667 (-1.03)	
Mam Interaction 2			0.866 (2.08**)	
Log - Likelihood	-231.25		-228.24	
Chi - Squared (15)(17)	218.66***		224.69***	
Number Of Observations	545		545	
Mac Fadden R^2	0.32		0.33	
% Correct Prediction	82.57		82.39	

Notes : As before. (for Table 4.30)

More extra chances for educated in RNFE in backward village because of distress diversification. It is odd result for 'education' happening because we (in effects) hold skills constant i.e., given skills, education is doing more for RNFE prospects if interacted with education in the backward village - but that is because education effect in inducing higher skills, which in turn increase RNFE chance, is between into the coefficients or skills, which induces, as expected, is significant in Veeravalli not Anandapuram.

To summarise it may thus be inferred from the results, land holding size, years of workers education, per acre value of agricultural output, social background such as caste, migration, seasonality, skills, absence of poverty are important factors of non-farm employment at the household level. It suggests that economic, environmental and social factors would matter for the RNFS.

4.3.2 Results for Modern/traditional Variable:

The results of the two logit models taking modern/ traditional non-farm employment as the dependent variable are presented in Table 4.29. We observe that two variables education and skilled/unskilled, are significant at the 1 per cent level. Migration into the villages, HH age, land holding size are significant at the 5 per cent level. March-May interacted with village dummy2 and land holding size are significant at the 10 per cent level. The chi-squared test of the hypothesis that this model was rejected was significant at the 1 per cent level.

The coefficients which have the expected signs are land holding size, education, caste 2, skilled/unskilled, village dummy, family size, September-November, March-May, household head age and poor.

Whether a HH is likely to have a main worker primarily in RNFS. Whether a HH, that does have such a worker, is likely to place him/her in the Modern RNFE. Especially if the traditional RNFS is a substantial part of (the total RNFS), there is no obvious reason to make the same predictions about what the determining variable will be, or about their signs.

However, caste dummy 2 and December-February have the opposite sign of what was predicted. The most important variables in terms of marginal effects of the model are education, skilled/unskilled.

Education is highly significant and positive. Thus, being educated matters in the determination of the probability of a household being engaged in the modern RNFS. The reverse also holds, so that the probability of participation in the traditional sector decreases with the level of education (schooling). It seems to be confirmed this for traditional as against modern activities - but not for traditional as against 'other activities' including farming. This is also possible.

As for skills, the positive sign means that the probability of participation in the modern sector is less for HHs that possess traditional skills. However, that participation in the RNFS is less than could be caused by a shift in production activities from the traditional to the modern sector following development. Skills are particularly important in the developed village which support the ODL hypothesis.

Land (the size of HH land holding) has a negative sign and is significant at the 10 per cent level suggesting that the probability of a household already in RNFE being engaged in modern non-farm activities may be lower in cases where the size of land holdings is comparatively higher.

It goes against the simple 'growth linkages' hypothesis at household level - though it supports the version that such a hypothesis works best for poorer/smaller farmers. The growth linkage impact on modern non-farm employment dominates the distress diversification (ADD) impact on traditional non-farm employment.

Affluent families in agriculture may not go for RNFE, particularly in the less developed village, whereas the poor sections of the village will work in the RNFS to ensure their survival, the RNFS acts for this group, as a residual sector. However, absence of growth linkages at household levels even if it is the case does not mean that much linkages are absent across households i.e., it may well still be true that villages showing greater agricultural prosperity also demand more villages non-farm products, i.e. as agricultural yields as land size increases. Thus the developed village has more participation in non-farm activities due to agriculture's location advantage.

The demographic variable HH age^2 is positive and significant at the 5 per cent level. HH head age was not significant although both have expected signs.

Households whose main activity (all activity) occurs in the December-February period are more likely - if in RNFE -to be in the modern non-farm sector. The probability of participation on modern activity is higher among the self employed. Most traditional activities are associated with self-employment, with not wage employment. As for the 'poor' variable, it is negatively associated with modern activities.

Two interaction variables were used: education with village dummy (not significant), and the season March-May with village dummy. If the households in the developed village engage in modern farm employment during March-May, the household scores 1 on the interaction March-may * village dummy. Thus March-May * Village dummy turned to be significant at the 5 per cent level. This shows that the seasonal effect varies across the villages.

The model of modern/traditional non-farm employment is better in identifying the key factors associated with modern non-farm employment at the HH level. Education, skills, season, land holding size are important factors. Migration into the villages, and per acre value of agricultural output the growth (AGL) linkage impact on modern non-farm employment play crucial roles the developed village.

We have identified landholding size as consistently unfavourable to RNFS to RNFS participation (and within RNFS, to modernity), years of education as consistently favourable; and in-migration, and a work peak in March-may, as generally favourable.

Thus more education, fewer big land holdings, would reduce poverty as well as increasing modernising RNFE; smaller families, older HH heads, would reduce poverty but not affect RNFE; and in-migration would increase modernise RNFE, but not affect poverty. The policies likely, on these findings, to raise and modern RNFS participation be good or bad for the poor is important. Education supports wider (ODL) hypothesis.

Table 4.29 presents key results (from Table 4.26, 4.27 and 4.28). For Anandapuram one acre increases in land holding decreases the probability of HH having non-farm employment by 3.91 percentage points. For Veeravalli village the corresponding figure is very high and it is 13.1 percentage points. For pooled regression the marginal effect close 9 percentage points (see Table 4.29).

The next explanatory variable is years of education. The marginal effect of education on the dependent variable is also higher in the village compared to Anandapuram, a one year increase in education of workers raise the probability of non-farm employment by 3.3 percentage points. the comparable figure for Anandapuram is 2.6 percentage points which almost similar for the pooled regression results.

Table 4.29 Key Results Table (from 4.27, 4.28 and 4.29 Tables)

	Marginal/impact effects				
Variables	*Anandapuram*	*Veeravalli*	*Pooled*	*Modern/tradi*	*Modern/tradi*
Land Holding Size	-0.0391***	-0.131***	-0.0898***	-0.04**	-0.05**
Education (years of education)	0.0261***	0.0332***	0.0247***	0.05***	0.06***
Per acre value of agri.output	-0.00000377*	-0.000028***	-0.000014***	0.00*	0.00*
HH head age	not significant	not significant	not significant	-0.02*	-0.02*
HH head age²	not significant	not significant	not significant	0.00**	0.00**
Caste dummy 1	not significant	-0.159*	-0.0104**	not significant	not significant
Caste dummy 2	not significant	-0.183*	-0.0141**	not significant	not significant
Migration in	not significant	0.211**	0.142***	0.11**	0.12**
September -November	-0.213***	not significant	-0.148**	not significant	not significant
December - February	-0.150**	not significant	not significant	not significant	not significant
March - May	not significant	0.659***	0.288***	not significant	not significant
Skilled 1, Unskilled 0	not significant	0.210**	0.856*	0.95***	0.17***
Poor 1, Non-poor 0	not significant	-0.210***	-0.116***	-0.09*	-0.10*
village dummy (A=1 V=0)	-	-	0.253***	-0.37*	not significant
log - Likelihood	-111.12	-184.79	-301.77	-231.25	-228.24
% correct prediction	86.16	84.52	85.10	82.57	82.39

Notes : *** Significant at 1 per cent level, ** Significant at 5 per cent level, * Significant at 10 per cent.

For per acre value of agricultural output it is found that in Veeravalli this particular variable is significant at 1 per cent level but in Anandapuram the variable was significant only to somewhat reduce the value of confidence (at 10 per cent). However, the same variable was also significant at 10 per cent level in the pooled regression. Although a significantly negative marginal effect is being detected what is very striking about these coefficients are that all very close to zero. For the impact effect of the caste variables is found that if the HH belong to backward caste with the given average characteristics the probability of non-farm employment decrease 1.04 percentage points in poled regression and exact the same impact can also be found in the case of caste dummy 2 variable.

The dummy variable for skilled and poor were found to significant only in the Veeravalli with and equal size of impact effect.

We can now conclude from the above discussion that land holding size per acre value of agricultural output can have a negative effect on non-farm employment. This is also expected *a priori* because the more land a HH possesses the more likely it is that it will be involved in agricultural activities. On the other hand, for education the relationship is positive because the higher the level of education the higher the chance of finding employment outside agriculture.

Some general observations moreover emerge. Much more of a HH's propensity to have a main worker principally in the RNFS is explained in Veeravalli than in Anandapuram (in terms of log-likelihood, c^2 tests, the number of significant variables, the size of marginal impact coefficients] and in pooled data than in dealing with Veeravalli and Anandapuram separately. Land holding size (- vely) and years of education (+vely) are significant in all cases. Migration-in is significant and positive, except in Anandapuram, similarly skills and absence of poverty.

4.3.3 Comparison of Household-level with District-level Determinants of RNFS Shares and Explanation for Differences

It is important for an assessment of the determinants of RNFE in AP to compare the regression analysis of the log model for pooled data and villages separately household model explaining per cent of households with a main worker in RNFE, with per cent of RNFE shares district model explaining presented in Chapter 3) and the logit model at the household level (presented in this Chapter 4). We are aware, however that 5 different models have been used for our analysis purposes. We start here by recalling the findings for the district before spelling out those for the households. We then try to generalise our findings.

The log model for RNFE shares and the linear model for growth between 1981-91 have identified some of the factors determining the proportion of main worker in RNFE at district level. The analysis showed that in all the models, the variables that were significantly associated with non-farm employment varied, depending on whether data was considered at the district level for the total labour force or was disaggregated-by gender and/or by RNF sub-sectors.

For RNFE shares, agricultural development (irrigation) is a significantly dominant factor, confirm the hypothesis that growth linkages from irrigated agriculture lead to modern RNFE whereas for RNFE growth, infrastructure and human capital i.e. roads and literacy (except for females) are significant factors for both males and females, support the wider/overall 'development' linkage (ODL) hypothesis that traditional RNFE share rises with lower levels of literacy.

In these two models the common significant factor for the sub-sectors are agricultural development and literacy. For most sub sectors, agricultural development is the main factor tending to raise the shares of RNFE (HHI, Mining, Construction) or in their growth (mining, non-HHI, Transport) again supporting growth linkages.

At the district level, poor women are less likely to participate in RNFE. Only one factor i.e. per cent of bank branches (see Table 3.16 part 2) is positively associated with female RNFE. All other factors (banks and bigger villages) have a negative impact on their participation. The determinants of female RNFE are distinct from those observed for male RNFE although for the latter, the year dummy matter suggested changes and increased participation in the RNFS between 1981 and1991. For females, it is negative at the district level. Just as the poor are generally less likely to participate in RNFE, the poor in the developed village and the self employed poor (compared with waged poor) are less likely to participate in RNFE. Most of the poor participate in agricultural labour work, oppose the hypothesised growth linkages (AGL).

From the HH level analysis, farm size is negative as expected in all the logit models. In the case of district shares, farm size is also negative except for mining and quarrying. This is one common interesting factor in all the models, support for the hypothesis (AGL) that traditional RNFE share rises with distress diversification by those with little or no land at district and household levels.

Turning to the education variable, this is positive for the developed and less developed village and for pooled data at household level. For growth at district level, education is also positive but a negative relationship is observed for total shares. It could be the case that at district level, traditional RNFE might dominate. The common finding for shares, growth and household level models is that traditional RNFE is dominated by relatively less literate people whereas modern RNFE is dominated by more literate people, support the wider/overall development linkage (ODL) hypothesis that traditional RNFE share rises with loser levels of literacy.

Demographic factors such as HH head age, family size, migration in, seasonality, and skills are important at the household level which are not included in district level data due to non-availability of data. Seasonality is important for RNFE because when agriculture is active, non-farm employment is less prevalent.

Conclusion: Positive linkages from agricultural development to RNFE are revealed at both district and household levels. Households with better agricultural resources are also more prone to have RNFS work. Modern RNFE requires human skills such as education, whereas traditional RNFE requires lower levels of education. Distress diversification is likely to be dominant in traditional occupations. Seasonality dominates participation in the RNFS during the agriculturally slack season.

Land holding size and the levels of literacy findings about the determinants of district level shares of total, males and females and key-sector (modern, traditional), RNFE are confirmed i.e. also significant and with same signs as household-level determinants of participation in RNFE.

Table 4.30 : Summary of the Signs and Significance of the Coefficients Obtained in the Logit

Independent variables	*Anandapuram RNFE = 1 all Farm = 0*	*Veeravalli RNFE = 1 all Farm = 0*	*Pooled RNFE =1 all Farm = 0*	*Modern: 1 Traditional: 0 (RNFE HHs only)*
Constant				
Land	(-)***	(-)***	(-)***	(-)**
Education	(+)***	(+)***	(+)***	(+)***
Agrl. Per Acre Value of Output	(-)*	(-)***	(-)***	(+)*
HH Head Age				(-)*
HH Head Age2				(+)**
Family Size				
Caste Dummy1		(-)*	(-)**	
Caste Dummy2		(-)*	(-)**	
Migration		(+)**	(+)***	(+)**
September-october	(-)***		(-)**	
December - February	(-)**			
March - May		(+)***	(+)***	
Skill		(+)**		(+)***
Poor		(-)***	(-)***	
Village Dummy			(+)***	
Linter2			(+)**	
Mamint2			(+)**	(+)***

Notes : The signs of the coefficients are reported in brackets unless insignificant.

*** Significant at 1 per cent, ** Significant at 5 per cent, *Significant at 10 per cent levels.

Other findings are (a) opposite or (b) not confirmed at household level, because somewhat different variables model differences or, reasonable to expect different causal processed for households and individuals.

Conclusions of Part 2 of the Logit Results of the Chapter

The logit regression results reported in this chapter are summarised in Table 4.30. The conclusion for the Logit Regression analysis of the determinants of whether a household has a main worker in non-farm employment in Anandapuram, in Veeravalli and in the pooled data for both villages, reveals that it is significantly negatively related to land holding size. This relationship is stronger (i.e. the decrease is greater) in the agriculturally developed village compared to less developed village. This suggests either that, for total RNFE, the growth (AGL) linkage impact on modern non-farm employment 'dominates' the distress diversification (ADD) impact on traditional non-farm employment, or that modern, 'agriculture-stimulated' activity has higher weight (or some of each). In either case, of big farmers are less likely to have a main RNFE, this suggests that farm land actively reduces total-RNFE participation. Households with less farm land do more RNFE supports distress diversification (ADD) dominates growth linkages. In the pooled data set; for a one acre increase in land holding size, the probability of household having any non-farm employment decreases by 9 percentage points, and in modern non-farm employment decreases marginal impact effect more in the developed village by 4 percentage points. The point strengthened by fact that

However, this is of course the multivariate effect of farm size; because there are higher levels of production following from ownership of more land, the production-consumption linkages mean that the likelihood of non-farm employment is increased through another channel. Wealthier villagers invest more in their children's education, which increases the likelihood of them taking non-farm employment; they also consume more, meaning more work for others. In the pooled data set one more year in education increases the chances of getting modern non-farm employment by 5 percentage points. It seems some of the results have economic and non-economic barriers.

The more land a household has, the less likely that this household itself will be involved in agricultural activity. But this 'same-house' approach conceals the fact that the production linkages between the farm and non-farm are strong consume more, meaning more work for other households. Also there are production linkages. Households with more land require agricultural mechanisation (tractors and threshing machines, etc.) which, in turn, creates more non-farm employment but less so than animal draught, so small farms have higher propensity to use local RNFE (e.g. Hazell and Ramasamy (1992)] Meanwhile, the capital generated from the agricultural output may be invested in non-farm activities.[12]

Education is significantly positively related to non-farm employment in each village, and on the pooled data. The marginal effect of education on the probability of HH having non-farm employment is greater in the more developed village compared to the less developed village. In this case, the effect of literacy in raising demand and/or supply for 'modern' RNFE appears to outweigh the effect in reducing them for traditional RNFE.

Per acre value of agricultural output is significant negatively related to household RNFE likelihood in Veeravalli and the pooled regression ($p = .01$) but in Anandapuram the variable was significant only to the reduced level of confidence ($p = .1$). This supports that for RNFE as a whole growth linkages to the modern sector, from agricultural growth, are very slightly outweighed in these villages by distress diversification to traditional RNFE. Land holding size and per acre value of agricultural output going opposite side in the case of modern RNFE. However, the elasticity for value of agricultural output is tiny and very close to zero.

If the household belongs to BC, SC or ST the probability of non-farm employment decreases by 1.04 percentage points in the pooled and Veeravalli regressions. For members of these castes (BC, SC and ST) there is less likelihood of non-farm employment: these groups are mainly agricultural labourers for non-farm employment requires resources such as capital, education, technology, and political influence, which are available mostly to the higher caste elite minority. The point is social status makes harder, social status effects economic status. These groups are often locked farm labour, then neither good nor bad agricultural growth will much affect their RNFE share, which will be below that of other households. But in villages with, tanneries the result would be the opposite, again very important but again saying little or nothing about distress diversification verses growth linkages. Lower caste people may feel inhibited from entering certain types of RNFE because they fear discrimination treatment from employment and fellow workers. Also lower castes even among poor this makes their children achieve higher levels of education, this intern restrict modern RNFE.

In Veeravalli one would expect these growth linkages a greater expansion of modern RNFE relative to traditional RNFE than in less developed village. This is likely to make it harder for backward castes to engage RNFE in the more developed village for both the referred identification earlier (education or fear of discrimination); hence the more significant link of RNFE to caste in Veeravalli.

The marginal effect of migration-in on the probability of HH having non-farm employment is also high i.e. 21.1 percentage points in the developed village, and for the pooled data 14.2 percentage points. This result can be interpreted more cautiously for the growth linkages (AGL) hypothesis on the following grounds. In the agriculturally more developed village one would expect these growth linkages and expansion of RNFE which might intern induce migration. If it is agricultural growth that induces migration (as migration will be; evidence was certainly more from Bihar, Eastern UP, to Punjab). This again suggests that at household level the 'linkage' effect of such growth in swelling total RNFE (via the modern sub-sector) outweighs its negative effect in shrinking the trade subsector of RNFE.

The dummy variable 'skills' (any marketable expertise, see p. 211, e.g. barber, motor mechanic, astrologer, photographer, radio repairs, etc.) is found to be significant only in Veeravalli, the developed village, supporting the growth linkages (AGL) hypothesis (even prosperous modern farmers use much more astrologers and barbers) of modern non-farm employment. A lack of skills provides an entry barrier into the wider market place.

Poverty was negatively related (p = .01) to the possibility of non-farm work for the developed village, and for the pooled data, which suggests does not support for the overall distress diversification (ODD) hypothesis. If non-farm work increases, poverty decreases. By implication in suggests that household development out of poverty is associated with increased RNFE prospects (ODL).

Both Caste dummy variables, as well as migration into villages and seasonality (September-November) have quite strong effects on non-farm employment. For example, a household with average characteristics in terms of in caste dummy 2 (if the household/ is from a Scheduled caste or from a Scheduled Tribe, the dummy takes the value 1, or 0 otherwise), has a 9 per cent greater chance of being employed in modern non-farming. However the effect of the March-May (agriculturally rough period) dummy is a 9 per cent lower chance of modern RNFE. It is very striking to see that the 'skill' and 'poverty' dummies have the expected signs *a priori*. A HH with a single main skilled worker has a 95 per cent greater chance of being involved in the modern sector. Again the requirement of special skills for entry into the modern non-farming sector is stressed. Similarly we can (see Table 4.32) that the poor/non-poor dummy variable is negatively related to modern non-farm employment (p = .1).

For the pooled data the probability of any household the higher the level of education, the greater the chance of engagement in modern non-farm employment (p = .05). The per acre value of agricultural output, and age^2, are significantly positively associated with modern RNFE, and household head age negatively so. The marginal effects are -0.02 for age and

0.0002 for household head age^2. The impact of per acre value of agricultural output is negligible.

These results highlight the fact that in many cases the critical variables modern and traditional RNFE vary significantly. Also, different factors are influential on the outcome of the dependent variable in the three models (the two villages separately and pooled). For example, land size (the growth (AGL) linkage impact on modern non-farm employment 'dominates' the distress diversification (ADD) impact on traditional non-farm employment], education (supports wider (ODL) hypothesis) and seasonality are equally important for both the villages separately (although different seasons are relevant in the different villages; September-November in Anandapuram and the pooled data, December-February season negatively, and March-May positively, for Veeravalli village only Work in March to May season which under line a particular set of activities (When the agriculture season was slack) and the pooled data. Poverty, migration into the villages, and per acre value of agricultural output (he growth (AGL) linkage impact on modern non-farm employment] lay crucial roles in the developed village and in the pooled data. Caste is also an important factor for developed village and the pooled data. Skills are particularly important in developed village which support the ODL hypothesis.

With a 1 per cent increase in age, the probability of the household being engaged in modern RNFE reduces by 1.8 per cent. In this model the relationship is not linear. The reason is that the coefficient on household age^2 is positively significant (beyond a certain age the probability will fall). Those households below average age experience a decline in probability of working in RNFE as age increases. But for those households aged above mean, the probability of working in modern RNFE increases. We have to interpret these two variables together. The sign patterns shows that the probability decreases for younger households and increases for older household heads. Younger household heads will be in traditional non-farm occupations whereas older household heads will be in modern RNFE. This is possibly because modern

RNFE requires certain skills which it are not possible to immediately acquire. As time passes the younger generations gradually acquire skills and move to the modern RNFE because of growth linkages effect.

For interaction between village dummy (less developed 1 and more developed 0), the relationship is positive. More education increases the probability of non-farm employment. An increase in education by one year i.e. 1 per cent increase in education leads to an increase of 2.47 per cent in RNFE. In each village for which the score 1, the village dummy (i.e. less developed village) those with less education are less likely to work in non-farm. This is possible because when agriculture development is poor, people go for relatively lower paid jobs because of distress diversification. The relationship between education and probability of working in RNFE is positive and significant. That means that if a person lives in the less developed village and everything else is constant, that person has a 25 per cent increased chance of working in the non-farm sector. For those who have the same level of education the probability of working in non-farm is higher in the less developed village.

NOTES

1 A study by the Agro-Economic Research Centre, Visakhapatnam (1974), selected indicators of resource base and of infrastructure so as to estimate input use and productivity for all the districts in AP. The districts were ranked and classified into high and low productivity districts on the basis of the value of agricultural production per acre cultivated. Of the two districts, Krishna emerged as an agriculturally developed and Visakhapatnam as agriculturally less developed district. The profile of these districts and of the villages Anandapuram and Veeravalli were selected so as to assess the differences in the pattern of non-farm employment at two development 'scales'.

On the basis of levels of output and growth patterns (variation in the growth of output is analysed by the method of decomposition of output) the districts of Krishna, Guntur, East Godavari and West Godavari are identified as developed while Srikakulam,

Vizianagarm and Visakhapatnam districts were identified as backward in terms of growth in agriculture. On the basis of a composite index, all Districts in AP were grouped according to their level of socio-economic development. Visakhapatnam is identified as one of the backward districts in AP.

2 Revenue-cum-development units. *Handbook of Statistics* Krishna District, 1991-92. Erstwhile '*taluks*' were divided into smaller units of '*mandals*' in 1984.

3 Directorate of Economics and Statistics, *Handbook of Statistics,* Visakhapatnam District, Government of AP, 1991-92, p. v.

4 *Ayacut* is defined as the area irrigated with the waters dependent on the release from the 'water resources' developed due to a dam, reservoir or *anicut.*

5 Note that in subsequent tables, the figures in brackets represent a percentage breakdown of India 1991, Series-2, Andhra Pradesh Final Population Totals, Office of the Director of Census Operations, AP: Hyderabad.

6 *Zamindari* tenure was introduced towards the end of the 19th century. Whilst Zamindars were intermediaries between the cultivators and the state, they behaved as land owners. More than 60 per cent of the total area was under the Zamindars tenure and exploitation of farmers was common. In 1947, after the attainment of independence, the government introduced abolition of the Zamindari system. The main objective was to replace the feudal agrarian structure with an equitable and just agrarian system. The early land legislation was concerned with regulating rents, protecting tenants and abolishing intermediaries.

7 Defined as ' all land occupied by buildings, roads and railways or under water, for example, rivers and canals, and other lands put to use other than agricultural'.

8 Handbook of Agriculture: Indian Council of Agricultural Research (ICAR) New Delhi (1984).

9 A popular stimulant made from decayed tobacco leaves, which are imported from Orissa, the neighbouring State.

10. Net sown area as percentage to arable land.

11. A study at the village level by Krishnaiah (1998) pointed out the withdrawal of labour from the labour market by certain groups (e.g. shepherds, toddy tappers), the change in cropping pattern from subsistence to commercial crops (mainly cotton) and increased pull migration that resulted in real agricultural wages

increasing rapidly during the 1990s. State intervention also played an important role in expanding non-farm employment. In addition, NGOs and labour unions participation in the labour market led to higher real wages [Khannnan (1998) and Sharma and Kumar (1998)]. Bhall (1993) points out that mechanisation was increasing because of rising real wages as well as the availability of cheap capital (institutional credit provided at subsidised rates). Hanumantha Rao (1998) also notes that substitution of capital for labour in agriculture during the 1980s in India.

12. Forward linkages occur from farming to the RNFS (such as agricultural processing and post-harvest activities). Backward linkages are related to agricultural use of local tools etc. These are backward from agriculture to RNFS, i.e. forward from RNFS to agriculture Consumption linkages derive from agricultural income spent on local RNFS consumer goods and services. Mellor (1986) and Hazell (1988) suggest on the basis of empirical evidence that (i) per unit of output, more backward and forward linkages originate from smaller farms, and (ii) that consumption linkages are the most powerful of the 3 types of linkages to RNFS, and arise from spending of agricultural income. This, in turn, leads to demand for the local RNFS. These backward and forward production linkages determine local RNFS levels and growth.

13. The term 'RNFS', is often used interchangeably with 'rural non-agricultural activities', 'rural non-farm activities', and even 'rural industries'. While there are subtle differences between these terms we have chosen to treat them as synonymous, since employment is the focus of this chapter. [Cf. Chuta and Liedholm (1979); Shand (1986); Islam (1987a) and Ranis and Stewart (1993)]. Definition of non-farm workers: All those who worked in any field of economic activity other than cultivation, agricultural labour. It includes categories IV (mining and quarrying), V (a) a household industry is one that is engaged in production, processing, servicing, repairing or making and selling (but not merely selling) or goods. It does not include professions such as those practised by a pleader or doctor or barber, musician, dancer, dhobi, astrologer or merely trade or business, even if such professions, trade or services are run at home by members of the household) V (b) manufacturing, processing, servicing and repairs in other than household industry, VI-IX 9 (constructions, trade and commerce, transport, storage and communications, other services) [Census of India (1991), Primary Census Abstract Part-II B (ii) p.xlvii].

14. Prof. G. Parthasarathy and the late Dr. Pramit Chaudhuri (both of whom worked extensively in these areas for more than 3 decades) were consulted in the design of the sample. AP is divided into 23 districts and each district was sub-divided into *Mandals* for administrative purpose. Each *Mandal* comprises a group of villages with a population of 5000 or below.
15. A 'household' as defined in the 1991 census, is a group of persons who commonly live together and take their meals from a common kitchen unless the exigencies of work prevented any of them from doing so. A household may comprise persons related with blood or a household of unrelated persons or having a mix of both. Examples of unrelated households are boarding houses, messes, hotels, residential hotels, rescue homes, jails, ashrams etc. These are called 'institutional households'. There may be one member households, two member households or multi-member households. For census purposes each one of these types is regarded as a 'household' (Census of India 1991, India, Final population totals paper-2 of 1992, Brief Analysis of Primary Census Abstract, p.4). I have used this definition for my analysis.
16. The poverty line cut off point which differentiates the poor from the non-poor households is Rs. 187.39 per person per month, which is the figure for 1993-94 rural per capita monthly expenditure used by the Directorate of Economics and Statistics, Government of AP, as its poverty line.
17. The statutory lists of scheduled castes and scheduled tribes are notified in pursuance of Articles 341 and 342 of the Constitution of India. "The President may with respect to any State or Union Territory, and where it is a State, after, consultation with the Governor thereof, by public notification, specify the castes, races or tribes or parts of or groups within castes, races or tribes which shall for the purpose of this Constitution be deemed to be Scheduled Castes and Scheduled Tribes in relation to that or Union territory, as the case may be".
18. In AP there are 59 castes in SCs (among them are the major caste systems such as *mala, madiga, relli, mastin, malasale, manne, aravamala, pamidi, ghasansi* and *saggali*). There are 29 ST castes (the major groups are *savara, jatapu, koya, konda reddy, yanidi, yerukala, chenchu, bagata* and *lambadi*).
19. Agricultural labourer are defined as those which derive more than half of their income from wages paid for manual labourer in agriculture. Hence, agricultural labourer can also cultivate a small piece of land, either owned or leased in.

20. Regular salaried/wage employee: persons working in other's farm or non-farm enterprises, both household and non-household, and getting in return salary or wages on a regular basis (and not on the basis of daily or periodic renewal of work contact) are the regular salaried/wage employees. This category not only includes persons getting time wage but also persons receiving piece wage or salary and paid apprentices, both full time and part-time.

21. The person may have worked for six months or 183 days or more in more than one activity in different seasons. For example s/he may have worked for 3 months in cultivation one month in gur making and 3 months as an agricultural labourer. S/he is requested to indicate which of these three activities according to him/her was main activity, i.e. in which capacity s/he spent more time in different seasons. In the instant case since the person has spent three months each in cultivation and as agricultural labourer the choice as to which of these two would be his/her main activity in which season maximum worked would be left to him/her.

22. Skill defined as in the 1996 NSS, "Any marketable expertise however acquired, irrespective of whether marketed or not, whether the intention is to market it or not, is considered as a skill". Sarvekshana, Vol.XX, No.1 68th Issue July-September 1996, p.6.

23. In order to obtain a basic understanding of the nature of the relationships between the endogenous and exogenous variables discussed earlier, a correlation matrix of all the variables was constructed. The highest correlation coefficient found was -0.65 (between March-May and December-February). Generally the coefficients are small although some are of the order of 0.5.

24. The effects for interaction variables cannot be directly interpreted.

25. Predictions which match the actual values of the dependent variable. I have also independently checked variables that can be eliminated on the basis of log likelihood ratio tests. However, in order to remain consistent in the results presented and to focus on the particular model tested full models are presented.

26. We thought there is a potential endogenity problem in the equations. We tested that the model was run by taking the ^ (fitted) values and residuals from the first model and then inserted in the non-farm model. It was found that the residuals term was not significant. The t-values on the residual was captured at only 0.964.

27. We know that the marginal effect computed for the logit for any variable is:

$$\frac{\delta prob\,[RNFE]}{\delta X_i} = \beta X_i * \frac{\exp[z]}{[1+\exp(z)]^2}$$ where z is the sum of coefficients multiplied by the means of the respective variables plus the constant term.

28. The results do not directly demonstrate this but it is what we would expect.

5

NON-FARM EMPLOYMENT– CASE STUDIES FROM TWO VILLAGES

Introduction

The regression analysis presented in Chapter IV has identified some of the factors influencing the level of RNFE in two villages of AP. Land holding size, household workers education, household head's age, family size and social background such as caste, migration in, poor or non-poor plus value of agricultural output and seasonality were found to have a significant association with non-farm employment in both villages. However, some factors differed between the 2 villages in their relationship with RNFE. For example, in the more developed village, social background had a negative relationship with non-farm employment, whereas it had an insignificant relationship in the less developed village. This is because of differences in the type of non-farm activities carried out. Similarly, literacy has an expected positive relationship with modern RNFE, while the same factor had a negative relationship with traditional RNFE. This may be explained by the fact that more traditional non-farm activities, for example toddy tapping, vegetable and/or flower vending, petty trading, shandy business, quarrying, and traditional occupations like washing do not require any educational skills whereas modern

RNFE requires higher levels of literacy. People without education are disproportionately likely to enter these occupations.

Chapter 3 has also identified factors associated with RNFE at more aggregated level. Irrigation, farm size, commercialisation, poverty, infrastructure (percentage of villages with banks, road length) literacy and urbanisation are significantly associated with shares and growth of RNFE. In this chapter male/female distinctions in these relationships were also noted.

The analysis of the two hypotheses growth linkages versus distress diversification was brought together in a single framework in chapters 3 & 4. In order to reflect in a more comprehensive way on the complex factors that are at work in the rural setting, this chapter presents some selected case studies. The chapter will enable us to identify selected factors operating at the household level, which may be hidden in the regression analysis and also illustrate the influence of some of the variables that are identified as significant in the regressions.

This chapter discusses specific features of certain non-farm activities, including the determination of income and hours of work. The account will indicate the variety of factors that affect the fortunes of individual families, for example: skill, resourcefulness, the families' credit worthiness, and physical factors such as the nature of soil and location. For example, seasonality is likely to be important in enabling RNFS work if there is a peak season labour constraint (or healthy labour constraint). The household survey reflected this aspect as did the case studies.

People are looking for additional avenues to supplement farm employment in terms of employment and income generation in rural areas. As the case studies show, also self-employment is an alternative to wage employment which is sometimes preferred and sometimes an occupation of last resort.

For the case studies, observation and interviewing techniques[1] were used and personal biographies were collected. A few families have been chosen from Veeravalli and

Anandapuram on the basis of either their occupational success or the nature of their non-farm activities. The families were selected following a detailed enquiry regarding their primary occupation, the reason for their choice of the non-farm activity, and its relation with the agricultural sector. In what follows we discuss the nature of these non-farm activities, the level of technology involved, the problems involved in sustaining or expanding income from them and the possible solutions to these and increasing non-farm employment opportunities.

Case studies are structured around: historical background of occupational lifestyle, i.e., social economic background, movements of non-farm employment in a particular occupation and linkages with farm sector.

5.1 Case Studies From Veeravalli

This section examines one key theme and its related issues. (1) the role of agriculture and transition to RNFS (a) the role of family background in RNFS (b) economic factors. In order to explore these issues in greater depth we interviewed 12 case study households in Veeravalli.

In Veeravalli a variety of non-farm activities are carried out: rice milling (husking), construction, tile and brick making, flour milling, hotel business, vending, motor repair, milk centres, tent house, wood cutting, chemical production, and traditional non-farm activities such as pottery, carpentry, gunny bag makers, washermen/women, cobbling, and petty trade, Leafco (local paper mill), Delta Chemicals Pvt. Ltd., and Venspra Chemicals Limited. This village has a relatively fast growing output and higher employment potential than the surrounding villages.

5.1.1 Key Characteristics of Labour Force in Selected Case Studies from Veeravalli (1995)

Key characteristics of the Veeravalli case study households are summarised in Table 5.1 features of their RNFE experience in Table.

Table 5.1 : Key Characteristics of Case Studies, Veeravalli (1995) - Part 1.

Interviewee	*Head Sex*	*age*	*No. of People in HH*	*Occupation of HHH*	*Occupation Since*	*Wife's Occupation*	*Occupation of HH head's Father*	*Reasons for Transformation into RNFS*	*Caste of HH*
A.Somaiah	M	70	10	Agriculturist + business	1990	Housewife	Agri. labourer	Agrl. income, family support and sons' education	B.C
J. Uma	M	29	3	Motor mechanic	1984	Housewife	Cultivation	Local demand for services	F.C
A. Rahiman	M	33	4	Tractor driver	1989	Agricultural labourer	Agri. labourer	Migration and demand for work	Muslim B.C
B.Bhimudu	M	35	4	Supplier of gunny bags	1987	Supplier of gunny bags + agrl. labour	Weaving gunny bags	Traditional, migration and modification in the nature of work	Lambadi S.T
S.Meeravalli	M	27	5	Vegetable, fruit vendor	1988	Agricultural labourer	Agri. labourer	Exploitation by the farmers	Muslim B.C
V. Achari	M	40	7	Carpenter	1974	House wife	Carpenter	Traditional and seasonal	B. C
Venkat. R	M	30	5	Pot maker	1973	Pot maker + agrl labourer	Pot-maker	Tradition and season	Kummari B.C
S. Husian	M	35	7	Tea stall owner	1980	Tea stall	Cotton Carder	Elderly people encouragement and no interest in tradition	Muslim B.C

Contd....

Table 5.1 : (Contd....)

Interviewee	*Head Sex*	*age*	*No. of People in HH*	*Occupation of HHH*	*Occupation Since*	*Wife's Occupation*	*Occupation of HH head's Father*	*Reasons for Transformation into RNFS*	*Caste of HH*
B.Raghavulu	M	60	4	Petty trade	1965	Petty trade	Agrl. labour+ vegetable vendor	Relatives support, migration, agrl. Income, and long experience	Gowdas B.C
M.Satyanarayana	M	29	4	Cycle shop owner	1981	Tailoring	Agrl. Labour + cycle shop	Father's job to son's job	Gowdas B.C
K. Prasad	M	40	4	Radio mechanic	1980	Housewife	Retired teacher	Urban to rural migration, location	S.C Christian
Mr. K. Tirapathiah	M	60	10	Cultivator + Business	1982	Housewife	Cultivation	Agrl.income, commu-ting, family support, and education	Koppula Velama

Notes : M= Male, F= Female, HHH = Household Head, HH = Household, BC = Backward Caste, FC= Forward Caste, SC= Scheduled Caste, ST= Scheduled Tribe.

Table 5.1 : Key Characteristics of Case Studies, Veeravalli (1995) - Part 2.

Interviewee	*No. of Children & Grand Children*	*Age of Children*	*Education level*	*Occupation of children*	*Previous Occupation of HH*
A. Somaiah	5+4		S.S.C	Same as father	Cowherd
J. Uma	1	2	S.S.C (failed)	Infant	Student
A. Rahiman	2	5, 2	Uneduca-ted	Student	Hotel cleaner
B.Bhimudu	2	10, 8	Uneducat-ed	Students 5th, 3rd	Weaver , palmayra fruits seller & agrl. labourer
S. Meeraval-li	3	6, 3, 1	Uneducat-ed	Student 1st class	Agrl. labourer
V. Chari	5	18, 14, 10, 8, 6	4th, 2nd	I.T.I, 10th, 5th,5th,1	Carpenter
Venkat. R	3	10, 7, 4	2nd, 1st	Students 5th, 4th	Pot maker
S. Husian	5	9, 7, 5, 3, 1	Head illiterate wife 5th	Infants	Rickshaw puller
B. Raghavulu	2	22, 16	S.S.L.C wife 4th	I.T.I, 9th	Petty trade
M.Satyanarayana	2	11, 9	3rd class, wife illiterate	6th, 4th	Cycle shop owner
K. Prasad	2	13, 10	I.T.I	7th, 6th	Sugar factory, grinder wife HH work
K. Tirapathiah	3 + 3	33, 25, 22	6th, wife illiterate	Engineer, Agriculture, employee	Agriculture + milk vendor

Note : HH = Household, S.S.C = Secondary school certificate (10th class), S.S.L.C =Secondary school leaving certificate (old 11th form), I.T.I = Industrial training institute (after 10th standard).

Source : Field work.

Table 5.2: Key Points Emerging from the Veeravalli Case Studies (1995)

Name of Interviewee	*Occupation of head of HH*	*The Importance of Each Case Study with Regard to Rural Non-Farm Sector*
A. Somaiah	Agriculturist + business	Expansion/transition into the RNFS from the agricultural sector (income earnings from growing pulses), role of family, role of capital, personal input into the agricultural sector (land is not leased out).
J. Uma	Motor mechanic	Role of mechanisation, role of personal skills, role of seasonality, demand is there for his services, change of vocation from father to son.
A. Rahiman	Tractor driver	Role of migration, change of occupation from hotel cleaner to driver, no link with traditional occupation cording cotton.
B.Bhimudu	Sheets supplier of gunny bags	Traditional non-farm activity, role of caste, education not required, role of migration (local semi nomadic), role of seasonality.
S. Meeravalli	Vegetable, fruit vendor	Role of commuting, no link to traditional occupation, change of occupation from agricultural labourer to vendor, role of seasonality.
V. Chari	Carpenter	Traditional non-farm occupation, linkage with agricultural sector, seasonality, skilled profession, declining importance due to mechanisation.
Venkat. R	Pot maker	Traditional non-farm activity, nature of work seasonal, shift of work according to seasons, cultivation is helpful to raise income.
S. Husian	Tea stall owner	Change of vocation from traditional non-farm to modern non-farm, role of family (5 children), lack of skills, seasonality (no business in the rainy season), lack of money, self -employment.

Contd....

Table 5.2: Key Points Emerging from the Veeravalli Case Studies (1995)

Name of Interviewee	*Occupation of head of HH*	*The Importance of Each Case Study with Regard to Rural Non-Farm Sector*
B. Raghavulu	Petty trade	Self-employment, change of vocation from agricultural to cycle-shop, no link with traditional occupation, demand high in summer, wife also earns income.
M. Satyam	Cycle shop owner	Role of migration, long experience in the business, role of family, role of owned land, no link with the traditional occupation.
K. Prasad	Radio mechanic	Role of migration, advantage of location of services, job not linked with his degree, no job satisfaction, income is not bad.
K. Tirapathiah	Cultivator + Business	Role of family, caste factor, advantage of location of business, role of large family, role of capital, role of agriculture.

5.1.2 *The Role of Agriculture: Original Occupation of Respondent, Transition to RNFS:*

Some of the case studies shed light on the transition out of agriculture to RNFS as well as the importance of agriculture in complementing income shortfalls. The continued involvement of some of the households with agriculture should also be noted. The role of land ownership (as a source of income for RNFS investment), seasonality and mechanisation are also noted in what follows.

5.1.2.1 *The Transition to the RNFS*

The inadequacy of agricultural incomes as well as lack of employment opportunities in farming have acted as a push factor into RNFS for some households in both villages. There is a need for alternative sources to raise family income and to keep people busy during the slack agricultural season. Yet, for some, links with agriculture have remained. Generally, land-related activities can be carried out on a seasonal basis, offering the possibility of securing short-term employment or generating complementary incomes. This means that, in many cases, the transition is not complete either way. The role played by agriculture was crucial in some of the case studies, for Mr. Somaiah, Mr. Shaik Meeravalli, Mr. Sheik Husian, and for Mr. Borra Raghavulu.

Mr. Somaiah started his working life as a cowherd and an agricultural labourer when he was young. At present he owns 30 acres of land but also runs a business in the RNFS (which is not normal in a B.C caste). He possesses his own tractor and takes a personal interest in looking after his land: no land is leased out and agriculture is carried out under his personal supervision. Pulses, an important income generating crop, are grown: of the annual 100 bags, there is a yield of 30 bags per acre in Kharif while in Rabi it is 35 bags. Of the total rice output nearly (1800 bags), 100 bags of paddy a year are for personal use and the rest is marketed. The investment crop growing amounted (per acre) to Rs. 3000 for Kharif and Rs. 6000 for Rabi per year approximately value of output. The income from agriculture supported Mr. Somaiah's investment in RNFS and in turn generated substantial profits.

Mr. Somaiah trades in cement, fertilisers, pesticides, seeds, shamianas (supplier of tents and other material for functions), furniture and cooking utensils. In addition he has undertaken various commission activities such as selling rice. (Even within RNFS, Mr. Somaiah undertakes a variety of activities depending on the local conditions. That is also one of the techniques for the success of business). The present business was started during 1990. There is a profit margin of Rs. 20 per bag of cement and his is the only shop which sells cement in that village. Of late, construction related activities in the village have grown, raising demand. Fertilisers are transported from Gudivada and Vijayawada and also yield a profit margin. Their sale is based on agricultural activity so that the primary sector has given rise to this non-farm income opportunity.

Mr. Somaiah has quite a large family and his four sons are competent in carrying out various tasks connected with the family business. In addition, two boys (not relatives) are employed in the shops helping the business. The particular significance in the use of family labour is that Mr. Somaiah, like many small-scale entrepreneurs, has less confidence in hired labour. The availability of family manpower is the prominent factor underpinning his prosperity. Of late the importance of non-farm activities has grown over agricultural activities.

The father of the interviewee was an agricultural labourer and in the third generation the vocation has changed from that of pure agriculture to, in part, non-farm activities. The main point I noted was that hardworking and careful management of money transactions male accumulating land possible i.e., every year out of the farm income he started buying land which was the first stage in the transition to prosperous farming.

According to Mr. Somaiah no loans are drawn from banks for business purposes. The business turnover is nearly Rs. 6 lakhs per year. Although his wife is illiterate his four sons are educated up to 10 level. Total family income is approximately Rs. 15000 per month. The family was in a satisfactory financial position and does not face any problems. This is one of the interesting cases where a change has been observed from a family of agricultural labourers to that of prosperous agriculturists and businessmen whose interest in non-farm activities is on the increase.

Mr. Shaik Meeravalli, a vegetable and fruit vendor trades various perishable agricultural goods (such as mangoes, vegetables and sapotas) depending on the season. He bicycles 25 kms between Veeravalli, Mallavalli and other villages per day to vend his goods. On an average he makes a profit of Rs. 40 to Rs. 70 per day. He has been involved with his business since 1987.

Prior to this he used to take part in agricultural activities as a wage labourer, but abstained from it as he felt that the farmers were mis-using him by giving extra work without any pay. Though his trade is irregular, since fruits and vegetables are not regularly available (this activity requires very little resources), he owns a house and has no debts. He does not have any land and he generally does good business during the summer months.His business declines in the rainy season. During January there is great demand for ripe chillies. On average he spends Rs. 40 for household expenses per day. This has implication for his ability to invest.

His non-farm activities provided him with a higher income than as an agricultural wage labour. This is a case of a self-employed person who is not adversely affected by the seasonal dimension of non-farm activities because when fruits and vegetables are not available he goes for ripe chillies. Though he has moved away from the agricultural sector, for Mr. Shaik Meeravalli the agricultural sector continues to play an indirect role in improving his livelihood by supplying the items which he sells. This is a case of forward linkages from agriculture.

Mr. Sheik Husian belongs to B.C. and runs a small hotel, referred to locally as a shad. His father used to ply a rickshaw. The village in which his family resides has been the traditional residence for generations. Elderly people in the village gave him credit (with kind i.e. to meet his large family daily expenditure) on an interest basis and encouraged him to set up a business. The bank has also given him a loan for Rs. 5000 which enabled him to buy all the necessary items and utensils for setting up the hotel.

Traditionally his forefathers carried out the occupation of carding cotton for making beds and pillows but Sheik Husian had little interest in pursuing this occupation. He stated that he was not able to be 'successful' in carding as he has five young children to look after. Husian's father had rickshaw the family was involved with the agricultural labour. However, at present the hotel also does not provide sufficient income and thus, the household also undertakes wage labour in agriculture. Sales in the hotel average Rs. 250 per day, of which nearly Rs.200 are invested in buying the necessary material.

The hotel business is affected in the rainy season when it may close temporarily because during rains no work is available and thus no pay, so people would not go to hotels. At that time, agricultural labour work is undertaken which is available on a daily basis. The income generated in this manner is however inadequate to satisfy the family's needs. This person does not own a house and pays Rs.150 monthly as rent for the hotel cum residence and Rs 50 for the electricity. Now and then, in order to pay the rent he takes private credit at an exorbitant rate. He also has to give credit to his customers to the extent of Rs. 400 per month and often this creates a strain for him as they do not pay up regularly. Out of the loan of Rs. 5000 that he has taken he has been able to repay only Rs. 1000. If some more money is invested in the business, there is good scope for development as it is located on the main road. He is running the business on marginal profits.

This household illustrates that where the non-farm activity is affected by seasons, agriculture may protect to some extent the livelihoods of people by providing additional wage employment. It also illustrates some of the consumption linkages from agriculture: if agriculture is able to generate more employment and income people spend this income on food items other than rice such as more coffee, tea and other beverages. This can generate more non-farm employment but only if the slack period of NFE corresponds to peak labour demand in agriculture.

Mr. Borra Raghavulu, a petty trader, was a native of Bandarugudem and migrated to Veeravalli 25 years ago. The household belongs to the caste of Gowdas (a backward caste which is by tradition toddy tappers) but no member of the household is engaged in the traditional vocation. Mr. Raghavulu's father once owned some land and was himself engaged in agriculture. In the past this was unusual for the gowda caste. Why his parents were not involved in the traditional vocation was not known to him. His main occupation is trading in small items which are disposed of quickly but he is also a cultivator. He has been engaged in the trading business for the past 25 years and regards himself as a success. He entered this business with the encouragement of relatives. His father was an agricultural labour and also a vendor of vegetables. He has sufficient work to keep him engaged except in the rainy season. His son and daughter-in-law also engage in petty trading, together with his wife.

This person has his own house and one acre of land on which he grows 25 bags of paddy per year. Seasonal annual farm input costs are around Rs. 2000 (including wages) and the work is done by labourers. The interesting point is that farm and non-farm income pay for the labour when it is required. His wife does not supervise the farm and looks after the trading business in his absence. He vends vegetables and green coconuts, cool drinks and confectionery to the extent of Rs. 200 to 300 per day and gains a profit in excess of Rs. 50 per day. The business is brisk between January and July. He was not able to invest more to improve his business as his daughter and grand-daughter are still at school, and some of the profits are being spent on his family's education. This person had applied for a bank loan on his land as collateral but his application was refused, because the loan authorities felt his case was not a priority.

Within his limits Raghavulu is a successful entrepreneur. He has been able to make a profit on his business and acquire some wealth. His careful monitoring of his resources and systematic planning have made him a successful man.

This case also shows that ownership of some land can be a support by providing paddy for his family's consumption and generate income by selling the excess output from farm leads the transition to RNFS. During the season Mr Raghavaulu makes some profits from the business. When the business is off season his concentration diverts towards agriculture. The reason for this business peak in the non-agricultural season lies with seasonal effect. During the summer there is a heavy demand for his trading goods, but no agricultural activity. While the profits gained from the non-farm business have sometimes been used partly as capital for agricultural operations such as ploughing, plantations of rice crop, weeding, and for water charges, electricity etc., the income from crop is also used as capital for the business at other times. The shift of capital when necessary plays a key role in the development of the RNFS activity.

5.1.2.2 *Role of Land Ownership (as Source of Income for RNFS Investment):*

The participation in RNFE of workers belonging to different types of households and their relative success may be influenced by the asset holdings of these households, especially the ownership of land. The regression results suggest that there is an inverse relationship between land ownership and participation in non-farm work; as the land ownership of the household increase, their participation in non-farm work declines. However, these case studies indicate that this conclusion is not always valid(especially for the more successful entrepreneurs). It is important to ascertain the land ownership characteristics of those households which are increasingly participating in non-farm work.

5.1.2.3 *The RNFS input to agriculture and agriculture's contribution to the RNFS: Evidence of interdependence linkages*

Through forward linkages some parts of RNFS output provide inputs to the farm sector. In terms of backward linkages, the RNFS provides a demand for the output of the farm sector. The growth of agricultural production and productivity may create a surplus which may be invested in the RNFS. Production linkages from non-farm to farm sector appear in the case studies of Mr. Somaiah (summarised above), and also of Mr. Achari, and of Mr. Venkata Ramanand. The next two case studies provide additional insights into the functioning of these linkages.

Mr. Veerabhadra Achari's family has traditionally worked in RNFE. Formerly the family members were goldsmiths but 20 years ago they switched to carpentry as well. The reason is traditionally they can be involved in both occupations. Carpentry work is mostly related to agriculture which can generate more income and employment. During the summer (February-July) demand for Mr. Achari's service increases and there is work for 5 days a week, because all agricultural related tools such as ploughs, bullock carts, knives etc. go for repairs during the summer when agriculture is not in operation. The household also manufactures knives, various types of cutters, ploughs, and other tools involving the skills of the blacksmith, an activity that lost its importance with the advent of tractors. On average there is 5 months work for carpentry occupation in the above mentioned activities throughout the year and the household also takes part in outdoor work such as fixing doors and windows. The average daily income is about Rs. 60. Mr. Achari does not own or lease land. The household incurs debts regularly, as he must feed 10 members and the women do not get any kind of paid work as traditionally in their family women are not accustomed to wage employment and are thus confined to household duties such as to look after the children and cooking food.

In the present generation young people who are educated do not show any interest in traditional jobs (out of 5 children only 1 works in the family profession). The household does not have any wealth or surplus to use in times of crisis and does not have sufficient work to keep every member busy. There has been no change in the primary occupation of carpentry for the last 50 or 60 years. They tried for credit but could not secure it. The volume of work is declining every year following the advent of tyre carts which have a greater carrying capacity. The family are unacquainted with the nature of work involving tyre carts.

In Mr. Achari's case, the linkage is traditional. RNFS' output like knives, various types of cutters, ploughs, bullock carts and other tools involving the skills of blacksmith serve as inputs to the farm sector. Yet this occupation has declined following inncvations in modern technology.

Mr. Venkata Ramanand engages in the traditional non-farm activity of clay pot making. His father was also a pot-maker by occupation. There are around 120 families engaged in this vocation in Veeravalli. The available work for clay pot-makers increases from January to June (during the summer people use more pots to keep water cold to drink in the highest temperature), and in the rainy season. This clay pot makers family relies on a series of agricultural activities like sowing, weaving and transplantation. In the humid atmosphere, the shape and strength of the pots are prone to distortion. On average, Mr. Venkata's monthly income will be around Rs. 2000 whenever a kiln is fired. Until after a kiln is emptied one does not know how many pots are fired/baked properly and how many are lost. Mr. Venkata does not possess land of his own at present but he has taken 2 acres on lease, from which he can save 10 bags of paddy after paying his tenancy. His primary occupation is seasonal. The family expenses are of the order of Rs. 50.

Mr. Venkata did not obtain much encouragement from his family nor did he learn much during his schooling. This has been a contributory factor in his lack of alternative skills which forced him to continue an occupation which he has had since he was 8 years old. At present his income just covers his expenditure. The nature of the job is dependent upon any unforeseen rain which may ruin the kiln, thus increasing losses. However, there is an adequate demand for the business on a commission basis for various pots and other form of ornamental work. He has sufficient work to keep him occupied.

He has secured a loan of Rs. 10,000 for installing an electric machine for making clay pots with different designs but somehow this investment has not been successful. However, he changed his items of production from traditional to new pieces, catering to the needs and tastes of the public which may even increase his income. Mr. Venkata's wife also participates in the work.

Mr. Venkata Ramanand's case signals that traditional clay pots are still well used by the rural community, even though plastic tools dominate the market. The pot makers supply all varieties of pots at low prices compared to plastic tools which are used in the farm sector. From the preceding case-study it appears that this individual has been more successful in adapting his product line. These traditional RNFS occupations which provide inputs to the farm sector are established with strong linkages. In the villages 80 per cent of the population depends on agriculture. These people go to the fields very frequently and they carry water along with them in pots (which will keep the drinking water cool and wet the land) made by these clay pot makers community. The significance of this case study in illustrating farm/non-farm linkages.

5.1.2.4 Seasonality:

Seasonality is likely to be important in enabling or constraining RNFS work, if there is a peak-season labour constraint (or healthy labour constraint). My household survey catches this in Chapter 4, so it is interesting to ask whether the case studies also reflect on this.

Farming is seasonal. Some forms of non-farm employment vary counter cyclically. A section of the rural workers seeks non-farm work when employment is not available in the farm sector. Even in the RNFS, employment is available in certain seasons, and it mainly employs casual and self-employed workers. Five case studies those illustrate of Mr Jami, Mr. Bhimudu, Mr. Meeravalli, Mr. Achri, and Mr. Raghavulu-in particular illustrate the seasonal nature of this work.

Mr. Jami Umamaheswara Rao (Mr. Uma) is a motor mechanic. His education was terminated by his failure in 10th class. When his education came to an end he was idle for some time before training as a motor mechanic for a period of 5 years. On and off he repaired vehicles whenever he had a chance to do so and later it became the mainstay of his life. During his training, he used to stay with his brother, a representative selling fertilisers. He learnt the mechanic's trade in Gudivada from 1984 -86 and in Tadepalli from 1987-88, and for some time worked in Rangapuram. These places are less than 100 kms away from Veeravalli. He learnt this professional activity while employed in a scooter and moped repair shed. He did not learn as an apprentice in a proper technical school. He did not pay training costs or get apprenticeship placement and offered free services to his supervisors.

He does not own land, but leases in one acre to cultivate paddy. As part of rent for the land 20 bags of paddy are paid in kind, leaving him with 8 bags for his own use. Pulses are also grown which together yield an income of Rs. 3000 per year. The cultivation is not done under his personal supervision but by his parents.

At present he maintains his own shed (Veeraanjayaneya Motor Works) in which two boys are employed as helpers. Recently he has changed the location of his shed to take advantage of business on the main road. His main work involves motor repairs and mending punctures. He now has an air compressor of his own which he bought second hand for Rs. 11,500 out of profit. Both the house and the shop are his own.

On average Mr. Uma's income is Rs. 40 per day and Rs. 1000 per month in the long run. He lives in his native village and he faces a greater demand for his services in the summer than in other seasons. He has one free day a week.

He is satisfied with his present state of income and does not expect any kind of problems until his children grow up and they are at school. At present he owns his house built at a cost of Rs. 60,000 financed by himself but financially he is not strong enough to start a new kind of business.

The grain he grows is adequate for his food needs. The main expense lies in the cultivation of Rabi crops which require more fertilisers (than Kharif crop) for an improved yield.

He is the only mechanic in the village and if the government can advance him a loan of more than Rs. 25,000, he can establish a spare parts shop which would increase his business turnover and potentially make him prosperous. There are 25 tractors in the village, and servicing these provides him with (in terms of demand for repairs) adequate employment. To acquire the necessary spare parts Mr. Uma frequently visits either Vijayawada or Hanuman junction which is 6 km distant.

He can be cited as an example of a self made man who switched to non-farm employment from a family dependent on agriculture as a source of livelihood. The tractors in the village are used only in the agricultural season. Repair work takes place only in that season. So, the RNFS activity has a seasonal dimension which is connected to farm activities. This case study shows there are more linkages from agriculture.

Mr. Bukkayaiah Bhimudu is 35 years of age and belongs to the ethnic group 'Lambadies', a local semi-nomadic tribe. His forefathers migrated from Suryapet (a town in Nalgonda District in AP) in search of a livelihood. Bhimudu's family of 5 brothers were engaged in weaving bags from gunny (a form of jute).

Whilst the basic nature of the family's profession did not change, it underwent a subtle change in terms of employment. They now make vast sheets by stretching and sewing cloth from gunny bags, which they then rent to farmers during harvest time. The spreads are folded on 4 sides and used as carriers for paddy and pulses. As such, the spreadouts are quite popular with farmers. They have been renting these out for the past 7 years.

Their main work is stretching and sewing together (the sheets have to be joined) the sheets of urea bags into large spreadouts and half of the year is spent on this task. The gunny bags are rented out at a rate of Rs. 5 per spread out of which an acre needs 15. They have to repair any damage to the sheets. The family's daily income is Rs. 125 per day when all the family members are employed. The household can expect to earn Rs. 125/day between 2 to 3 months of each year and this does not cover the cost of materials. This person also cultivates a leased in 2 acres of land which yields 7 bags of rice per acre per year after paying tenancy.

Mr. Bhimudu buys the urea bags necessary for making these spread-outs from Gudivada, the nearest town. A lot of 2000 bags is bought per term (in the agricultural season). He takes part in work whenever possible and incurs debts whenever not employed. During the summer the household sells the fruits of palmayra, which are quite popular in AP. His wife is engaged in the same trade and when there is no employment they go for daily labour in agriculture. At the time of the survey Mr. Bhimudu requested loans to be granted or at least the raw material to be supplied.

Formerly, when the family wove gunny bags, they had to handle heavy material. Now the spread-out has made their work easier, relieving them of the responsibilities of loading the produce in gunny bags. The family gave up weaving gunny bags 6 years ago.

The household lives a hand to mouth existence. The livelihood of these tribes cannot be termed a success as it does not guarantee them a continuous source of income, while on the other hand it helps them to maintain their basic lifestyle. Mr. Bhimudu's case is one of a RNFS activity that is dependent on the agricultural season.

Mr. Shaik Meeravalli a vegetable and fruit vendor whose activity has been detailed earlier is distinct from the above, as he is not obviously adversely affectedby the seasonal dimension of his non-farm activities. The reason lies in the very nature of his job. Mr. Meeravalli's sales are relatively 'regular', even though the goods themselves vary with the season and some product is always in season.

In Mr. Veerabhadra Achari's (carpenter) case the linkage is traditional. In Mr. Achari's case there are fluctuations of demand during the year, following the activity carried out in the fields. This irregularity of income (recall that there is work for only 5-6 months during the year) combined with declining demand, has meant that the household has had to become involved with the vicious circle of loans and debts.

Mr. Venkata Ramanand belonged to the traditional non-farm activity of pot making. The available work for pot-makers increases from January to June, and in the rainy season people depend on various agricultural activities like sowing, weaving and transplantation. This persons household is more successful in supplementing the main non-farm income source than the previous three case-studies because the margin of profit for his product is comparatively higher and the demand for the product is also higher.

5.1.2.5 Mechanisation of agriculture:

In the 'forward' linkages from the RNFS, rural non-farm outputs such as; manufacture and repair of agricultural implements, transport and distribution of fertiliser serve as inputs to agriculture. This mechanisation positively influences the demand for the products and services of the RNFS. However, mechanisation can also have a negative impact for traditional RNFE. Mr Somaih, Mr. Jami Umamaheswara Rao, and Mr. Abdul Rahiman represent cases that are positively influenced and Mr. Veerabhadra Chari's case is negatively influenced by mechanisation because following the advent of tyre carts demand for his traditional occupation fell.

Mr. Arannapalli Somaiah supplied fertilisers and pesticides to the village. Mechanisation of transport (using tractors) played a crucial role for earning more profits. Mechanisation provides transportation of fertilisers, pesticides, cement, paddy, pulses, organic manure, dried grass and sugar-cane, where tractors are also being used for agricultural operations such as ploughing, threshing, and turning the soil over after watering the fields.

Mr. Jami Umamaheswara Rao, was successfully involved with motor repairs mending punctures and servicing the village's tractors for instance.

As for *Mr. Abdul Rahiman*, he is directly involved with agricultural mechanisation as he is, by profession a tractor driver. In fact his knowledge is limited to that of driving a tractor and he does not opt for another job. His father used to work as an agricultural labourer, and a wood cutter. Mr. Rahiman's native village is Sobhanapuram, one km away from

Veeravalli. There was only one tractor in that village, which was sold years ago. Thus Mr. Rahiman migrated to Veeravalli (where there are 25 tractors) and decided to stay there. He started his career by working in a hotel doing menial jobs in Sobhanapuram and later he learnt driving by going around in the tractor before migration for which he was paid (for cleaning the tractor) Rs. 20 or Rs.15 depending on the season. After migration his income increased. Given the large number of tractors, he is regularly employed except when it rains, as the tractors get stranded in the mud. He was only unemployed two months of the year because of lack of work and was paid wages of Rs. 30 per day or Rs. 900 per month.

His household expenditure is more or less matched by his income and he does not face any debts. He does not own land although he does have a house in his native village. Yet, he does not enjoy his present job and on an average he has to make at least one trip in a day on a tractor.

In his opinion he is just working for survival. His income does not satisfy adequately for his needs and whenever he is absent his wages are cut. Also, the employer frequently fails to pay up, which results in arguments and temporary loss of employment. Following irregular timings and night work (and over-time that is badly remunerated) he is developing health problems. He has been trying for a government job as a driver for a long time. From his meagre income he sends Rs. 100 per month to his parents. His wife frequently goes for agricultural labour work (so as to complement the household income) and is paid at a similar rate of Rs.15 or Rs. 20 per day. As a professional he has asked for higher wages. This impeded regular contract and competition with other tractor drivers who without the necessary driving licences are employed at a lower rate.

On the whole his life can be termed as a prosperous and as a successful one compared to agricultural labour even though he faces problems in this sector. Because the proportion of the driver's work in on farm (classifiable agriculture) and the proportion is off-farm.This is an interesting instance of a skill required in both sectors. He gets ten months employment and a higher wage and there is a link between mechanisation of agriculture and RNFE.

5.1.2.6 *The Role of the Family and of the Caste*

Both household economic status and the activities carried out are influenced by socio-economic factors. Both family relationships and caste play an important role in influencing the choice of the activity. Lower caste groups in the society have inferior positions of influence in the village social hierarchy and are also placed in a disadvantageous position in receiving public resources.

Family relations and caste ties are strong in rural AP. The household as a whole take part in decision making about economic matters affecting the family.

In the case of Mr. Sheik Husian, presented earlier in the discussion of the transition to the RNFS, an important constraint in the perception of the success lies with the number of children (3 girls and 2 boys) he has to look after. At present the hotel does not provide sufficient income for the household which are compounded by personal problems (gambling and drinking). Yet, it was reported that the village (elderly people) did provide some financial support. His wife also contributes to the family income by doing agricultural labour work

On the whole his case is not a success. If the family size is big sometimes the household is not in a position to secure sufficient money to invest, even though there are good prospects for the business. Additionally because of the family size he could not take the advantage of the loan provided by the bank and other money lenders to improve his business.

Mr. Karanam Tirapathiah (supplier of tent house and utensils for functions) has 3 sons. The household consists of 7 grown ups and 3 children. He studied up to 6th standard, but his wife is illiterate. The first son studied in the Polytechnic (technological training college), the second one is engaged in agriculture while the third is a government employee. His three sons are also involved part-time in this business. He resides in Umamaheswarapuram, one km away from Veeravalli but his business is in Veeravalli. He has sufficient work to keep him busy throughout the year and in the season he takes up the shamiyana (thick cloth which can be used for temporary shelter) business. He started his business in 1982 and was engaged in agriculture and milk vending in the past whilst at present he does not have a milk business. Both his grand father and father were engaged in agriculture.

He cultivates 5 acres of land on his own and has taken on lease another two acres. He produces a yield of 25 bags per acre and 10 bags of pulses on the whole.

The shamiyana is an additional business in this generation from which he gains an income of Rs. 20000 minus expenses of Rs. 10000. Also given the damage to the shamiyana, the articles of trade frequently need to be renovated or purchased. Two boys are employed as helpers and the business is brisk from March to July, and slack in other months. He educated his son to be an engineer after selling two and half acres of land. He detailed the problems related to his work regarding the repossession of his material, their cleaning and reparation of the damages incurred. Yet he says that it is a part of trade and he does not complain. Up to now he invested a capital of Rs. 150,000 as well as goods to the tune of 10 to 15 thousand per year. He advises that for any unemployed youth this is a reasonable career without seeking government help.

All in all this can be termed a successful case in which the expectations of life are fulfilled and the problems associated with the vocation are taken in their stride. A part of success gives choice to the children. However, the case above is peculiar in that one son is engaged in agriculture. His big family has been positively influenced by the RNFS which has created additional employment and income. The role of the big family in this case seem to matter for RNFS.

5.1.2.7 The Role of Female Household Member (Wife) also Matters to RNFS

In the above discussion, cases have been reported of the important role of the wife in supplementing the household income. Cash-income generating activity undertaken by the wife is often flexible and carried out during lean periods. At times, however the engagement role of the wife is more substantial. Occasionally as well, some of the children carry out the RNFS activity.

Mr. Borra Raghavulu has a wife and two children, a son who passed the I.T.I, a technical course and a daughter in her 9th class. Both his son and daughter-in-law are also engaged in petty trading. Both himself and his wife are engaged in the trade.

Here the important point is that there is no link to son's job as a business man in petty trade and his education. If the business is profitable, people can take advantage of pursuing RNFS even if it is unrelated to their education.

5.1.3 The Role of Economic Factors

5.1.3.1 *Access to Capital and Lack of Skills*

Mr. Karanam Tirapathiah's has a high economic profile. His case informs on a series of possibilities that are open within the RNFS. The fact that he has been educated up to the 6th standard, his first son studied in the Polytechnic, and his second and third sons are also educated up to graduation level might have contributed to his success and to his determination in supporting the education of his children.

5.1.3.2 *Migration/commuting*

Several people in the survey have had to migrate so as to carry out their RNFS activity and to improve success. Mr. Abdul Rahiman moved from Sobhanapuram, 3 km away from Veeravalli because of better-location specific prospects. Similarly, the forefathers of Mr. Bukkayaiah Bhimudu migrated from Suryapet (300 km away from Veeravalli) in search of a livelihood. Mr. Karanam Tirapathiah resides in his native village of Umamaheswarapuram one km away from Veeravalli. His property and relatives are in that village but his business is in Veeravalli. While one cannot talk here of migration in the conventional sense, it would appear that the Veeravalli centre, on the main national highway, has offered additional employment prospects. The location of his business has been an important determinant as his shop is on the main road and in the centre of the village.

Also, Mr. Katur Prasad, a radio mechanic, is a migrant from Eluru a nearby city 20 kms away from Veeravalli village. His migration from a city to a village is a very rare case. The reasons for his migration are that in the village a house can be rented without paying any advance and the village happens to be at the centre of many villages. He earns an income of Rs. 50 each day and pays the rent of Rs. 100 per month for the shop and his house. In his case, migration is associated with him securing a good income in the RNFS.

Mr. Shaik Meeravalli is a native of Mallavalli, a village very near Veeravalli. His activity involves some movement. In order to sell his mangoes, sapotas and other fruits and vegetables, he cycles 25 kms every day between Veeravalli, Mallavalli and other villages when the items are in season

Wherever opportunities for non-farm pursuits exist men show a sufficient degree of mobility to take advantage of them. In general mobility of female members into non-farm pursuits is much lower. However, landless labourer females households show a higher degree of mobility towards non-farm pursuits.

5.1.3.3 The economic factors

(a) Location : For Mr. Jami Umamaheswara Rao, whose case has already been presented, the RNFS activity has been related to a demand for his motor mechanic services. Even, he has been able to supply employment for 2 helpers. Recently he has changed the location of his shed. His shop is located on the main road which is a national high way, so there is heavy traffic throughout the day. This creates demand from outside villages as well.

(b) Educational qualification : For Mr. Sheik Husian one relevant point was his lack of managerial skills due to the lack of education (he cannot sign his name).

Mr. Katur Prasad is a radio mechanic who studied up to 10th class and passed the trade of fitter I.T.I. He has two children, a boy and a girl and his wife looks after household work. He studied in I.T.I from 1972-74 and worked as an apprentice from 1974-75 and he was employed in a sugar factory from 1975-76 for some time; he also worked as a grinder. He became a mechanic in 1980. He also does various types of electrical house work and undertakes commissioned work in paintings sign boards, banners etc. He mentioned that he is engaged in this vocation because he could not effort to pay for a bribe to get a permanent government job or seek recommendation and even at his age he was barred and finally he is settled in this present job.

He does not own any land but earns an amount of Rs. 1500 per month, his father is a retired teacher and his grand father an agricultural labourer. He is not satisfied with his present level of income. He is hopeful that he can maintain himself in this vocation. He feels that the time he spent on education and resources were wasted and he took up this mode of living. It is distress diversification. He complains that the prices of electrical parts have gone up and he is maintaining the shop according to the market and his customers. The person can not be termed successful in terms of his career, but does fulfil his minimum needs. His dissatisfaction is to some extent related to the mis match between his expectations and the reality of his life.

(c) Other economic factors : Mr. Marla Satyanarayana's primary occupation is maintaining a cycle shop which he started in 1981. He has a wife and two children and belongs to the caste of Gowdas, the toddy tapers. His father also used to maintain a cycle shop and his grandfather was engaged in agriculture. The vocation changed in his father's time from agriculture to services.

He studied up to 3rd class and his wife is illiterate but knows tailoring and sews whenever possible. Summer is the peak season for his business. In the off seasons he will deal with repair work and he earns between Rs. 50 to 60 per day and Rs. 1200 per month. His wife earn an additional Rs. 20 per day.

The expenses of the household amount to Rs. 30 per day and he has saved Rs. 5000. He owns a house but pays rent for the shop. He does not have any land and he is not acquainted with any other work. He balances his budget with his income. He has one helper in his shop who is paid Rs.250 per month. He is confident his work will face a better demand in the future. He has extensive experience in his work and he believes that his income will be commensurate with his commitment. He does not face any problems and has secured a loan of Rs. 5000, some of which has been repaid. He is satisfied with his present level of income. There are 5 cycle shops in the village and he has 5 cycles of his own for rent which he acquired by investing Rs. 8000. There are 15 Gowda families in the village out of which 5 or 6 are engaged in traditional vocations. His family in this sense is not representative of traditional occupation.

He can be termed a successful man as he does not suffer from minimum needs problem, he has hope in the future and he is satisfied with the present income. The long experience in the RNFS pursuit made his life secure and stable.

5.2 Case Studies from Anandapuram

Several non-farm activities observed in Anandapuram are such that the occupations provide just an enough income for the families to lead a life above subsistence level. However, the level which would provide a comfortable income has not yet been reached by the majority of the families. There are 15 families living from blacksmithing and carpentry providing them a reasonable income. 70 families live as toddy tappers, a product which is in demand in the village. 20 families work in oil mills, an area of work from which they are able to obtain a sufficient income. 19 families live as manual labourers, often involving the transportation of rice bags. 25 families eke out their livelihood by plying rickshaws.

A recent innovation is the cultivation of flowers for marketing, and a number of families (between 20 to 50) gain their livelihood in this manner. The families of washermen serving the village number about 25 and there are 7 families of barbers. 40 families live by trading in shandies, 20 from quarrying and 30 are employed in the manufacture of plywood for which there is a growing demand. Poultry farms are run by

4 families. 10 families live by producing a local stimulant called *guudaku*, which is a mild intoxicant and is quite popular in the neighbouring State. 3 families live from quality grading of groundnuts and 4 families gain their livelihood by manufacturing plastic bags which are sold in local markets. 3 families maintain cycle shops, repairing and renting out cycles. Auto rickshaws are plied by 4 families and 2 live by trading in mangoes. There are 12 hotels, and 6 fertiliser stores. Besides these there are several small time businessmen doing petty business and several workers digging the earth (information collected during survey) (see Tables 5.3 & 5.4).

5.2.1 The Role of Agriculture : Transition into the RNFS

We have already pointed out that Anandapuram is agriculturally less developed compared to Veeravalli. A transition of occupation which incidentally may also be made by the self- employed. Four factors influence the incomes and living levels of wage earning households: the number of workers per household, worker-dependent ratio, the days of employment and the rate of wages. The cases of Mr. Narayana Rao, and Mr. Raminaidu are relevant to this theme

Mr. Kotyada Narayana Rao's family consists of 12 members (5 Men, 5 women and 2 infants). He has studied up to Standard 6 and his wife is educated up to Standard 4. His elder son received I.T.I (Industrial Training Institute) as a fitter training from a local industrial training Institute. The second son after being unsuccessful in his attempt to attain Standard 10 (school final) gave up his studies and entered into petty trading business. The third son is studying in class 7. Mr. Rao's main occupation is petty trading in seasonal commodities and two of his sons are also involved in the business in parallel.

He owns land and runs a small trading. They had 10 acres of land but 8 acres have been sold for the maintenance of the big family for which agriculture failed to provide sufficient income. The remaining 2 acres are let to tenants to grow rice. For this they will receive Rs. 1000 (which is very small) rental per year. Narayana Rao has also done some building contract work in the past but, following financial losses, he gave

Table 5.3 : Key Characteristics of Case Study Households in Anandapuram

Name of Interviewee	Sex	Age	No. of People in HH	Occupation of HH	Caste	Years in occupation	Reasons for transformation into RNFS	No. of children	Age of children	Level ofschooling	Occupation of children if any	Previous occupation of HH	HH head father's occupation
K. Appala Naidu	M	30	5	Toddy tapping + quarrying	Settibalia	Quarrying since 1984	Traditional and Demand			-	-	Toddy tapping	Agrl. labourer
G. Rumunaidu	M	28	4	Local factory worker	Yadavas	Since January 1995	Better wages, job security	None	-	-	-	Ricksha-puller	Cultivation
M. Appalaswamy	M	50	6	Masonry	Throup Kapu (B. C)	Since beginning	Acquired skills	4	19, 16, 14, 12,	One daughter 7th	2 sons masonry	Agril labourer	Bullock cart
E. Narasimha Rao	M	30	3	Khalasi (porter)	Yadava	1982	Distress diversification	no	-	-	-	Dormitory based labour	Agrl labourer
K. Narayana Rao	M	58	12	Shandy business+ Cultivation	Komati business (O. C)	Since Beginning	Family support and education	4	25, 21, 17, 12	I.T.I, S.S.C, 7th	2 sons shandi business	Cultivation	Shandy business
P. Murari	M	42	5	Owns teak and ply wood industry	Marvadis	Since Beginning	Capital, education location	2	15, 11	12, S.S.C	Students	Business	Business
E. Appala Konda	F	23	3	Flower-picker	Yadava	1992	Distress	1	5	-	-	Husband rearing goats+ rickshaw	Shepherd
C.B. Naidu	M	47	6	Cultivation + poultry farm	Naidu	1991	Additional income	4	18, 12, 7, 5	10th, 6th, 2nd, 1st	None	Cultivation	Cultivation

Notes : H H: household head, M= male, F= female, BC: Backward Caste, FC: Forward Caste

Table 5.4 : Key Points Emerging from the Anandapuram Case Studies 1995

Name of Interviewee	
K. Appala Naidu	Role of caste, traditional and seasonal link with agriculture, shifting occupation petty trade and quarrying. Wife also an income earner.
G. Rumunaidu	Change of occupation following no role of education, wife contributes an extra income, would have been better off as agricultural labourer.
M.Appalaswamy	No role of education, skilled occupation, seasonal, provides wage employment for 8 people, linkage with agricultural allied activity, change of vocation from agricultural to skilled profession
E. Narasimha Rao	No role of education, change of profession (agricultural labourer to porter) consequent to social difficulties, seasonal link with agriculture, flexibility in working hours.
Narayāna Rao	Role of secondary education, seasonal work, profitable activity, required organisational skills.
P. Murari	Role of education, role of capital, managerial skills, location advantage, profits and employment generation, role of caste, migration,
E. Appala Konda	Lower wages (for 4 hours worked earn only Rs. 5 as a wage), seasonal employment, husband earns money as rickshaw puller.
C.B. Naidu	Role of capital and credit, role of agriculture, marketing techniques, self employment, personal skills

up this particular business and had a panshop (such a shop caters for people who enjoy this particular pastime of chewing betel leaves and nuts, lime and some sweet and hot pan masala) for a period of 5 years. Currently, he has no panshop.

His first two son's job is trading chilli and cashews. The elder son of Mr. Rao buys and sells goods at weekly village markets (shandys). Seasonally there is a high demand for the business from April to July. In the remaining period, he lends money 5 days a week. Shandys are organised in nearby villages during different days of the week. The household head's main job consists of buying the bags of chillies and cashews from farmers and carrying them on bullock carts and buses to the shandies of Tagarapu Valasa, Boya Palam, Madhuravada, and of Anandapuram. These business people do not entirely depend on their own villages. He made an initial capital of Rs. 5,000 on the panshop, and his sales are worth Rs. 150 per day, of which Rs. 40 to Rs. 50 is profit (10 Manugulu are equivalent to 100 kgs load of chillies and cashews carries to the shandy). He buys 1 kg of chillies for Rs. 39 and sells of at Rs. 42, making a profit of Rs. 3 per Kg. He gets on average Rs. 300 profit on each weekly village market. For cashew the market price is Rs. 26 per kg. which he buys for Rs. 23 from the farmer. In 4 months he earns Rs. 5,000 in net profit. Mr. Rao's second son is also involved in the family business so there is a continuity in their business from father to sons. During the interview, as well as during personal observation, the son was worried because of increasing competition from newcomers, hence he expects less business in his otherwise profitable enterprise. Of late this trading business requires a Government licence, and for every Rs. 100 worth of profit he has to pay a Rs. 2 tax. Mr. Rao's parents also participate the same business doing shandy. Together they earn Rs. 4,000 in a month. They are satisfied with their present income.

As is clear from the foregoing case-study the demand for non-farm activities, especially for petty trade business, is increasing. The extent of marketing by the marginal farmers is influenced by first, the composition of agricultural output between food crops and commercial crops, second, the output of foodgrains in relation to the requirements of the family. The profits being made generate the setting up petty-trading activities which in the long-run might erode the profits being made. There has been a transition away from agriculture to the RNFS business sector for a larger number of family households.

The point we want to make with this case study is that partly agriculture is responsible (even though farm output is not adequate) for the diversification into non-farm activity.

Mr. Golagani Raminaidu (Mr. Naidu) (by caste Yadava, B.C community) works in a local factory which produces a popular stimulant called *'guudaku'* from decayed tobacco leaves imported from Orissa. The leaves are combined with lime molasses, and clay soil and then processed and packed into small tins which are then sold in the market. It is applied to tooth and gums and induces mild intoxication. Two lorries of the manufactured product are exported to Cuttack.

He is a native of the village and illiterate, and used to tend goats. Then for some time he worked in the same job that he is doing now, then for 9 years was engaged in rickshaw pulling. Golagani Raminaidu's father was engaged in agriculture and used to own an acre of land which was sold due to the increase in household expenditure. There are 4 persons in the household. All are adults and the interviewee does not have children.

Mr. Naidu has worked in this factory since January 1995. The factory was started in 1974 by M.K. Khan a businessman from Cuttack (the former capital of border State of Orissa). The significance of this is an example of job creation by an immigrant entrepreneur.

At present, the factory employs 40 men of which 21 are employed permanently earning Rs. 950 per month, and these salaries are enhanced based on the duration of the service. The main market for the factory's output is in the border State of Orissa. Formerly they were paid a wage of Rs. 350 per month. (Due to a dispute between the workers and the owner they approached the court and the workers won the case so that there has been a big pay rise]. The interviewee gets Rs. 31.50

per day. His salary has been enhanced of late and his job has also become permanent. This job is available throughout the year, so at present he enjoys job security. Formerly, women were also employed but they were recently discharged, due to inadequate work.

Frequently Mr. Naidu's wife engages in agricultural labour on the commercial flower plantations and is paid Rs. 10 per day. The market for the flowers is in near by city of Visakhapatnam. Here it is worth pointing out that women are ruthlessly exploited and that no consideration is shown for their long hours of work.

A bag of rice is consumed by the family members each month. The family borrowed an amount to Rs. 2000 at 2 per cent interest monthly. Once a year during the Dasera festival a bonus equivalent to one month's salary is given. The only complaint Golagani Raminaidu made was that during his work period, due to the dust of the product manufactured, workers vomit and feel nauseous.

The life of the interviewee can be regarded as a partial success, he has job security but his income is not sufficient to ensure a secure future because of this low income and the lack of pension, gratuity and leave facilities. There has been a transition form agriculture to factory employment. Compared to the primary job the current job is better in terms of employment and income, but the conditions apparently pose a threat to health. The interesting feature of this account is the presence of 2 capitalist, wage-labour based, enterprises in a poor village due to the village's proximity to wider markets; also it has a location advantage as cheap labour is available, and if the factory is within the villages it will be given small scale concessions such as tax reduction, and other financial facilitates for the industry bank loans.

Again in this case also the finding is that this family belonged to a traditional occupation along with agricultural labour work. There is a transition from agriculture labour to permanent factory employment even though he is illiterate. For this transition agriculture is partly responsible.

5.2.2 *Farm Income Diversification into RNFE*

In Anandapuram people are seeking channels for raising income through farm diversification to RNFS, which is providing non-farm employment. For instance commercial crops; vegetables, flowers, horticulture, dairy farming, and provision of irrigation facilities; poultry farming, sheep-rearing.

5.2.2.1 Land Ownership/agricultural Commercialisation/farm Income Diversification Leads to RNFS

In order to supplement income a number of farm households are involved in subsidiary and allied occupations. Land ownership is the one deciding factor in decision making to choose the type of activity in the RNFS.

Mr. Chandraka Bangaru Naidu was educated up to graduation. He has 4 children, 1 son and 3 daughters. The eldest daughter has studied up to the 10th standard, the second daughter is studying 6th standard, the third daughter 2nd standard and the son 1st standard. He is a land-owning middle farmer and additionally owns a poultry farm. The household has 4 acres of wet land and 2 acres of dry land. In the wet land rice is grown yielding 20 bags an acre, and on the dry land he grows 3 to 4 bags of groundnut. Mr. Naidu is also involved in civil contracts like road construction and small building (officially termed as self-employed). This work is normally carried out for Praja Prashid (local elected body) and the Department of Education in nearby sites.

There is little guarantee for farmers in the area that they will make a profit from their crops. For this reason they constantly shift crops in search of an alternative source of income. Because they live near the city they found it profitable to grow fruits and vegetables to sell at the city market. Mainly marginal farmers are facing problems. Some of them are leaving their own villages and lands in search of other means to make a living. There is also little interest amongst the present generation in carrying on farming on the family-based traditional land. That is why farmers have shifted from paddy and ragi farming to vegetable growing and rose plantations. Farmers grow (1) rose plants and hybrid vegetables 'Beerakaya' (bottle guard) in February and June, (2) groundnut (which is a profitable product) in June and August and (3) In July-August (the beginning of the monsoon) farmers start agriculture plantations.

Between January and June they would normally have less work. It is during this period that they produce plants and vegetables, as there is no problem with insects during the summer months. The air will also be very fresh and should there be a problem with insects the farmer will spray the crop, usually only once. The Government offers a 15 per cent subsidy on seeds.

This case signals it is profitable to engage in both activities. Farm income diversification generates employment opportunities through agricultural growth linkages. Farmers can fall back on one or the other in case of a crop failure or a loss in the non-farm sector, but that happens very rarely and generally rich farmers make a profit from both activities. This case mostly shows diversification within farming (defined as crop and livestock development). It is important to record that such developments generate non-farm linkages.

The point we are making from this case study is that shifting occupation is inevitable in the less agriculturally developed village. Farm activity alone cannot provide sufficient income for the livelihood of the households. Consumption and production linkages are very important for the generation of adequate incomes for the middle farmers also.

5.2.2.2 Distress Diversification

One dimension to the growth of non-farm activities in rural areas can be termed 'distress diversification' into unproductive or low paid non-farm jobs. This happens where total labour is not employed in the farm sector and the non-farm sector acts as cushion for the excess labour. Mr. Egala Narasimha Rao' case illustrates such distress diversification.

Mr. Egala Narasimha Rao (Mr. Rao) a *khalasi* or porter[2] is 30 years old, unmarried, native of and still living in Anandapuram. The household does not have any land. They belong to the Yadava caste (declared a B.C. by the AP Government). For the last 3 generations no one in his family has been educated. His mother is an agricultural labourer earning 5 Rs. for 4 hours of work in the middle of the 1990s. The women gets Rs. 10 per day of work. Because of old age his father is unable to work at all. On average no work is available to Narasimha Rao for two days each week.

His main occupation for the last 15 years has been as a *khalasi*. Previously, he worked for 5 years as a paleru (dormitory-based labourer for a rich farmer), where he used to earn Rs. 300 per month and free food for himself. His work now as a porter is seasonal even though he works solely for a particular merchant, unloading bags. For each bag he receives 1 Rupee although he also unloads 15 Kg oil tins for which he gets 50 paise, and 25 paise for jaggory cubes. The amount paid by the merchant for unloading is matched by a similar sum from the farmer. If he works during the high season between 6 am and 1 p.m. he earns between Rs. 20-30.

Mr. Rao changed his occupation from a dormitory-based agricultural labourer to a porter, because as a porter working 6 hours a day is better than working throughout the year under a farmer as a bonded labourer. There are no problems with the work although he had to borrow Rs. 4000 for his sister's wedding. He had to repay the debt at the rate of Rs. 3 for Rs. 100 per month. Consequently they had to eat Ragi (they make gruel out of ragi) rather than more costly rice.

There are specific occupational problems; due to the recession in farming (yields are low because mostly in that villages agriculture depends on rainfed) there is not much demand for his work as a *khalasi*. The business (selling provisions) has been decentralised in line with Government policy. The Government made arrangements to supply rice through civil supply organisations under government schemas. Supplies have however been irregular and the Government has imposed limits on rice stocks. Because of this policy, business persons (these persons are supposed to buy rice and sell to the people directly) buy less rice from the wholesale shop which ultimately reduced the hours he works as a porter. Another reason for falling demand for *khalasi* labour relates to the tradition of the *Komatis* - the trading community - who look after the business. Mr.Rao has been working for this community. Because of the diffusion of trading amongst non *komati* businessmen he gets less and less work. In addition porters do not work individually. They collectively contract loading and unloading, and distribute the money earned among themselves at the end of day. Moreover cooking oil is sold in the market at a subsidised rate to the public through the public distribution system managed by the Ministry of Civil Supplies. Thus, the distribution of food items has reduced in the open market in which workers such as Mr. rao are involved.

Another point lies in the fact that the demand for the above mentioned items depends on the purchasing power of people. If people have more money they will consume more rice, oil and pulses, ultimately creating more work. After the withdrawal of subsidies, prices of fertilisers went up considerably. As a result, small and middle-scale farmers bought less of it and distribution of fertilisers reduced sharply together with the demand for porters' work. Some farmers are currently thinking of using traditional fertiliser techniques. In parallel, increases in the price of essential commodities meant that the demand for supply and distribution of such commodities went down, affecting the demand for labour of people like Mr.Rao.

This worker breakfasts on gruel which is left over from the previous night's food, which mainly consists of rice, chilli salt and water. Lunch is Ragi gruel (because it is very cheap compared to rice). Once a day, normally in the evenings, he will eat rice. It can be clearly seen from the foregoing case study that because of macro-economic changes, the demand, the supply and the distribution of all commodities (essential and non-essential) have fallen very sharply, as has unskilled labour like *khalasi.*

The point we make from this case study is that seasonal non-farm activities are important for a poor person like Mr. Narasimha Rao. It clearly displays distress diversification from a dormitory-based labourer to porter even though the income is very marginal. His working hours are limited to six hours.

5.2.3 Locational Advantage/the Role Education and of Skills

The level of literacy can be an important factor of influence on economic position. We have also noticed in our empirical logit regression results for Anandapuram the potential significance of education attainment for RNFE The educational skills influence the economic position in Mr. Pairu's case.

Mr. Pairu Murari Badruka is educated up to graduation. He is a 42 year old industrialist who owns a teak and plywood industry. His father was also an industrialist in Visakhapatnam city. He belong to the Marvadi communities. (The Marvadies are a traditional and generally highly successful trading and business community. They originally belong to the Marwadi region of the Western State of Rajastan).

Mr. Pairu owns Andhra Wood Product (Private) Ltd. This was registered in 1989 but production started in August 1992. There are 53 people working in the factory: 9 supervisors; 6 operators; 29 permanent workers; and the remainder are casual labourers. They produce veneer top surfaces for plywood, which they supply to order for various product wholesalers and retailers throughout India. Inside the factory the main units are peeling clipper, flattening and dry machine.

The owner has made an initial investment of Rs.3 million. The money came from banks, Government and other financial institutions. They import raw material (logs of wood) from Malaysia, Myanmaar (Burma), and Kombodia (Kampuchea). To minimise import costs, 4-5 small industrialists generally jointly import from foreign destinations and once in India the raw material is distributed according to requirements. Generally, shipments are 2000 tonnes of log-wood which first comes to the port of Visakhapatnam and reaches different destinations by lorry/four wheeler. After processing the log wood through cutting, peeling, clipping and drying, the factory then supplies the finished product to various furniture makers, to builders for sealing purposes, and to decorators for laminations.

The Manager is paid Rs. 3000 per month, the Supervisor Rs. 1200-1600, and the trainee and probationary supervisor around Rs. 1000. The wage of unskilled male labour is Rs. 20 per working day and that of a female unskilled labourer Rs. 17 per working day. The main operators of the various units receive Rs. 2500 per month, because their task involves skilled and technical expertise.

In September 1989, the total production of teak and plywood was 488.02 cubic feet (this figure is cross-checked with trade union leaders of the factory affiliated to CITU[3]). In February 1995, the production had gone up to 270,564.03 (meters). They supplied 17 trucks of material in that month, each truck carrying a 24,000 to 25,000 Sq. metres load.

The main reasons, according to Pairu for establishing a ply and teak wood industry in this place are: that there is sufficient supply of water for the industry, and labour is available at a cheaper rate than in a city. In addition, the initial investment of only Rs. 3 million rupees makes it a small scale industry and, as the factory is located in a backward area, the factory owner gets substantial tax concessions (as specified by the Govern-ment). Consequently loans at low interest are available from the commercial banks as per order of the Government. A last motive for the choice of location relates to the fact that the excise duty and sales taxes are fixed by the central Government, and that a small-scale industry is exempted from these for a period of up to 5 years. There are similar factories in the nearby places of Sabbavaram, Boddupalem, Bogapuram, and Aripaka, which is convenient for joint imports of log wood from overseas. The port of Visakhapatnam is only 45 Kms away from Anandapuram.

The point from this case study is that even in backward areas like Anandapuram there are plenty of opportunities for expanding the industrial infrastructure and thereby expanding employment opportunities in the non-farm sector. The main economic constraint is securing sufficient capital to run the business. Here education, traditional experience and locational advantage helped to acquire adequate managerial skills for the success of business.

5.2.4. Caste vis-a-vis Traditional Non-farm Occupation

Traditional non-farm, wage, seasonal employment and self-employment are the most predominant form of employment in the rural areas. Within any year there are considerable shifts in demand for work depending mainly upon the seasons. In the peak season of the crop (e.g. paddy) i.e., during trans-planting, harvesting and threshing the demand curve for labour shifts to the right. During this season, there is an urgency in completing the operation of the crop. The reason is that working hours are also longer when compared to operations in other seasons.

Opportunities for earning wages in non-farm work are many, particularly in villages around urban centres, fishing villages and villages situated in forest areas. In villages around urban centres, construction work, rickshaw pulling and quarrying are important. These are occupations pursued mainly in the slack seasons of agriculture. Caste continues to play a decisive role in influencing the employment opportunities. Wage rates earned from these pursuits compare favourably with slack season wages in the farm sector. Mr. Appalanaidu's case is related to caste theme.

Mr. Koppula Appalanaidu's primary job is toddy tapping. His secondary occupation is working in the quarry, loading and unloading lorries. He is 30 years old and both he and his wife are uneducated. His father worked as a labourer under a local farmer while his grand father used to tend buffaloes. However, both his father and grandfather engaged in toddy tapping, an occupation which is seasonal in nature.

The peak period for the activity is from mid January to the end of May. Mr Naidu draws toddy from 20 trees. The family suspend a pot from each source of toddy and collect the liquid daily. Each tree has 4 to 12 point spots of toddy and those who have a higher number of points are called feminine trees. Each pot yields one to two earthen tumblers of toddy, and if 20 trees are tapped they yield some 40 pots. On average a tree has to be climbed 3 times a day and (with virtually no exception) all the male members in the families consume toddy. Women do not consume toddy.

The toddy is usually sold at the bottom of the tree itself. Most trees are located in farmers' field, and the tappers pay a tax to the farmer for using the products of the tree. Additionally, the farmer receives 4 to 5 tumblers of toddy gratis per day. A tax of Rs. 55 has to be paid, of which Rs. 16 are paid as a prohibition tax (new tax) for a period of 11 months. A tax of Rs. 28 is payable for making the mark (signifying temporary possession) on the tree. There is also a traditional bribe to be paid to the constable. Farmers frequently threaten that unless toddy tappers support them on various village-related issues the trees will be cut including toddy. As long as toddy is available from the trees the tappers will be adequately remunerated, especially after the Government declared prohibition on various intoxicants (excluding toddy).

Koppula Appalanaidu will switch to his other work (lorry loader) from June to January. He has been engaged in this lorry work for the past 10 years. The work will be available for 4 days a week and he will be paid Rs. 30 per single load and Rs. 60 per double load. If a person is engaged in this work at 8 o'clock in the morning he is relieved at the same time the next day. Women do not engage in lorry loading work as it is considered too strenuous. In the village of Endada, there are two quarries quarrying hills and it is there that most workers are engaged. The output of quarrying (i.e. stones) is transported to the steel plants at Visakhapatnam and Nadipalli. Additionally lorries transport other building materials to various construction sites.

The interviewee does not possess any land and he is a native of the village. His wife does not work in quarrying but she sells toddy. In seasons when employment is scanty the household engage in pig rearing, selling meat in local shandies and also in marketing fish from the Gambheram reservoir and the sea in nearby Bhimili.

As far as the primary vocation of the household is concerned, it is seasonal in nature and does not sustain the family throughout the year. Though the 2 occupations appear to be of equal importance the toddy tapping is classified as primary because the quarrying activity emerged only recently after the Steel Plant construction started in Visakhapatnam. As Koppula Appalanaidu's main livelihood is not a viable one his life cannot be termed as a success in material prosperity. The only connection with agriculture is traditional toddy (palm) trees which are located in the fields of farmers.

The point we make from this case study is that for traditional non-farm occupations, caste is the barrier in rural villages even today. This a kind of distress diversification. If people are illiterate in that particular caste they are bound to associate to those occupations.

5.2.5 Skilled Professions

In rural areas skilled occupations are pursued by people belonging to particular communities such as carpentry, barbers, cobblers, blacksmiths, cotton carders, butchers etc. These skills are transferred from generation to generation within that particular community only. Other communities do not take part in these activities. Mr. Mamidi Appalasawmy's case is related to this theme.

Mr. Mamidi Appalaswamy is a resident of Anandapuram. He has a wife, two sons, and two daughters. All but one are illiterate, a daughter who is studying in 7th standard. Mamidi's primary vocation is masonry, and his sons are also engaged in the same occupation. One of his sons is married and set up a separate household while the other, unmarried, entered this trade in1993. There are around 15 masons in the village. According to him alternative employment is limited in the village. Work is available for 6 days a week. He has 8 people working under him, the men are paid a wage of Rs. 50 per day, and the women Rs.20 per day His and his sons' work is seasonal because people prefer major construction work in summer only but not in the rainy season, and he goes wherever his services are needed.

In the absence of his primary vocation, the household sometimes engages in transporting organic fertiliser to the fields, for which he is paid Rs. 30 per day. Mr. Appalaswamy has not learnt another trade. The household head encouraged and taught his sons. There is a continuity in inter-generational employment, the father of the interviewee was an agricultural labourer as well as mason. The nature of work changed during the present generation. Masonry is skilled work. On the day of shandy he spends Rs. 200 to Rs. 300 to pay for the necessary provisions for a week. The expenditure sometimes exceeds that of the necessities. One problem with this vocation is that those engaged in it are prone to accidents. The occupation is hazardous, stilts and supports on which they work collapse or workers fall resulting in injury. There is no protection or insurance on the side of the employer. There is no law to protect the workers' interest, although they are now requesting adequate legal welfare provisions from the government particularly those who work in this occupation. An amount of Rs. 4000 was borrowed on an interest-free loan for his daughter's marriage. He earns an income of Rs. 1200 per month. Once the expenditure is subtracted it leaves a savings of Rs. 200 to Rs. 300 per month.

A number of suggestions were made by the interviewee regarding security and welfare. All Government construction works are given to private contractors, who then sub-contract the work to them. The interviewee is opposed to this system, in which the majority of the profit goes to the contractor and not to the workers. The abolition of the contract system in this occupation is necessary to avoid exploitation and corruption and to increase these peoples' living standards. A law should be introduced and implemented to protect their rights. Also, construction workers have to use certain instruments in their occupation. The Government should provide credit facilities to buy these instruments, as they are paying interest at the rate of 6 per cent per month. If the banks offered loans to these people the interest could be reduced 1.90 per cent. Masons need bicycles to reach distant work places and hiring a bicycle for one month cost Rs. 150. If the banks were to give a loan at low rate interest to buy a bicycle it would be a great help to them. In this occupation there are possibilities of frequent illness from handling cement, as inhalation of the dust makes some of them permanently very weak. In such times they would need free medical care and money for a good food supply.

The case study illustrates another way in which farm and non-farm complement each other. If people have more income through agricultural out put there is a demand for construction. There is a linkage effect we have also seen this effect in our secondary data regressions.

5.2.6 The Economic Factors

Economic factors such as education, capital, wages of the workers, raw material availability, managerial skills, production techniques, and marketing skills are the important dynamic economic factors which centre on the relative profit, savings and reinvestment rates of RNFS activities. This capital growth issue is significant for policy because it sheds light on the economy's growth rate. Mr. Pairu Murari Badruka's case is relevant to this theme.

5.2.7 Commercialisation of Agriculture: Non-farm Wage Labour

Commercialisation is expected to encourage RNFS activity by supplying vegetables, flowers etc., creating greater demand for such goods and services, raising demand for consumer goods and generating surplus for investment. Mrs Eagala Appala Konda's wage labour created in that process is an example for this theme.

Mrs Eagala Appala Konda, aged 23, lives with her husband, Eagala Narayana Rao, aged 25, and their child of 5. They belong to the Yadava caste. Her main occupation is working as a plucker and picker of flowers and fruits for petty trading. The land and crops are owned by her employer who is a middle farmer. She works from 7 am to 12 noon.

Recently, the flower business has been flourishing in the cluster of nearby villages. Jasmine, roses, kanakambralu jajulu, virajajulu and banti are the different kinds of flowers grown on the land where she works. The farmer supplies these flowers to the nearby cities and towns of Visakhapatnam, Gopalapatnam, Pendurti, Narsipatnam, Subbavaram through wholesalers in kilograms. One kilo of flower is sold at a minimum of Rs. 40. These prices go up, according to season and demand, to Rs. 100 or Rs. 180.

The farmer in the peak season can harvest 50 kg of jasmine flowers and 10 kg of jaji per day by employing 6 labourers, mostly women. The peak season for these flowers is between February and July. During the summer season the yield is high for jasmine whereas for jaji the peak season is March to July. There is normally a heavy demand for flowers during the marriage and election seasons.

Under the District Rural Development Agency (DRDA) programme, the Government has offered subsidies to such farmers for the last 3 years. Moreover, banks offer soft loan facilities. Even though there is plenty of work available the wage is normally only Rs. 10 per day.

Before growing the flowers farmers grew *ragi, ganti,* cholu black gram, and green gram on the same land. The shift to the present yield of flowers is important in this context because of its profitability and capacity for generating instant cash. For growing flowers the farmers need to use less water. The present Government agricultural policy is to export more flowers thus reducing the production of traditional crops.

Mrs. Konda's husband, who is illiterate, has been engaged in rearing goats since the age of 5. He owns a rickshaw and every day he earns Rs. 20 by rickshaw pulling. During the summer there was much demand for the rickshaw puller. Similarly to Mrs. Konda's case, her mother also picks flowers and her father is a shepherd. The government provides a small house to both families under Indira Awaas Yojana (IAY Indira Gandhi's housing scheme for the poor). They incurred a debt of Rs. 5000 to meet expenses of Mrs Konda's husband sister's marriage and are paying interest on it. They are obviously not satisfied with their present wages. Compared to previous yields of ragi, ganti, chollu, green gram, and black gram which are locally consumed, flowers are exported commodities. The switch has also resulted in a decrease in demand for synthetic fertilisers and an increase in the use of bio-manure products (whereas traditional pulses need comparatively high amounts of fertilisers).

The switch to cash crop means very good earnings for the land owner and to the national economy in terms of foreign export earning. But, as this case study shows, the wages/or labourers have remained static even though the demand for labour has marginally increased.

Given the absence of a trade union in the unorganised sector land-owners continue to give very low wages, even though their own income has increased. Even the minimum wage specified by the Government is not observed.

The main point I intended to illustrate in this section is that the rainfed village of Anandapuram does raise commercial crops with high value added which gives more returns, and consumption linkages are strong.

Conclusions

The case studies presented indicate the wide range of non-farm activities in the two villages, and their varied impact on the levels of household income. Other points highlighted include the following.

1. Mr. Somaih and Mr. Uma's cases in Veeravalli illustrate that the growth of the RNFS is associated with backward and forward production linkages to farm activities.
2. Seasonality and weather conditions affect non-farm employment.
3. In the process of economic growth certain traditional activities such as handloom weaving and carding cotton (Mr. Sheik Husian), traditional gunny bags (Mr. Bhimudu), pottery (Mr. Ramananda), carpentry (Mr. Achari), toddy tapping (Mr. Raghavuly and Mr. Satyanaraya) lose out to modern activities.
4. Technological changes in agriculture such as mechanisation and tractorisation are leading to the emergence of new opportunities for employment outside the farm. Especially tractorisation has led to the emergence of a new non-farm

occupations like repairs, maintenance of the tractors including sale of spare parts and sales.

5. People are successful in RNFS when they are able to capture the opportunity at the right moment of entry into services sector, catering to the needs of modern life and expanding agriculture.

6. Where the man-power is family-based and RNFS households had relatively successful agricultural activity to fall back on to meet the daily consumption, a comfortable position in agriculture, coupled with an available market and man power led to the success of the venture. This in short is a situation where capital, man power, market, and infrastructure facilities have all come together to make non-farm employment.

7. Non-farm employment which involves seasonality characterised by low wages, irregular timings etc. This irregularity necessitates taking up other jobs in RNFE which involve instability, lower wages, dissatisfaction and ill-health. Where no demand for agricultural activities exists, the present generation is getting absorbed into these jobs. This situation keeps them always on the lookout for alternative if not better opportunities.

8. Small vendors of vegetables and fruits are restricted by lack of raw materials and capital as it involves the purchase of materials for cash every day.

9. Some traditional RNFE is affected by technological changes. For example a blacksmith finds it difficult to change over to repairing tyre carts, a potter who installed electric machinery to improve on designs and quality also could not cope with it.

10. The present generation prefers to obtain education in polytechnics and industrial training institutes and try to get secure RNFE. But this kind of situation usually depends on the family's possession of agricultural land as well as exploitation of non-farm employment as a source of additional income. For the uneducated in Anandapuram,

the shift is observed from toddy tapping to work on trucks (loading and unloading of materials) or to factory work different from educated work. The jobs then have fixed monthly salaries or daily wage.

11. There is a frequent occupational mobility of people within the non-farm sector. The reason is seasonality of work, new options, insufficient incomes and large numbers of entrants into the non-farm employment.

12. In the case where investment was made on a small or medium scale with the advantage of the availability of cheap labour, the non-farm venture gets stabilised. This brings out the fact that for RNFE to be of a permanent nature, use of local resources and investment is required to commence a technology based unit.

13. The income earned the non-farm employment based on a single activity was sometimes very meagre and therefore, some people have to engage in more than one activity according to opportunity and seasonality. This implies that no particular skill or experience is imparted for the worker involved in non-farm employment.

NOTES

1. This background effects RNFS activity i.e. caste specialisation or caught in formal survey.
2. A *Khalasi*, otherwise known as a coolie, is a porter who loads and unloads food grain bags from lorries.
3. CITU is a Federation of the Centre for Indian Trade Unions.

6

SUMMARY AND SOME CONCLUSIONS

Non-farm activities, whether rural or urban, reduce the pressure on land, and produce goods and services. The RNFS is normally more labour-intensive than the urban, and hence creates employment and extra income for the rural poor. Rural non-farm activities began to receive increased attention in India only after employment elasticities began to decline in agriculture. The need for generating employment in RNFS is now an important issue in India and policies to do this are vital for alleviating poverty by reducing unemployment.

In AP more clearly than in India as a whole, labour absorption in agriculture and in the urban-industrial sectors has not grown fast enough to match the growth of the labour force. Unemployment has persisted, and in some cases increased in rural areas. Though agriculture continues to be the largest employer, in the light of declining employment elasticity (e.g. Bhalla, 1987; Jayasuriya & Shand, 1986) any future rise in employment may increasingly have to be found beyond the agricultural sector.

Does agricultural growth stimulate rural non-farm growth ('growth linkages') or does agriculture stagnation compel rural non-farm growth ('distress-diversification')? This thesis seeks to test 'distress diversification' against 'growth linkages' as explanations of rural non-farm employment, or - more precisely

- of the propensity of rural workforce participants in AP to be involved in the RNFS. The 'strict' growth linkages hypothesis is that of agricultural growth linkages (AGL): higher - or a faster growing - agricultural income/output/employment tends to cause more, or faster-growing, nearby rural non-farm share. Then on the agricultural distress diversification hypothesis (ADD) is the opposite hypothesis that lower (or slower growing) agricultural production (or 'performance' in agriculture) causes higher (or faster-growing) RNFE share.

A wider 'development linkage/diversification hypothesis' has also been tested, that of this overall development linkage hypothesis (ODL) is that higher (or faster-growing) development indicators such as literacy, bank branches, urbanisation, tend to cause more (or faster-growing) nearby RNFE. Then on the converse, overall distress diversification hypothesis (ODD) is that lower (or slower-growing) development indicators cause higher (or faster-growing) RNFE share.

These hypotheses have been explored using (a) district level (secondary data) and (b) household level (primary data) in regressions designed to explain differences in RNFE labour force shares and, in the case of (a), RNFE growth rates. The primary question is whether agricultural prosperity (and related factors) increase or decrease RNFS employment share. In the course of the thesis, some other explanations of inter-district and inter-household variations in RNFE are also tested.

A central hypothesis, tested in Chapter 3 and Chapter 4, is that different factors determine 'traditional' and 'modern' RNFE shares in total employment. A high traditional rural non-farm share is likely to be associated with workers having relatively few years of education, with lower castes, and with agricultural indicators suggesting distress diversification. A high modern rural non-farm share is likely to be associated with better-educated household members, with upper castes, and with agricultural indicators suggesting rural growth linkages from agriculture.

Our evidence suggests that traditional-sector RNFE growth does tend to be in part due to 'distress-diversification' out of agriculture into non-farm activities; whereas modern-sector RNFE growth tends to be in part due to rural growth linkages of agriculture to RNFE. When rural labour is not fully absorbed in the farm sector, the traditional non-farm sector acts as a sponge for labour spillover into low productivity and low paid non-farm activities. Overall, however, growth linkages predominate, i.e. it is good performance of the agricultural sector (and, more generally, development) that favourably influences the share of total (traditional plus modern) RNFE, at both inter-district and inter-household levels.

Several studies have been carried out in the past to find out the determinants of RNFE, but few, if any, emphasise the determinants of RNFE at micro level. Most empirical research on RNFE in India is based on secondary data at all-India or state levels. Apart form the lack of household-level (and even cross-district) studies, work on the composition of the RNFS is rare. Our literature review emphasised the need for further careful testing of disaggregated responses, for instance at the district-level and household-level, in order to find out causes of growth of RNFE.

Evidence of several studies in the Indian context indicate that RNFE is important for the poor. However, it appears from the literature that no attempt has been made so far to examine the determinants of RNFE in the agriculturally developed regions vis-à-vis agriculturally less developed regions. One new contribution of our study is to compare the causes of RNFE growth between a more developed and a less developed village. The main conclusion here is that a household's probability of having the main worker in RNFE rises faster in Veeravalli, the developed village, compared to Anandapuram. Households in Veeravalli are more likely to have a main worker, in particular in modern employment. Also the marginal effect of education on the probability of a household having RNFE is greater in the more developed village compared to less developed village.

There follows a summary of the main findings of this study of RNFE in AP.

Trends in RNFE and its Composition in AP and India (1981 and 1991)

There has been an increasing trend in the shares of RNFE in AP and India. However, the RNFE share has been less, and slower-growing in the 1980s, in AP than elsewhere in India, despite slower improvement in output (and in labour absorption) in agriculture. So AP is a good place to examine the causes of high - or low - RNFE growth.

Census data confirms the rise in RNFE both at the national and state levels, and the predominance of males in RNFE, in 1981 and 1991 both in India and AP. But AP, unlike all-India has a rising percentage of agricultural labourers in the rural workforce. Furthermore, with development, poverty is being concentrated among the agricultural labour households in several districts of AP.

The size of the RNFE, viz., the rural percentage of total main workers principally engaged in the non-farm sector, in AP was at 16.8 per cent and 17.1 per cent in 1981 and 1991 respectively, compared with all-India's 17.7 per cent in 1991 (and has been growing relatively more slowly since 1981 at 2.2 per cent a year compared to 2.8 per cent nationally). AP's share is not far below all-India's, but AP's share is growing slower while that of India is growing faster. There is considerable inter-district variation in the industrial distribution of AP's rural workforce, and in its change in 1981-91. In 1981 the proportion of non-farm workers in rural areas was relatively high in Nizamabad and low in Mahabubnagar districts. The share has either declined or increased very little in the districts of Srikakulam and East Godavari. In the remaining parts of the state the increase was moderate. In 1981, the Ranga Reddy district had the highest (22.5 per cent) while Ananthapur has the lowest (12.1 per cent) figure. In 1991, the Nizamabad district had the highest (26.8 per cent) while Ananthapur had lowest size (13.3 per cent). The inter-district coefficient of variation of RNFE share, in 1981-91 increased marginally. The districts which obtained top ten ranks in 1981 more or less obtained the same ranks in 1991.

The pattern of change in the size of RNFE would not necessarily appear encouraging in terms of economic development; in 12 of 22 districts there was a decrease in the proportion of RNFE between the two periods. However, across the time span and for most of these districts, the proportion of people below the poverty line has decreased, urbanisation has possibly absorbed some of those engaged in RNFS activities, and the per capita value of agricultural output has also increased. One potential cause for concern was the district of Mahabubnagar where a steady, low share of RNFE coincided with an increase in the percentage of persons below the poverty line.

Trends in RNFE in Visakhapatnam and Krishna (1981 and 1991)

We chose a less developed and a more developed district, respectively Visakhapatnam and Krishna, to explore underlying reasons for district-level RNFE trends in more detail. Visakhapatnam has higher illiteracy, more agricultural dependency, less irrigation cultivation agriculture and is more drought affected than Krishna.

Although agriculture is the dominant source of employment for the rural population in these two districts, there was a trend towards a decrease in RNFE by -2.49 in Visakhapatnam and -0.42 in Krishna per annum growth rate between 1981-91. These shares fall because urbanisation has been growing faster in both the districts. Early absorption of the green revolution with good canal irrigation facilities explains the higher position occupied by only traditional male RNFE in Visakhapatnam and modern RNFE for totals in Krishna district and for males both traditional and modern. The growth of agro-processing in Krishna district accounts for the higher proportion of males in RNFE.

Determinants of RNFE in the Study Area : (a) Districts

Results of the log-linear analysis at the district level showed that for the pooled sample for 1980-90 for totals (males+ females), irrigation is positively significant, whereas farm size and literacy are negatively significant, in explaining district-level RNFE shares. For males also irrigation is positively significant and literacy is negatively significant. However, for females the results are different: only infrastructure (percentage of villages with bank branches), big villages and poverty are negatively significant.

The results for irrigation suggest higher agricultural productivity (associated with irrigation) is linked to a high RNFE share for male workers. The analysis of determinants of workforce composition confirm the hypothesis that growth linkages from irrigated agriculture lead to modern RNFE.

Conversely, the compositional results for farm size imply support for the hypothesis (AGL) that RNFE share rises with distress diversification by those with little or no land. The result for literacy supports the wider/overall 'development linkage' (ODL) hypothesis that RNFE share rises with lower levels of literacy. The results, for males only supports the AGL hypothesis in the case of irrigation and ODL (overall development linkages) in the case of literacy. The possible explanation for this is that males are affected by fewer cultural constraints. The results for big villages and percentage of villages with bank branches in the case of female labour (both for women only), oppose the hypothesised growth linkages (AGL) relationship. There is no obvious explanation for this result.

The overall results for RNFE subsectors support the AGL hypothesis that there is a large dynamic linkage effect from expanded irrigation (i.e. districts with a 1 per cent more irrigation have 0.13 per cent higher RNFE share at point of mean). Similarly the impact of poverty reduction for female RNFE share is also quite high in promoting RNFE which supports ODL.

Conclusions for Disaggregating Sub-sectors of RNFE

The conclusion for the log pooled sample for the share of the 7 sub-sectors is that irrigation is significant positively for HHI, supporting the strict growth linkages (AGL) hypothesis to modern RNFE. Percentage of villages with banks is negatively significant for HHI, which supports the wider 'development linkages' (ODL) hypothesis. Given our assumption that HHI is traditional, the fact that irrigation is significantly positive for HHI is surprising. However, percentage of villages with banks is negatively significant for HHI and supports (ODL). Farm size is positively significant for construction (which may suggests that distress linkages decline as average farm size rises) and negatively significant for other services, again suggesting agricultural distress linkages to this traditional RNFE subsector.

Poverty is negatively associated with percentage of the workforce employed in trades which tends to rise as poverty falls; if trade is a 'modern' subsector of RNFE this supports the 'wider linkages hypothesis' (ODL). For such sectors so does the fact that RNFE literacy is positively significant for growth in such sectors as trade and transport. Conversely, it is negative for HHI, thus supporting the 'wider' distress diversification hypothesis (ODD). The fact that literacy is positively significant for other services, however, opposes my hypothesis that such services, if seen as predominantly tradition-oriented, are linked to distress diversification (ODD).

Urbanisation is positively significant for mining, non-HHI and transport; since for non-HHI urban options may pull away rural non-farm workers, this positive net link provides an especially strong indication in support of the wider hypothesis (ODL), that development raises the modern RNFE share. As urbanisation increases employment is generated for the remaining resident rural non-farm people; nearby villages take advantage of modern local (not just urban) employment opportunities.

The size of villages is positively significant for non-HHI, which supports only the wider hypothesis (ODL), not AGL. Demand for the products of RNFS is higher in larger villages. The real argument is that in a big village, different types of activity provide enough demand to 'take in each other's washing' across sub-sectors of RNFE. This is a sort of 'economies of scope' but has nothing obvious to do with strict 'growth linkages' from agriculture to RNFE.

The results showed that agricultural development as reflected in agricultural irrigation, has a significant bearing on the level and composition of RNFE.

The strict agricultural growth-linkages (AGL) and ODL hypotheses 'wins' for total RNFE share and male RNFE share, and ODD and ADD 'lose'. For females RNFE share opposes the AGL hypothesis and wins the ODD hypothesis.

Conclusion from the Growth of RNFE Shares Regressions

In the regression results for the growth in the total RNFE labour force, urbanisation and commercialisation are negatively significant. This implies that the districts with high growth of urban share, and of agricultural commercialisation, tend to show slower growth of total RNFE. This suggests, on balance, distress diversification (ADD). Literacy and infrastructure, being positively significant, support the (ODL) hypothesis. For males, infrastructure is also positively significant, as are infrastructure (banks) and literacy for females, also supporting the wider (ODL) hypothesis, but commercialisation and irrigation are negatively associated which opposes the narrow growth linkages (AGL) hypothesis. It seems that as irrigation expands women wage workers find additional employment chiefly in farming itself.

The agricultural distress diversification (ADD) and strict overall growth-linkages (ODL) hypotheses wins for total RNFE growth. For male RNFE growth the ODL hypothesis wins and the ODD hypothesis loses. For females RNFE growth wins the ODL, and opposes the AGL hypothesis.

Conclusions for all the 7 Sub-sectors Growth Regression Results

RNFE differences in growth at district level strongly support the 'wider hypothesis' (ODL) that modernising factors assist RNFE expansion, but they tend to run against the 'narrow growth linkages from agriculture' (AGL) hypothesis, at least for women.

The growth in percentage terms of villages with banks has a positive association with RNFE growth for construction only, supporting the wider (ODL) hypothesis to modern RNFE. Agricultural commercialisation growth is negatively significant for growth in mining, trade and transport. In the case of mining one would not expect a direct link to agriculture. The negative relationship suggests that mining employment has grown fastest in areas of low agricultural potential (supporting ADD) hypothesis. The negative relationship between agricultural commercialisation growth and employment, and growth in trade and transport was very surprising. More agricultural surplus surely has to mean more trade and transport, not less. On the other hand agricultural development (irrigation growth) is positively significant for non-HHI and transport employment growth, supporting growth linkages (AGL), but is negatively significant, for services. This also supports our central hypothesis that agricultural development leads to growth linkages in modern RNFE and distress diversification in traditional RNFE.

Poverty growth is positively significant for non-HHI growth, however it runs against the central hypothesis. Infrastructure development (road length) is positively significant for construction, trade and transport, supporting 'wider' ODL for the modern sectors, and hence our central hypothesis. Growth of literacy is positively significant for growth of employment in HHI. This result is surprising. There is no obvious explanation for this result. For transport and services employment growth, however, literacy is positively significant, supporting the wider (ODL) hypothesis for these modern sectors. However, districts with faster growing "village size" tend to have slower growing employment shares in trade and transport, which opposes DDL and the central hypothesis.

We are rather less concerned about the inconclusive nature of the significant results of district growth regressions for our central hypothesis - as compared with the general support given by the 'district level' and 'household level' regressions- because of the generally small 'district growth' elasticities. These indicate that growth in some RNFS variables does not have a strong effect on RNFE (totals and sub-sectors) growth. Perhaps because in most cases, the effects of the variables on employers' demand for RNFS labour, absolutely or relatively to farm labour, are opposite to the effect on the employees' willingness to supply such labour, absolutely or as compared to farm work.[1]

One of the other findings is that growth of literacy is positively associated with modern RNFE growth in districts, and negatively associated with traditional RNFE growth (except, surprisingly in HHI) in districts. The problem, though, is that education affects both labour supply and labour demand in different stages of socio-economic and technological development. Making inferences about its effect and relation with development level can only be tentative; in other words, its influence needs to be considered cautiously.

The district level data analysis in most respects supports the hypothesis that growth linkages (AGL) are the main explanation for high shares in, and the growth of, 'modern' RNFE, and distress diversification (ADD) for 'traditional' RNFE. Also in most respects this supports the wider hypothesis (ODL) that linkages are the main explanation for high shares in and growth of, 'modern' RNFE, and overall distress diversification (ODD) for 'traditional' RNFE. But the 'shares' results are more convincing than the 'growth' results.

Determinants of RNFE (b) at Household Level

Within the 'developed' district, Krishna, we selected a developed village, Veeravalli, and within the 'less developed' district, Visakhapatnam, we selected a less developed village Anandapuram.

Logit Regressions Results

A household's probability of having the main worker in non-farm employment (in Anandapuram, in Veeravalli and in the pooled data for both villages), is significantly negatively related to land holding size in all three cases. This relationship is stronger (i.e. the decrease in probability is greater) in the agriculturally developed village. This suggests either that, for total RNFE, the growth (AGL) linkage impact on modern RNFE 'dominates' the distress diversification (ADD) impact on traditional RNFE, or that modern, 'agriculture-stimulated' activity has more weight, (or some of each). In either case, if big farmers are less likely to have a main RNFE, this suggests that farmland actively reduces total-RNFE participation. Households with less farm land 'do' more RNFE-distress diversification (ADD) dominates growth linkages. In the pooled data set, for a one acre increase in land holding size, the probability of household having any non-farm employment decreases by 9 percentage points, and in modern RNFE decreases marginal impact effect more in the developed village by 4 percentage points compared to less developed village.

However, this result from our multivariate logit regression is of course the multivariate effect of farm size; because there are higher levels of production following from ownership of more land, the production-consumption linkages mean that the likelihood of non-farm employment is increased through other channels. Within the large-farm households wealthier villagers invest more in their children's education, which increases the likelihood of them taking non-farm employment; (see below).

The more land a household has, the less likely that this household itself will be involved in RNFE. But this 'same-household' approach conceals the fact that the linkages between the farm and non-farm are strong, larger farms also consume more, meaning more work for other households. Also there are production linkages. Households with more land require agricultural mechanisation (tractors and threshing machines, etc.) which, in turn, creates more non-farm employment - though less so than animal draught-so small farms have a higher propensity to use local RNFE [e.g. Hazell and Ramasamy (1992)] Meanwhile, the capital generated from the agricultural output may be invested in non-farm activities.[2]

Education is significantly positively related to RNFE in each village, and on the pooled data, this supports the wider (ODL) hypothesis. In the pooled data set one more year in education increases the chances of getting modern RNFE by 5 percentage points. The marginal effect of education on the probability of household having non-farm employment is greater in the more developed village compared to the less developed village. The effect of literacy in raising demand and/or supply for 'modern' RNFE appears to outweigh the effect in reducing them for traditional RNFE.

Per acre value of agricultural output is significantly negatively related to household RNFE likelihood in Veeravalli and the pooled regression (p = .01) but in Anandapuram the variable was significant only at the reduced level of confidence (p = .1). This suggests that for RNFE as a whole growth linkages (AGL) to the modern sector, from agricultural growth, are very slightly outweighed in these villages by distress diversification to traditional RNFE. However, the elasticity for value of agricultural output is tiny and very close to zero.

There are other factors, helping to explain a household's probability of having main worker in non-farm employment, not directly associated with either AGL/ADD or ODL/ODD such as caste, household head age, household head age-squared.

If the household belongs to BC, SC or ST the probability of non-farm employment decreases by 1.04 percentage points in the pooled and 15.9 percentage points in Veeravalli regressions. For members of these castes (BC, SC and ST) there is less likelihood of non-farm employment: these groups are mainly agricultural labourers and are often locked in farm labour and live far away from the village even after 50 years of independence, so that neither good nor bad agricultural growth will much affect their RNFE share, which will be below that of other households. Lower caste people may feel inhibited from entering certain types of RNFE because they fear discriminatory treatment from employers and fellow workers. Furthermore, modern non-farm employment requires resources such as capital, education, technology, and political influence, which are available mostly to the higher caste elite minority. Most lower caste households, being poor, are less likely to have their children achieve higher levels of education, which in turn restricts modern RNFE.

In Veeravalli one would expect, through growth linkages, to induce a greater expansion of modern RNFE relative to traditional RNFE than in the less developed village. This is likely to make it harder for backward castes to engage in RNFE in the more developed village for both the reasons identified earlier (education or fear of discrimination); hence the more significant link of RNFE to caste in Veeravalli.

The marginal effect of migration-in on the probability of a household having non-farm employment is apparently also high i.e. 21.1 percentage points in the developed village, and for the pooled data 14.2 percentage points. However, the direction of causation should be interpreted cautiously. In the agriculturally more developed village one would expect growth (AGL) linkages and expansion of RNFE which might in turn induce migration.

The dummy variable 'skills' (any marketable expertise, e.g. barber, motor mechanic, astrologer, photographer, radio repairs, etc.) is found to be significant only in Veeravalli, the developed village, supporting the growth linkages (AGL) hypothesis (even prosperous modern farmers use much more astrologers and barbers). A lack of skills provides an entry barrier into the wider market place.

Poverty was negatively related (p = .01) to the possibility of non-farm work for the developed village, and for the pooled data, which does not support the overall distress diversification (ODD) hypothesis. If non-farm work increases, poverty decreases. By implication this suggests that household 'development' out of poverty is associated with increased RNFE prospects (ODL).

Seasonality also has quite strong effects on non-farm employment. The effect of the March-May (agriculturally slack period) dummy is a 9 per cent lower chance of modern RNFE. It is very striking to see that the 'skill' and 'poverty' dummies have the expected signs a priori. A household with a single main skilled worker has a 95 per cent greater chance of being involved in the modern sector. This supports the wider (ODL) hypothesis. Again the requirement of special skills for entry into the modern non-farming sector is stressed. Similarly we can see (Table 4.32) that the poor/non-poor dummy variable is negatively related to modern non-farm employment (p = .1).

For the pooled data the probability of any household is that the higher the level of education, the greater the chance of engagement in modern non-farm employment (p = .05). The per acre value of agricultural output, and age^2, are significantly positively associated with modern RNFE, and household head age negatively so. The marginal effects are -0.02 for age and 0.0002 for household head age^2. The impact of per acre value of agricultural output is negligible.

These results highlight the fact that in many cases the critical variables for modern and traditional RNFE vary significantly. Also, different factors are influential on the outcome of the dependent variable in the three models (the two villages separately and pooled). For example, land size (the growth (AGL) linkage impact on modern non-farm employment 'dominates' the distress diversification (ADD) impact on traditional non-farm employment), education (supporting the wider (ODL) hypothesis) and seasonality are equally important for both the villages separately (although different seasons are relevant for RNFE in the different villages; September-November in Anandapuram and the pooled data, December-February season negatively, and March-May positively, for Veeravalli village only Work in March to May season which underline a particular set of activities when the agriculture season was slack) and the pooled data. Poverty, migration into the villages, and per acre value of agricultural output (the growth (AGL) linkage impact on modern non-farm employment) play crucial roles in the developed village and in the pooled data. Caste is also an important factor for developed village and the pooled data. Skills are particularly important in the developed village which supports the ODL hypothesis.

The case studies presented indicate the wide range of activities in the two villages, the varied impact on levels of RNFE and the scope for further development of RNFS. The case studies illustrated that growth of RNFE is associated with backward and forward production linkages. Seasonality and weather conditions are important for RNFE. In the process of economic development certain traditional activities lose out to modern RNFE. Technological changes in agriculture such as agricultural mechanisation is leading to the emergence of new opportunities for employment outside the farm. Where the man-power is family-based and RNFE households had relatively successful agricultural activity this had led to success in the RNFS. Some traditional RNFE activities are affected by technological changes. Small vendors are pinned down by lack of raw materials and capital. The RNFE is seasonal in nature leads to frequent occupational mobility of people within the RNFS.

The data analysis supports the hypothesis that growth linkages are the main explanation for high shares in, and the growth of, 'modern' RNFE, and distress diversification for 'traditional' RNFE. It also demonstrates a strong, significant association between traditional RNFE and low literacy and modern RNFE and high literacy.

Some Policy Matters for RNFE

RNFE is often seen as an offshoot of bad agricultural performance - a distress diversification in India. That is where the problem arises. Our work suggests that more RNFE emerges primarily out of prosperity of agriculture. This will lead to a healthy employment environment and also boost demand for non-traditional consumer goods. Thus, an increase in investment on irrigation, and infrastructural facilities coupled with large scale non-farm activities would generate a significant increase in non-farm employment. Our results support these recommendations, for example the variable 'skills' (any marketable expertise) is found to be significant at household level only in a developed village supporting the growth linkages hypothesis into modern RNFE.

The problems of non-farm employment in agriculturally developed and underdeveloped areas must be identified separately. Area specific non-farm programmes must be conceived and implemented. Skilled man power development must be encouraged. Government must promote training centres and encourage skill development in the rural areas. Old skills may not be suitable for the people to undertake any new non-farm activity. For the new generation skills have to be developed to enable them to engage in some non-farm activity other than the old one they are accustomed to the present.

Marginal farmers and agricultural labourers who constitute the largest section of the rural poor have not adequately benefited from the progress of agriculture for the last two and half decades (AERC, 1975).[3] Several studies (Parthasarathy, 1971; Pranab Bardhan, 1970) have highlighted the point that these groups need special assistance and support. There is a need to assist the marginal farmers and agricultural labourers to improve their incomes by means of subsidiary occupations and off-season employment. In this context the role played by agriculture is important in terms of employment and income generation in the non-farm sector. Government self-employment schemes as well as the development of agricultural infrastructure, e.g. irrigation, and improvements in rural educational standards are therefore policies likely to accelerate the growth of RNFE shares.

For Further Research

The results of our study have important implications for future research in India and other developing countries. In our study, which is based on district-level and household level data from AP, the analysis of the changes in the non-farm employment of the rural work-force is somewhat incomplete, because the study does not analyse the corresponding changes in urban areas. There is also a need for more studies covering different regions in AP and in different states of India.

NOTES

1. However, one or two literacy should raise both supply of and demand for modern RNFE labour (so we would expect high elasticity).
2. The results do not directly demonstrate this but it is what we would expect.
3. Agro-Economic Research Centre, (1975), 'Study of the Marginal Farmers and Agricultural Labourers Development Agency', Visakhapatnam District, Andhra Pradesh, Andhra University, Visakhapatnam.)

BIBLIOGRAPHY

Adelman, I. (1984) 'Beyond Export-Led Growth', *World Development,* Vol. 12, No.9 , pp. 937-949.

Ahammad, (1984)

Alagh, Y. K.; Bhalla, G. S. and Bhaduri A. (1978) 'Agricultural Growth and Manpower Absorption in India', in Bardhan P. K. et al. (ed.), Labour Absorption in Indian Agriculture: Some Exploratory Investigations. Bangkok: ILO, ARTEP.

Anderson, D. (1982), 'Small Industries in Developing Countries: A Discussion of Issues', *World Development,* Vol. 10, No. 1.

Anderson, D. and Leiserson, M. (1978), 'Rural Enterprise and Non-farm Employment', Washington D.C: The World Bank.

Anderson, D. and Leiserson, M. (1980), 'Rural Non-farm Employment in Developing Countries', *Economic Development and Cultural Change,* Vol. 28, No. 2.

B. D. Dhawan (1993) *Trends and New Tendencies in Indian Irrigated Agriculture.* New Delhi: India, Commonwealth Publishers.

Barbara, H. (1984) *Exchange Relations and Poverty in Dry Land Agriculture.* New Delhi: India, Concept Publishing Company.

Barbara, H. (1984) State and Market' State Intervention in Agricultural Exchange in a Dry Region of Tamil Nadu: South India. New Delhi: India, Concept Publishing Company,.

Barbara, H. (1984) Transitional Trade and Rural Development: the Nature and Role of Agriculture Trade in South Indian Districts. India: New Delhi, Vikas.

Bardhan, K. (1977) 'Rural Employment, Wages and Labour Markets in India: A Survey of Research', *Economic and Political Weekly,* Vol. 12, Nos. 26, 27 and 28, 25 June (Review of Agriculture), 2 July and 9 July.

Bardhan, K. (1983) 'Economic Growth, Poverty and Rural Labour Markets in India: A Survey of Research'. ILO, World Employment Programme, Rural Employment Policy Research Programme Working Paper No. 54.

Bardhan, P. K. (1978) 'Labour Absorption in Asian Agriculture with Particular Reference to India', in Bardhan P. K; et al, Labour Absorption in Indian Agriculture: Some Exploratory Investigations. Bangkok: ILO, ARTEP.

Bardhan, P. K., Vaidyanathan, A and Alagh, Y. K. (1978) Labour Absorption in Indian Agriculture: Some Exploratory Investigations. ILO, ARTEP.

Basant, R. and Joshi, H. (1989) 'Non-Agricultural Employment in Rural Gujarat: Some Evidence from an Agriculturally Developed Region'. India: Paper presented at the seminar on Non-agricultural Employment in India: Trends and Prospects, The Gujarat Institute of Area Planning, Ahmedabad.

Basant, R. (1990)

Basant, R. and Kumar, B. L. (Jan.-Feb. 1989) 'Rural Non-agricultural Activities in India: A Review of Available Evidence', *Social Scientist*, Vol. 17, Nos 1-2, pp. 188-1.

Basant, R. and Parthasarathy, R. (March 1991) 'Inter-Regional Variations in Rural Non-Agricultural Employment in Gujarat, 1961-81'. Ahmedabad, India: The Gujarat Institute of Area Planning, Working Paper No. 36.

Basu, K. (1984) The Less Developed Economy. New Delhi: India, Basil Blackwell.

Bell, C. Hazell

Berry, A. and Sabot, R. (1978) 'Labour Market Performance in Developing Countries: A Survey' *World Development*, Vol. 6, No 11/12, pp. 1199-1242.

Bhalla, G. S. (June 1981) 'Labour Absorption in Indian Agriculture. A Regional Analysis', *Anvesak*, Vol. II, No. 1.

Bhalla, G. S. and Chadha, G. K. (1983) Green Revolution and the Small Peasant. India: Concept Publishing Company, New Delhi.

Bhalla, S. (Oct-Dec 1987) 'Trends in Employment in Indian Agriculture, Land and Asset Distribution', *Indian Journal of Agricultural Economics*, Vol. 10L11, No. 4, pp. 537-560.

Bhalla, S. (1989) 'Employment in Indian Agriculture: Retrospect and Prospect', *Social Scientist*, No. pp 192-193.

Bhalla, S. (1990) 'Jobs for Rural People'. Ahmedabad, India: Paper presented at the All India Seminar on 'Agro-Climatic Regional Planning', March 5-6.

Bhardwaj, Krishna (1988) 'On the Formation of the Labour Markets in Rural Asia', Center for Economic Studies and Planning, Jawaharlal Nehru University, New Delhi (mimeo).

Bhatty, I. Z. and Vashishtha, P. (1987) 'Structure of the Rural Non-farm Sector and Stages of Economic Development in India' in R. H. Syed (ed.) The Rural Non-farm Sector and Process of Economic Development. Kuala Lumpur, Malaysia: ADIPA, pp. 116-130.

Binswanger, H. P. and Rosenzweig, M. R. (April 1986) 'Behavioural and Material Determinants of Production Relations in Agriculture', *Journal of Development Studies,* Vol. 22, No. 3, pp. 507-510 and 513-517.

Binswanger, Hans et al (1983), Thailand: Rural Growth and Employment, The World Bank, Washington D. C.

Binswanger, Hans p. and Khandker. S. (1995) 'The Impact of Formal Finance on the Rural Economy of India', *Journal of Development Studies,* Vol. 32, No. 2, pp.234-62.

Booth, A. and Sundarum, R. M. (1984) Labour Absorption in Agriculture: Theoretical Analysis and Empirical Investigations. Delhi India: OUP,.

Brahamanada, P. R. (1982) Productivity in the Indian Economy. Bombay, India: Himalaya Publishing House.

Byrd, W.A. and Qungson Lin (Eds) (1989) 'China's Rural Industry: Structure, Development and Reform', World Bank.

C. S. Murty (1996) 'Some Causes of Changes in Workforce Structure in a Delta village', *The Indian Journal of Labour Economics,* Vol. 39. No.4.

Census of Andhra Pradesh (1971) District Census Hand Book Series 2 Andhra Pradesh Parts X- A&B, Visakhapatnam District.

Census of Andhra Pradesh, (1971), Series 2 Andhra Pradesh District Census Handbook Parts X A & B, Village & Town Primary Census Abstract Krishna District.

Census of India (1961) Volume 1, India part 11-B(i) General Economic Tables [for AP pp. 90- 91 for All India pp. 86-87].

Census of India (1971) District Census Hand Book Series 2 Andhra Pradesh Parts X- A & B, village/Town Primary Census Abstract 1991 Krishna District.

Census of India (1971) Series 1, India, ii B (i) General Economic Tables, Table B-I, Part A.

Census of India (1971) Series 1, India, part-ii-B (ii), General Economic Tables, office of the Registrar General and Census Commissioner of India.

Census of India (1971) Series 1, part-ii-B (iii), General Economic Tables (Table B-1V parts A, B, C & D) for all-India and AP p. 440.

Census of India (1981) Part II, 'Special Report and Tables Based on 5 per cent Sample Data for Various States', Tables B-3 and B-7.

Census of India (1981) Series-1, India Part-iii A (i) General Economic Tables (for all-India pp. 134 and 135 for AP pp. 136-7).

Census of India (1981) Series-2 Andhra Pradesh District Census Hand Book Parts XIII- A & B (II) Visakhapatnam District, Volume 2.

Census of India (1983) Registrar General and Census Commissioner Series 1, India, Part II - B (i), Primary Census Abstract- General Population.

Census of India (1991) Andhra Pradesh Final Population office of the Director of Census Operation A.P. Hyderabad.

Census of India (1991) Andhra Pradesh Series-2 paper-1 of 1991 Supplement Provisional Population Totals.

Census of India (1991) Andhra Pradesh, Population Totals, Series-2, pp. 10, 66-73.

Census of India (1991) District Census Hand book, Village/ Town Primary Census Abstract Krishna District, Visakhapatnam District.

Census of India (1991) Government of India, Provisional Population Totals, AP, Series 2, Paper-1, Supplement Table 6A, pp. 66-73.

Census of India (1991) India, Andhra Pradesh series-2, Provisional Population Totals, Paper-1 Supplement, pp. 23-25.

Census of India (1991) Series-1 India, Paper-3 of 1991 Provisional Population Totals: Workers and their Distribution, p.5.

Census of India (1991) Series-1, Final Population totals. Paper 2 of 1992, Brief Analysis of primary Census abstract pp. 126-127.

Census of India (1991) Village/Town Primary Census Abstract 1991 Krishna district, Visakhapatnam district.

Census of India, (1981) as cited in VII Plan Vol. I, AP (Parthasarathy, 1989) .

Chadha, G.K (1984) The Off-farm Economic Structure Agriculturally Growing Regions - A Study of India Punjab, p. 147.

Chadha, G. K. (1986) 'Agricultural Growth and Rural Non-farm Activities: An Analysis of Indian Experience' in (Eds) Choe Yang-Boo and Lo Fu-Chen, Rural Industrialisation and Non-farm Activities of Indian farmers Korea Rural Economic Institute, Seoul, Korea.

Chadha, G. K. (1990) 'The On and Off Farm Employment and Incomes in Developing Rural Asia', Report on the Indo-Dutch Research Project, Centre for the Study of Regional Development, School of Social Sciences, JNU, New Delhi.

Chadha, G. K. (1993) Non-farm Sector in Rural China: Trends and Variations in Labour Productivity. Bangkok ILO (ARTEP).

Chadha, G.K. (1992) 'Non-farm Sector in Rural China: Trends and Variations in Labour Productivity' Asian Regional Team for Employment Promotion, ILO, World Employment Programme, New Delhi.

Chadha, G.K. (1996) 'The Industrialisation Strategy and Growth of Rural Industry in India'. ILO, South Asia Multidisciplinary Advisory Team (SAAT) New Delhi.

Chandrasekhar, C.P. (1993) 'Agrarian change and occupational diversification: non-agricultural employment and rural development in West Bengal', *Journal of Peasant Studies* 20 (2): 205-70.

Chaudhuri, P. (1978) Indian Economy, Poverty and Development. India: Vikas, Delhi.

Chaudhuri, P. (ed.) (1972), Readings in Indian Agricultural Development. London: Allen and Unwinpress.

Chenery, B.H. and Syrquin, M. (1975) Patterns of Development 1950-1970, Oxford University Press.

Chenery, H.B. and S.S Watanabe (1976) 'The role of Industrilisation in Japanese development, 1914-65' unpublished manuscript.

Chinnappa Nanjamma and Silva, W.P.T. (1980) 'Impact of the Cultivation of High-Yielding Varieties of Paddy on Income and Employment,' B.H. Farmer (eds.): Green Revolution, Macmillan, pp. 204-224.

Choe, Sang-Chul and Kim, Jong-Gie (1986) 'Rural Industrial Policy in Korea: Past Experience and a New Approach' in(Eds) Choe Yong-Boo and Lo Fu-Chen, Rural Industrialisation and Non-Farm Activities of Asian Farmers KREI, Seoul.

Choe, Y. B. (1981) 'Rural Industrialisation in Korea: A Critical Assessment, Korea Rural Economic Institute, Chs. 9-10.

Chuta, E. and Liedholm C. (1979) 'Rural Non-farm Employment: A Review of the State of the Art', Michigan: MSU Rural Development Papers, Paper No. 4, Department of Agricultural Economics, Michigan State University; East Lonsing.

Chuta, E. and Liedholm C. (1990) 'Rural Small-Scale Industry: Empirical Evidence and Policy Issues', in Eicher and Staatz (Eds.), Agricultural Development in the Third World, Baltimore, MD: Johns Hopkins University Press, Second Edition.

Clark, C. (1960) 'The conditions of economic Progress', New York, Memillan and Co. Ltd.

Clark, C. (1960) The Conditions of Economic Progress. New York: Macmillan Ltd.

Connell, John, Biplab. D, Laishley, Roy, Lipton Michael, (1976) Migration from Rural Areas: The Evidence from Village Studies. India: Oxford University Press, Delhi.

Dadibhavi, R. V. (1990) 'Agricultural Growth, Structural Changes and Implications for Employment Generation: with Special Reference to Karnataka', Southern Regional Seminar on Agricultural Policy, Nov. 20-22. Seminar organised by ISEC, paper presented at the Bangalore and the Indian Society for Agricultural Economics.

Dakshina Murthy, K.S. (May 1986) 'Politics of Environment', Economic and Political Weekly, Vol. XX1, No. 18, pp. 773-775.

Dantwala, M. L. (July-Sept 1987), 'Rural Assets Distribution and Composition of Labour Force', *Indian Journal of Agricultural Economics,* Vol. XLII, No. 3, pp.

Dantwala, M. L. (June 1979), 'Rural Employment: Facts and Issues', *Economic and Political Weekly,* Vol. XXIV, No. 25, pp. 1048-1057.

Dasgupta, B. (1977) The New Agrarian Technology and India. Macmillan.

Dasgupta, B. et al (1977) Village Society and Labour Use. New Delhi: Oxford University Press.

Datt G. and M. Ravallion (1996), Why have some India States done better than others at reducing rural poverty?, world Bank Research Working Paper 1594, Washington DC.

De Haan, A. (1994) 'Towards a Single Male Earner: The Decline of Child and Female Employment in an Indian Industry', in Economic and Social History in the Netherlands: Family Strategies and Changing Labour Relations. Netherlands Economic History Archives.

Deb. N.C. (1984).

Deb. S.M. (14 July 1990).

Dev. S.M. (Jan-March 1988).

Dev. S.M. (July 1990).

Dev. S.M. (Sept. 1988).

Dhavan B.D. (1993).

Dixit, A. K. (1973) 'Models of Dual Economies Discussion'. in Models of Economic Growth (ed.) James A. Mirrlees and N. H. Stren. Macmillan: International Economic Association.

Dreze, J. (1986) 'Rural Labour Markets in India: Theories and Evidence', Paper presented at the 8th World Congress of International Economics, New Delhi.

Dreze, J. and Mukerjee, A. (1987) 'Labour Contracts in Rural India: Theories and Evidence', Discussion Paper Series No. 7, Development Research Program, Suntory Toyoto International Center for Economics and Related Disciplines, London School of Economics, London.

Dreze, J. and Sen A. (1989) Hunger and Public Action. Oxford: Clarendon Press.

Eapen, Mridul (1994) 'Rural non-agricultural employment in Kerala: Some emerging tendencies' *Economic and Political Weekly*, Vol. 29, No.21.

Ellis, F. (1988) Peasant Economics - Farm Households and Agrarian Development. Cambridge, U.K: Cambridge University Press.

Fallon, P. (1987) 'The Labour Market in Zimbabwe: Historical Trends and an Evaluation of Recent Policy'. Wahington D.C.: IBRD Development Research Dept., Economics Research Staff Discussion paper No. 296.

FAO of the United Nations (1998) 'Rural Non-farm Income in Developing Countries' in the State of Food and Agriculture.

Fei, J.C.H. and Ranis, G. (1961) 'A Theory Economic Development', American Economic Review.

Fisher Thomas and Mahajan Vijay with Singha Ashok, (1997) 'The Forgotten Sector-Non-farm Employment and Enterprises in rural India'. Intermediate Technology Publications.

Fureng, D. (1988) 'Rural Reform, Non-farm Development, and Modernisation in China'. Washington, D.C.: EDI Seminar paper No. 38, World Bank (Economic Development Institute), pp. 12-30.

Ghayur, S. (Jan.-March 1990) 'Non-farm Employment in rural Areas of SAARC Region', *Journal of Rural Development and Administration*, Vol. XXII, No. 1, pp. 17-37.

Government of Andhra Pradesh (1972) Area Under Paddy: Season & Crop reports 1972-84, Bureau of Economic & Statistics, Hyderabad.

Government of Andhra Pradesh (1981) Andhra Pradesh District Census handbook parts XIII- A&B (11) Visakhapatnam, Series-2 District Volume 2.

Government of Andhra Pradesh (1981) Data Gross Value of Agricultural Output, Directorate of Economics and Statistics, Hyderabad.

Government of Andhra Pradesh (1981) Series-2 Andhra Pradesh District Census handbook parts A&B Village and town primary Krishna District.

Government of Andhra Pradesh (1982, 1983, 1986, 1988, 1991, 1992 p. 476 and 207) Statistical Abstracts.

Government of Andhra Pradesh (1984) "Season & Crop Reports 1972-84". Hyderabad: Bureau of Economics and Statistics.

Government of Andhra Pradesh (1990), Third Economic Census Directorate of economic & Statistics Hyderabad 1992.

Government of Andhra Pradesh (1991) Village/Town primary census abstract Krishna district, Visakhapatnam district.

Government of Andhra Pradesh (1991), Based on Cost of Cultivation of Principal Crops in India, Directorate of Economics & Statistics, Department of Agriculture & Co-operation, Ministry of Agriculture, New Delhi p. 1.

Government of Andhra Pradesh (1993) An Outline of Agricultural Situation in A.P. 1993-94, Directorate of Economics and Statistics, Hyderabad.

Government of Andhra Pradesh (1999), Vision 2020.

Government of Andhra Pradesh, Annual Season and Crop reports for the years 1970-71 to 1990-91, Bureau of Economics and Statistics, Hyderabad.

Government of India (1981) "Sixth Five-year Plan", 1980-85. Planning Commission.

Government of India (1991) "Cost of Cultivation of Principal Crops in India". India: Directorate of Economics and Statistics, Department of Agriculture and Co-operation, Ministry of Agriculture, New Delhi.

Government of India (1991) Draft Eighth five year plan Planning Commission, Vol. II, New Delhi, Computed from NSS Employment date on the usual principle plus subsidiary status basis and CSO National Accounts Statistics; Quoted in S. Bhalla (1993).

Government of India, (1973) *Report of the Committee on Unemployment,* Vol. 1, part A, May.

Government of India, (March 1978) Planning Commission (Plan Evaluation Organisation), Evaluation Study of Rural Industries Project, New Delhi, pp. V-VI.

Greeley, M. (1987) Postharvest Losses, Technology, and Employment: The Case of Rice in Bangladesh. Boulder and London: Westview press.

Haggblade, S. and Hazel, P. (1980) NCAER as given in Rural urban growth linkages in India.

Haggblade, S. and Hazel, P. (1988) Agricultural Income Data from Economic Intelligence Service as Given in Rural Urban Growth Linkages in India.

Haggblade, S. and Hazel, P. (1989) 'Agricultural Technology and Farm Non-farm Growth Linkages', Agricultural Economics, Vol. 3, No.

Haggblade, S. Hazel, P. and Brown, J. (1987) 'Farm/Non-Farm Linkages in Rural Sub-Saharan Africa: Evidence and Policy Implications'. Washington, D, C.: Discussion paper Report No. ARU 67, World Bank (Research Unit, Agriculture and Rural Development dept.)

Haggblade, S. Liedholm, C. and Mead, D. (1986) 'The Effect of Policy and Policy Reforms on non-agricultural Enterprises and Employment in Developing countries: A Review of Past Experiences'. Cambridge, Mass: Harvard Institute of International Development. Employment and Enterprises policy Analysis Discussion paper, No. 1.

Haggblade, S. P. Hazell and Brown, J. (1989) 'Farm Non-farm Linkages in rural Sub-Saharan Africa', *World Development,* Vol. 17, No. 8, pp.

Hanumantha Rao, Ch. (1977) 'Agricultural Growth and Rural Poverty: some Lessons from Past Experiences', *Economic and Political Weekly,* Vol. 11, No.33 & 34, August.

Harris, B. (1987), 'Regional Growth linkage from Agriculture' *the Journal of Development Studies.*

Harris, B. (Jan. 1987) 'Regional Growth Linkages from Agriculture and Resource Flows in Non-Farm Economy', *Economic and Political Weekly,* Vol. XXII, Nos. 1 & 2, pp. 31-46.

Harris, B. (1984), 3 of these.

Harris-White, Barbara (1995) 'Economic Restructuring, State, Market, Collective and household Action in India's Social Sector', European *Journal of Development Research,* Vol. 7, No. 1, pp.

Hart, G. (1998).

Hassman J.A. (Nov. 1978).

Hazell P. (1989).

Hazell P. and Haggblade S. (Oct.-Dec. 1991) 'Rural-Urban Growth Linkages in India', *Indian Journal of Agricultural Economics,* Vol. XL V1, pp. 515-29.

Hazell, P. and Haggblade S. (1991) 'Rural - Urban Growth Linkages in India', *Indian Journal of Agriculture Economics,* Vol. 46, No. 4, pp. 515-529.

Hazell, P. and Haggblade S. (1992) Farm Non-farm Linkages and the Welfare of the Poor.

Hazell, P and Ramasamy C. (1991) The Green Revolution Reconsidered: The Impact of High-Yielding Rice Varieties in South India. Johns Hopkins University Press, Baltimore and London.

Hazell P. & Roell, A. (1983)

Hirschman, A. E. (1958), 'The Strategy of Economic Development' New Haven: Yalw University Press, pp. 109-10.

Ho Samuel P. (1986) 'Asian Experience in Rural Non-agricultural Development and its Relevance for China'. Washington D.C.: World Bank Staff Working Paper 757.

Hunt, D. (1991) 'Farm System and Household Economy as Frameworks for Prioritising and Appraising Technical Research: A Critical Appraisal of Current Approaches' in Haswell, M. and Hund, D. (Eds) Rural Households in Emerging Societies: Technology and rural Change in Sub-Saharan Africa, pp. 49-50, Berg Press.

Hymer, S. and s. Resnick (1969) 'A model of an agrarian economy with nonagricultural activities', *American Economic Review* 59 (4): 493-506.

ILO (1973) Mechanisation and Employment in Agriculture: Case studies from four Countries, Geneva.

ILO (1978) Labour Absorption in Asian Agriculture: An Issue Paper. Bangkok: ILO-ARTEP.

ILO (1979) 'Employment expansion in Indian Agriculture'- Proceedings of a National Seminar held in Bangalore.

ILO (1980) Employment expansion in Asian Agriculture: A Comparative Analysis of South Asian Experience, ILO, ARTEP, BANGKOK.

ILO (1982) Labour Absorption in Rice based Agriculture. Bangkok: ILO, ARTEP.

ILO (1983) Promotion of Employment and Incomes for the Rural Poor, Including rural Women, Through Non-farm Activities, Geneva.

Ishikawa, Shigeru (1982) Labour Absorption and Growth in Agriculture-China and Japan, ILO, ARTEP, Bangkok.

Islam, R, (1987) 'Non-farm Employment in Rural Asia: Issues and Evidence' in R. Islam (Ed.), Rural Industrialisation and Employment in Asia. New Delhi: ILO, ARTEP, pp. 60.

Islam, R. (1991) 'Growth of Rural Industries in Post- Reform China: Patterns, Determinants and Consequences'. ARTEP working papers, ILO, New Delhi.

J.A. Hausman, (1978) "Specification Tests in Econometrics," Econometrica, Vol. 46, No. 6. November, pp. 1251-1271.

Jagadeswara Rao M. (1990) Problems of Tank Irrigation in Visakhapatnam-A case Study of Anandapuram Mandal Center for Planning and Development studies Andhra University.

Jarque, C.M. and Bera, A.K. (1987) 'A Test for Normality of Observations and Regression Residuals', International Statistical Review, Vol. 55, pp. 163-172.

Jayaraj, D. (1989) 'Rural Non-farm Employment: An Analysis of the Village Level Data for Tamil Nadu'. Madras: Madras Institute of Development Studies, Working paper No. 91.

Jayasuriya, S.K. and Shand, R.T. (1986) 'Technical Change and Labour Absorption in Asian Agriculture: Some Emerging Trends', World Development, Vol. 14, No. 3, pp. 415-418.

Johnston B. & Kilby. P. (1975).

Jorgenson, D. W. (June 1961) 'The Development of Dual Economy', *Economic Journal,* Vol. L21.

Kanakalatha, Mukund (1990) Andhra Pradesh Economy in Transition. India: Fine Art Press, Delhi.

Kannan, K.P. (1990) 'Towards Understanding the Dynamics of rural Labour Markets: An Approach Based on India Evidence', *The Indian Journal of Labour Economics,* Vol. 33, No. 3, pp.

Kilby, P. and Liedholm, C. (1989) 'The Role of Non-farm Activities in the Rural Economy, in the Balance between Industry and

Agriculture in Economic Development', Proceedings of the Eighth world Congress of the International Economics Association India, Delhi, Macmillan Press.

Kin, R.P. & Byerlee, D. (1977).

Krishnaiah, J. and Krishnamurthy, S. (Jan.-March 1988) 'Inter- Regional Allocation of Major Food Grains in Andhra Pradesh: An Application of Spatial Equilibrium Model', *Indian Journal of Agricultural Economics,* Vol. 10L111, No. 4, pp. 35-43.

Krishnamurthy, J. (1970) 'Long term Changes in the Industrial Distribution of the Working Force in the Indian Union and the States: 1901-1971', in the Report of the committee of Experts on Unemployment Estimates, Planning Commission of India.

Krishnamurthy, J. (Dec. 1984) 'Changes in the Indian Work Force', Economic and Political Weekly, Vol. XIX, No. 50, pp. 2121-2128.

Kundu, A. (1985) 'Analysing Structural Changes in the Indian Economy -Certain Avoidable Anomalies in the Usage of Population Census Data', *Population Geography,* Vol. 7, Nos. 1 & 2, pp. 66-82.

Kuznets, S. (1971) 'Economic Growth of Nations', The Belknap Press of Harvard University Press, Cambridge, Massachusetts.

Kuznets, S. (1971) Economic Growth of Nations. Cambridge Massachusetts: The Belknap Press of Harvard University Press.

Lewis, Arthur (1958) 'Economic Development with Unlimited Supplies of Labour', in Agarwal and Singh (eds.), Economics of Under-Development. India: Oxford University press, New Delhi (p. 400).

Lewis, W.A. (Sep. 1979) 'Dual Economy Revisited', Manchester School Journal, Vol. No. p.

Liedholm, C. and Kilby, P. (1985) 'The Role of Non-farm Activities in the Rural Economy' in Williamson, G. and Panchamukhi V. R. (eds.) The Balance between Industry and Agriculture in Economic Development. Proceedings of the Eighth World Congress of the IEA, Delhi, India, (Volume 2).

Liedholm. C, & Mead, D. (1987).

Lipton, M. with Longhurst, (1989) 'New Seeds and Poor People', Johns Hopkins, Baltimore.

Lipton, M. (1969) 'Transfer of Resources from Agriculture to Non-agricultural Activities: The Case of India'. Sussex University: IDS Communication 109, p. 1.

Lipton, M. (1977) Why Poor People Stay Poor. Cambridge Mass: Harvard University Press.

Lipton, M. (1983) 'Labour and Poverty', World Bank Staff Working Papers Number 616, The World Bank Washington, D.C:

Lipton, M. (1995) 'Growing Points in Poverty Research: Labour issues' in Gerry Rodgers (Ed.) New Approaches to Poverty Analysis and Policy I, The Poverty Agenda and the ILO Issues for Research and Action. Geneva: ILO, pp. 101-168.

Little, I.M., Mazumdar, D.D. and Page, J.M. (1987) 'Small Manufacturing Enterprises: A Comparative Study of India and other Economies'. Washington, D.C: World Bank.

Majumdar, D. (1983).

Mahendra, Dev (Sept. 1988) 'Prospects of Enhancing Labour productive'. *Indian Journal of Agricultural Economics*, Vol. xxiii, No. 39, pp. 106.

Mahendra, Dev S. (Jan.-March 1988) 'Poverty of Agricultural Labour Households in India: A State level Analysis', *Indian Journal of Agricultural Economics*, Vol. 10L111, No. 1, pp. 14-25.

Mahendra, Dev S. (July 1990) 'Non- Agricultural Employment in Rural India: Evidence at a Disaggregate Level', *Economic and Political Weekly*, pp. 1526-1536.

Mahendra, Dev S. (July 1990), 'Non- Agricultural employment in rural India', *Indian Journal of Agricultural Economics*, Vol. No.

Mazamdar, D. (1983) 'Segmented Labour Markets in LDCs', American Economic Review, Vol. 1. pp.

Mehra, Shakuntala (1976) 'Some Aspects of Labour use in Indian Agriculture', Department of Agricultural Economics, Cornell University, Occasional paper No. 88 (Mimeo), June also in *Indian Journal of Agriculture Economics*, Vol. 31, No. 4. October-December.

Mehra, Shakuntala (April 1966) 'Surplus Labour in Indian Agriculture', *The Indian Economic Review*, Vol. 1 (new series), No. 1. (Also reprinted in Chaudhuri (1972)).

Mellor, J. and U. Lele (1973), 'Growth linkages of the new foodgrain technologies', *Indian Journal of Agricultural Economics* 28 (1) : 35-55

Mellor, J. & Mudahar M.S. (1974).

Mellor, J.W. (1976) The New Economics of Growth: A Strategy for India and the Developing World. London: Cornell University Press.

Minhas, B.S. and Majumdar, Grace (January 1987) 'For 27th and 32nd Rounds, Unemployment and Casual Labour', *Indian journal of Industrial Relations*, Vol No. pp.

Mitra, A. K. (July 1976) 'Surplus Labour in Agriculture: Some Estimates', *Economic and Political Weekly*, Vol. 11, No. 28, 10.

Mitra, Ashok (1983) 'Unemployment in Agriculture and its Measurement', in Ghosh B.N. (ed.), Economics of Under-employment. New Delhi : Deep and Deep publications, pp.

Mukhopadyaya, S. (1985) June.

Murthy J.L.N. (1992).

Mohan Rao R.M. (1986) 'Commercialisation and Agriculture Growth in Asia: A Comparative Study of South Korea and Coastal Andhra', International Workshop on Rural Transformation in Asia, New Delhi, October 2-4, 1986 (Mimeo).

Murty C.S. (1996) 'Some Causes of Changes in Workforce Structure in a Delta Village', *The Indian Journal of Labour Economics*, Vol. 39, No. 4. pp.

Murty, C.S. and Durga C. (Oct.-Dec. 1992) 'Rural Non-Farm Employment with Reference to Employment in Handloom Weaving in Andhra Pradesh', *Manpower Journal*, Vol. XXVIII, No. 3, pp. 1-22.

Myrdal, G. (1972) 'Asian Drama an inquiry into the poverty of nations' Penguin Publishers Oxford, Allen lane.

Nanjamma, C. & Silva, W. (1980).

Narasimham, M et al. (1991) Report of the Committee on Financial System, RBI.

Narayana Murthy J.L. (1992) 'Issues Relating to Employment in Andhra Pradesh' in T. Koteswara Rao, and S. Sudhakara Reddy (eds.), Development of Andhra Pradesh Problems and Prospects. Delhi: D.K. Fine Art Press, pp.

Natarajan, K. S. (1982) '1981 Census Economic Data', *Economic and Political Weekly*, Vol. XVII, No. 34, pp.

National Sample Survey Organisation (NSSO) (October 1977) 'Employment Unemployment Situation At a Glance: A Brief Note Based on Data of All the Four Sub-rounds of the NSS 27th Round Survey on Employment-Unemployment, 1972 - 73', Sarvekshana, Vol. V, No.2.

NSS (1983) 38th Round Sarvekeshna, Vol. 1X. No. 4, April 1988 pp. 14-5 Population data, 25-6 UPAS, 28-9 UPAS & SS

NSS (1987-88) NSS 43rd Round, Sarvekshna, For NSS July 1987-June 1988 Key Results of the fourth Quinquennial survey on employment and unemployment (All-India) September 1990 pp. 45-6. Population data, 65-6 UPSS, pp. 74-6, 46-8 UPAS + UPSS.

NSS (1990) 43rd Round, Sarvekshna, For NSS July 1987-June 1988 Key Results of the fourth Quinquennial survey on employment and unemployment (All-India) September pp. 45-6. Population Data, 65-6 UPSS, pp. 74-6, 46-8 UPAS + UPSS.

NSS (1994) 43rd Round (1987-88) pp. s-163 & s-294 as given in NSF Study Group.

NSS (Jan. 1990) 'Key Results of Employment and Unemployment Survey (July 1987-June 1988) All-India (Part-1)'. Delhi: Data for 43rd Round, Special report No. 1, pp. 114 - 116.

NSS (July 1987-June 1988) Key Results of employment and unemployment survey All-India (part-1) Special report 43rd Round No. 1 January 1990 pp. 114-116.

NSSO (1978) 'Some Findings of the Survey on Self-Employment in Non-agricultural Enterprises-29th round'. *Sarvekshana,* Vol. 1, No. 4. April.

NSSO (1981) 32nd round, 'Some Key Results from the Survey on Employment and Unemployment', Department of Statistics, New Delhi.

NSSO (1981) 'Survey Results of the Second Quinquennial Survey on Employment and Unemployment: All India NSS Thirty Second Round'. *Sarvekshana,* Vol. V, No. 1&2, July-October.

NSSO (1983) 38th Round, No. 341, 'Report on the Third Quinquennial Survey on Employment and Unemployment'', All India, Table 14.

NSSO (1984) 32nd Round, 1977-78, No. 301/2, Wages and Earnings of Rural Labour Households.

NSSO (1987) 38th Round, 1983, No. 341. Report on the Third Quinquennial Survey on Employment and Unemployment Survey Results, All India.

NSSO Government of India (1990) Department of Statistics, 'Key Results of Employment and Unemployment Survey All-India (part-1) 43rd Round (July-June)'.

NSSO Sarvekshana (1987), Vol. IX, No. 4, Table 1.

NSSO Sarvekshana, (1984), Vol. V, No. 1 & 2, 1981, Tables 29; Vol. VI. No. 1 & 2, 1982; Vol. VI, No. 3 & 4, 1983; Vol. VII, No. 3 & 4, Table 6.

Ody, A. J. (1992) 'Rural Enterprise Development in China, 1986-90'. Washington, D.C: World Bank, World Bank Discussion paper No. 162.

Office of the Director of Census Operation (1991) AP Final Population, Hyderabad.

Oshima, H.T. (1984), The Significance of Off-Farm Employment and Incomes in Post-War East Asian Growth, Asian Development Bank Econic Staff paper 21, Manila.

Osmani, S.R. (Dec. 1989) 'Limits to Allevation of Poverty through Non-farm Credit', *Bangladesh Development Studies,* Vol. 17, No. 4, pp.

Ozlen, Datt, Ravallin, 1996 (data on disk) (Agricultural wage Rs/day at October 1973 June 74 all India rural prices).

Papola, T.S. (1987) 'Rural Industrialisation and Agricultural Growth: A Case Study of India' in Rizanul Islam (Ed.) Rural Industrialisation and Employment In Asia. New Delhi: ILO, ARTEP, pp.

Papola, T.S. (1988) Restructuring in Indian Industry: Implications for Employment and Industrial Relations. New Delhi: ILO-ARTEP.

Papola, T.S. (Dec. 1983) 'Rural Industrialisation Approaches and Potential', Himalaya Publishing House, Bombay, 1982: Reviewed by P.V. Narayanan in RBI Occasional papers, Vol. 4, No. 2.

Papola, T.S. (May 1991) 'Industry and Employment in Large Scale Industry', Monthly Commentary, Vol. XXXII, No. 9. pp.

Parthasarathy (1995) For 27th and 32nd Rounds, Minhas B.S. and Grace Majumdar (January. 1987) 'Unemployment and Casual Labour', *Indian Journal of Industrial Relations.*

Parthasarathy, G (June 1982) 'Growth Fluctuations and Real Wages in Andhra Pradesh', Agro-Economic Research, Andhra University, Waltair.

Parthasarathy, G. (1988) 'Growth, Stability and Equity within the Agrarian Sector of Andhra Pradesh', in Agricultural Growth, Rural Development and Poverty, Dept. of Cupertino and Applied Economics, Andhra University, Visakhapatnam.

Parthasarathy, G. (1989) 'Growth Development and State Planning in Andhra Pradesh', paper presented at the seminar on 'Eighth plan perspectives of AP, Centre for Economic and social Studies, Hyderabad. February 2-3.

Parthasarathy, G. (4 Jan 1962) 'Manpower Utilisation within Agriculture', *Economic Review.*

Parthasarathy, G. and Jayshree, A. (1994) 'Trends and Dimensions in Employment and Unemployment in Andhra Pradesh', *Economic and Political Weekly,* Vol.

Parthasarathy. G. (Jan-March 1987) 'Changes in the Incidence of Rural Poverty and Recent Trends in Some Aspects of Agrarian Economy', *Indian Journal of Agricultural Economics,* Vol. 42, No. 1, pp. 1-21.

Parthasarthy, G (1979) 'Inter-State Variations in Rural Unemployment and Growth of Agriculture', *Indian Journal of Labour Economics,* Vol. XL ll No. 1.

Planning Commission, (1981) Sixth Five-year Plan 1980-85, Government of India (GOI) p.100

Planning Commission, 1991, Draft Eighth Five Year Plan, Vol. ll, New Delhi, Computed from NSS Employment date on the usual principle plus subsidiary status basis and CSO National Accounts Statistics: Quoted in Bhalla (1993).

Planning Commission, Govt of India (May 1990), 'Employment: Past Trends and Prospects for 1990s: A working Paper', New Delhi.

R. Radhakrishna and Alakh N. Sharma (1998) 'Empowering Rural Labour in India: Market, State and Mobilisation'. New Delhi: Institute for Human Development, D.K. Fine Art Press.

Radhakrishna R. (1990) 'Growth Scenario for India in 2000: Persistence of Basic Problems', *Social Scientist,* Vol.18, No. 4 No. 203,

Radhakrishna. R, et al. (1977) 'An Explanatory Study on Slums: Employment, Poverty and Liquor Consumption', SPIESR, Ahmedabad, Mimeo.

Raghav Gaiha (1987) 'Impoverishment, Technology and Growth in Rural India' Cambridge, *Journal of Economics,* 11.

Raghav Gaiha (1987) 'Impoverishment, Technology and Growth in Rural India,' *Cambridge Journal of Economics,* Vol. 11, pp. 23-46.

Raghav, Gaiha (July 1987) 'Inequality, Earnings and Participation among the Poor in Rural India', Journal of Development studies, Vol. 23, No. 4, pp.

Raj, K. (Jan.-March 1973) 'Presidential Address-on Unemployment in India', *Indian Journal of Agricultural Economics,* Vol. 28, No. 1, p. 6.

Raj, K. (March 1973) 'Unemployment in India', *Economic and Political Weekly,* Vol. 8, No. 9, p. 477.

Raj, K.N. (Aug. 1976) 'Trends in Rural Unemployment in India: An Analysis with Reference to Conceptual and Measurement Problems', *Economic and Political Weekly,* Special Number, pp.

Ramasamy, C.; Hazell, P.; Rajagopalan, V. and Aiyasamy P.K. (1986) 'Changes in Paddy Technology, Input use and Returns', IFRI/ TNAU Workshop on Growth Linkages, Ootacamund, February 14-16 (mimeo).

Ramsey, J.B. (1969) 'Tests for specification Errors in classical linear least squares regression Analysis', *Journal of the Royal Statistical Society*, Series B, Vol. 31, pp. 350-371.

Rangarajan, C. (1982) Agricultural Growth and Industrial Performance in India, Research Report No.33, International Food Policy, Research Institute, Washington D.C.

Ranis Gustav and Stewart Frances (1993) 'Rural Non-agricultural Activities in Development: Theory and Application,' *Journal of Development Economics*, Volume 40, No.1, pp.

Ranis, G. and Fei, J. (Sept. 1961) 'A Theory of Economic Development', *American Economic Review*, Vol. L1, No. 4, pp. 533-565.

Ranis, G. and Stewart F. (Feb. 1993) 'Non-agricultural Activities in Development: Theory and Application', *Journal of Development Economics*, Vol. 40, No. 1, pp.

Rao, C.H. Hanumantha (14 Dec. 1973) 'Farm Size and Economies of Scale', *Economic and Political Weekly*, Vol. 15, No. 50, p.

Rao, C.H. Hanumantha (1979) August.

Rao, V.K.R.V. (Feb. 1955) 'Marginal Analysis and Subsistence Agriculture', *Indian Economic Review*, Vol. 11, No . 3, p.

Rao, V.M. (29 June 1996) 'Agricultural Development with a Human Face: Experience and Prospects', *Economic and Political Weekly*, pp. A50-A73.

Rao, M. Jagadeswara (1990).

Rao, R.M. Mohan (1986).

Rathna Reddy, A. (1988) 'Surplus Labour, poverty and Agricultural Development-A Case Study of Andhra Pradesh', Artha Vijnana, Vol. 30, No. 4, pp.

Reardon, T and Matlon, P. (1989) 'Seasonal Food Insecurity and Vulnerability in Drought-Affected Regions of Burkina Faso', in D. Sahn (ed.) Causes and Implications of Seasonal Variability in Household Food Security. Baltimore, MD: Johns Hopkins University Press.

Reardon, T.; Matlon, P and Delgado, C. (Sept. 1988) 'Coping with Household Level Food Insecurity in Drought-affected Areas of Burkina Faso', *World Development*, Vol. 16, No. 9, pp. 1065-74.

Reardon, T.; Taylor, J..; Stamoulis, K.; Lanjouw, P.; Balisacan, A. (May 2000) 'Effects of Nonfarm Employment on Rural Income Inequality in Developing Countries: An Investment Perspective', Vol. 51, No. 2 forthcoming.

Reddy, R.A. (1988).

Reddy, S.S. (1991).

Report of the Expert Group (1993) on; Estimation of proportion and number of poor; Perspective Planning Division, Planning Commission, Government of India, July, pp.36, Table 4.1).

Robinson, A. (1983) Employment Policy in a Developing Country: A Case study of India. Macmillan Press, Vol. 1.

Rudra, Ashok (1973) 'Direct Estimates of Surplus Labour in Agriculture', *Economic and Political Weekly,* (Annual Number), Vol. 8, Nos. 4, 5 and 6, February.

Rudra, Ashok and Sen Amertya (Feb. 1980) 'Farm size and Labour Use', *Economic and Political Weekly,* (Annual Number), Vol. 15, Nos. 5, 6 and 7.

Saith, A. (1986) ' Contrasting Experiences in Rural Industrialisation: Are the East Asian Success Transferable?' in R. Islam (ed.) Rural Industrialisation and Employment in Asia, ILO, (ARTEP), New Delhi, pp. 273-303.

Saith, A. (1992) 'The Rural Non-farm economy: Processes and Policies', ILO, Geneva, pp. 1-16 and 21-24 (Analytical framework), pp. 27-32 (empirical evidence), pp. 86-96 (critical overview of Grameen and IRDP) and pp. 99-114 (Concluding observations: macro-development strategy).

Sankaranarayana, V (1980) 'Inter - State Variation in rural Non - Agricultural employment - Some Tentative Results'. Trivandrum: Centre for Development Studies, working paper No. 104,

Sardana Parveen K, Manocha V. and Gangwar A.C. (1995) 'Nature and Pattern of Changes in Rural Non-farm Employment in Haryana' *Indian Journal of Agricultural Economics,* Conference Number, July-September.

Sarvekeshana (1986) 27th Round, 32nd Round and 38th Rounds from Vol. 1X. No. 4, April pp. S-119-S-122.

Sarvekeshana (1986) 27th Round, 32nd Round and 38th Rounds from Vol. 1X. No. 4, April, pp. S-119-S-122.

Sarvekshana (1990) NSS 43rd Round (July 1987-June 1988) and on Key Results of employment and Unemployment Survey All-India (part-1), Special Report No. 1, January. Sarvekshana 43rd Round, Jan 1992 Special issue, AP.

Sarvekshana (April 1986) Vol. 1X, No. 4, pp. 5-184.

Sarvekshana (April 1988) Vol. X1, No. 4, Issue No. 35, *Journal of NSSO*, Government of India for 38th Round pp. 23 and 43.

Sarvekshana (July-October 1981) Vol. 5, Nos. 1 & 2 for 32nd Round pp. 14 and 31 for all-India 27th Round, p. 11.

Sarvekshana for 43rd Round, (July 1987-June 1988), and on Key Results of Employment and Unemployment survey, All-India (Part-1), Special Report No. 1 January 1990 pp. 63 and 111.

Sarvekshana, (1978) 'Some Findings of the Survey on self-employment in non-agricultural Enterprises' 29th Round, July 1974-June 1975. NSS, 1 (1978) 4.

Satyapriya, V S (1984) Labour utilisation in Agriculture. (Tumkur District, Karnataka). Bangalore: Shiny Publications.

Scarlett, Penny David H, (Eds) (1972) Opportunity and Response: Case Studies in Economic Development. London: Hurst.

Scarlett, T. (1962) Economic development and social Change in South India, Manchester.

Scarlett, T. (1973) South India: Yesterday, Today, and Tomorrow. Mysore Villages Revisited. London: Macmillan.

Seal, K C (1980) 'Women in the Labour force in India: A Macro-Level statistical Profile', Chapter 2, pp 22-92, in 'Women in the Labour Force', Papers and Proceedings of a Workshop held in Trivandrum, July 24-25, ARTEP Publication.

Sen, A K (1975) Employment Technology and Development. Oxford: Clarendon Press. A Study prepared for the ILO within the frame work of the World Employment Programme.

Sen, Amartya K (1972) Choice of Techniques: An Aspect of the Theory of Economic Development. Oxford (Third Edition).

Sen, Amartya K (1972) 'Farm Mechanisation in a labour abundant economy', *Economic and political Weekly*, Annual Number.

Sen, Amartya K (1975) Technological Change and Distribution of Gains in Indian Agriculture. New Delhi: Macmillan.

Sen, Amartya K (Feb. 1962) 'An aspect of Indian Agriculture', *The Economic Weekly*, Annual Number.

Set, A. (October-Dec. 1994) 'Rural Labour Markets and Poverty', *The Indian Journal of Labour Economics*.

Shand, K.T. (Ed.), (1986) Off-farm employment in the Development of Rural Asia, 2 Vols., Australian National University, Canberra.

Sharma A.K. Saksena (1984).

Shand, R.T. (1983) Off-Farm Employment in the Development of Rural Asia. Vol. 1&2.

Sharma, Alakh. N. (1997A) 'Labour Markets and Employment in Bihar', Institute of Economic Growth, Delhi (Mimeo).

Sharma, Alakh. N. (1997a) 'Labour Markets and employment in Bihar', Institute of Economic growth, Delhi (Mimeo).

Sharma, P. V (Jan.-March 1975) 'Regional Variations in the Growth of Agricultural Output in A.P *Economic and Statistical Bulletin*, Bureau of Economics and Statistics, Government of A.P, pp 9-39.

Shramshakti (1988) 'The Report of the National Commission on Self Employed Women and Women in Informal Sector', New Delhi: Reviewed by Howard Spodek in Economic Development and Cultural Change, in July 1990.

Shukla Vibhooti and Shukla Tara (1990) 'Regional Determinants of Rural Non-farm Employment in Maharashtra' (Revised) Paper presented at the National Seminar on Non-agricultural Employment in India: Trends and Prospects (Ahmedabad, India: March 1989).

Shukla, V (19 Oct. 1991) 'Rural Non-farm Activity: A Regional Model and Its Application to Maharashtra', *Economic and Political Weekly*, pp. 2423-26.

Shylendra H.S. and P. Thomas, (1995) 'Non-farm Employment: Nature, Magnitude and Determinants in a Semi-Arid Village of Western India', *Indian Journal of Agricultural Economics*, Conference Number, July-September.

Sigurdson, J (May 1978) 'Rural Industrialisation: A Comparison of Development Planning in China and India', World Development, Vol. 6. No. 5, pp. 667-680.

Simmons Colin and Supri Salinder (1995) 'Off-farm Activities and Employment Generation in Rural India: A Case Study of Household Enterprises in Jalandar District, Punjab', (Mimeo).

Singer, H.W. (Oct. 1970) 'Dualism Revisited: A New Approach to the Problems of the Dual Society in Developing countries', *Journal of Development Studies*, Vol. 7, No. 1, October, pp. 60-75.

Singh, Andrea Menefee (1984) 'Rural-to-Urban Migration of Women in India: Patterns and Implications', in J.T. Fawcett et al, Women in the Cities of Asia. Migration and Urban Adoption. Boulder: Westview Press, pp. 83-85.

Singh, S. (1993) 'Some Aspects of Rural Non-Farm Sector Development in Developing Countries', in Chadha (1993a)

Singh, Surjeet (17 Nov. 1990) 'Rural Credit: Issues for the 1990s', *Economic and Political Weekly*, pp. 2531-2535.

Sinha.J.N. (1 Sep. 1979) 'Employment and Agriculture in the Draft plan, 1978-83' *Economic and Political Weekly*, Vol.XIV, No.35, pp. 1503-1510.

Sirohi, A.S. (1985) 'Presidential Address: Impact of Agricultural Subsidies and Procurement Prices on Production and Income Distribution in India', Forty Fourth All India Agricultural Economics.

Sixth Five-year plan 1980-85 (1981) Planning Commission, Government of India p. 100.

Smita, J.N. (1982) '1981 Census Economic Data: A Note', *Economic and Political Weekly*, X V II 6.

Smith, A.D. (1971) Concepts of Labour Under Utilisation. ILO, Geneva.

Sreerammurty. K. (1986) Urban Labour in the Informal Sector. B.R. Publishing Corporation, New Delhi.

Standing, G. (1978) Labour Force Participation and Development. ILO, Geneva.

Statistical Abstract of Andhra Pradesh, 1982 and 1983, 1988 to 1991, 1992, pp 207. Government of Andhra Pradesh, Table 13.1.

Stewart, F., (1977) 'Technology and underdevelopment', Hong Kong, The Macmillan Press Ltd., second edition.

Sudhakar, Reddy. S. (1991) 'Poverty and Agricultural Growth in Rural Andhra Pradesh' Inter District Analysis, Centre for Economic and social studies, (CESS) Poverty Project Monograph No.1.

Sundaram, K. and S. D. Tendulkar (1988) 'Towards an Explanation of Inter-Regional Variations in Poverty and Unemployment in Rural India', In T.N. Srinivasan and P.K. Bardhan (eds) 'Rural Poverty in South Asia', Oxford University Press, Delhi.

Sundaram, K. and Tendulkar, S.D. (1988) 'Towards an Explanation of Inter-Regional Variations in Poverty and Unemployment in Rural India', Srinivasan T N and Bardhan P K (Eds), Rural Poverty in South Asia, Oxford University Press.

Swamy, Dalip, S. and Gulati, Ashok (1986) 'Farm Prosperity to Retrogression: Indian Cultivators during the 1970s', *Economic and Political Weekly*, Vol, XX1, No. 25 and 26, June 21-28, pp. A-57-A-64.

Swapana Mukhopadhyay (June 1985) 'Non-Farm Sector in Asia: A Characterisation', *Economic and Political Weekly*, Vol. XX, No. 22,.

Syed, R.H. (ed.) (1987) 'The Rural Non-farm Sector and Process of Economic Development', ADIPA, Kuala Lumpur.

Timberg, T.A. (1990) 'Small Enterprises among village women in Tanzania' in Small Enterprise Development, Vol. 2, No. 1, March, pp. 20-31.

Timmer, P.C. (1975).

Tyabji, Nasir (1989) The Industries Policy in India. Calcutta: Oxford University Press.

Tyagi D S (1981), 'Growth of Agricultural output and labour Absorption in India'. *Journal of Development Studies,* Vol. 18, No. 1, October 1981, p. 112.

Unni, J. (19 Jan. 1991), 'Regional Variations in Rural Non-Agricultural Employment: An Explanatory Analysis', *Economic and Political Weekly,* pp 109-122.

Unni, Jeemol (1989) 'Changes in Women' s Employment in Rural areas, 1961-83', *Economic and Political Weekly,* Vol. XX1V, No. 17.

Unni, J. (1990).

Vaidyanathan, A. (1978) 'Labour Use in Indian Agriculture: Analysis based on Farm Management Survey Data', in ILO, Labour Absorption in Indian Agriculture, Some Exploratory Inventions. Bangkok: ARTEP.

Vaidyanathan, A. (1986) 'Labour Use in Rural India', *Indian Journal of Agricultural Economics.*

Vaidyanathan, A. (1986) 'Labour Use in Rural India: A Study of Spatial and Temporal Variations', *Economic and Political Weekly,* Vol. 21, No 52.

Vaidyanathan, A. (1987) 'Irrigation and Agricultural Growth', *Indian Journal of Agricultural Economics,* Vol. 42, No. 4, October-December. vol. L11 No. 4. pp 503-527.

Vaidyanathan, A. and Jose, A. (1977) 'Absorption of Human Labour in Agriculture: A Comparative Study of some Asian countries', in Annexures of ILO-ARTEP (1978).

Vibhuti Shukla (1991) 'Rural Non-farm activity-A Regional Model and its Empirical Application to Maharashtra', *Economic and Political Weekly,* Vol.XXVII, No. 45, November 9, pp.2587-95

Vibhuti Shukla (1992) 'Rural non-farm employment in India Issues and Policy' *Economic and Political Weekly,* Vol.XXVII, No. 28, July, pp.1477-88.

Visaria, P. (1980) 'Poverty and Unemployment in India', *Indian Journal of Agricultural Economics,* XXX V, No. 3, July-Sept., pp. 1-19.

Visaria, P. (1981) 'Poverty and Unemployment in India: An Analysis of Recent Evidence', 'World Development', Vol. ll, No. 3.

Visaria, P. (1984) 'The Growth of Population and Labour Force in India: 1961-2001', A paper presented at the Workshop on Population growth and Labour Absorption in the Developing World: 1960-2000, Bellagio, July 1-6.

Visaria, P. (1989) 'Concepts and Measurement of Unemployment and Under-Employment in Asian Countries: A Comparative Study', ILO ARTEP Working Paper.

Visaria, P. (1989) 'Sectoral Distribution of the Work Force in India-A Review'. Seminar on Non-Agricultural Employment in India-Trends and prospects, Ahmedabad, March 29-31 .

Visaria, P. and Minhas, B. S. (13 April 1991) 'Evolving an Employment Policy for the 1990s: What Do the Data Tell us?', in *Economic and Political Weekly,* pp. 969-979.

Visaria, P. and R. Basant (1994), 'Non-Agricultural Employment in India: Trends and Prospects', Sage, Delhi.

Visaria, P. and Visaria, L. (1990) Concepts and Measurement of Unemployment and Underemployment in Asian Countries: A Comparative Study. New Delhi: ILO, Asian Employment Programme (ARTEP).

Visaria. Pravin, (1995), 'Rural Non-farm Employment in India: Trends and Issues for Research' *Indian Journal of Agricultural Economics,* Conference Number, July-September.

Vyas, V.S. (1968) 'Rural Labour Utilisation and Agricultural Development', Artha Vikas, Vol. 6, Jan.

Vyas, V.S. (1979) 'Some Aspects of Structural Change in Indian Agriculture', *Indian Journal of Agricultural Economics,* Vol. 34, No 1, Jan.-March.

Vyas, V.S. (1990) 'Rural Labour: Strategies for Employment Creation' Economic Times, May 30.

Vyas, V.S., and Mathai, G. (1978) 'Farm and non-farm Employment in Rural Areas', *Economic and Political Weekly,* Annual Number, February.

Vyasulu, Vinod (1990), ' The Non-Farm Sector in the Indian Economy: A Discussion Note on Research Priorities', *The Indian Journal of Social Science,* July-Sept., pp. 443-451.

Walker Thomas, S. and Ryan James, G. (1990), Village and household economies in India's semi-arid Tropics. The johns Hopkins University press.

Walker, T.S and J.G Ryan (1990), Village Household Economies in India's Semi-arid Tropics. The Hopkins University Press Baltimore and London.

Walker, T.S. and J. G. Ryan (1990) 'Village and household Economies in India's Semi-arid Tropics', Johns Hopkins University Press, Baltimore and London.

White, H. (1980) "A Heteroscedasticity Consistent Covariance Matrix Estimator and a Direct Test of Heteroscedasticity", *Econometrica,* Vol.48. pp. 817-818.

Wong, C P W (1988), 'Interpreting Rural Industrial Growth in Post-Mao Period' in Modern China, Vol. 14, No. 2, Jan, pp. 3-30.

World Bank, (1978), 'Rural Enterprise and Non-farm' Employment', A World Bank Paper, Washington DC.

World Bank, (1983), Growth and Employment in Rural Thailand, World Bank Report, (Summary).

APPENDIX

Appendix Table 1.1 : Percentage distribution of total main rural workers in Andhra Pradesh and India (1961 to 1991).

	Andhra Pradesh				*India*			
	1961	*1971*	*1981*	*1991*	*1961*	*1971*	*1981*	*1991*
Cultivators	44.5	36.5	38.4	33.4	60.3	50.9	51.1	48.5
Agricultural Labourers	31.3	41.7	42.0 (2.8)*	47.4 (1.9)*	18.9	30.0	29.9 (2.4)*	31.8 (2.0)*
Rural Non-agriculture	24.1	21.8	16.8	17.3	20.8	19.1	16.6	17.7
Total	100	100	100	100	100	100	100	100

Sources : Census of India (1971), "Supplement Provisional Population Totals", Series 1, India, Paper 1 of 1971, pp. 30-31; Census of India (1991), "Provisional Population Totals: Workers and their Distribution", Series 1, India, Paper - 3 of 1991, New Delhi, p. 433. Note: * indicates Agricultural allied activities.

Appendix Table 1.2 : 1981 and 1991 Rural Work Participation Rates from Census data in AP and All-India (Main and Marginal Workers):

AP				*All-India*			
Males		*Females*		*Males*		*Females*	
1981	*1991*	*1981*	*1991*	*1981*	*1991*	*1981*	*1991*
60.19 (59.56) *0.63	58.01 (57.31) *0.7	40.03 (31.95) *8.08	42.92 (37.30) *5.62	53.80 (52.61) *1.19	52.43 (51.29) *1.14	23.18 (16.00) *7.18	27.06 (19.07) *8.00

Remarks: The figures in parentheses give the labour force participation rates of main workers;
- *: workforce participation rates of marginal workers.

Sources : 1981 & 1991 Census data: Census of 1991, India, Andhra Pradesh series-2, Provisional Population Totals, Paper-1 of 1991 Supplement pp. 23-25.

Appendix Table 1.3 : Age and Gender-Specific Labour Force Participation rates: Census data (main and marginal workers) 1961 and 1981, and NSS Usual Principal Activity Status (UPAS)and UPAS + UPSS (Usual Principal Subsidiary Status) 1983, 1987-88, for AP and All-India (figures in percentages):

	Andhra Pradesh							*All India*						
	Census			*NSS*				*Census*			*NSS*			
Years/ Age group	*1961*	*1981 Main workers only*	*1981 Main+ marginal*	*1983 UPSS*	*1987-88 UPSS*	*1983 UPAS+ UPSS*	*1987-88 UPAS+ UPSS*	*1961*	*1981 Main workers only*	*1981 Main+ marginal*	*1983 UPSS*	*1987-88 UPSS*	*1983 UPAS+ UPSS*	*1987-88 UPAS+ UPSS*
Males														
5-14	17.7	11.5	12.0	23.2	17.6	24.2	20.8	10.6	6.3	6.9	11.3	7.2	13.5	10.2
15-59	96.6	92.9	93.6	92.4	90.3	93.4	92.3	93.8	86.8	88.4	88.4	81.4	90.4	88.7
60 & above	80.4	70.8	71.8	61.8	59.4	64.1	62.1	79.9	67.8	69.1	64.1	64.6	66.8	66.8
all ages	64.3	59.6	60.2	69.1	57.5	70.1	59.5	58.2	52.6	53.8	61.3	51.7	63.5	53.9
Females														
5-14	12.8	8.8	10.7	18.1	17.6	20.4	21.7	7.63	3.5	5.3	8.8	6.1	12.5	9.6
15-59	71.8	49.9	62.7	64.2	63.4	72.7	72.0	50.8	26.1	37.7	40.1	40.2	54.5	51.6
60 & above	33.3	22.2	28.1	21.5	18.8	25.5	24.2	24.3	11.3	15.9	15.5	16.0	22.6	21.8
all ages	46.0	32.0	40.0	47.9	40.9	54.4	47.0	31.4	16.0	23.2	28.7	24.5	39.3	32.3

Contd....

Appendix Table 1.3 : (Contd....)

Notes : (1) 1961 & 1981 data cannot be compared because of a change in the definitions of worker. It is probably mostly because of this change in definitions that the proportions of female workers in 1981 is much lower than in 1961.

(2) Census and NSS data are not comparable.

(3) The calculation of the NSS labour force participation rates for age groups 5-14, 15-59, 60> & all ages has taken account of the weight of different age groups.

Sources : 1961 Census data: calculated on the basis of the Census of India 1961, Volume 1, India part 11-B(i) General Economic Tables for AP pp. 90 and 91 for All India pp. 86-7.

1981 Census data: calculated on the basis of the Census of India 1981, Series-1, India Part-111 A (i) General Economic Tables for all-India pp. 134 and 135 for AP pp. 136-7.

1983 NSS data: calculated on the basis of the 38th Round Sarvekeshna, Vol. 1X. No. 4, April 1988 pp. 14-5 Population data, 25-6 UPAS, 28-9 UPAS & SS -

1987 - 88 NSS data: calculated on the basis of the 43rd Round, Sarvekshna, For NSS July 1987-June 1988 Key Results of the Fourth Quinquennial Survey on Employment and Unemployment (All-India) September 1990 pp. 45-6. Population data, 65-6 UPSS, pp. 74-6, 46-8 UPAS + UPSS.

Appendix Table 1.4 : Percentage of Workers aged 5 + according to Usual Principal Status, Current Weekly Status and Current Day Status during the 27th, 32nd, 38th, and 43rd Rounds of NSS: for AP and All-India - Rural (main and marginal workers):

	Andhra Pradesh				*All India*			
Rounds/	*27th Round (72-73)*	*32nd Round (77-78)*	*38th Round 1983*	*43rd Round (87-88)*	*27th Round (72-73)*	*32nd Round (77-78)*	*38th Round 1983*	*43rd Round (87-88)*
	Current Day Status				**Current Day Status**			
Rural Males	63.5	62.1	60.5	54.5	58.9	56.6	55.9	50.1
Rural Females	29.8	33.9	35.1	32.7	27.2	22.6	22.9	20.7
	Weekly Status				**Weekly Status**			
Rural Males	67.7	66.7	64.9	55.2	62.1	60.2	59.3	50.4
Rural Females	37.0	39.1	40.8	35.5	32.6	26.9	26.3	22.0
	Usual Status				**Usual Status**			
Rural Males	72.4	71.2 (69.7) *1.5	70.1 (69.1) *1.1	59.5 (57.5) *2.0	63.8	64.1 (62.3) *1.8	63.5 (61.3) *2.2	53.9 (51.7) *2.2
Rural Females	52.5	51.7 (45.4) *6.3	54.4 (47.9) *6.5	47.0 (40.9) *6.1	37.5	38.5 (28.8) *9.7	39.3 (28.7) *10.6	32.3 (24.5) *7.8

Note : The Figures in parentheses give the labour force participation rates of main workers (*indicates subsidiary status).

Sources : Sarvekshana, Vol. X1, No. 4, Issue No. 35, April 1988, Journal of NSSO, Government of India for 38th Round pp. 23 and 43.

Sarvekshana, Vol. 5, Nos. 1 & 2 July-October 1981, for 32nd Round pp. 14 and 31 for all-India 27th Round, p. 11.

Sarvekshana for 43rd Round, Key Results of Employment and Unemployment survey, All-India (Part-1), (July 1987-June 1988), Special Report No. 1 January 1990 pp. 63 and 111.

Comment : The high WFPR [= workers + work seekers/population] in AP is an indication that a larger percentage of economically active [= employed/workers+work seekers] population is available/engaging themselves in work to earn their subsistence.

Appendix Table 1.5 Rural Non-farm Employment and Ratios of farm Labourers to Cultivators for 1981 and 1991 in the Indian States

	RNFE 81 (%)	*RNFE 91 (%)*	*Growth/ year (%)*	*81 agrl. lab (%)*	*91 agrl. lab (%)*	*Agri/cul for 91*	*Agri/cul for 81*
All India	16.6	17.7	0.4	30.8	32.2	0.6045	0.668
Andhra Pradesh	16.8	17.1	0.3	42.0	47.5	1.094	1.420

Source : Census of India 1991, Andhra Pradesh, Population Totals, Series-2, pp. 10, 66-73.

Comment : The share of the total workforce in RNFE declined by 0.29 per cent per year in AP between 1981 and 1991. For the same period, RNFE for India increased by 0.37 per cent per year, giving some support to the idea that RNFE in AP is not doing well. These figures have to be interpreted with great caution because this change has been calculated for the only two years for which data are available (the 1981 RNFE and the 1991 RNFE figure). In relation to the change to the agriculture labourer/cultivators ratio, it has increased from 1.09 to 1.4 for AP between 1981 and 1991. The figure for India has also increased (from 0.60 to 0.67) but not by as much as AP where agricultural labour dominates. Behind these figures is the fact that the proportion of agricultural labour increased more rapidly than the proportion of cultivators declined. Whilst the trend is the same as that observed for India, the Indian increase in agricultural labour has been offset by the decrease in cultivators.The proportion of cultivators has declined significantly while that of agricultural labourers has increased sharply.

Appendix Table 1.6 - Part 1: Proportions in RNFS Employment, Across States between 1981 and 1991

States	*Year*	*I*	*II*	*I+II*	*III*	*IV*	*V(a)*	*V(b)*	*VI*	*VII*	*VIII*	*IX*	*Total RNFS*
India	**1981**	50.95	30.80	81.75	2.37	0.45	3.07	3.43	1.02	2.79	1.10	4.73	16.59
	1991	48.15	32.17	80.32	1.96	0.47	2.20	3.60	1.04	3.26	1.23	5.92	17.72
Andhra	**1981**	38.39	42.01	80.4	2.74	0.29	4.49	2.80	0.83	3.13	0.89	4.43	16.86
Pradesh	1991	33.45	47.51	80.96	1.89	0.67	3.22	3.00	0.78	3.33	1.02	5.13	17.15
Arunachal	**1981**	75.04	2.57	77.61	1.45	0.01	0.24	1.48	6.15	1.74	0.30	11.02	20.94
Pradesh	1991	66.68	5.52	72.2	1.73	0.20	0.18	2.16	5.16	2.31	0.81	15.25	26.07
Assam	**1981**	na	na	na	na	na	na	na	na	na	na	na	na
	1991	56.62	13.35	69.97	11.39	0.42	0.81	2.00	1.07	4.20	1.41	8.73	18.64
Bihar	**1981**	47.95	38.71	86.66	0.74	0.94	2.27	2.21	0.45	2.26	0.99	3.48	12.6
	1991	47.77	40.23	88	0.31	0.70	1.57	1.17	0.41	2.13	0.72	4.99	11.69
Goa	**1981**	26.21	13.56	39.77	5.88	7.27	3.81	10.61	4.85	7.90	5.36	14.54	54.34
	1991	22.31	13.26	35.57	4.66	5.72	2.70	12.95	5.45	10.82	6.67	15.46	59.77
Gujarat	**1981**	50.34	29.62	79.96	2.61	0.30	2.31	5.17	0.87	2.93	1.51	4.34	17.43
	1991	46.11	30.68	76.79	3.58	3.34	1.42	7.19	0.95	3.19	1.70	4.86	22.65
Haryana	**1981**	55.80	19.68	75.48	0.91	0.09	2.57	5.36	1.92	3.46	1.91	8.30	23.61
	1991	49.56	23.38	72.94	0.82	0.09	1.28	4.99	1.93	3.56	2.33	12.06	26.24
Himachal	**1981**	73.14	2.86	76	2.51	0.24	1.82	2.82	4.90	2.44	1.39	7.88	21.49
Pradesh	1991	68.58	3.48	72.06	2.46	0.25	1.45	3.23	4.38	2.96	1.57	11.64	25.48
Jammu	**1981**	69.07	3.78	72.85	3.51	0.15	4.46	3.51	2.20	2.63	1.68	9.01	23.64
& Kashmir	1991	na	na	na	na	na	na	na	na	na	na	na	na
Karnataka	**1981**	47.81	32.37	80.18	4.46	0.41	3.53	3.32	1.13	2.73	0.87	3.37	15.36
	1991	43.79	35.94	79.73	4.18	0.62	1.61	3.97	1.11	3.36	0.95	4.47	16.09

Contd....

Appendix Table 1.6 - Part 1 : (Contd....)

States	*Year*	*I*	*II*	*I+II*	*III*	*IV*	*V(a)*	*V(b)*	*VI*	*VII*	*VIII*	*IX*	*Total RNFS*
Kerala	**1981**	15.31	32.46	47.77	10.28	0.80	3.86	10.35	2.60	9.16	3.86	11.22	41.85
	1991	15.09	30.56	45.65	10.42	1.11	2.48	9.43	3.28	10.04	4.58	13.01	43.93
Madhya	**1981**	59.95	27.45	87.4	1.80	0.62	3.05	1.43	1.02	1.43	0.42	2.83	10.8
Pradesh	1991	61.05	27.03	88.08	1.20	0.54	2.08	1.71	0.70	1.63	0.46	3.60	10.72
Maharashtra	**1981**	47.86	35.14	83	2.20	0.26	2.22	3.55	1.44	2.22	0.89	4.22	14.8
	1991	46.26	36.61	82.87	1.66	0.27	1.47	3.86	1.13	2.73	1.16	4.85	15.47
Manipur	**1981**	72.02	4.90	76.92	0.85	0.01	8.40	1.06	1.07	1.53	0.56	9.60	22.23
	1991	69.65	6.49	76.14	1.23	0.02	5.20	1.29	1.08	1.93	0.80	12.31	22.63
Meghalaya	**1981**	71.80	11.12	82.92	7.03	0.65	0.72	0.64	0.76	1.73	0.37	5.54	10.41
	1991	64.16	14.12	78.28	7.15	0.58	0.37	0.79	0.88	2.88	0.64	8.43	14.57
Mizoram	**1981**	82.86	1.32	84.18	0.54	0.01	0.44	0.41	2.06	0.93	0.36	11.07	15.28
	1991	81.51	1.65	83.16	0.52	0.01	0.41	0.24	1.39	1.14	0.20	12.93	16.32
Nagaland	**1981**	80.74	0.78	81.52	0.34	0.04	0.22	0.97	0.81	0.95	0.32	14.83	18.14
	1991	82.34	1.37	83.71	0.83	0.03	0.33	0.92	1.19	1.23	0.37	11.39	15.46
Orissa	**1981**	51.79	30.14	81.93	2.26	0.70	3.26	2.11	0.71	2.51	0.77	5.75	15.81
	1991	49.38	31.43	80.81	1.66	0.80	3.20	2.00	0.49	3.42	0.86	6.76	17.53
Punjab	**1981**	47.73	28.52	76.25	0.95	0.02	2.27	5.08	1.55	3.97	2.31	7.60	22.8
	1991	42.81	30.75	73.56	0.67	0.01	1.17	5.47	1.87	4.09	2.57	10.59	25.77
Rajasthan	**1981**	73.13	8.36	81.49	3.27	0.86	2.74	2.57	1.17	2.41	0.99	4.50	15.24
	1991	71.02	11.54	82.56	1.88	0.95	1.64	2.34	1.32	2.71	1.09	5.51	15.56
Sikkim	**1981**	69.96	3.77	73.73	1.69	0.13	0.81	1.24	7.79	1.58	0.47	12.56	24.58
	1991	63.23	8.49	71.72	2.44	0.21	0.64	2.58	6.82	2.79	1.45	11.35	25.84

Contd....

Appendix Table 1.6 - Part 1 : (Contd....)

States	*Year*	*I*	*II*	*I+II*	*III*	*IV*	*V(a)*	*V(b)*	*VI*	*VII*	*VIII*	*IX*	*Total RNFS*
Tamil nadu	**1981**	38.28	40.27	78.55	2.44	0.23	3.81	4.96	0.93	3.70	1.02	4.31	18.96
	1991	32.76	44.73	77.49	1.86	0.27	3.06	5.31	1.11	3.63	1.35	5.92	20.65
Tripura	**1981**	47.71	26.29	74	2.78	0.12	1.45	3.55	1.51	4.62	1.59	10.38	23.22
	1991	44.13	26.50	70.63	2.60	0.15	1.46	2.73	1.04	5.48	1.83	14.08	26.77
Uttar	**1981**	68.41	17.91	86.32	0.44	0.06	2.83	2.59	0.56	1.68	0.92	4.63	13.27
Pradesh	1991	63.01	21.47	84.48	0.57	0.09	1.80	2.78	0.76	2.53	0.87	6.12	14.95
West Bengal	**1981**	40.20	33.58	73.78	3.98	0.78	3.55	5.55	0.82	4.29	1.66	5.58	22.23
	1991	37.97	32.24	70.21	3.32	0.43	4.22	6.22	1.24	5.98	2.15	6.23	26.47

Notes : I: Cultivators; II: Agricultural labour; III: Agral. allied activities; IV: Mining and quarrying; V (a): Household Industry; V(b): Non-household industry; VI: Construction; VII: Trade; VIII: Transport; IX: Services, [I to IX add to 100].

Sources : Census of India 1991, Andhra Pradesh, Population Totals, Series-2, pp. 10, 66-73

Comment : For AP, the agricultural allied sector III has lost out over time compared to India. For India, II has grown in India and in AP although AP has had a larger proportion in agricultural labour throughout the period. The reverse holds true for cultivators. Expansion (in particular in AP compared to all-India) occurred in sector IV. While VI has remained relatively small and stable for all-India, it declined for AP. Another sector where a modest increase has been observed in compared to India is in the trade sector. A strong increase in AP in the transport sector VIII has occurred in comparison to India. A moderate increase in AP for services compared to India. For V(a) household industry although AP's share is grater than that of all-India. There has been a decline for both, AP and India V(b) share's is greater in India than AP, the share has grown in both cases but in AP slightly less fast than in India. RNFE increased for all-India by over 0.5 percentage points but there was a decline by a relatively similar order of magnitude for AP.

Appendix Table 1.7: Percentage of Unemployed to Total Persons of Age 5 Years and Above According to Usual Status, Current Weekly Status and Current Day Status during the 27th, 32nd, 38th, and 43rd Rounds of NSS.

	Andhra Pradesh				*All India*			
Rounds/	*27th Round (72-73)*	*32nd Round (77-78)*	*38th Round 1983*	*43rd Round (87-88)*	*27th Round (72-73)*	*32nd Round (77-78)*	*38th Round 1983*	*43rd Round (87-88)*
	Current Day Status				**Current Day Status**			
Rural males	6.9	5.7	5.6	4.9	4.8	4.5	4.8	4.6
Rural females	8.4	6.3	4.7	9.4	3.7	2.5	2.5	6.7
Urban males	6.9	6.8	5.0	10.1	4.8	5.4	5.5	8.8
Urban females	3.3	2.8	1.8	13.2	2.0	2.1	1.7	12.0
	Weekly Status				**Weekly Status**			
Rural males	3.7	3.0	2.7	4.0	2.2	2.3	2.6	4.2
Rural females	5.8	4.3	2.8	5.3	2.3	1.4	1.6	4.4
Urban males	5.2	5.4	3.4	6.8	3.5	4.1	4.0	6.6
Urban females	2.4	2.1	0.8	9.1	1.5	1.7	1.3	9.2
	Usual Status				**Usual Status**			
Rural males	0.5	1.5	1.2	2.5	0.8	1.4	1.5	2.8
Rural females	0.1	2.5	0.6	4.5	0.2	1.7	0.5	3.5
Urban males	4.1	4.4	2.9	6.4	2.9	3.9	3.6	6.1
Urban females	1.5	4.1	0.9	9.0	1.0	3.0	2.5	8.5

Note : 38th round NSS survey is based on 5+ population and for 43rd Round NSS based on 15 + active population. The differences in the percentages of unemployed over the two rounds have to be viewed therefore with caution.

Sources : Data for all India and AP figures 27th Round, 32nd Round and 38th Rounds from Sarvekeshana, Vol. 1X. No. 4, April 1986 pp. S-119-S-122.

Data for NSS 43rd Round (July 1987-June 1988) Key Results of Employment and Unemployment Survey All-India (part-1) Special report No. 1 January 1990 pp. 114-116.

Definition of Unemployment

A person not working, but either seeking or available for work (activity code 81: sought work) for more than 183 days or equal to 183 days of the previous year was assigned the UPAS of 'seeking or available for work' or unemployed. A person who had not worked even one hour on any one day of the week, but had been seeking work or had been available for work (although not seeking) at any time during the week, was considered 'seeking/available for work' (or unemployed). If the respondent was not engaged in any 'work' for even one hour on the day, but was seeking or available for 'work' for four hours or more, s/he was defined as 'unemployed' for the entire day. If s/he was available for 'work' for less than four hours only, s/he was considered 'unemployed' for a half day and not 'in labour force' for the other half of the day.

Appendix table 1.8 : Incidence of Unemployment (As Percentage of Labour Force)

	Andhra Pradesh		*India*	
	Males	*Females*	*Males*	*Females*
Usual Status (Principal Workers)				
Rural 1977-78	2.1	4.8	2.2	4.4
1983	1.7	1.1	2.3	1.3
1987-88	4.2	9.6	5.2	10.8
Current Weekly status				
1977-78	4.6	11.0	3.9	5.2
1983	4.2	6.8	4.4	5.9
1987-88	7.3	14.9	8.3	20.0
Current Day Status				
Rural 1977-78	9.1	18.5	7.9	10.9
1983	9.2	13.4	8.6	11.0
1987-88	9.0	28.8	9.2	32.4

Source : Computed.

Farm and non-farm employment elasticities:

The elasticity of employment to the Sectoral Gross Domestic Product (SGDP) both in the farm and non-farm sector in AP has shown a considerable decline. Between these sectors the agricultural sector shows much lower elasticity (see Appendix Table 1.9). Also the observed low elasticity of employment in AP contrasts with earlier studies which noted AP to be among the states with high elasticity of employment in agriculture (Parthasarathy, 1995). A number of factors have contributed to the falling elasticity. First, over the period there was a rapid decline in maintenance of plough-cattle (particularly in coastal AP) and a decline in the number of attached agricultural labour; second, tractor-usage has increased at a rapid pace, and displacement of labour in specific occupations (like threshing and ploughing) is no longer compensated by employment in the third crop (growing pulses) as the rate of growth of irrigation began to decline. Third, the slowing down of the Green Revolution has had its effects. Fourth, changes in cropping patterns from labour-intensive crops (like rice) to value-added but capital-intensive crops (such as social forestry and pisciculture) have taken place. As a result labour use per hectare in net-sown hectare has declined from 420 persons in 1977-78 to 379 persons in 1987-88.

Appendix Table 1.9 : Estimated Sectoral Employment Elasticities with Respect to Sectoral GDP:

Sector	*Period - 1 1972-73 to 1977-78*	*Period -11 1977-78 to 1983*	*Period -11 1 1983 to 1987-88*
Agriculture	0.5	0.5	0.4
Mining	1.0	0.7	0.9
Manufacturing	1.1	0.7	0.3
Construction	0.4	1.0	1.0
Electricity, Gas & Water	1.7	0.7	0.5
Transport, Storage & Communications	0.8	0.9	0.4
Services	0.8	1.0	0.4
All sectors	0.6	0.6	0.4

Source : Planning Commission, 1991, Draft Eighth Five Year Plan, Vol. ll, New Delhi, Computed from NSS Employment date on the Usual Principal plus Subsidiary Status basis and CSO National Accounts Statistics: Quoted in Bhalla (1993).

Bhalla's (1987) study based on cost of cultivation data gives an employment elasticity of 0.59 for agriculture during the period 1971-72 to 1983-84. Another study by Bhalla (1993) extends the analysis on employment trends to 1989-90. The latter shows no decline in that the growth rate of employment of the male workforce from 1983 to 1989-90, as compared to the period 1977-78 to 1983. This might be due to a rise in public expenditure on employment programmes and growing absorption of casual labour in these programmes and, during the good agricultural years 1983 and 1988-89, falling unemployment rates.

Appendix Table 1.10 : Casual Labourers as a Per cent of Total Usual Principal Subsidiary Status (for hired labour only)

	Andhra Pradesh				*All-India*			
	Rural		*Urban*		*Rural*		*Urban*	
Round	*Males*	*Females*	*Males*	*Females*	*Males*	*Females*	*Males*	*Females*
27thR 1972	27.3	48.9	11.5	30.7	22.0	31.4	10.1	23.7
32ndR 1977-78	32.7	50.6	14.0	30.2	26.6	35.1	13.2	25.6
38thR 1983	34.3	50.4	14.3	31.7	29.2	35.3	15.4	28.4
43rd R 1987-88	38.1	49.7	21.0	37.2	31.4	35.5	14.6	25.4
45thR 1989-90	38.7	50.8	17.8	27.6	30.4	36.3	16.4	22.2
46thR 1990-91	46.0	56.8	19.4	32.8	31.5	37.7	15.0	25.2

Source : For 27th and 32nd Rounds, Minhas B.S. and Grace Majumdar (January. 1987) 'Unemployment and Casual labour; Indian Journal of Industrial Relations. For other rounds, as cited in Parthasarathy (1995).

Usual Principal Activity Status (UPAS)

All respondents are counted as either 'main workers' or 'marginal workers'. The UPAS of a respondent was defined as

Appendix Table 1.11 : Growth Rates of Rural Working Age Population (15 years and above) in AP and India 1961-71 and 1971-81: per cent/year

	AP			*India*		
Period	*Total Population*	*Males*	*Females*	*Total Population*	*Males*	*Females*
1961-71	1.5	1.5	1.5	1.8	1.9	1.7
1971-81	1.9	1.9	1.9	1.8	1.8	1.9

Sources : Calculated on the basis of Census of India:
1961, Volume 1, India, part 11-B (i) General Economic Tables. For India p.86, for AP p. 90.
1971, Series 1, part-11-B (111), General Economic Tables (Table B-1V parts A, B, C&D), for all-India and AP p. 440.
1981, Series-1, India Part-111 A (i) General Economic Tables for all-India p.134, for AP p. 136.

Appendix Table 1.12 : Overview of Definitions of Employment/ Unemployment According to CDAS, CWAS, UPAS, UPSS.

	Current Daily Status (Time-rate)	*Current Weekly Activity Status*	*Usual Principal Activity Status: UPAS and UPSS*
Employment	(1) Full Day: ≥ 4 hours each day (last week) (2) 1/ 2 day: 1-4 hours per day (last week)	≥ 1 hour any day (last week)	(1) ≥ 183 days per year UPAS (2) < 183 days per year UPSS UPAS+UPSS = All workers.
Unemployment	<1 hour each day, seeking work for ≥ 4 hours	< 1 hour, seeking any amount of time	Not working, seeking ≥ 183 days per year
Participation	(1) Full Day: if ≥ 4 hours per day (last week) (2) 1/ 2 day: if 1-4 hours per day (last week)	≥ 1 hour per day (last week)	(1) ≥ 183 days per year UPAS (2) < 183 days per year UPSS
Non-participation	No work, not available (each day) / Last week	< 1 hour per day (last week)	engaged in non-gainful activity.

Sources : Based on Sarvekshana NSS 43rd Round (July 1987-June 1988), and on Key Results of Employment and Unemployment Survey All-India (part-1), Special Report No. 1, January 1990.

'working' or 'employed' if, and only if, that respondent worked for 183 days or more in any gainful work activities (coded 11 to 51) during the 365 days preceding the day of survey. These respondents are termed as main workers.

Usual Principal Subsidiary Status (UPSS): A respondent was defined as 'marginal worker' if, and only if, that respondent worked in some gainful activity more or less regularly (but for less than 183 days), even if it was intermittent in nature. Only main workers can have UPAS, and only marginal workers can have UPSS. These two groups, viz. those with the UPAS status of workers and those with UPSS status together constituted all workers according to the usual status classification.

A person not working, but either seeking or available for work (activity code 81: sought work) for more than 183 days or equal to 183 days of the previous year was assigned the UPAS of 'seeking or available for work' or unemployed.

Persons categorised as 'working (or employed)' and categorised as 'seeking or available for work (or unemployed)' together constitute the labour force. They are also termed as persons 'economically active'. A person engaged for a relatively longer period in any one or more of the non-gainful activities was considered 'not in labour force'.

Current Weekly Activity Status (CWAS): A respondent was assigned the CWAS of 'working' or 'employed' if, and only if, (s)he was engaged in any one or more of the gainful activities for at least one hour on any one day of the reference week. Further, (s)he was assigned that gainful activity category on which spent the major part (the largest single amount) of the working time during the reference week. A person who had not worked even one hour on any one day of the week, but had been seeking work or had been available for work (although not seeking) at any time during the week, was considered 'seeking/available for work' (or unemployed). Others were considered 'not available for work' (or 'not in labour force').

Current Daily Activity Status (CDAS): The day-to-day activity status of a person is termed 'current-day activity of a person'. The activity pattern of the population, particularly in the unorganised sector (the agricultural sector is considered as almost entirely unorganised), is such that a person might be pursuing more than one activity during a week and sometimes even during a day. Many people, particularly women, might undertake nominal work[1] in their household enterprises along with other non-gainful activities, thus pursuing both gainful and non-gainful activities on the same day. Therefore CDAS recorded up to two activity statuses, on each day of the reference week to persons pursuing more than one activity during the seven days of the reference week. Thus the unit of classification was 'half day', according to CDAS. This means that a worker, working 7 hours on her farm and 1 hour spinning, is classified 'CDAS half-day agriculture, half-day textiles'. A CDAS of a respondent was defined as 'working' (employed) if, and only if, that respondent worked for 4 hours or more during the day. In the CDAS approach, the reference period was counted as each day of the 7 days preceding the date of survey. This approach attempts classification of person-days and not persons. If the respondent worked for one hour or more, but less than 4 hours, s/he was defined as 'working' (employed) for half a day, and either 'seeking/available for work' (unemployed) or 'not available for work' (not in labour force) for the other half of the day. If the respondent was not engaged in any 'work' for even one hour of the day, but was seeking or available for 'work' for four hours or more, s/he was defined as 'unemployed' for the entire day. If s/he was available for 'work' for less than four hours only, s/he was considered 'unemployed' for a half day and not 'in labour force' for the other half of the day. A respondent who neither had 'work' to do nor was 'available for work' even for half of the day was considered 'not in labour force' for the entire day.

The 'employed' and 'unemployed' together constitute the 'labour force', i.e. the available labour supply in the State or country, or the 'economically active' population. The relevant estimates of labour force are calculated from the data available through all the three approaches adopted for classification of the population: usual status, current weekly status and current daily status [current daily approach gives the labour force person-days]. For the usual status approach, the 'economically active' population is based on the principal status. Here, however, we shall also consider both the principal and the subsidiary status.

Labour force participation rate (LFPR), or the proportion of economically active population is defined as *w/p*: the ratio of the 'economically active' (i.e. 'members of the workforce') to the population of potential members, *p*, (i.e., equal in working-age). W includes all workforce of whatever age, P is usually ages between 15-59 or 15-64 only. The relevant rates are presented in (Appendix Table 1.5). It is observed that in rural areas, the usual status labour force is rather above the corresponding current status labour force, both in the case of males and females-indicating that some of the usually employed withdraw from the labour force when there is no work during some part of the year rather than reporting as unemployed. (LFPR is a weighted function of AGSPR's and of the percentage of persons in each age-group).

Our interest in the participation rate derives from the fact that the income of a household depends partly on the daily status workforce participation[2] rates in the household. Though income depends also on the type of jobs held by members, the number of participants in a household can serve as a broad indicator of its economic activity, and age/gender specific of workers in a household are the key person-characteristics to be linked with participation for an in-depth analysis. In order to concentrate on the different trends in RNFE the thesis will first focus on workforce participation rates in AP.

***Appendix to chapter* 2:** Alternative definitions of the concept of RNFS found in the literature G.K. Chadha (1993) defined non-farm as a composite and catch-all term which includes a wide range of economic activities whose composition may vary from country to country. The most common convention is to include animal husbandry, hunting and trapping, forestry and logging, fishing, etc. in agricultural activities, and accordingly, all other economic activities would constitute the 'non-farm' sector. Thus, a variety of industry and manufacturing, transport and communications, trade and hotelling, community and per-

Appendix Table 2.1 : Area, Production and Yield Per Hectare of Rice 1956-57 to 1997-98

	Area	*In Lakh*	*Hectare*	*Production*	*In Lakh*	*Tons*	*Yield*	*KGs/ha.*	
years	*Kharif*	*Rabi*	*Total*	*Kharif*	*Rabi*	*Total*	*Kharif*	*Rabi*	*Total*
1956-57	26.38	5.59	29.27	N/A	N/A	N/A	N/A	N/A	N/A
1957-58	21.63	6.68	28.31	N/A	N/A	N/A	N/A	N/A	N/A
1958-59	23	7.1	30.1	N/A	N/A	N/A	N/A	N/A	N/A
1959-60	24.69	6.11	30.8	N/A	N/A	N/A	N/A	N/A	N/A
1960-61	23.88	5.73	29.61	N/A	N/A	N/A	N/A	N/A	N/A
1961-62	26.98	6.95	33.93	N/A	N/A	N/A	N/A	N/A	N/A
1962-63	27.48	7.27	34.75	N/A	N/A	N/A	N/A	N/A	N/A
1963-64	27.16	6.42	33.58	N/A	N/A	N/A	N/A	N/A	N/A
1964-65	27.71	6.89	34.6	N/A	N/A	N/A	N/A	N/A	N/A
1965-66	25.27	6.13	31.4	31.73	7.88	39.61	1319	1285	1263
1966-67	25.51	7.72	33.23	33.66	10.49	44.15	1319	1358	1329
1967-68	26.05	7.94	33.99	34.68	12.06	46.74	1331	1518	1375
1968-69	20.63	7.86	28.49	25.74	9.34	35.08	1248	1188	1231
1969-70	25.62	9.07	34.69	30.55	12.75	43.3	1193	1405	1248
1970-71	27.65	7.56	35.21	38.05	9.82	47.87	1376	1299	1359
1971-72	23.21	7.2	30.41	35.35	11.82	47.17	1523	1641	1551
1972-73	22.03	7.25	29.28	30.62	11.94	42.56	1390	1648	1458
1973-74	24.84	8.94	33.78	41.77	14.06	55.83	1681	1573	1653
1974-75	25.27	10.24	35.53	38.82	18.18	57	1534	1774	1604
1975-76	28.3	10.65	38.95	44.98	19.53	64.51	1590	1835	1657
1976-77	29.6	6.05	35.65	38.61	10.69	49.3	1332	1800	1410

Contd....

Appendix Table 2.1 : Area, Production and Yield Per Hectare of Rice 1956-57 to 1997-98

	Area	*In Lakh*	*Hectare*	*Production*	*In Lakh*	*Tons*	*Yield*	*KGs/ha.*	
years	*Kharif*	*Rabi*	*Total*	*Kharif*	*Rabi*	*Total*	*Kharif*	*Rabi*	*Total*
1977-78	27.08	9.54	36.62	37.74	18.31	56.05	1424	1966	1565
1978-79	29.79	10	39.79	53.15	21.17	74.32	1820	2163	1907
1979-80	25.03	9.66	34.69	42.22	20.85	63.07	1724	2211	1859
1980-81	28.09	7.91	36	53.76	16.35	70.11	1955	2123	1991
1981-82	28.94	9.3	38.24	57.48	21.2	78.68	2029	2338	2102
1982-83	26.91	9.47	36.38	55.18	21.53	76.71	2095	2329	2156
1983-84	30.48	11.16	41.64	62.1	25.81	87.91	2085	2370	2161
1984-85	25.93	9.05	34.98	48.58	20.51	69.09	1916	2328	2021
1985-86	26.6	7.92	34.52	57.04	19.09	76.13	2198	2483	2264
1986-87	26.25	8.34	34.59	45.87	20.04	65.91	1786	2473	1951
1987-88	22.34	9.73	32.07	46.69	24.18	70.87	2132	2551	2258
1988-89	30.61	11.57	42.18	74.43	31.78	106.21	2483	2809	2572
1989-90	31.34	10.72	42.06	71.15	28.44	99.59	2316	2715	2403
1990-91	30.46	9.9	40.36	69.85	26.69	96.54	2340	2578	2442
1991-92	30.29	9.07	39.36	67.48	25.01	92.49	2273	2828	2400
1992-93	27.05	8.52	35.62	62.63	23.13	85.89	2454	2786	2534
1993-94	N/A	N/A	35.47	N/A	N/A	95.62	N/A	N/A	2700
1994-95	N/A	N/A	36.38	N/A	N/A	92.77	N/A	N/A	2550
1995-96	N/A	N/A	36.92	N/A	N/A	90.14	N/A	N/A	2440
1996-97	N/A	N/A	41.09	N/A	N/A	106.86	N/A	N/A	2490
1997-98	N/A	N/A	35	N/A	N/A	85.1	N/A	N/A	N/A

Source : Season and crop reports

sonal services put together constitute the non-farm sector. For a typically developing economy, agricultural activities are very largely spread partly in the rural and partly in the urban areas. At any point in time, the share of rural areas depends on numerous policy, institutional and historical factors operating in each specific country".

Unni, J. (1991) defined as the size of the rural non-agricultural sector in India can be measured in terms of employment using Census and National Sample Survey (NSS) data. Non-agricultural activities include all economic activities other than crop production and allied agricultural activities such as animal husbandry, plantations, fishing forestry, etc. Non-agricultural work may often be undertaken as a secondary activity, such work under taken by women in particular may be under counted. Given the multiple occupational status of individuals it is difficult to identify the main occupation of a worker. We have included both principal and subsidiary or marginal workers in our estimates of non-agricultural worker.

For Colin Simmons and Salinder Supri (November 1995), non-farm activities are defined as those activities undertaken in rural areas covered by the Census of India 1981 and 1991 occupational categories IV-IX. This enables us to define 'non-farm household' as one where a simple majority of working persons pursued such activities. There were two types of non-farm households: First those were had historically followed non-farm activities, in that both the parents and grandparents of the current head of household (always male) were non-agriculturists. Second were those who had recently diversified into these activities but hailed from a cultivating background.

Notes: There is no formal official definition of 'non-farm activities'. It has often been treated as a residual category lying somewhere between agriculture (generally stopping at the harvest marketing stage but occasionally proceeding upstream to agro-processing), and the secondary tertiary sectors. As a result, there is a little agreement over the use of the term non-farm activities, which is often used interchangeably with rural non-agricultural activities', 'rural non-farm activities', and even 'rural industries'. While there are subtle differences between these terms, we have chosen to treat them as synonymous since the employment dimension is the focus of this thesis. Cf. Chuta and Liedholm (1979); Shand (1986); Islam (1987a) and Ranis and Stewart (1993).

Parthasarathy and Shameem (1998) definition of non-agriculture in Census varies from the definition given in the NSS. NSS agricultural workers include those engaged in allied occupations while Census agricultural workers include only those engaged in crop production i.e. cultivators and agricultural labourers. In fact, since the Census definition is much more restrictive the percentage occupied in agriculture should be lower as compared to NSS. Yet, it is found to be higher. It is possible that Census investigators do not find adequate time to capture details related to other occupations (whereas NSS investigators could capture these).It is not only the levels which are different between the Census and NSS sources but also the trends. Trends as seen from NSS show a rise though the rate of increase lowers between 1983 and 1987-8.In contrast, the Census

Figure 2.1 : Area Under Rice in Andhra Pradesh.

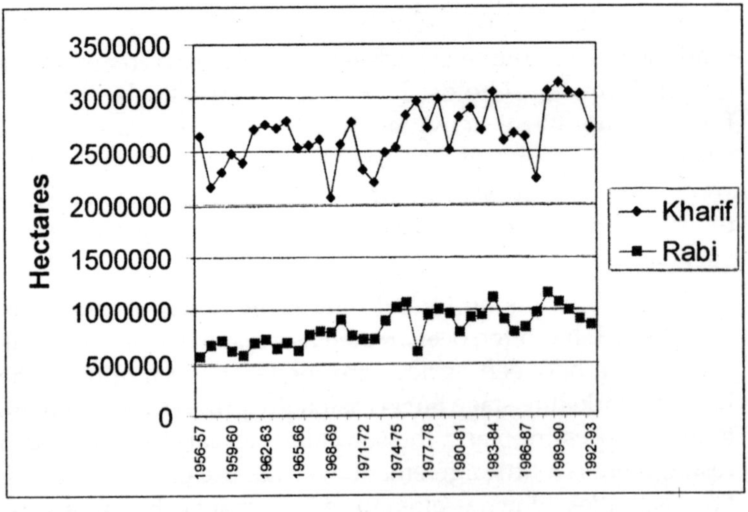

Figure 2.2 : Rice Production in Andhra Pradesh.

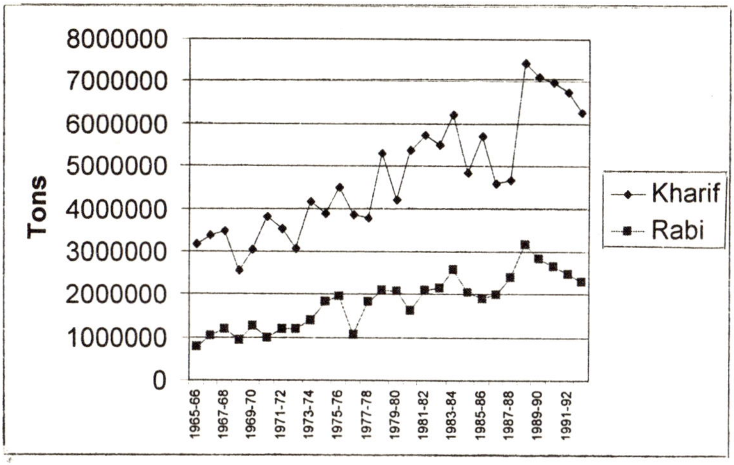

Figure 2.3 : Rice Yield Per Hectare in Andhra Pradesh

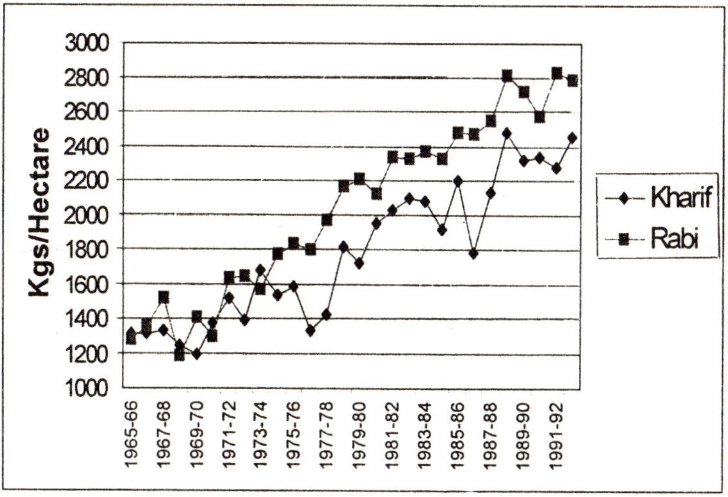

shows a continuous fall in non-agricultural proportions from 19.70 per cent in 1971 to 19.20 per cent in 1991.The NSS, it may be noted does not show a decline. But there is evidence of slack in of rate of growth of non-farm employment.

G. Gangadhara Rao, (1997) the author, based on the survey of literature, the concept of rural non-farm employment (RNFE) is defined as employment in pursuits other than cultivation, livestock, forestry, fishing, hunting, plantations, orchards and allied activities. In brief, it covers employment in mining and quarrying, manufacturing (manufacturing, processing, servicing and repairs in household industry and other than household industry), construction, trade and commerce transport, storage and communications and other services.

Appendix Table 3.1 : Classification of Non-farm Activities

Category	*Description*
Mining and Quarrying	This sector covers mining of coal and lignite, extraction of crude petroleum, production of natural gas, mining of iron ore, metal ores uranium, thorium ores, non metal ores.
Non-household Manufacturing	This sector includes manufacture of food products, beverages, tobacco, cotton textiles, wool, silk, jute, wood, paper, leather, repair of capital goods. Generation, transmission and distribution of electricity, generation and distribution of gas, steam distribution, water supply.
Household industry (HH)	An industry conducted by the head of the household himself or herself and/or by the members of the household at home or within the village in rural areas. Household industry relates to production, processing, servicing, repairing or making and selling of goods. It does not include professions such as pleader, doctor, barber, musician, dancer, weather man, washer person, astrologer, or merle trade or business, even if such professions, trade or services are run at home by members of the household.
Construction	This sector includes construction of buildings (residential and non-residential) construction and maintenance of roads, buildings. Construction and maintenance of power plants except hydroelectric plants and all other activities allied to construction.

Contd....

Appendix Table 3.1 : (Contd....)

Category	*Description*
Trade	This sector covers wholesale / retail trade in cereals, pluses, fruits and vegetables, cotton, jute, wood, paper, machinery equipment. Restaurants, hotels, resting houses, mess, lodging places.
Transport	This sector includes all types of land, water, and air transport and services incidental to transport.
Other services	This includes public administration and defence services, sanitary services, education and scientific research services, health and medical services, religious services, recreational and cultural services, personal services like laundry, cleaning, dyeing, hair dressing. Postal, telegraphic, wireless, signal communication, courier activities other than post. Godowns, warehousing of agricultural products without refrigeration and cold storage, other storage and ware housing facilities. Banking and similar types of financial institutions, provident fund, insurance, real estate, business services.

Source : Government of Andhra Pradesh, (1992), Report on third Economic Census 1990, Directorate of Economics and Statistics, pp 9-10.

Appendix Table 3.2 Income Distribution by Functional Classification, India 1975/76

Income Level (Rs/Household) Rural Areas	*Farming*	*Wages**	*Salary*	*Business*	*Rent Dividends Transfers*	*Total*
Less than 3,600	40.1	45.0	2.3	6.0	6.3	100
3,601-7,500	58.5	16.2	11.7	7.0	6.6	100
7,501-15000	64.5	2.1	18.8	8.4	6.2	100
15,001-30,000	74.5	.2	10.8	9.8	5.5	100
Over 30,000	40.5	0	7.5	38.8	13.2	100

* Include farm and non-farm wages together. Non-farm wages account for roughly 40 per cent of rural wages and 95 per cent of Urban wages.

Source : NCAER, 1980 as given in Haggblade, S. and Hazel, P.

Appendix Table 3.3 : Land Distribution

	For Rural Total Workers					
Category	*Working Population (11-72)* in person days/1000*			*Actually Worked (11-51)** Persons/1000*		
Household land cultivated class in Hectares	*Non-agril (1-9)*	*Total (0.9)*	*Proportion of non-agril to total (%)*	*Non-agril (1-9)*	*Total (0.9)*	*Proportion of non-agril to total (%)*
0.00	157	342	45.9	165	415	39.8
0.01-0.20	112	336	33.3	121	425	28.5
0.21-0.40	91	358	25.4	94	447	21.0
0.41-1.00	70	366	19.1	68	447	15.2
0.01-1.00	86	357	24.1	88	441	20.0
1.01-2.00	52	371	14.0	50	444	11.3
2.01-3.00	46	370	12.4	44	439	10.0
3.01-4.00	41	376	10.9	38	444	8.6
2.01-4.00	44	373	11.8	41	441	9.3
4.01-6.00	34	373	9.1	32	440	7.3
6.01-8.00	34	384	8.9	29	452	6.4
8.01& above	32	376	8.5	28	440	6.4
4.01& above	34	376	9.0	30	443	6.8
all	92	358	25.7	95	434	21.9

Notes : * Per thousand distribution of person-days by current daily activity for each household land cultivated class for rural areas.

** Per thousand distribution of persons by usual activity category taking into consideration of subsidiary gainful status of persons categorised not-working for each household land cultivated class.

Source : NSS 43rd Round (1987-88), pages s-163 & s-294 as given in NSF study group (1994)

Appendix Table 3.4 : Percentage of Irrigated area to Total Cropped Area.

1956-57		*1960-61*		*1970-71*		*1980-81*		*1990-91*		*1991-92*	
gross	*net*	*gross*	*net*	*gross*	*net*	*gross*	*net*	*gross*	*net*	*gross*	*net*
27.2	25.1	29.0	27.0	31.6	28.2	35.3	32.2	40.7	39.07	40.8	39.4

Source : Directrate of Economics and Statisitcs Government of AP.

Appendix Table 3.5 : Correlation Between Agricultural Productivity, Population and Location of Non-farm Activity, Indian States, 1981

	Correlation Coefficient between Agricultural Income per Agricultural population and share in each locality size of			
	Non-farm employment		*Population*	
	All States	*All Except Kerala*	*All States*	*All Except Kerala*
Rural Areas	-.23	-.28	-.23	-.24
Rural Towns 5-100	.33	.38	.41	.41
5-250	.49	.57	.44	.45
Large Urban 100+	.08	.10	.08	.09
250+	-.06	-.05	-.04	-.04

Sources : Employment and population data from India (1981b).

Agricultural income data from Economic Intelligence Service (1988) as given in Rural urban growth linkages in India by Haggblade, S. and Hazel, P.

Appendix Table 3.6 : Correlation Matrix of all Variables Used in the Log-linear Model at District Level

Variable	*RNFE*	*Male*	*Female*	*Comcrop*	*Irri*	*Farm*	*Pov*	*Lit*	*Urban*	*Villages*	*Roadleng*	*Banks*
RNFE	1											
Male	0.69	1										
Female	0.89	0.36	1									
Comcrop	-0.39	-0.21	-0.35	1								
Irri	0.40	0.27	0.33	-0.37	1							
Farm	-0.36	-0.32	-0.28	0.36	-0.61	1						
Pov	-0.26	-0.47	-0.02	0.12	-0.36	0.24	1					
Lit	-0.04	0.35	-0.20	0.26	0.49	-0.30	-0.62	1				
Urban	0.11	0.39	-0.05	-0.06	0.08	-0.10	-0.37	0.36	1			
Villages	-0.16	-0.05	-0.10	0.15	0.22	0.19	-0.22	0.41	-0.03	1		
Roadleng	0.22	0.36	0.11	0.00	0.39	-0.49	-0.33	0.47	0.29	-0.11	1	
Banks	-0.04	0.30	-0.12	0.24	0.02	-0.08	-0.43	0.52	0.31	-0.03	0.37	1

Note : There are no correlation problems that were deemed worth reporting.

Appendix Table 3.7 : Estimated Coefficients of multiple Regression of the percentage of non-farm to total employment in rural areas and selected variables for 1981-91 pooled data:

Variables *Y = % RNFE*	*Total 1*	*Male 2*	*Female 3*	*Total 4*	*Male 5*	*Female 6*
Constant	27.347	32.184	13.993	25.43	31.020	10.842
	(5.40)***	(5.81)***	(1.94)***	(8.93)***	(12.992)***	(7.427)***
comcrp	0.002	-0.035	-0.017		-0.057	
	(0.04)	(-0.75)	(-033)		(-2.207)**	
Farmsize	0.107	0.507	0.031			
	(0.11)	(0.50)	(0.03)			
Irri	0.107	0.037	0.172	0.097		0.182
	(2.76)***	(0.94)	(3.07)***	(3.93)***		(4.678)***
Bank	-0.399	-0.646	-0.194			
	(-0.74)	(-1.12)	(-0.25)			
Pov	-0.064	-0.058	-0.048	-0.065	-0.067	
	(-1.97)**	(-1.71)	(-1.04)	(-2.31)***	(-2.593)***	
Lit	-0.286	-0.093	-0.465	-0.226		-0.394
	(-2.46)	(-0.72)	(-3.39)***	(-3.58)***		(-3.907)***
Urbanisation	0.0488	0.489	0.046			
	(0.734)	(0.69)	(0.49)			
Road length	1.28	-0.582	2.076			
	(0.30)	(-0.13)	(0.33)			

Contd....

Appendix Table 3.7 : (Contd....)

Variables *Y = % RNFE*	*Total 1*	*Male 2*	*Female 3*	*Total 4*	*Male 5*	*Female 6*
Villages	-0.032	-0.043	-0.001			
	(-0.97)	(-1.15)	(-0.02)			
Year dummy	2.082	2.460	2.730			2.674
	(1.35)	(1.34)	(1.30)			(1.869)*
$\overline{R}^2$	0.28	0.09	0.23	0.32	0.21	0.32
F =	2.677	1.41	2.31	7.72***	4.820	7.84
	(0.016)	(0.22)	(4.68)			
Heteroscedasticity	2.38	1.38	13.66	3.066		
	(0.123)	(0.240)	(0.000)	(0.08)		
Normality	3.239	20.89	13.250	3.01		
	(0.20)	(0.000)	(0.001)	(0.22)		
Functional Form	2.56	0.088	20.921	0.667		
	(2.56)	(0.767)	(0.000)	(0.41)		

Notes : The figures in brackets are t-values; - Number of observations: 44;
*** significant at 1 per cent ** significant at 5 per cent * significant at 10 per cent.

Appendix Table 3. 8 : Estimated Coefficients of Multiple Regression of the Percentage of Non-farm Categories to Total Employment in Rural Areas and Selected Variables for Pool Data Results

Variables Independent	*Y = % RNFS mini*	*HHI*	*NON HHI*	*Construc-tion*	*Trade*	*Transport*	*Service*	*Mini*	*HHI*	*NON HHI*	*Construc-tion*	*trade*	*Transport*	*Services*
Constant	0.745	10.32	4.17	0.312	3.746	0.264	5.29			3.319	0.593		4.52	
	(0.72)	(3.031)***	(2.50)***	(0.56)	(3.50)	(0.63)	(4.70)***			(6.23)***	(5.12)***		(9.60)***	
Bank	-0.042	-0.031	-0.169	0.089	-0.039	0.027	-0.223						-0.240	
	(-0.38)	(-0.09)	(-0.95)	(1.50)	(-0.34)	(0.61)	(-1.85)*						(-2.60)*	
comcrp	-0.018	0.040	-0.005	0.002	-0.006	0.0001	-0.007						-0.012	
	(-2.23)**	(1.55)	(-0.359)	(0.54)	(-0.79)	(0.30)	(-0.81)						(-2.11)**	
Farm	0.159	-0.251	-0.011	0.076	0.012	-0.034	-0.035				0.124			
	(0.82)	(-0.40)	(-0.035)	(0.74)	(0.06)	(-0.44)	(-0.17)				(2.04)**			
Irri	-0.016	0.084	0.016	0.002	0.006	0.002	0.005			0.021				
	(-2.058)**	(3.21)***	(1.28)	(0.54)	(0.68)	(0.55)	(0.58)			(2.44)**				
Lit	0.012	-0.384	-0.093	-0.009	0.055	0.020	0.102			-0.058			0.110	
	(0.51)	(-4.92)***	(-2.44)**	(-0.68)	(2.22)**	(2.12)**	(3.90)***			(-2.21)**			(8.14)***	
Pov	0.006	-0.039	-0.014	-0.0002	-0.008	-0.004	-0.005							
	(0.96)	(-1.80)*	(-1.30)	(-0.07)	(-1.20)	(-1.50)	(-0.75)							
Roadlength	-0.565	0.848	0.782	-0.257	-0.149	0.322	-0.780							
	(-0.64)	(0.29)	(0.55)	(-0.55)	(-0.157)	(0.90)	(-0.811)							
Urban	0.020	-0.004	0.028	0.007	-0.003	0.019	-0.0004							
	(1.43)	(-0.10)	(1.27)	(1.00)	(-0.18)	(3.53)***	(-0.03)							

Contd....

Appendix Table 3. 8 : (Contd....)

Variables Independent	*Y = % RNFS mini*	*HHI*	*NON HHI*	*Construc-tion*	*Trade*	*Transport*	*Service*	*Mini*	*HHI*	*NON HHI*	*Construc-tion*	*trade*	*Transport*	*Services*
Villages	-0.006	0.272	0.013	0.002	-0.022	-0.005	-0.027						-0.026	
	(-0.87)	(1.21)	(1.22)	(0.60)	(-3.05)***	(-1.79)*	(-3.65)***						(-4.30)***	
Yeardum	0.806	1.72	1.119	-0.108	-0.346	-0.338	-0.019			0.815				
	(2.54)**	(1.66)	(2.20)**	(-0.64)	(-1.06)	(-2.65)***	(-0.06)			(1.97)*				
$\overline{R}^2$	0.28	0.40	0.11	-0.06	0.34	0.60	0.57			0.10	0.07		0.62	
F=	2.66	3.87	1.53	0.74	3.24	7.56	6.59			2.565*	4.15 **		18.17***	
	(0.02)	(0.002)	(0.17)	(.68)	(.005)	(0.000)	(0.000)							
Hetroscedi	12.32	13.25	5.377	2.86	4.39	0.011	0.264			3.90	3.79		0.745	
	(.000)	(0.000)	(0.02)	(.09)	(.036)	(.917)	(0.607)			(0.05)			(0.39)	
Normality	34.64	16.50	0.728	3.31	0.193	13.23	0.822			4.70	2.79		1.069	
	(.000)	(.000)	(0.70)	(.19)	(0.908)	(0.001)	(0.66)			(0.95)			(0.59)	
Functional	10.51	24.26	8.38	0.22	2.89	4.59	5.21			2.24	8.29		3.428	
	(.001)	(.000)	(.004)	(.64)	(0.09)	(3.73)	(0.22)			(0.14)			(0.06)	

Notes : The figures in brackets are t-values; - Number of observations: 22;
*** significant at 1 per cent
** significant at 5 per cent
* significant at 10 per cent.

Appendix Table 3.9 : Estimated Coefficients of Multiple Regression of the Percentage of Non-farm to Total Employment in Rural Areas and Selected Variables for 1981-91 pooled data

Variables *Y = % RNFE*	*Total* 1	*Male* 2	*Female* 3	*Total* 4	*Male* 5	*Female* 6
Constant	27.347 (5.40)***	42.965 (8.54)***	63.283 (9.79)***	25.43 (8.93)***	38.400 (12.88)***	62.597 (13.39)***
comcrp	0.002 (0.04)	-0.012 (-0.32)	-0.023 (-0.85)			
farmsize	0.107 (0.11)	-0.540 (-0.66)	0.077 (0.11)			
Irri	0.107 (2.76)***	0.048 (1.59)	0.061 (1.81)*	0.097 (3.93)***	0.077 (3.84)***	0.063 (3.52)***
Bank	-0.399 (-0.74)	-0.595 (-1.33)	-1.77 (-3.93)***			-1.723 (-4.43)***
Pov	-0.064 (-1.97)**	-0.026 (-0.98)	-0.034 (-1.36)	-0.065 (-2.31)***		
Lit	-0.286 (-2.46)	-0.147 (-1.44)	-0.075 (-0.89)	-0.226 (-3.58)***	-0.160 (-2.55)***	
Urbanisation	0.0488 (0.734)	0.059 (1.07)	0.015 (0.30)			
Road length	1.28 (0.30)	-0.009 (-0.003)	0.902 (0.27)			
Villages	-0.032 (-0.97)	-0.010 (-0.35)	-0.034 (-1.34)			-0.041 (-2.10)**
Year dummy	2.082 (1.35)	3.257 (2.28)	2.269 (2.05)***		2.99 (2.57)***	1.872 2.07**

Contd....

Appendix Table 3.9 : (Contd....)

Variables *Y = % RNFE*	*Total* *1*	*Male* *2*	*Female* *3*	*Total* *4*	*Male* *5*	*Female* *6*
District dummies						
Ranga Reddy15	-	12.815 (-4.80)***			-13.416 (-5.58)***	
Nizamabad 17	-		-13.298 (-5.65)***			-13.513 (-6.226)***
Nizamabad 39	-		-20.28 (-7.64)***			-21.193 (-9.39)***
Adilabad 40	-		-9.15 (-3.76)***			-9.675 (-4.16)***
$\bar{R}^2$	0.28	0.45	0.78	0.32	0.46	0.80
F =	2.677 (0.016)	4.22***	13.37***	7.72***	10.229***	25.339***
Heteroscedasticity $\lambda^2(1)$	2.38 (0.123)	0.003	0.443	3.066 (0.08)	0.122	0.516
Normality $\lambda^2(2)$	3.239 (0.20)	1.396	0.781	3.01 (0.22)	2.312	1.128
Functional Form $\lambda^2(1)$	2.56 (2.56)	0.031	6.544 (0.011)	0.667 (0.41)	0.417	5.497

Notes : The figures in brackets are t-values; - Number of observations: 44;
*** significant at 1 per cent ** significant at 5 per cent * significant at 10 per cent.
Dum15 Rangareddy, Dummy 17 and 39 Nizamabad, Dummy 40 Adilabad districts.

Appendix Table 3.10 : Part 1. Estimated Coefficients of the Multiple Regressions. Pooled data Results on the Percentage of Non-farm Employment in the Listed Sectors of Activities to Total Employment in Rural Areas.

Y/X	*Mining*	*HHI*	*NON HHI*	*Construc-tion*	*Trade*	*Transport*	*Services*	*Mini*	*HHI*	*NON HHI*	*Construc-tion*	*trade*	*Transport*	*Services*
Constant	3.321	34.280	8.592	1.459	3.746	1.820	2.916	2.976	35.128	9.130	0.593	5.278	1.962	2.956
	(3.56)***	(13.19)***	(5.10)***	(2.40)**	(3.38)***	(4.10)***	(2.06)**	(5.93)***	(16.47)***	(7.51)***	(5.12)***	(7.65)***	(5.844)***	(3.60)***
Bank	-0.131	-0.717	0.249	0.050	0.018		-0.220		-0.671	0.317			-0.240	-0.225
	(-1.54)	(-4.03)***	(1.30)	(0.95)	(0.541)	(0.61)	(-1.98)*		(4.45)***	(2.44)**			(-2.60)*	(-2.55)**
Comcrp	-0.012	0.013	-0.002	0.005	-0.006	-0.446-E	-0.009	-0.009					-0.012	-0.015
	(-2.02)**	(1.04)	(-0.15)	(1.33)	(-0.82)	(-0.18)	(-1.04)	(-1.91*					(-2.11)**	(-2.70)***
Farm	0.143	-0.013	-0.332	0.049	0.012	-0.02	-0.003			-0.558	0.124			
	(0.98)	(-0.045)	(-1.26)	(0.54)	(0.07)	(-0.38)	(-0.02)			(-2.93)***	(2.04)**			
Irri	-0.010	0.023	0.009	0.004	0.006	0.001	0.005	-0.014				0.014		
	(-1.68)*	(1.70)*	(0.85)	(1.07)	(0.61)	(0.46)	(0.60)	(-3.42)***				(2.88)***		
Lit	0.010	-0.120	-0.078	-0.014	0.055	0.026	0.099		-0.063	-0.051			0.029	0.116
	(0.56)	(-2.87)***	(-2.44)**	(-1.26)	(2.94)***	(3.58)***	(3.98)***		(-2.98)***	(-2.59)**			(5.67)***	(8.84)***
Pov	0.005	-0.032	-0.010	-0.002	-0.008	-0.006	-0.010		-0.028			-0.012	-0.006	
	(1.03)	(-3.24)***	(-1.07)	(-0.52)	(-1.43)	(-2.80)***	(-1.39)		(-3.08)***			(-2.40)**	(-3.59)***	
Roadlength	-0.821	0.475	0.524	-0.349	-0.174	0.065	-0.696							
	(-1.22)	(0.37)	(0.451)	(-0.84)	(-0.162)	(0.24)	(-0.77)							
Urban	0.023	-0.037	0.028	0.010	-0.003	0.015	-0.004	0.017	-0.045				0.015	
	(2.25)**	(-1.84)*	(1.27)	(1.54)	(-0.21)	(3.41)***	(-0.25)	(1.93)*	(-2.37)**				(3.74)***	
Villages	-0.003	-0.008	0.017	0.002	-0.004	-0.005	-0.025			0.017		-0.015	-0.05	-0.025
	(-0.63)	(-0.72)	(1.80)*	(0.87)	(-1.78)*	(-1.79)*	(-3.63)***			(2.03)**		(-2.89)***	(-2.56)**	(-4.36)***
Yeardum	0.748	0.605	0.180	-0.016	-0.346	-0.339	0.056	0.423					-0.329	
	(3.12)***	(1.29)	(0.34)	(-0.11)	(-1.15)	(-3.42)***	(0.17)	(2.68)***					(-4.35)***	

Appendix Table 3.10 : Part 2. Estimated Coefficients of Multiple Regression of the percentage of Non-farm Categories to total Employment in Rural areas and Selected Variables for pool data Results:

Y / Dist. Dummies	*Mining*	*HHI*	*NON HHI*	*Construc-tion*	*Trade*	*Transport*	*Services*	*Mining*	*HHI*	*NON HHI*	*Construc-tion*	*trade*	*Transport*	*Services*
Visak. 3						-0.956 (-4.51)***								
Adilab. 40	-2.503 (-5.09)***	-3.12 (3.28)***						-2.285 (-4.80)***	-3.107 (-3.28)***					
Ran. R 15			-2.042 (-2.34)**							-2.376 (-3.01)***				
Nizam. 17	-6.589 (7.04)***								-7.158 (-8.04)***					
Karimn. 19	-3.186 (-3.44)***					-0.450 (-2.27)**			-3.242 (-3.56)***					
Kham. 21				-0.935 (-3.14)***										
E. God. 26												-1.168 (-1.96)*		
Krishna 28							1.202 (1.83)*							1.380 (2.28)**
Nizam. 39		-10.183 (-9.80)***							-10.987 (-11.77)***					

Contd....

Appendix Table 3.10 : Part 2. (Contd.....)

Y / Dist. Dummies	*Mining*	*HHI*	*NON HHI*	*Construction*	*Trade*	*Transport*	*Services*	*Mining*	*HHI*	*NON HHI*	*Construction*	*trade*	*Transport*	*Services*
Kham. 41			-3.668							-3.994				
			(-3.24)***							(-4.707)***				
Nalg. 44							1.383							
							(1.99)*							
$\bar{R}^2$	0.59	0.88	0.42	0.15	0.34	0.76	0.63	0.58	0.88	0.44	0.07	0.41	0.80	0.65
F	6.589***	24.124***	3.544***	1.72	3.24***	13.458	7.135***	12.860***	39.31***	6.622***	4.15 **	8.439***	24.89***	17.130***
Heteros.	0.009	1.221	0.006	0.135	—	0.067	0.056	0.017	0.945	0.154	3.79	1.101	0.305	0.006
Normality	3.144	1.072	0.196	2.269	0.193	0.902	1.713	10.227	0.388	0.583	2.79	0.543	1.024	2.706
Function.	7.323	3.009	0.637	1.691	2.89	0.380	3.763	1.676	2.806	0.613	8.29	3.591	0.019	3.909

Notes : The figures in brackets are t-values; Number of observations: 44; *** significant at 1 per cent; ** significant at 5 per cent; * significant at 10 per cent.
Heteroscedasticity $\chi^2(1)$; Normality $\chi^2(2)$; Functional $\chi^2(1)$

Appendix to Chapter 4 (a)

The villages covered in the study are: (1) Veeravalli (Census 1991, population 5,437) in the district of Krishna; (2) Anandapuram (census 1991 population 5,573) in the district of Visakhapatnam.[3] In Visakhapatnam most irrigation is performed through tanks and most of the tanks are rainfed. In Ananda-puram rainfed tanks are also the predominant source (77.8 per cent) of irrigation, the remaining 23.7 per cent originating from tube and dug wells. The cropping pattern in the village resembles that of a dry region. Most farmers in the area have marginal farms (less than 2.46 acres). Indeed, the majority of the land holdings (51.61 per cent in Veeravalli and 77.93 per cent in Anandapuram) are concentrated in the lowest size groups viz. 0.5 to 2.46 acres. A detailed land-holding pattern is presented in Chapter 4. A study of the village of Anandapuram village enables us to understand the relationship between less-developed agriculture and the growth of non-farm employment.

In Veeravalli a canal is the predominant source of irrigation supplying 77 per cent of the Gross Irrigated Area. The remaining 23 per cent is irrigated from tube and dug wells. The entire village is located in the delta region. Cropping patterns and labour use are different from those of Anandapuram. Veeravalli is endowed with a rich soil, and is agriculturally advanced (in terms of yield rates) with paddy being the main food crop produced. The net irrigated area in the village is 4,000 acres occupying 84 per cent of the cropped area. The unirrigated area is only 238 acres. Paddy is the main crop with 3,486 acres, with sugar cane (378 acres) and groundnut (192 acres). The main source of irrigation for the village is the river Krishna. The village will be studied to examine the relationships between the prosperity of agriculture and the development of non-farm activities. In both villages 35 per cent of the total households were randomly selected for interview, these yielding a total of 465 households in Veeravalli, and 354 households in Anandapuram. From each selected household, information relating to a number of variables was collected by canvassing a pre-designed schedule which included information on a number of demographic, social, and economic characteristics, such as the number and size of households, family members' occupation, social status, land holding status, value of agricultural output, number of working days, percentage of non-farm employment to total employment, migration/ commuting in and out, literacy, income and expenditure.

The important consideration was the presence of various non-farm activities alongside agriculture activities. Almost all occupations under different categories of non-farm activities (traditional and modern) are covered in the two villages. The survey covered small and marginal farmers and agricultural labourers, households with exclusively non-farm employment, as well as households with both farm and non-farm employment. It covered traditional and modern varieties of non-farm employment.

An in-depth survey among a sub-sample of households was then conducted with a comprehensive questionnaire. The field work involving the household surveys in the villages, collection of secondary data at district level, the primary data of two villages, was completed over 6 months (June 1993 to January 1994), and a second phase of field-work took place (March 1995 to April 1995). Further visits were made to the two villages at regular intervals throughout the second phase of the study. Data collection and interviews were carried out by the researcher.

The village survey findings help to understand the employment (occupational distribution of the population) pattern in the village. It is possible to compare the survey results with the occupational distribution of the populations of the villages as revealed historically by the Census (from 1971, 1981, 1991). This will help to ascertain whether the significance of traditional occupations is decreasing. The employment and income levels of the non-farm sector are compared with those of the farm sector. Such a comparison can help to establish whether there is distress-diversification (people employed in the non-farm sector because there is no place for them in the farm sector).

For the purpose of case-studies a few individual households were chosen by random sampling covering major farm and non-farm occupations, some of which were successful in non-farm activities. Only a selection of case studies is presented in the Chapter 5. The families were selected for detailed enquiry regarding their primary occupation, their reason for choosing the non-farm activity, and its relation to agricultural activities. The nature of non-farm activities, the level of technology involved and its relationship with the agricultural sector were also covered. The problems faced, the possible solutions to these problems, and the increase of non-farm employment opportunities are also examined. The case-studies also analysed historical factors affecting households. The case-studies were conducted by participant observation and interviewing. Biographical method was used to construct the background of the individuals.

Statistical tools (such as growth rates, multiple (OLS) and log linear regressions as well as LOGIT models, and correlations) have been used in the present study. The details of these techniques is given in relevant chapters.

In order to analyse socio-economic characteristics of the sample households, simple percentages are used. To identify the inequalities in the distribution of land assets and income Gini coefficients and Theil indices are estimated. To estimate the impact of various factors on non-farm employment, both at the macro (District) level and at the micro (village) level, single linear and log linear model regression techniques and elasticity estimates are used (detailed techniques are presented in the respective chapters).

Appendix to Chapter 4 (b): The Model Specification

A number of authors have argued for the use of the qualitative response model when survey data are available. Considering the occurrence or non-occurrence of an event, for example, "a household is engaged in non-farm occupation" let it be represented by a dichotomous random variable Y. If the event occurs (i.e., a household is engaged in non-farm

Appendix Table 4.1 : Correlation Matrix of all Variables Used in the Logit Model at Household Level

Variables	*Non-farm*	*Land*	*HH age*	*Family size*	*Casted 1*	*Casted 2*	*Migra-tion*	*Sep-Nov*	*Dec-Feb*	*Poor*	*Educa-tion*	*Skill*	*Agrl. value*	*March-may*
Non-farm	1													
Land	-0.33	1.00												
HH age	-0.10	0.16	1.00											
Familysize	0.01	0.06	0.05	1.00										
Casted1	0.07	-0.18	-0.07	0.01	1.00									
Casted2	-0.09	-0.10	-0.02	0.02	-0.51	1.00								
Migration	0.14	-0.07	-0.07	-0.07	-0.09	0.12	1.00							
Sep-Nov	-0.33	0.09	0.08	0.04	-0.06	0.11	-0.07	1.00						
Dec-Feb	-0.14	0.12	0.03	-0.06	-0.01	-0.06	0.03	-0.36	1.00					
Poor	0.42	-0.18	-0.07	0.02	0.11	-0.12	0.00	-0.46	-0.50	1.00				
Education	0.12	0.24	-0.02	-0.02	-0.30	-0.07	0.20	-0.08	0.05	0.06	1.00			
Skill	-0.06	0.30	0.05	0.05	0.00	-0.21	-0.03	-0.02	-0.04	0.11	0.28	1.00		
Agrl.Value	-0.33	0.42	0.15	0.09	-0.01	-0.14	-0.11	0.18	0.11	-0.22	0.10	0.47	1.00	
March-May	0.42	-0.17	-0.08	0.02	0.11	-0.10	0.02	-0.43	-0.50	0.89	0.07	0.08	-0.21	1.00

Comment : In the majority of cases, the variables are not correlated at a high level.

occupation) the value is 1 and the value is 0 if the household is not so engaged.

Given a random sample of size n.

Let Pi be the probability[4] that Yi = 1 For the ith household (i = 1, 2...n).

Let Pi be dependent on a vector of K independent variables X = (X1, X2,.......Xk) and a vector of (K+1) unknown parameters β = (β0 β1, β2, βk). The general model is Pi = P(Yi = 1) = G(X, β) for i = 1,2....n. It is also assumed that the random variables Y1,Y2,......Yn are independently distributed. Considering a linear function of the independent variables (X1,X2,...Xk), i.e., H (X,B), we assume that the probability that a household is non-farm depends upon the value taken by H(X,B) for that household. Thus P(Yi = 1) = f (β0+β1X2+....+βkXk) For I = 1,2...n. There are three different probability distribution functions (F) that are commonly used in the literature. The Linear Probability model, F(β0+β1X1+β2X2+....+βkXk) = (β0+β1X1i+β2X2i....+βkXki). For the Probit model: P (β0+β1X1i+β2X2i....+βkXki) = (1/√2π-1/2t2). Finally The standard normal distribution function.

The logit model:

$$F\ (\beta_0+\beta_1X_{1i}+....+\beta_kX_{ki}) = \frac{EXP(\beta_0+\beta_1X_{1i}+....+\beta_kX_{ki})}{1+\ EXP(\beta_0+\beta_1X_{1i}+....+\beta_kX_{ki})}$$

The linear probability model has defects. The linear function (β0+β1X1i+....+βkXki) = e(β0+β1X1i+....+βkXki) may not always lie between 0 and 1 as any probability should. This can be rectified by placing constraints on the expression $((\beta_0+\beta_1X_{1i}+....+\beta_kX_{ki})$ at 0 and 1. Another difficulty arises because the variance of the error term is V(ui) = V(Yi) = Pi (1-Pi)=[($\beta_0+\beta_1X_{1i}+....+\beta_kX_{ki}$) (1-($\beta_0+\beta_1X_{1i}+....+\beta_kX_{ki}$))]. V (ui) is not constant and hence gives rise to the problem of heteroscedasticity. On the other hand, the Probit model uses the standard normal distribution function while the logit model uses the logistic distribution function.[5] In both cases they take values between 0 and 1 because they are probability distribution functions. The variance of the logistic distribution is ($\pi/3$). These two distribution functions are very similar and hence 'in the univariate dichotomous model, it does not matter much whether one uses a Probit model or a logit model except in cases where data are heavily concentrated in the tails'[6] [Amemiya, T., (1981)].

For our model the data pertain to a sample of N households; these households are classified into two categories. The households either have one or number engaged in non-farm occupations as a primary occupation or they do not. Thus

Yi = 1 if the ith household has one or members engaged in non-farm employment as a primary occupation

Yi = 0 if the ith household has one or members engaged in farming as the primary occupation

Let the probability of the ith household having one or members engaged in non-farm occupation be

Pi = Prob(Yi =1), then the probability the ith household is not a rnfs household is (1-pi) = prob(yi=o). We also have data on a set of explanatory variables (X1, X2...Xk). Some of the variables are continuous such as the wage ratio, per capita value of the agricultural output, land-holding size. Others are discrete, size of household, migration in, skilled/unskilled and some variables are categorical (such as caste).

we combine these variables using a linear function. Let wi $= -(\beta_0+\beta_1 X_{1i}+....+\beta_k X_{ki})$,

wi is a linear combination of the explanatory variables (X1,X2...Xk) and the set of unknown parameters $(\beta_0, \beta_1....+\beta_k)$ is transformed into a measure of the probability that a household is engaged in non-farm taking values in the range of 0 to 1. That is, we use the logistic cumulative probability distribution function to relate Pi and Wi giving rise to the logit model.

Pi = prob(Yi) = $F(\beta_0+\beta_1 X_{1i}+....+\beta_k X_{ki})$

The logit form is: Pi = $1/(1+\exp(-(\beta_0+\beta_1 X_{1i}+....+\beta_k X_{ki}))$ or Pi = 1/ (1+exp(-wi))

The latter expression is the logistic cumulative probability distribution, exp is the constant representing the base of natural logarithms. Rewriting this equation as

(1+exp(-w)) Pi = 1, then Pi +Pi exp(-W) = 1

Pi exp (-W) = 1 1-Pi /Pi Taking natural logarithms

-W = log (1-Pi/Pi) or Wi = log (pi/1-pi). Therefore log (pi/1-pi) = wi = $(\beta_0+\beta_1X_{1i}+....+\beta_kX_{ki})$

This equation is treated as regression equation in which the dependent variable in the equation is a monatomic transformation of the original dependent variable p1: it is the logarithm of the odds[7] of the ith household being classified as engaged in non-farm occupation. This transformation helps in using the logit model for prediction purposes because the range of values pi can take in the interval (0,1) whereas log (pi/1-pi) can take any real value from minus infinity to plus infinity. Since the above equation is similar to a regression equation, the interpretation of the parameters bi is as follows, taking partial derivative of log (pi/1-pi) with respect to Xk

$$\frac{\delta \log (pi/1-pi)}{\delta Xk} = \beta_k$$

Which means β_k measures the change in log of the odds that the ith household is classified as engaged in non-farm employment when there is a unit change in the independent variable Xk. If $\beta_k > 0$ the effect is direct (positive) on the dependent variable. If $\beta_k < 0$ the effect is negative i.e., indicating an inverse relationship. The logistic function is not linear, its slope (i.e., δ log (pi/1-pi)/ δ wi is not constant, it takes maximum value when Σ(pi)= Σ[p(yi)]=1/2 or Pi= P(Yi) = ½, i.e., the mid point of the distribution. This means that it is at this point that changes in the independent variables show maximum effect on the dependent variable. The parameters $\beta_0+\beta_1,.....\beta_k$ are unknown and have to be estimated with the help of sample information. When individual observations are available from a survey i.e. ungrouped date accessible the maximum likelihood method of estimation is preferred.[8]

NOTES

1. The activities were grouped into three categories: 1 Activities relating to agricultural production like maintenance of kitchen garden, work in household poultry dairy, non-remittances collection of fish, including free collection of agricultural products for household consumption; 2 Processing of primary products produced by the households for household consumption; 3 other activities such as husking of paddy, grinding of food grain, preparation of gur, preservation of meat; making baskets etc., preparation of cowdung cakes; sewing, tailoring, tutoring of own children, fetching water, for own consumption but resulting in economic benefits to the households (not gainful). Activities in 1 and 2 categories are considered as gainful.

2. 'Participation' is defined as work in any economically-productive activity. It may be physical or mental in nature. Work involves not only actual work but also effective supervision and direction of work. It also includes unpaid work on farm or in family enterprise. (Census of India (1991), Series-1 India, Paper-3 of 1991 Provisional Population Totals: Workers and their distribution p.5)

3. Visakhapatnam city is the district headquarter. It is a port city and the industrial centre of North Coastal Andhra.

4. Klecka, W.R (1980), Discriminate Analysis, Sage University paper Series on Quantitative Applications in the Social Science, 07-019 Beverly Hills, C.A.Sage.

5. The logistic function is

   Pi = exp (Wi)/(1+exp(Wi))

   Pi =exp (-Wi). Exp(W1)/(exp(-Wi).Exp(-Wi))

   Pi = 1 / (1+exp(-Wi))

6. Amemiya, T. (Dec. 1981) "Qualitative Response Models: A Survey", *Journal of Economic Literature*, Vol. 19.

7. The Logit means 'Log odds' or natural logarithm of the odds. By odds we mean the relative probability of falling into one of two possible categories for some variable.

8. For example it the probability of a household being engaged in non-farm activity is 0.4/0.6=0.67. This implies that households are about two thirds as likely to be categorised as engaged in

farm, with given the probability that the household will be non-poor from the following equation: prob of household will be poor = (odds ratio)* Prob. Of household being engaged in farm 0.40 = 0.67*0.6. The maximum likelihood method of estimation is preferred.